Feeding the Mind

Feeding the Mind explores how European intellectual life was rebuilt after the cataclysm of the First World War. Learned communities were left in ruins by the conflict and its consequences; cultural and educational sites were destroyed, writers and artists were killed in battle, and tens of thousands of others were displaced. Against the backdrop of an unprecedented post-war humanitarian crisis which threatened millions with starvation and disease, many organizations chose to focus on assisting intellectuals and their institutions, giving them food, medicine, and books in order to stabilize European democracies and build a peaceful international order. Drawing on examples from Austria to Russia and Belgium to Serbia, *Feeding the Mind* analyses the role of humanitarianism in post-conflict reconstruction and explores why ideas and intellectuals were deemed to be worth protecting at a time of widespread crisis. This issue was pertinent in the century that followed and remains so today.

TOMÁS IRISH is Associate Professor of Modern History at Swansea University. A specialist in the cultural history of the First World War and its aftermath, his books include the prizewinning *The University at War 1914–25: Britain, France and the United States* (2015) and *Trinity in War and Revolution, 1912–23* (2015).

Studies in the Social and Cultural History of Modern Warfare

General Editor
Robert Gerwarth, *University College Dublin*
Jay Winter, *Yale University*

Advisory Editors
Heather Jones, *University College London*
Rana Mitter, *University of Oxford*
Michelle Moyd, *Michigan State University*
Martin Thomas, *University of Exeter*

In recent years the field of modern history has been enriched by the exploration of two parallel histories. These are the social and cultural history of armed conflict, and the impact of military events on social and cultural history.

Studies in the Social and Cultural History of Modern Warfare presents the fruits of this growing area of research, reflecting both the colonization of military history by cultural historians and the reciprocal interest of military historians in social and cultural history, to the benefit of both. The series offers the latest scholarship in European and non-European events from the 1850s to the present day.

A full list of titles in the series can be found at: www.cambridge.org/modernwarfare

Feeding the Mind

Humanitarianism and the Reconstruction of European Intellectual Life, 1919–1933

TOMÁS IRISH
Swansea University

CAMBRIDGE
UNIVERSITY PRESS

Shaftesbury Road, Cambridge CB2 8EA, United Kingdom

One Liberty Plaza, 20th Floor, New York, NY 10006, USA

477 Williamstown Road, Port Melbourne, VIC 3207, Australia

314–321, 3rd Floor, Plot 3, Splendor Forum, Jasola District Centre, New Delhi – 110025, India

103 Penang Road, #05–06/07, Visioncrest Commercial, Singapore 238467

Cambridge University Press is part of Cambridge University Press & Assessment, a department of the University of Cambridge.

We share the University's mission to contribute to society through the pursuit of education, learning and research at the highest international levels of excellence.

www.cambridge.org
Information on this title: www.cambridge.org/9781009123228

DOI: 10.1017/9781009128476

© Tomás Irish 2024

This publication is in copyright. Subject to statutory exception and to the provisions of relevant collective licensing agreements, no reproduction of any part may take place without the written permission of Cambridge University Press & Assessment.

First published 2024

A catalogue record for this publication is available from the British Library.

A Cataloging-in-Publication data record for this book is available from the Library of Congress.

ISBN 978-1-009-12322-8 Hardback

Cambridge University Press & Assessment has no responsibility for the persistence or accuracy of URLs for external or third-party internet websites referred to in this publication and does not guarantee that any content on such websites is, or will remain, accurate or appropriate.

Contents

Figures

Acknowledgements

This book has been in development since 2016, in which time I have accumulated many scholarly debts. I am very grateful to colleagues who read and commented on draft chapters of the book. Michael Bresalier, Rebecca Clifford, Dónal Hassett, John Horne, Martin Johnes, Kevin O'Sullivan, Elisabeth Piller, Julie M. Powell, and Katharina Rietzler were all exceptionally generous with their time and expertise and have helped to shape the direction of the book for the better. I am also indebted to academic colleagues around the world for conversations that have helped me to refine my ideas. They include Michael Clinton, Boyd van Dijk, Charlotte Faucher, Peter Gatrell, Rebecca Gill, Martin Grandjean, Daniel Laqua, Branden Little, Heather Jones, Mahon Murphy, Craig Owen, Tammy Proctor, Ilaria Scaglia, Jan Stöckmann, James Allen Smith, Anastassiya Schacht, Ciarán Wallace, Elizabeth White, Susannah Wright, and Neville Wylie. The two anonymous readers for Cambridge University Press also provided constructive advice about how to strengthen the manuscript. All errors of detail and interpretation are mine.

Swansea University, where I arrived in 2015, has been a supportive and convivial home for this project, and colleagues past and present have been a great source of encouragement during the research and writing of the book, of whom I would like to thank Tom Allbeson, Jonathan Dunnage, Ute Keller, Eugene Miakinkov, Louise Miskell, Adam Mosley, and Trish Skinner. I am especially grateful to the wonderful students who have taken my special subject module on interwar internationalism over the years, who, through our navigation of international history, have helped me develop many of the ideas in this book.

The research for *Feeding the Mind* would not have been possible without the generous support of the Research Support Fund in Swansea University's College of Arts and Humanities, the Rockefeller Archive Center, and the British Academy/Leverhulme Small Research Grants scheme. This book is the result of research conducted in archives on both sides of the Atlantic, and I wish to acknowledge archivists at the following institutions for permission to access materials: La contemporaine; Archives nationales; Bodleian Libraries Archives and Manuscripts; British Library; British Academy Archives; Columbia University Archives; Columbia University Rare Book and Manuscript Library; Harvard University Archives; Library of the Society of Friends; London School of Economics Archives and Special Collections; The National Archives (UK); National Library of Wales; Rockefeller Archive Center; Royal Society Archives; UNESCO Archives; United Nations Library and Archives; West Glamorgan Archive Service; and Yale University Divinity Library Special Collections. I would like to thank staff at the following institutions for making materials available to me in digital form: Parliamentary Archives; American Philosophical Society Library; M. E. Grenander Department of Special Collections and Archives, University at Albany, State University of New York. Every effort has been made to track copyright holders and to obtain permission for the use of copyright material. I apologize for any omissions and correction and acknowledgement will be made in any future editions of this book.

I am indebted to Robert Gerwarth for suggesting Cambridge University Press as a home for this book and to Michael Watson, Emily Plater, Erin Cunningham, and Natasha Whelan at CUP for steering the work through peer review and production. I also wish to thank Michelle Brumby for the creation of book's index. Some elements of Chapter 3 have been published as 'The "Moral Basis" of Reconstruction? Humanitarianism, Intellectual Relief and the League of Nations, 1918–1925', *Modern Intellectual History,* 17.3, pp. 769–800, while elements of Chapter 4 have been published as 'Educating Those Who Matter: Thomas Whittemore, Russian Refugees and the Transnational Organization of Elite Humanitarianism After the First World War', *European Review of History/Revue européenne d'histoire*, 28.3, pp. 441–62.

My parents, Tom and Irene, have been a wonderful support during the writing of this book – and my whole life. Kate has lived with this book for almost as long as I have; she has been the greatest source of intellectual critique and loving support throughout. The book is dedicated to her.

Abbreviations

AAC	Academic Assistance Council
AAULCE	Anglo-American University Library for Central Europe
AMBA	Arbeitsmittel-Beschaffungs-Ausschuss
AN	Archives nationales
APSL	American Philosophical Society Library
ARA	American Relief Administration
ARAEOR	American Relief Administration European Operational Records
ARAROR	American Relief Administration Russian Operational Records
ARC	American Red Cross
ASESR	American Section European Student Relief
BA	British Academy
BAA	British Academy Archives
BAR	Bakhmeteff Archive of Russian and Eastern European Culture
BL	British Library
CAME	Conference of Allied Ministers of Education
CARA	Council for At-Risk Academics
CCNY	Carnegie Corporation of New York
CEIP	Carnegie Endowment for International Peace
CERYE	Committee for the Education of Russian Youth in Exile
CF	Commonwealth Fund
CITI	Confédération internationale des travailleurs intellectuels
CRAWEP	Commission on the Responsibility of the Authors of the War and on Enforcement of Penalties
CRB	Commission for Relief in Belgium
CRD	Commission on the Reparation of Damage
CRRI	Committee for the Relief of Russian Intellectuals
CRRR	Committee for the Relief of Russian Refugees

CTI	Confédération des travailleurs intellectuels
CUA	Columbia University Archives
CURBML	Columbia University Rare Book and Manuscript Library
ESR	European Student Relief
FEWVRC	Friends' Emergency and War Victims' Relief Committee
FGP	Frank Golder Papers
GKP	Grayson Kefauver Papers
HILA	Hoover Institution Library and Archives
HUA	Harvard University Archives
ICIC	International Committee on Intellectual Cooperation
ICRC	International Committee of the Red Cross
IEB	International Education Board
IIIC	International Institute of Intellectual Cooperation
IIE	Institute of International Education
ILO	International Labour Organization
IRC	International Research Council
ISC	International Studies Conference
ISS	International Student Service
IUA	International Union of Academies
IWRF	Imperial War Relief Fund
JDC	Jewish Joint Distribution Committee
LAC	La contemporaine
LNA	League of Nations Archives
LSEASC	London School of Economics Archives and Special Collections
LSF	Library of the Society of Friends
LSRM	Laura Spelman Rockefeller Memorial
MEGDSCA	M. E. Grenander Department of Special Collections and Archives
NER	Near East Relief
NLW	National Library of Wales
NYPLAM	New York Public Library Archives and Manuscripts
OIC	Organization for Intellectual Cooperation
OMR	Office of the Messrs. Rockefeller
PA	Parliamentary Archives
PROI	Public Record Office of Ireland
RAC	Rockefeller Archive Center
RF	Rockefeller Foundation
RSA	Royal Society Archives

SCF	Save the Children Fund
SFF	Student Friendship Fund
SRF	Science Relief Fund
TIU	Tokyo Imperial University
TNA	The National Archives (UK)
UIA	Union of International Associations
UN	United Nations
UNESCO	United Nations Educational, Scientific and Cultural Organization
WCTP	Winifred Coombe Tennant Papers
WGAS	West Glamorgan Archive Service
WILPF	Women's International League for Peace and Freedom
WKP	Walter Kotschnig Papers
WSCF	World Student Christian Federation
YMCA	Young Men's Christian Association
YUDLSC	Yale University Divinity Library Special Collections

Note on the Text

I have referred to places as they appeared in contemporary sources using the generally accepted English-language version of their names. Where place names have subsequently changed, their current name is indicated in a footnote at their first mention in the text. In specific cases where sites were contested at a point in time, such as the former Habsburg lands in the immediate aftermath of the First World War, two names are provided to highlight this contemporary contestation.

Introduction

'We all had the impression, I think, of having passed out of the modern world back into a vanished civilization.' These were the words of the American historian James Shotwell following a visit to the devastated towns of Reims and Soissons in northern France in the spring of 1919.[1] Shotwell was a prominent internationalist who taught at Columbia University, was heavily involved in the work of the Carnegie Endowment for International Peace, and was a member of President Woodrow Wilson's Inquiry, a team of experts brought together to plan the post-war peace.[2] It was in the latter capacity that he was in Paris in 1919 as part of the American delegation to the peace conference. During his time in Paris, Shotwell visited the nearby battlefields and *régions dévastées*, confronting the material damage of total war face on, and writing of his experiences in graphic detail in his diary. The battlefields of Verdun and the Belgian town of Ypres, he recounted, symbolized 'the utmost that has ever been suffered and endured by men from the beginning of the world'.[3] And yet Shotwell argued that while wartime destruction needed to be understood in a manner which was tangible and graphic, it also took more subtle forms where 'there was no marching army in evidence'. This was the cultural war. 'There are devastated regions in the realms of philosophy and religion', he argued, 'as well as on the desolate fields of Northern France'.[4] At the heart of this book lies Shotwell's assertion that the war had caused physical harm but also damage to more abstract entities like the production of different branches of

---

[1] Diary entry for 6 April 1919, James T. Shotwell, *At the Paris Peace Conference* (New York, NY, 1937), p. 247.
[2] Harold Josephson, *James T. Shotwell and the Rise of Internationalism in America* (Cranbury, NJ, 1975).
[3] Diary entry for 23 May 1919. Shotwell, *At the Paris Peace Conference*, p. 331.
[4] James Shotwell, 'The Social History of the War: Preliminary Considerations', *Columbia University Quarterly*, 21 (1919), p. 291.

knowledge. In the wake of the most destructive conflict in human memory, which was an intellectual as well as a military confrontation, how might intellectual life, its institutions, and its practitioners be rebuilt from the ruins of war?

The First World War ushered new ways of waging war into the twentieth century. The logic of total war meant that whole societies were mobilized in prosecuting industrial and mechanized warfare where the distinction between civilian and combatant was increasingly blurred.[5] This was evident not only in the wider societal mobilization for war, but also in the conflict's targets and victims, with this war seeing the first aerial bombardment of civilian populations, mass internment of enemy alien civilians, and the vast displacement of populations.[6] The conflict was inaugurated by infamous instances of cultural destruction in 1914, such as the burning of Louvain library in August and the shelling of Reims Cathedral the following month, both by the German army. These acts quickly became notorious around the world as examples of the wanton excess of modern warfare.

Beyond the well-known examples of Louvain and Reims cultural life sustained severe damage across Europe in a series of interconnected ways that took years, and sometimes decades, to resolve.[7] Universities, libraries, churches, schools, and other sites of cultural importance were destroyed by long-range artillery fire, aerial bombing raids, or deliberate acts of vandalism by armies as they advanced or retreated. In eastern Serbia, the Bulgarian army sought to eradicate Serbian cultural influence through the destruction of books, manuscripts, and archives, while, in northern Italy, Austrian and German forces conducted bombing raids that caused significant damage to churches, museums, libraries, and archives.[8] These examples are far

---

[5] John Horne, 'Introduction: Mobilizing for "Total" War', in Horne ed., *State, Society and Mobilization in Europe during the First World War* (Cambridge, 1997), pp. 1–17; Roger Chickering and Stig Förster eds., *Great War, Total War: Combat and Mobilization on the Western Front, 1914–1918* (Cambridge, 2000).

[6] Tammy Proctor, *Civilians in a World at War, 1914–1918* (New York, 2010), p. 3.

[7] Alan Kramer has argued that cultural destruction was 'intrinsic' to the war itself. Kramer, *Dynamic of Destruction: Culture and Mass Killing in the First World War* (Oxford, 2007), p. 159.

[8] Milovan Pisarri, 'Bulgarian Crimes against Civilians in Occupied Serbia during the First World War', *Balcanica*, 44 (2013), pp. 357–90; Kramer, *Dynamic of Destruction*, pp. 55–57; Robert Bevan, *The Destruction of Memory: Architecture at War*, 2nd ed. (London, 2016).

from exhaustive.[9] The deliberate destruction of sites of cultural importance in wartime contravened the 1907 Hague Convention, which stipulated
that 'buildings dedicated to religion, art, science, or charitable purposes'
should not be targeted unless they were being used for military reasons.[10]

Beyond built infrastructure, cultural life suffered severe and direct
damage through the loss of human life: many young scholars, writers,
and artists died in combat at the front lines. The mass deployment of
troops at the beginning of the war meant that those with specialist skills
were often mobilized in regular fighting units. As the war progressed,
these men began to be 'combed out' to work on war-related projects more
closely aligned with their skills. Nevertheless, the move came too late for
promising intellectuals, such as the British physicist Henry Moseley and
the French sociologist Robert Hertz, both of whom had already been
killed in action. The deaths of individuals constituted a loss to wider
intellectual life that was understood as such by contemporaries.[11]

International cultural life suffered in more subtle ways during the war;
the disruption caused by the conflict to international communications
mechanisms meant that, in many cases, the exchange of people, books,
and ideas – essential to much pre-war intellectual activity – was severely
impeded. Cultural destruction, such as that which took place at Louvain
in 1914, was central to wartime cultural mobilization and the creation of
an image of the barbaric enemy.[12] The conflict was fought as a cultural

---

[9] Vėjas Gabriel Liulevičius, *War Land on the Eastern Front: Culture, National
Identity, and German Occupation in World War I* (Cambridge, 2000), p. 129;
Roger O'Keefe, *The Protection of Cultural Property in Armed Conflict*
(Cambridge, 2006), p. 37; James Wilford Garner, *International Law and the
World War*, vol. 1 (London, 1920), p. 451.

[10] O'Keefe, *The Protection of Cultural Property*, p. 24.

[11] Tomás Irish, 'Fractured Families: Educated Elites in Britain and France and the
Challenge of the Great War', *Historical Journal*, 57.2 (2014), pp. 509–30;
Jay Winter, *The Great War and the British People* (London, 1985), pp. 92–9;
Jean-François Sirinelli, *Génération intellectuelle: khâgneux et normaliens dans
l'entre-deux-guerres* (Paris, 1988), pp. 26–30.

[12] Pierre Purseigle, 'La Cité de demain: French Urbanism in War and
Reconstruction, 1914–1928', *French History*, 35.4 (2021), pp. 508–9. On
reconstruction, see Tammy Proctor, 'The Louvain Library and US Ambition in
Interwar Belgium', *Journal of Contemporary History*, 50.2 (2015), pp. 147–67;
Luc Verpoest, Leen Engelen, Rajesh Heynickx, et al. eds., *Revival after the Great
War: Rebuild, Remember, Repair, Reform* (Leuven, 2020); Nicholas Bullock
and Luc Verpoest eds., *Living with History, 1914–1964: Rebuilding Europe
after the First and Second World Wars and the Role of Heritage Preservation*
(Leuven, 2011).

war with intellectuals trading bitter manifestos across borders in defence of their national cause, with the Allies claiming to defend Western 'civilization' and Germany invoking its *Kultur*.[13] The most infamous intellectual manifesto was the German 'Appeal to the Civilized World', published in October 1914. Signed by ninety-three eminent German intellectuals, it defended Germany's conduct in the war while denying that atrocities had been committed by the German army in Belgium.[14] It elicited a strong international reaction with many intellectuals and institutions in allied and neutral countries severing ties with their erstwhile colleagues as a consequence.[15] The bitterness of wartime divisions meant that international connections, too, would need to be rebuilt in a process that took years.

Against the backdrop of unprecedented violence being waged on cultural life, the war saw the beginning of humanitarian efforts to assist intellectual communities and institutions. Aid of this type was often presented as a demonstration of solidarity between allied nations and a means through which nations mobilized culturally during the conflict. Following the German invasion of 1914, hundreds of Belgian refugee scholars were accommodated at institutions across Europe and North America. A 'Belgian University' was formed at Cambridge to allow exiles to continue their studies and to conduct research, where one observer claimed that it was evidence that 'the sacred hopes of our country have come through all her trials undiminished'.[16] Serbian scholars were afforded a similar welcome in allied countries from the onset of the Central Powers' offensive in late 1915.[17] The housing of refugee intellectuals privileged them as symbols and custodians of national life in exile. These relief efforts emphasized the importance of ensuring not only the good health of intellectual refugees, but the

---

[13] Anne Rasmussen, 'Mobilising Minds', in Jay Winter ed., *The Cambridge History of the First World War*, vol. 3 (Cambridge, 2013), pp. 390–418.

[14] Rasmussen, 'Mobilising Minds', pp. 390–9; Tomás Irish, *The University at War 1914–25: Britain, France and the United States* (Basingstoke, 2015), pp. 25–7; 32–25.

[15] Robert Fox, *Science Without Frontiers: Cosmopolitan and National Interests in the World of Learning, 1870–1940* (Corvallis, OR, 2016), pp. 45–52; Irish, *The University at War*, pp. 83–7.

[16] Charles Dejace, 'The Belgian University at Cambridge', *A Book of Belgium's Gratitude* (London, 1916), p. 299.

[17] Miloš Paunović, Milan Igrutinovic, Dejan Zec, et al., *Exile in the Classroom: Serbian Students and Pupils in Great Britain During the First World War* (Belgrade, 2016), p. 59.

continuity of their scholarly work and, in turn, national cultural life. This paradigm would be replicated on a larger scale in the post-war years.

Wartime relief to intellectuals had value in demonstrating solidarity with fellow allied states in wartime but it also spoke to the belief that cultural pursuits might form a protective bulwark against the barbarism of modern warfare. In many belligerent states, war libraries were established to send books to troops at the front, keeping their minds healthy and active against the ravages of total war.[18] Book relief emerged in other ways that spoke to intellectual, educational, and class differentiation, notably where soldiers and civilians were being held in internment or prisoner-of-war camps.[19] While the Hague Convention of 1907 made no specific provision for the treatment of interned intellectuals, many relief organizations sent specialist reading and laboratory equipment to camps, with informal 'universities' set up to structure learning.[20] Alfred T. Davies, who oversaw a British book relief scheme, stated that his work was 'absolutely essential to save the prisoners from mental starvation'.[21] A French prisoner of war newspaper described the camp library as 'a wonderful intellectual dining room where we can satisfy our literary and scientific appetites'.[22] The use of this humanitarian metaphor equated literal hunger with an

---

[18] T. W. Koch, *Books in the War: The Romance of Library War* Service (New York, 1919); Sara Haslam, 'Reading, Trauma and Literary Caregiving 1914–1918: Helen Mary Gaskell and the War Library', *Journal of Medical Humanities*, 41 (2020), pp. 305–21.

[19] *Report of the International Committee of the Red Cross on its Activities During the Second World War, Volume I, General Activities* (Geneva, 1948), p. 276; Alfred T. Davies, *Student Captives: an Account of the Work of the British Prisoners of War Book Scheme* (London, 1917); T. W. Koch, *War Libraries and Allied Studies* (New York, 1918).

[20] 'Convention (IV) Respecting the Laws and Customs of War on Land and its Annex: Regulations Concerning the Laws and Customs of War on Land. The Hague, 18 October 1907', ihl-databases.icrc.org/applic/ihl/ihl.nsf/Treaty.xsp? action=openDocument&documentId=4D47F92DF3966A7EC12563CD 002D6788 [accessed 1 August 2022]; Matthew Stibbe, *British Civilian Internees in Germany: The Ruhleben Camp, 1914–18* (Manchester, 2008), pp. 80–94; Alon Rachaminov, *POWs and the Great War: Captivity on the Eastern Front* (Oxford, 2002), pp. 99–101.

[21] 'Books for Prisoners', *The Times*, 29 December 1916, p. 11; Davies, *Student Captives*, p. 17; Edmund G.C. King, '"Books Are More To Me Than Food": British Prisoners of War as Readers, 1914–1918', *Book History*, 16 (2013), pp. 246–71.

[22] *L'intermède: Camp de Würzburg*, 14 January 1917, p. 47.

Figure 0.1 British war library workers prepare book parcels to send to wounded British soldiers, 1916 (Topical Press Agency/Stringer/Getty)

absence of specialist reading material; in this way, it also claimed that the needs of middle-class intellectuals differed from those of other sufferers as they needed intellectual as well as corporeal sustenance. As will be shown throughout this book, this metaphor became widespread in the early 1920s across a range of organizations and initiatives.

While the war posed an existential threat to European intellectual life, the conditions underpinning this threat did not abate with the signing of the armistice in November 1918. Violence of different types continued with great intensity across much of the continent into the early 1920s.[23] Hunger and disease were rife in Central and Eastern Europe by 1919, while the mass displacement caused by the Bolshevik Revolution and the Russian Civil War led to a major refugee crisis. Spiralling inflation gripped countries like Germany and Austria, meaning that practitioners of intellectual pursuits were unable to purchase books, periodicals, or laboratory equipment. Cumulatively, these

---

[23] Robert Gerwarth, *The Vanquished: Why the First World War Failed to End, 1917–1923* (London, 2016).

events put millions of lives in Europe at risk, among them thousands of intellectuals and their institutions, many of whom had already suffered severe disruption owing to the First World War.

All of this meant that when James Shotwell wrote of the damage wrought by the war on intellectual life in 1919, the worst was still to come. What followed was not just an act of reconstruction, but an improvised humanitarian intervention to save Europe's intellectual life. Governments, philanthropists, and humanitarian organizations oversaw a vast range of initiatives designed to save intellectuals and rebuild cultural institutions in the face of widespread fears over the fate of European civilization and the perceived threat of disorder across the continent. This book tells the story of how intellectual lives were saved from starvation and disease, libraries were rebuilt and restocked, and refugees were placed in new homes because they were deemed to be intellectuals. It argues that intellectuals and intellectual life were seen as an important emblem of the old, pre-war European order; thus, their salvation and restoration were symbolic means of safeguarding peace and stability following the terrible bloodshed of the Great War and the humanitarian crisis that followed.

Intellectual Relief: Definitions and Contexts

Feeding the Mind shows how the reconstruction of intellectual life formed a distinct and important part of the broader effort to rebuild Europe and save lives in the aftermath of the First World War. I term all of this intellectual relief. This form of relief was highly elitist, in that it was directed towards educated, middle-class communities, and was also seen as an emergency measure in response to a crisis of European intellectual life. Intellectual relief was both literal and metaphorical; it proceeded from the conviction that not only did the physical lives of intellectuals need to be saved, but that intellectual life itself – an abstract, intangible entity – needed salvation in the face of a mortal threat. Intellectual relief stressed that it was insufficient to merely restore intellectuals to physical health through feeding and medicines; their minds, too, required sustenance and restoration. Humanitarian organizations of differing sizes led schemes that provided food and medical aid to intellectuals at risk of death, but also supplied books, laboratory equipment, and other materials so that they could continue their creative work as both producers and imparters of knowledge. Beyond this, intellectual relief entailed the reconstruction of institutions like libraries and universities that had been destroyed by the violence of total war. Cumulatively, it sought to reconstruct Europe's intellectual life as it had been in 1914.

This type of humanitarian activity constituted an important element in the quest for stability in post-war Europe; it was, in many cases, directed towards new states in Central and Eastern Europe where democracies replaced deposed multi-ethnic empires. Here, the study of humanitarian aid offers a unique perspective on how philanthropists and policy makers sought to build stable states through the work of intellectuals; not so much in terms of what they researched or wrote, but what they represented as figures who were deeply embedded in the pursuit and dissemination of knowledge and who embodied middle-class interests. It is an example of what Charles Maier called 'recasting bourgeois Europe', a reaffirmation of middle-class interests against the perceived threats to order posed by Bolshevism, the growing strength of the working classes, or calls for self-determination from empire.[24]

Intellectual relief utilized both the practices and the language of post-war humanitarianism. In Austria, Poland, and Russia, 'intellectual kitchens' were set up to provide food and nourishment exclusively for those labelled intellectuals. In a similar manner, intellectuals were identified for special assistance among the 150,000 Russian refugees stranded in Constantinople in 1920 and 1921, with the League of Nations resolving in August 1921 that it was 'especially desirable' that they receive 'special protection and employment'.[25] Across Europe, from Vienna to Berlin, Budapest to Warsaw, Paris to Odesa, and Belgrade to Moscow, there is much evidence of a similar emphasis on ensuring the wellbeing of those involved in intellectual and cultural pursuits which marked them as a distinct category of sufferers. *Feeding the Mind* explores the contours of intellectual reconstruction and humanitarianism as a discrete project

---

[24] Charles S. Maier, *Recasting Bourgeois Europe: Stabilization in France, Germany, and Italy in the Decade after World War I* (Princeton, NJ, 1975). This idea has also been explored in histories of humanitarianism such as Michelle Tusan, 'Genocide, Famine and Refugees on Film: Humanitarianism and the First World War', *Past & Present*, 237.1 (2017), pp. 197–235; Emily Baughan, 'International Adoption and Anglo-American Internationalism, c 1918-1925', *Past & Present*, 239.1 (2018), pp. 181–217.

[25] 'Conference on the Question of Russian Refugees', 24 August, 1921, League of Nations Archives (LNA), Geneva, C-277-M-203–1921-VII.

because that is how it was viewed by a wide range of contemporary actors, including politicians, diplomats, philanthropists, aid workers, and intellectuals. Across organizations such as the American Relief Administration (ARA), the Imperial War Relief Fund (IWRF), the Friends' Emergency and War Victims' Relief Committee (FEWVRC), and the Rockefeller philanthropies, the category of the intellectual (and the related field of 'intellectual life') emerged again and again as necessitating bespoke, distinct, and discrete aid in post-war Europe. Seen as emblematic of wounded European civilization, intellectual relief was almost existential.

Alongside threats to human life presented by post-war famine, disease, and displacement, the peril of cultural death loomed large over post-war Europe. Discourses of civilizational decline, famously articulated by Paul Valéry and Oswald Spengler, were widespread among European intellectual elites following the end of the First World War and, in this reading, ideas and culture themselves faced extinction. A 1921 appeal by the British Quakers stated its fear that 'Austria, the beggared nation, will starve in her rags; a noble and splendid civilization will have passed away'.[26] Following the example of aid to prisoners of war in the recently-ended conflict, humanitarian appeals frequently spoke of the 'intellectual hunger' or 'intellectual starvation' of individuals in central and Eastern Europe who could not access recent literature and continue their cerebral work for the cause of civilization. The breakdown of cultural life was further evidence of post-war disorder which in turn provided an impetus for aid programmes to disperse literature and laboratory equipment to those in need. In the words of the ARA's head, Herbert Hoover, it was a matter of 'keeping their minds alive well as their bodies'.[27] This phrasing showed how those engaged in intellectual relief drew on fears of civilizational decline but utilized the language of humanitarianism in order to locate their work firmly within that sphere.[28]

---

[26] *Hidden Tragedy in Vienna* (London: Friends Relief Committee, Vienna, 1921), Library of the Society of Friends (LSF), London, YM/MfS/FEWVRC/4/3/7/4, pp. 26–7.

[27] Memorandum regarding talk of Mr. Whittemore, 1 January 1921, Columbia University Rare Book and Manuscript Library (CURBML), Bakhmeteff Archive of Russian and Eastern European Culture, Columbia University, New York, Committee for the Education of Russian Youth in Exile Records (BAR Ms Coll/CERYE), 1914–1939, Box 99, Folder 10.

[28] Didier Fassin, *Humanitarian Reason: A Moral History of the Present* (Berkeley, CA, 2012), pp. 2–3.

Feeding the Mind has two overlapping and mutually reinforcing themes, being the fate of intellectuals and intellectual life in post-war Europe and the humanitarian effort undertaken to reconstruct Europe in the same period. Neither of these themes is examined in isolation; indeed, I argue that each elucidates the other in a reciprocal manner. Humanitarianism shaped the organization of post-war intellectual life and the squalid conditions and cultural destruction of the war informed the humanitarian response that followed. In this manner, the two themes – seemingly distant and traditionally occupying distant places in the historiography – are deeply interconnected.

Intellectual relief was a widespread but limited element of post-First World War humanitarianism which sheds important light on the emergence of humanitarian practices in this key transitional period.[29] 'Intellectuals' were identified as especially deserving of aid owing to their societal and cultural eminence, which, in the eyes of philanthropists, politicians and many aid workers, differentiated their needs from those of other sufferers in the wider humanitarian landscape. Davide Rodogno has shown that 'civilization' was a key political and moral norm underpinning early twentieth-century humanitarianism; the concern to bolster civilization in areas seen as 'less civilized', such as Eastern Europe and the Near East, was fundamental to much humanitarian activity.[30] The idea of civilization was premised upon racial and gendered visions of global order. The same preoccupation with civilization informed intellectual relief and cast scholars, writers, artists, and students, as well as the institutions that supported them, as the elite embodiments of European

---

[29] Bruno Cabanes, *The Great War and the Origins of Humanitarianism 1918–1924* (Cambridge, 2014); Julia F. Irwin, *Making the World Safe: The American Red Cross and a Nation's Humanitarian Awakening* (Oxford, 2013); Tammy M. Proctor, 'An American Enterprise: British Participation in US Food Relief Programmes (1914–1923)', *First World War Studies*, 5.1 (2014), pp. 29–42; Keith David Watenpaugh, *Bread from Stones: The Middle East and the Making of Modern Humanitarianism* (Oakland, CA, 2015); Branden Little, 'An Explosion of New Endeavours: Global Humanitarian Responses to Industrialised Warfare in the First World War Era', *First World War Studies*, 5.1 (2014), pp. 1–16; Heather Jones, 'International or Transnational? Humanitarian Action During the First World War', *European Review of History/Revue européenne d'histoire*, 16.5 (2009), pp. 697–713; Davide Rodogno, *Night on Earth: A History of International Humanitarianism in the Near East, 1918–1930* (Cambridge, 2021); Daniel Maul, *The Politics of Service: US-amerikanische Quäker und internationale humanitäre Hilfe 1917–1945* (Berlin, 2022).

[30] Rodogno, *Night on Earth*, pp. 2–4.

civilization or, as one appeal put it, 'civilizing influences'.[31] As politicians, diplomats, philanthropists, and aid workers frequently invoked threats to European civilization in making the case for the importance of their work, the suffering of intellectuals, overwhelmingly men, came to take on an acute and symbolic importance. In this way, the humanitarian salvaging of intellectual life was portrayed as an imperative for the buttressing of civilization.

Many humanitarian initiatives in the aftermath of the First World War operated on the idea that 'need, not identity' was a key motivation for those who received attention.[32] This type of humanitarian rhetoric was best exemplified by schemes that sought to assist children who were suffering in the aftermath of war, with the image of the destitute child seeking to mobilize universal empathy, even when assistance served national or imperial ends.[33] Intellectual relief was explicitly premised upon the opposite of universal suffering as it identified a specific elite and educated group as especially deserving of assistance. Because it implicitly denied that all suffering was equal, it spoke to a different universalism, emphasizing that the production, dissemination, and cultivation of knowledge were universal phenomena of universal concern.

Post-First World War relief is a crucial indicator of how Europe sought to attain peaceful equilibrium against the persistence of wartime hostilities in the early 1920s. The humanitarian issues that followed were more complex than those of wartime because the worst suffering was experienced not among fellow allies, but in the territories of former enemies such as Germany and Austria. In wartime, cultural reconstruction constituted a form of ongoing mobilization against a demonized enemy. In the aftermath of war, reconstruction simultaneously presented opportunities for the hardening of wartime belligerence as well as for international reconciliation, meaning that the transition from hostile wartime mentalities to conciliatory post-war mindsets was neither immediate nor

---

[31] 'American Assistance for Families of German and Austrian Scientists and Teachers', 1921, Hoover Institution Library and Archives (HILA), Stanford University, Palo Alto, CA., American Relief Administration European Operational Records (ARAEOR), Box 551, Folder 7, Reel 652.

[32] Michael Barnett, *Empire of Humanity: A History of Humanitarianism* (Ithaca, NY, 2011), p. 82.

[33] Emily Baughan, '"Every Citizen of Empire Implored to Save the Children!" Empire, Internationalism and the Save the Children Fund in Inter-war Britain', *Historical Research*, 86.231 (2013), pp. 116–37.

straightforward.[34] Seen in this context, relief was both a measure and a facilitator of post-war cultural demobilization, although it was not always articulated as such. Instead, sweeping invocations of the collapse of civilization itself were made to justify assistance to intellectuals in post-war Austria, while their counterparts in Germany were overlooked by a range of agencies owing to lingering wartime bitterness.

This book was researched and written a century after the events in question, at a time when there is widespread cynicism and scepticism in political discourse about intellectual pursuits, the authority of experts, and the veracity of facts.[35] From the vantage point of 2023, the prevalence of projects to assist and support intellectuals and their institutions as part of the wider reconstruction of Europe suggests that an implicit faith was placed in these figures as agents of stabilization and reconstruction. Against the backdrop of modern-day anti-intellectualism, this appears almost utopian. In the aftermath of the First World War, assistance to intellectuals was consistent with a wider liberal internationalist belief in a rational and progressive international order where educated public opinion regulated international relations and sought to provide a safeguard against aggression.[36] In a world where educated public opinion was the ultimate sanction, intellectuals had an important role to play in building a stable order.[37]

The idea of intellectual relief opens up important definitional questions. Who was an intellectual and what function they were expected to perform? The intellectual has been variously invoked, assailed, defended, mourned, and celebrated in the historiography of twentieth-century Europe. There is a vast scholarship concerning intellectuals which generally analyses them in specific national contexts, meaning that they are frequently taken to have particular qualities specific to

---

[34] John Horne, 'Demobilizing the Mind: France and the Legacy of the Great War, 1919-1939', in Vesna Drapac and André Lambelet eds., *French History and Civilization: Papers from the George Rudé Seminar*, 2 (2009), pp. 101–19.

[35] William Davies, *Nervous States: How Feeling Took Over the World* (London, 2018).

[36] Stephen Wertheim, *Tomorrow, the World: The Birth of U.S. Global Supremacy* (Cambridge, MA, 2020), pp. 17–8, 28–9; Sakiko Kaiga, *Britain and the Intellectual Origins of the League of Nations, 1914–1919* (Cambridge, 2021), pp. 59–60.

[37] Leonard V. Smith, *Sovereignty at the Paris Peace Conference of 1919* (Oxford, 2018), p. 10.

national settings.[38] *Feeding the Mind* argues that in the aftermath of the First World War, intellectuals began being defined in an international (rather than national) context, with shared responsibilities and challenges, all of which were a product of the conflict and post-war social and economic conditions. This collective definition was highly gendered, in that it usually referred to men, as well as Eurocentric. In this period, tens of thousands of 'intellectuals' were referred to and assisted as a collective, whether that was in France, Germany, Austria, Hungary, Czechoslovakia, Poland, or Russia. The widespread invocation of intellectuals in this period suggests a growing but uneven transnational consensus regarding their importance, further evidence of which can be seen in the multiplicity of national and international associations set up in this period to protect intellectual interests. These organizations, such as the Confédération internationale des travailleurs intellectuels (CITI, established 1923), spoke of protections to be afforded to safeguard the social and cultural standing of international intellectuals. The frequent collective mention of intellectuals is evidence that, in the context of the post-war humanitarian moment and the reconstruction of the continent after the cataclysm of war, intellectuals mattered.

This book relies upon the archives of a number of humanitarian organizations and initiatives, some large and permanent, others small and fleeting. The archives of Western humanitarian organizations are

[38] Michel Winock, *Le siècle des intellectuels* (Paris, 1999); Stefan Collini, *Absent Minds: Intellectuals in Britain* (Oxford, 2006); Dietz Bering, *Die Intellektuellen: Geschichte eines Schimpfwortes* (Stuttgart, 1978); Schlomo Sand, *La fin de l'intellectuel français? De Zola à Houllebecq* (Paris, 2016); Jean-François Sirinelli, *Intellectuels et passions françaises* (Paris, 1990); Jeremy Jennings and Anthony Kemp-Welsh eds., *Intellectuals in Politics: From the Dreyfus Affair to Salman Rushdie* (London, 1997); Jeremy Jennings ed., *Intellectuals in Twentieth-Century France: Mandarins and Samurais* (London, 1993); Christopher Lasch, *The New Radicalism in America, 1889–1963: The Intellectual as Social Type* (New York, 1965); Richard Hofstadter, *Anti-Intellectualism in American Life* (New York, 1963); T. W. Heyck, *The Transformation of Intellectual Life in Victorian England* (London, 1982); Jurgen Habermas, 'Heinrich Heine and the role of the Intellectual in Germany', in Habermas ed., *The New Conservatism: Cultural Criticism and the Historians' Debate* (Cambridge, 1989), pp. 71–99; Richard Pipes ed., *The Russian Intelligentsia* (New York, 1961); Marc Raeff, *Origins of the Russian Intelligentsia: the Eighteenth Century Nobility* (New York, 1966); Stuart Finkel, *On the Ideological Front: The Russian Intelligentsia and the Making of the Soviet Public Sphere* (New Haven, CT, 2006).

notable for the story that they seek to convey, generally of good inten-
tions and successful outcomes where the absences can be as revealing as
that which is present.[39] Western humanitarian actors frequently initiated action based upon their perception of what was 'best' for populations based on racist, colonial, religious, political, and other
motivations. As Davide Rodogno notes, the voices of local populations
are often absent in these archives.[40] An interrogation of the plight of
intellectuals in this period highlights a different issue: these people were
educated, often multilingual, and sometimes had access to influential
intellectual and philanthropic networks. Crucially, they were equipped
with the vocabulary to speak the language of civilizational decline and
intellectual relief; they could, in many cases, 'write up' to humanitarian
organizations and philanthropists in a manner that other sufferers
could not.[41] In a humanitarian context, intellectual voices were heard
loud and clear.

***

Feeding the Mind explores the phenomenon of intellectual relief and
cultural reconstruction from the end of the First World War through to
1933 when, following the Great Depression and the rise to power of the
Nazis in Germany, European intellectual life was confronted by a new
set of challenges. Chapter 1 begins in Paris in 1919 as the peacemakers
sought to remake the post-war world. It analyses the emergence of
discourses of civilizational decline and different schemes to rebuild
the world which saw intellectuals at their heart. As news of the privations being experienced in Central Europe began to reach philanthropists, politicians, and intellectuals in Western Europe and North
America, the reconstruction of intellectual life was presented as
a means of averting civilizational collapse. This chapter shows how,
by mid-1920, the problems of post-war reconstruction and the needs of
intellectual communities had been identified by foundations such as the
Commonwealth Fund and humanitarian organizations like the British
Quakers as important objects of humanitarian action.

---

[39] Rodogno, *Night on Earth*, p. 311.   [40] Rodogno, *Night on Earth*, p. 6.
[41] Peter Gatrell, Alex Dowdall and Anindita Ghoshal et al., 'Reckoning with
Refugeedom: Refugee Voices in Modern History', *Social History*, 46.1 (2021),
pp. 70–95; Norbert Göltz, Georgina Brewis and Steffen Werther,
Humanitarianism in the Modern World: The Moral Economy of Famine Relief
(Cambridge, 2020), pp. 113–6.

Chapters 2 and 3 explore two distinct dimensions of post-war intellectual relief. Chapter 2 begins in Vienna, the epicentre for intellectual starvation in the early 1920s and widely described as one of Europe's 'centres of civilization', where different food aid schemes identified starving and impoverished intellectuals as a key demographic for assistance. Here, intellectuals were often fed and clothed away from the wider populations in which they lived. Despite the widespread invocation of 'intellectuals' as a category to be assisted, the practical distribution of aid demonstrated challenges in clearly defining who this encompassed. Chapter 3 analyses the emergence of book relief, the metaphorical counterpart of 'intellectual feeding', which operated on the understanding that the minds – as well as the bodies – of intellectuals needed nourishment. The provision of specialist literature and laboratory equipment to intellectuals across Central and Eastern Europe was articulated as an emergency humanitarian measure that overlapped with the provision of food and medicine to scholars. Book relief necessitated a more nuanced process than its corporeal counterpart; the ultimate resolution to Europe's book famine could not be found in emergency aid but rather in the restoration of international flows of publications that had ended abruptly with the outbreak of war, which meant that many libraries in Central and Eastern Europe had received no new overseas literature since 1914. For this reason, the normalization of international cultural relations occasioned by 1925's Locarno treaties was a key point in the resolution of this issue.

While the issues of intellectual feeding and provision of literature were two sides of the same coin, Chapter 4 explores the theme of intellectual displacement of both people and institutions. Starting in Constantinople in 1920, it assesses how and why thousands of intellectuals were combed out of the wider body of Russian refugees from the civil war and relocated to sites across Europe and the wider world, much as Belgian refugees had been during the First World War. The chapter also looks at how other forms of intellectual capital were displaced following post-war treaties and the redrawing of international borders, such as Hungarian universities and libraries which found themselves 'exiled' to new states. The displacement of knowledge demonstrated how individuals, institutions, and even modes of thinking were portrayed as synonymous with certain national identities and thus 'deserving' of emergency assistance for that reason.

Chapter 5 explores the reconstruction of intellectual sites in the aftermath of the war and various attempts to replace the knowledge that had been lost in warfare. It focuses on the rebuilding of the university libraries of Louvain and Belgrade and pays particular attention to not only the physical rebuilding of buildings, but the reconstruction of knowledge itself through the replacement of library and manuscript collections. Cultural reconstruction was not just about repairing sites that had suffered war damage; it also sought to support the production and dissemination of new knowledge and to symbolically push back against the 'collapse' of civilization. Reconstruction of sites destroyed in the war, and the replenishment of their collections, was an international phenomenon in which different countries, generally erstwhile allies, could make their own symbolic contribution to the buttressing of civilization; thus, this chapter also explores the reconstruction of the library of Tokyo Imperial University, destroyed in the Great Kantō earthquake of 1923, as a continuation of schemes to rebuild Louvain.

Whereas the preceding chapters focus on sites of humanitarian action, Chapter 6 centres on Geneva as a crucible for bureaucracy and attempts to categorize and organize international intellectual life. It addresses a question that underpins all of the preceding chapters: given widespread claims of their suffering in early 1920s Europe, who were the intellectuals? Beyond the famous analyses of figures like Julien Benda, Antonio Gramsci, and Karl Mannheim, this was a widely discussed transnational issue in the period. Europe's humanitarian crisis shone a light on the suffering of intellectuals as a distinct category, while, in the same period, a wide range of national and international organizations came into being in order to codify and safeguard their international standing. The post-war humanitarian crisis generated international interest in the position of intellectuals because, grappling with rampant inflation, precarious employment, and other material concerns, they had much in common across post-war Europe. The Epilogue discusses the legacies of post-1918 intellectual relief and how the memory of its failures – and the practical experience gained by those involved in the schemes of the early 1920s – informed how European intellectual life was rebuilt again from the ruins of the Second World War.

1 | *1919*

Rebuilding Civilization

At 3 pm on 25 January 1919, Woodrow Wilson rose to address the gathered delegates at the Paris Peace Conference about the establishment of a League of Nations. The formation of a general association of nations was the key desire of the American president in Paris; it had been the centrepiece of his famous fourteen points and an essential element of his vision to craft global peace.[1] The first piece of business that afternoon was to appoint a commission to draft a covenant for the League. Given his personal stake in the project, Wilson would chair this committee and personally oversee the drafting process.[2] In his address to delegates drawn from twenty-six states and territories, Wilson initially touched upon what were by then familiar themes; the establishment of the League would, he asserted, complete the work of the peace conference and was deemed urgent because the burden of modern warfare touched the 'heart of humanity' itself.[3]

The American president then turned to matters of the mind. Wilson decried the wartime mobilization of one of the great markers of civilizational progress, science, and its subversion by destructive forces. 'Is it not a startling circumstance', he asked, 'that the great discoveries of science, that the quiet study of men in laboratories, that the thoughtful developments which have taken place in quiet lecture rooms, have now been turned to the destruction of civilization?' Wilson felt that the victorious allies had a responsibility to ensure that intellect was never again corrupted in the same manner, and thus he urged greater international cooperation as a safeguard against further regression. 'Only

---

[1] Adam Tooze, *The Deluge: The Great War and the Remaking of Global Order* (London, 2014), p. 255.

[2] Margaret MacMillan, *Peacemakers: The Paris Conference of 1919 and Its Attempt to End War* (London, 2001), p. 94.

[3] Speech of Woodrow Wilson, 25 January 1919, *Papers Relating to the Foreign Relations of the United States: The Paris Peace Conference, 1919*, vol. 3 (Washington, DC, 1943), p. 178.

the watchful, continuous co-operation of men', he claimed, 'can see to it that science, as well as armed men, is kept within the harness of civilization'.[4]

Perhaps it should not come as a surprise that Wilson would speak in such terms. After all, before he was a politician, initially as governor of New Jersey and then as president of the United States, he was a successful historian, political scientist, and president of Princeton University.[5] However, the American president was not alone in taking up this theme in making the case for the League of Nations. Léon Bourgeois, the veteran French politician and a long-time advocate of a world association who had attended the pre-war peace conferences at the Hague, also touched upon the connection between science and war. Global interdependence in the 'economic, financial, moral and intellectual spheres' meant that that 'every wound inflicted at some point threatens to poison the whole organs'. For Bourgeois, the application of science towards warfare turned the former away from its 'proper object' of furnishing 'hope for the future'.[6]

Wilson and Bourgeois articulated a widespread sense of unease with matters of the mind that had gathered pace during the war and came to a crescendo upon its conclusion. This can be seen as part of a general loss of faith in the idea of 'civilization', which had been premised upon the idea of progress in history and which was, in turn, used to emphasize Euro-American political, racial, and cultural superiority.[7] By the end of the First World War, many authors voiced anxieties about the consequences of the conflict for Europe's high culture and intellectual achievement, which was, in turn, frequently portrayed as an emblem of civilization itself. As people began to take stock of the damage wrought by the war, intellectual life emerged as a distinct field that required

---

[4] Speech of Woodrow Wilson, 25 January 1919, *Papers Relating to the Foreign Relations of the United States,* vol. 3, p. 179.

[5] John Milton Cooper, *Woodrow Wilson: A Biography* (New York, 2011); A. Scott Berg, *Wilson* (London, 2014).

[6] Speech of Léon Bourgeois, 25 January 1919, *Papers Relating to the Foreign Relations of the United States*, vol. 3, pp. 183–4.

[7] Jan Ifversen, 'The Crisis of European Civilisation after 1918', in Menno Spiering and Michael Wintle, eds., *Ideas of Europe Since 1914: The Legacy of the First World War* (Basingstoke, 2002), pp. 14–31; Mark Mazower, 'An International Civilization? Empire, Internationalism, and the Crisis of the Mid-Twentieth Century', *International Affairs* 82.3 (2006) pp. 553–66; Paul Betts, *Ruin and Renewal: Civilising Europe after the Second World War* (London, 2020), pp. 1–29.

reconstruction, and one which simultaneously provided the tools to effect the wider reconstitution of civilization. By the summer of 1920, extreme food shortages in Central and Eastern Europe meant that the need to aid intellectual life had taken on greater urgency and engendered a new humanitarian preoccupation: the salvation of European intellectuals.

***

Intellectual reconstruction was conceptualized as both a metaphorical and a material issue from the start of 1919 until the middle of 1920, by which time many humanitarian initiatives had begun to take shape. It was metaphorical in the sense that the events of the war led to much introspection among intellectuals about how a previously deeply held belief in the idea of progress – as they understood it – had come to a grinding halt with the global cataclysm of 1914. Framed in this manner, reconstruction was an intellectual process, which posed difficult questions about ideas and the nature of knowledge itself, as well as about the function of intellectuals in their respective societies. There were also more tangible issues at stake in the immediate aftermath of the war; physical institutions, many of which had been destroyed by fighting, needed to be rebuilt, while international connections required cultivation after over four years of bitter cultural warfare. The year 1919 was a time for taking stock and enumerating the material losses of wartime as well as interpreting their meaning for the worlds of learning and high culture. In the words of historian Jörn Leonhard, the end of the war marked a point 'between the past and the future'.[8]

Nineteen nineteen was the year of the Paris Peace Conference, when politicians, diplomats, lobbyists, intellectuals, journalists, and observers descended upon the French capital. The conference itself had the daunting aim of ensuring peace in Europe and, given the breadth of issues involved and the scale of the problems, it acts as a prism through which post-war issues, be they political, social, or cultural, can be viewed. The mood of the time was somewhat paradoxical. Pessimism was widespread across Europe as contemporaries grappled with the scale and significance of wartime losses and sought to imbue them with a wider meaning for their individual nations and civilization more generally. At the same time, 1919 was a chance to remake the world

---

[8] Jörn Leonhard, *Der überforderte Frieden: Versailles und die Welt, 1918–1923* (Munich, 2018), p. 22.

anew in order to ensure enduring peace, and thus there was a fleeting sense of hope and possibility. This was encapsulated in the aspiration of Wilsonian self-determination and the promise of a League of Nations.[9] In this way, the formal end of the First World War afforded contemporaries a moment to contemplate the meaning of what had been lost while also mapping out visions of how things might change in the years ahead. Intellectuals were deeply involved in these processes as thinkers, embodiments of wartime decline, and potential agents of better futures.

The immediate post-war period was marked by three related developments which saw Europe's cultural crisis transformed from an intellectual matter to one that required large-scale material assistance. First, many prognostications of civilizational decline followed the end of the war and contributed to a widespread sense that Europe was experiencing, in the resonant words of the French poet Paul Valéry, a 'crisis of the mind'. The second development was the way in which intellectual reconstruction was discussed at the Paris Peace Conference as both a measure of wartime loss and reason for reparation as well as a means of building a lasting peace. Furthermore, the discussions in Paris demonstrated a preoccupation with the rise of Bolshevism and the fear, widely held by many politicians and diplomats, that it might take root in the emerging successor states of Central and Eastern Europe. This fear of Bolshevism was linked to a third dynamic – the emerging humanitarian crisis in Central Europe and the growing realization that hundreds of thousands of people faced starvation and required immediate aid. Early 1920 saw organizations like the British Quakers providing bespoke assistance to intellectuals in Central Europe and many others followed. The post-war crisis of civilization had, by the middle of 1920, become a humanitarian issue whereby aid to Europe's intellectuals was formally organized and justified as a means of stabilizing European societies in order to ward off the collapse of civilization itself.

Crisis of Civilization, Crisis of the Mind

The American ambassador to the Ottoman Empire, Henry Morgenthau, argued in late 1918 that had Germany emerged victorious from the conflict, 'civilization would have been set back in its march of progress

---

[9] Jay Winter, *Dreams of Peace and Freedom: Utopian Moments in the Twentieth Century* (New Haven, CT, 2006), pp. 48–9.

possibly one thousand years, at least five hundred'.[10] The total violence of the First World War led to a wave of cultural pessimism and widespread claims that European civilization was on its last legs. While thinkers had been preoccupied with ideas of civilizational decline before the First World War, the conflict's culmination saw a resurgence of reflection on the issue.[11] From passing comments in diplomatic correspondence at the peace conference to metaphors that underscored the importance of a particular issue or elaborate tracts that sought to explore the issue systematically, invocations of civilizational collapse were widespread in 1919.

The crisis of civilization has been dealt with extensively by historians but provides important context for the intellectual reconstruction that emerged in the aftermath of the First World War.[12] Discourses of civilizational decline usually sought to historicize the present crisis through comparison to dead civilizations of antiquity. The best-known articulation of the crisis of civilization was Oswald Spengler's *Der Untergang des Abendlandes (The Decline of the West)*, the first volume of which was published in April 1918. Spengler argued that civilization was in its old age and on the cusp of inevitable decline, as many historic civilizations before had declined.[13] Although the majority of the book had been written before the war, its publication at the end of the war resonated in Germany and it had sold 100,000 copies by 1926, as well as being translated into many languages.[14] Other authors

---

[10] 'Hold High the Light of Liberty', *Wisconsin State Journal*, 15 December 1918, p. 14.

[11] Richard Overy, *The Morbid Age: Britain and the Crisis of Civilization, 1919–1939* (London, 2010), p. 10; Fritz Ringer, *The Decline of the German Mandarins: The German Academic Community, 1890–1933* (Cambridge, MA, 1969), p. 2; Zeev Sternhell, *The Anti-Enlightenment Tradition* (New Haven, CT, 2010), pp. 369–70.

[12] Ifversen, 'The Crisis of European Civilisation after 1918', p. 14; Mark Hewitson and Matthew d'Auria, 'Introduction: Europe during the Forty Years' Crisis', in Hewitson and d'Auria eds., *Europe in Crisis: Intellectuals and the European Idea 1917–1957* (New York, 2012), pp. 1–11.

[13] Oswald Spengler, *Der Untergang des Abendlandes: Umrisse einer Morphologie der Weltgeschichte* (Munich, 1963; orig. 1918); Peter Watson, *A Terrible Beauty: The People and Ideas that Shaped the Modern Mind* (London, 2000), pp. 171–2; Christophe Charle, *Discordance des temps: une brève histoire de la modernité* (Paris, 2011), pp. 339–42; Leonhard, *Der überforderte Frieden*, pp. 622–38.

[14] Philipp Blom, *Fracture: Life and Culture in the West 1918–1938* (London, 2015), pp. 45–6.

made similar dark comparisons. In his book about post-war social reconstruction, the American sociologist Charles A. Ellwood claimed that 'careful students of civilization' had pointed out the 'disturbing resemblances' between contemporary Europe and the deposed civilization of ancient Rome.[15] The Italian historian Guglielmo Ferrero published widely on this topic in the immediate aftermath of the war, offering comparisons between post-war Europe and ancient Rome.[16]

Civilization has been defined in myriad ways since the Enlightenment. The term emerged in the eighteenth century in the context of jurisprudence but had, by the century's end, become synonymous with advancement and refinement. All of these qualities were held to be antithetical to barbarism, and the binary quality of civilization existing in opposition to a barbaric other remained an important characteristic into the early twentieth century.[17] The nineteenth century saw the emergence of a 'standard of civilization', a legal framework utilized to denote the global extent of international law, all of which was premised upon European superiority. This facilitated, according to Mark Mazower's recent analysis, a 'cultural mapping of the world' which placed Europe at its heart.[18] The legal utilization of the term meant that civilization could be invoked as both a claim to power and a rationale for colonial violence.[19] By the start of the twentieth century, civilization was frequently cited as a justification for European imperial rule, while also becoming increasingly fractured according to national characteristics, traditions, and cultures.[20]

[15] Charles A. Ellwood, *The Social Problem: A Reconstructive Analysis* (New York, 1919), p. 3.
[16] Guglielmo Ferrero, 'La ruine de la civilisation antique: réflexions et comparaisons', *Revue des deux mondes*, 53 (1919), pp. 311–29; Guglielmo Ferrero, *The Ruin of the Ancient Civilization and the Triumph of Christianity: With Some Consideration of Conditions in the Europe of Today* (London, 1921).
[17] Betts, *Ruin and Renewal*, pp. 11–12; Larry Wolff, *Inventing Eastern Europe: The Map of Civilization on the Mind of the Enlightenment* (Stanford, CA, 1994), pp. 4–5.
[18] Mark Mazower, *Governing the World: The History of an Idea* (London, 2012), p. 71.
[19] Mazower, 'An International Civilization?' p. 554.
[20] Betts, *Ruin and Renewal*, p. 12; Sternhell, *The Anti-Enlightenment Tradition*, pp. 316–70.

Writing in 2019, Eric D. Weitz claimed that the term contained 'both humanitarian and exterminatory possibilities'.[21]

The First World War was fought and portrayed in allied countries as a struggle to defend civilization; days after the German invasion of Belgium, the French philosopher Henri Bergson who would later chair the League of Nations' International Committee on Intellectual Cooperation (ICIC), proclaimed that 'the struggle against Germany is the struggle of civilization against barbarism'.[22] For the Allies, their war for civilization meant fighting for a number of (sometimes contradictory) concepts, such as the ideas of 1789 and the rights of man, democracy, universalism, Christianity, and the heritage of ancient Greece and Rome. In opposition, German intellectuals claimed to be fighting to defend German *Kultur*, which was more rooted in regionality, encompassed civic ideas like self-sacrifice and heroism, and viewed civilization as materialistic.[23] These opposing visions of the war had the effect of popularizing the idea that the war was being fought in defence of not only territory but also a cultural ideal.[24] The Inter-Allied victory medal, issued in 1919, proclaimed that the conflict should be known as 'the Great War for Civilisation' and ensured that the association of the allied cause with that of civilization would be cast in bronze for eternity.

Intellectual Responses to the Crisis of Civilization

While civilization held multiple meanings in different contexts, it was frequently associated with high culture and intellectual life. Seen this way, the problems facing the world of intellect following the First World War symbolized the wider perceived threat to European civilization itself. This was the argument of Paul Valéry, who wrote, as the peace conference was sitting in April 1919, that 'a civilization is as fragile as a life'.[25] For Valéry, the war had not only grievously damaged

---

[21] Eric D. Weitz, *A World Divided: The Global Struggle for Human Rights in the Age of Nation-States* (Princeton, NJ, 2019), p. 109.

[22] Irish, *The University at War*, p. 24.

[23] Wolfgang J. Mommsen, 'German Artists, Writers, and Intellectuals, and the Meaning of War 1914–1918', in John Horne ed., *State, Society and Mobilization in Europe During the First World War* (Cambridge, 1997), pp. 21–38; Stéphane Audoin-Rouzeau and Annette Becker, *14–18: Understanding the Great War* (New York, 2002), p. 116.

[24] Rasmussen, 'Mobilising Minds', p. 396.

[25] Paul Valéry, 'The Spiritual Crisis', *The Athenaeum*, 11 April 1919, p. 182.

European culture through its destructiveness and the 'thousands of young writers and young artists who are dead', but also presented the troubling phenomenon whereby the accumulated knowledge and science of Europe – formerly evidence of its supposed civilizational superiority – had been applied to warfare.[26] Valéry identified three crises threatening Europe by 1919: military, economic, and intellectual.[27] For Valéry, Europe's crisis of the mind was also linked to a more general fear of European decline and the rise of Asia.[28]

Many thinkers reflected on the fate of civilization in the same period. The influential Belgian historian of science George Sarton wrote that intellectual reconstruction was just as important as material reconstruction in order to 'preserve the sacred ideals which are the essence of our civilization'.[29] Other writers engaged in discussions of civilizational collapse in a more critical manner. In June 1919, the French pacifist Romain Rolland wrote sarcastically of the decline of civilization, seeing it as euphemism for colonial rule: 'goodbye, Europe, queen of thought, guide of humanity. You have lost your way, you lie trampled in a cemetery. Your place is there. Go to sleep! And let others lead the world.'[30] Conservative Germans were also critical of the idea of civilization (or Zivilisation) because it was antithetical to the *Kultur* for which they had fought the war; the novelist Thomas Mann argued at the conflict's end that civilization was un-German and thus equated to support for the allied cause.[31] Writing a number of years later, the historian Arnold Toynbee, who attended the Paris Peace Conference as part of the British delegation and spent much of his career preoccupied with the study of civilizations, was critical of 'the rational Western intellectual' because, while they could admit the fallibility of civilization after the war, they had not identified its fragility before 1914.[32]

The crisis of civilization was, for the most part, an intangible, intellectual construct; it was given primary expression in the world of books and journals which discussed the fallibility of a culture

[26] Valéry, 'The Spiritual Crisis', pp. 182–3.
[27] Valéry, 'The Spiritual Crisis', p. 183.
[28] Paul Valéry, 'The Intellectual Crisis', *The Athenaeum*, 2 May 1919, pp. 279–80.
[29] George Sarton, 'War and Civilization', *Isis*, 2.2 (1919), pp. 317–8.
[30] Romain Rolland, 'Aux peuples assassinés', *L'Art Libre*, 15 June 1919, p. 66.
[31] Thomas Mann, *Reflections of a Nonpolitical Man* (New York, 1983), p. 36.
[32] Arnold J. Toynbee, *The World After the Peace Conference* (London, 1926), p. 88.

which was built upon ideas of perennial progress and argued that examples from antiquity formed instructive precedents. It was, in that respect, an imagined crisis, but one which would provide a crucial part of the lexicon utilized to explain the material threat posed to intellectual life thereafter. The language of civilizational crisis would also be used to explain and justify the imperative of humanitarian relief in the early 1920s.

By the end of the First World War, intellectual life was seen as both a symptom of Europe's wider decline and also as a unique resource that could bring about its recovery. As Valéry wrote in his diagnosis of Europe's 'spiritual crisis', the world faced a problem of disorder.[33] While the war had disrupted intellectual life, many felt that intellectuals could also play a particular role in helping to re-establish European order. Alongside pessimistic assertions of the imminent decline of intellectual life, schemes emerged which sought to leverage organized intellectual life to build stable and peaceful societies. The key issue which most of these initiatives encountered was their international composition and the (un)willingness of participants to cooperate with the former enemy. Before the war, intellectual life was characterized by its international mindedness; after the conflict, the international community of scholars and writers was theoretically well-placed to rebuild international links, symbolically making peace with the former enemy and providing an example to their wider communities.[34]

International pacifists saw a distinct role for intellectuals in salving the wounds of the war. This line of thinking developed during the conflict itself, where international appeals specifically targeted intellectuals as agents of peace. In October 1914, a petition drawn up by the German scientists Georg Friedrich Nicolai and Albert Einstein identified 'those who are esteemed and considered as authorities by their fellow-men' as crucial in salvaging European civilization in the face of destruction.[35] In early 1915, the International Peace Bureau in Berne issued an appeal 'to intellectual leaders in all nations' which urged them to 'bear aloft the banner of civilisation' and remain aloof from national hatred. It mapped out a special role for these intellectual leaders on the conclusion of peace when their

---

[33] Valéry, 'The Spiritual Crisis', p. 184.
[34] Fox, *Science Without Frontiers*, pp. 11–44.
[35] Georg Friedrich Nicolai, *The Biology of War* (New York, 1919), p. xix.

'words and deeds' would 'help to heal the wounds which are bleeding today'.[36]

Following the formal cessation of hostilities, pacifist intellectuals were quick to propose international organization as a means of repudiating war and as a demonstration of transnational solidarity. Many of these proposals, while international in scope, centred on the French capital. On 26 June 1919, two days before the signing of the Treaty of Versailles, an appeal called the 'Proud Declaration of Intellectuals' appeared in the French socialist newspaper *l'Humanité*.[37] The petition was authored by the Romain Rolland, who had been an outspoken opponent of the conflict while it was ongoing. In 1914, Rolland wrote *Au-dessus de la mêlée*, a tract that was deeply critical of the recourse to aggressive nationalism by his erstwhile colleagues in the course of the war. Rolland addressed his appeal to 'workers of the mind, colleagues dispersed across the world and separated for five years by armies, censorship and the hatred of nations at war'. His declaration called on not only the reconstruction of the world of the mind that had existed before the war, but also its re-imagining as something 'more solid and more sure than that which existed before'. Rolland argued that the shared humanity of intellectuals ought to override everything else. His appeal was signed by more than 140 intellectuals representing nations such as France, Germany, Britain, Belgium, Italy, Russia, Switzerland, Greece, the United States, Austria, Argentina, Sweden, Hungary, India, Spain, and Hungary.[38]

Rolland's appeal sparked a debate in France where conservative authors challenged the internationalism of the pacifist proposal and a reignited debate from the Dreyfus Affair of twenty years prior.[39] On 19 July 1919, a counter-appeal was published on the front page of *Le Figaro* by the conservative Catholic author Henri Massis. He criticized Rolland's 'bolshevism of the mind' in appealing to universal humanity over national identity. For Massis, the task of reconstruction should

[36] Henri La Fontaine and Henri Golay, 'To Intellectual Leaders in All Nations', January 1915. Harvard University Archives (HUA), Cambridge, MA, Charles W. Eliot Papers, UAI 15.894, Box 101, War Societies, 1915–18, M-P, 5 of 7.

[37] Romain Rolland, 'Fière déclaration d'intellectuels', *L'Humanité*, 26 June 1919, p. 1.

[38] Romain Rolland, 'Déclaration de l'Independence de l'esprit', in Rolland ed., *Quinze ans de combat (1919–1934)* (Paris, 1935), pp. 7–9.

[39] On the Dreyfus Affair, see Ruth Harris, *The Man on Devil's Island: Alfred Dreyfus and the Affair that Divided France* (London, 2011).

focus on defending French intellectual values, which would, in turn, be beneficial to humanity. 'Victorious France wishes to retake its sovereign place in the order of the mind', he claimed, suggesting that it was too early to talk about reconciliation with former enemies.[40] In a similar vein, the right-wing author and politician Maurice Barrès wrote a series of articles in the conservative *Écho de Paris* newspaper in 1919 on the theme of 'the intellectual reconstruction of France'. Rather than seeing it as evidence of a collapsing civilization, Barrès praised the application of French science to warfare during the conflict.[41] For Barrès, the war proved French intellectual superiority because it had salvaged 'the accumulated treasures of high civilization', meaning that there was no reason for the establishment of equal international intellectual relations.[42] Both Massis and Barrès were opponents of universal ideas of the Enlightenment and French Revolution and their positions in 1919 were consistent with this.[43] For both, civilization was a national, rather than a universal endeavour, and a means by which France could lead the world.

Other pacifists viewed the war as an opportunity to reorganize intellectual life. The French socialist Henri Barbusse fought in the conflict and wrote one of its most famous anti-war treatises, *Le Feu*.[44] During the conflict he began to collaborate with a number of fellow combatants, as well as figures like Rolland, in the hope of creating an intellectual movement that could create a better social order.[45] Barbusse, like so many other intellectuals of the period, justified the need for action in terms of civilizational decline, writing: 'we are the same as these hopeless and paralysed witnesses from antique

---

[40] 'Pour un parti de l'intelligence', *Le Figaro*, 19 July 1919, p. 1. Julien Benda later criticized Massis for his position, which Benda claimed was no different to that of Germany in 1871. Julien Benda, *La trahison des clercs* (Paris, 1927), pp. 297–8.

[41] Maurice Barrès, 'Le rôle de la science française pendant la guerre', *L'Écho de Paris*, 26 May 1919, p. 1.

[42] Maurice Barrès, 'La reconstitution intellectuelle', *L'Écho de Paris*, 7 April 1919, p. 1.

[43] Sternhell, *The Anti-Enlightenment Tradition*, pp. 316–8; Robert Wohl, *The Generation of 1914* (Cambridge, MA, 1979), pp. 5–18.

[44] Henri Barbusse, *Le Feu* (Paris, 1916).

[45] Henri Barbusse, *La lueur dans l'abîme: ce que veut le Groupe Clarté* (Paris, 1920), pp. 130–1; Nicole Racine, 'The Clarté Movement in France, 1919-21', *Journal of Contemporary History*, 2.2 (1967), pp. 195–201; Raymond Lefebvre, 'L'organisation de l'internationale intellectuelle', *l'Art Libre*, 15 November 1919, p. 185.

cataclysms'.[46] The result was a group called *Clarté*, which felt that the international organization of intellectual life was key to ensuring global peace. Charles Richet, a pacifist, eugenicist, and physiologist, wrote in 1919 that *Clarté* aspired to create an 'internationalism of intelligence', by which he meant the adoption of inclusive international modes of thinking in science and art irrespective of whether one had been belligerent in the war. For Richet, the idea of nationalism in art and science was 'just as absurd as if the animals in a zoo or the plants in a botanic garden had national claims'.[47] *Clarté* held its first meeting in Paris in September 1919, by which time it had the support of writers with international reputations such as H. G. Wells, Upton Sinclair, Thomas Hardy, E. D. Morel, Rabindranath Tagore, and Stefan Zweig.[48] However, *Clarté* was short-lived; it planned to hold an international congress in Switzerland in 1920 but had fractured by that point over the issue of its adherence to the Third International and the use of violence.

The pacifist Women's International League for Peace and Freedom (WILPF) also saw an important role for international intellect in the reconstruction of the world. Its position was mapped out at a conference held in Zurich in May 1919, which overlapped with the peace conference in Paris and was intended as an alternative to it. The Zurich conference was attended by 146 women from fifteen different countries and, unlike the gathering of victors in Paris, ex-enemy states were well-represented. Despite these differences, the Zurich conference proceeded from the same point of departure as so many post-war analyses, asserting that 'the events of the past five years have proved that our civilization has completely failed'. The conference resolved to set up an educational committee under the leadership of the Norwegian zoologist Emily Arnesen, with the goal of creating an international spirit in young people through education.[49] In a more detailed proposal written the following year, Arnesen stated that members of this committee needed to be selected carefully to imbue it with 'prestige and authority' with which to counter chauvinism. Such a committee, once

---

[46] Barbusse, *La lueur dans l'abîme*, p. 5.
[47] Charles Richet, 'L'internationalisme de l'intelligence', *L'Art Libre*, 15 October 1919, p. 165.
[48] Barbusse, *La lueur dans l'abîme*, p. 148.
[49] 'Proposals: Educational Programme', in *Rapport du congrès international de femmes* (Geneva, 1919) pp. 267–268, 314–315.

functioning, would constitute a 'civilizing institution' engaged in a 'great communal civilizational task'.[50]

Pacifists could articulate a vision for the full cooperation of international intellectuals as they had not engaged in the divisive discourse of wartime. For those who had been belligerent in their attitudes during the conflict, the task was much more complicated. Many international academic organizations dissolved following the outbreak of war in 1914, fracturing much of the intense internationalization that had taken place over the preceding half-century.[51] Around the midpoint of the conflict, allied nations began reviving international collaboration while ensuring the ongoing exclusion of scholars from the Central Powers and instead casting the new bodies as inter-allied, rather than fully international bodies.[52] This inter-allied emphasis continued into the post-war period, often becoming embedded into the structure of larger organizations.

Two major international organizations were established in 1919, the International Research Council (IRC) and the International Union of Academies (IUA), which represented the sciences and the humanities, respectively. The example of the IUA demonstrated the difficulties of resuming international cooperation after the war. In the spring of 1919, the Institut de France contacted their counterparts at the British Academy (BA) with a proposal to form a new body to replace the pre-war International Association of Academies. The proposal called for the continued exclusion of scholars from the Central Powers in the new organization. While the British Academy worried about 'Europe being divided into two intellectual leagues', it ultimately agreed to participate in the French initiative until such time as 'it may be possible to readmit Germany and Austria to fellowship of civilized nations'.[53] It was

---

[50] Emily Arnesen, 'Conseil international d'éducation et d'instruction publique', La contemporaine (LAC), Nanterre, Fonds Duchêne, F/DELTA/RES/244/6, pp. 1–6.

[51] A good overview of this phenomenon can be found in Martin H. Geyer and Johannes Paulmann, 'Introduction: The Mechanics of Internationalism', in Geyer and Paulmann eds., *The Mechanics of Internationalism* (Oxford, 2001), pp. 1–26.

[52] Tomás Irish, 'From International to Inter-allied: Transatlantic University Relations in the Era of the First World War, 1905–1920', *Journal of Transatlantic Studies*, 13.4 (2015), pp. 311–25.

[53] Sir Frederic Kenyon to President of Académie des Inscriptions et Belles Lettres, 19 July 1919, British Academy Archives (BAA), London, Minutebook of the British Academy, 1912–1919, 189–90; 204.

a similar story with the IRC, which was established following two inter-allied conferences towards the end of the war.[54] The IRC's statutes explicitly excluded the former Central Powers and allowed neutrals to be admitted only by a three-quarters majority vote.[55] The non-inclusion of German scholars from many international intellectual organizations mirrored the wider exclusion of Germany from the League of Nations, which persisted until 1926.[56]

The discourse of civilizational decline was widespread in 1919 and framed how many thought about post-war reconstruction, from issues of building peace, to the practice of intellectual work, to the issue of who was and was not admitted to the circle of 'civilized' nations after the war. Valéry's 'crisis of the mind' was a symptom of a wider malaise that had come to the fore during the war. The association of high culture and intellectual life with civilization meant that intellectuals could play an important and highly symbolic role in re-establishing European stability. The impediments to the stabilization of international relations, especially when it came to the reintegration of the former enemy, would present an ongoing challenge. All of these issues were apparent at the Paris Peace Conference.

The Paris Peace Conference

In his famous account of the Paris Peace Conference, John Maynard Keynes described Europe as exhibiting the 'fearful convulsions of a dying civilization'.[57] When the peace conference opened in January 1919, the victor states were tasked with building peace from Europe's ruins. The challenges facing the conference were exceptionally complex; four empires had collapsed in the course of the war and new polities had emerged to fill this power vacuum. The conference was to

---

[54] Fox, *Science without Frontiers*, pp. 72–82.

[55] A. G. Cock, 'Chauvinism and Internationalism in Science: The International Research Council, 1919-1926', *Notes and Records of the Royal Society of London*, 37.2 (1983), p. 249.

[56] Daniel J. Kevles, '"Into Hostile Political Camps": The Reorganization of International Science in World War I', *Isis*, 62. 1 (1971), pp. 47–60; Elisabeth Piller, *Selling Weimar: German Public Diplomacy and the United States, 1918–1933* (Stuttgart, 2021), p. 134; Horne, 'Demobilizing the Mind: France and the Legacy of the Great War, 1919-1939', pp. 101–19.

[57] John Maynard Keynes, *The Economic Consequences of the Peace* (New York, 1920), p. 4.

agree the specific boundaries of many new states, while also deciding what to do with the vanquished powers of the war and determining what reparations they might pay for war damage. Woodrow Wilson was committed to the idea of setting up a League of Nations to prevent the outbreak of future wars. The Paris conference led to the drafting of peace treaties with the five defeated powers which were signed between June 1919 and August 1920, although the last of these, with the Ottoman Empire, was superseded in 1923 by the Lausanne Treaty.[58] Paris in 1919 was thronged with delegations, journalists, interested observers, and lobbyists who sought to influence the peace treaties on myriad issues. The French capital became the centre of the international world, minus formal representatives from vanquished states and Bolshevik Russia.

The Russian Civil War, a series of conflicts fought between reds, whites, and nationalists and other groups across Russia's western borderlands, constituted an ominous backdrop to the discussions in Paris, as did the associated fear that Bolshevism would spread into Eastern and Central Europe.[59] Bolshevism quickly came to take place of the barbaric 'other' in the allied imagination that had been occupied by the Central Powers during the war.[60] Throughout 1919, the struggle to 'save' Western civilization was both a matter of dealing with the vanquished powers in Europe as well as ensuring that Bolshevism did not advance further, especially into the new and unstable successor states. As the delegates were assembling in Paris in January 1919, the Spartacist uprising in Germany had just been suppressed. In London, the Fabian socialist Beatrice Webb wrote at the start of the peace conference in her diary that the 'future of the civilised world' depended upon the successful reconstruction of Germany.[61] Bela Kun's communist revolution in

---

[58] On the peace conference, see: MacMillan, *Peacemakers*; Erez Manela, *The Wilsonian Moment: Self-Determination and the International Origins of Anticolonial Nationalism* (Oxford, 2007); Smith, *Sovereignty at the Paris Peace Conference*; Zara Steiner, *The Lights that Failed: European International History, 1919–1933* (Oxford, 2005). On Lausanne, see Jay Winter, *The Day the Great War Ended, 24 July 1923: The Civilization of War* (Oxford, 2022).

[59] Gerwarth, *The Vanquished*, p. 86.

[60] John Horne and Robert Gerwarth, 'Bolshevism as Fantasy: Fear of Revolution and Counter-Revolutionary Violence, 1917-1923', in Horne and Gerwarth eds., *War in Peace: Paramilitary Violence in Europe after the Great War* (Oxford, 2012), pp. 42–3.

[61] Beatrice Webb, diary entry for 14 January 1919, London School of Economics Archives and Special Collections (LSEASC), London, Beatrice Webb Typescript Diaries, LSE Archives/PASSFIELD/1/2/3666.

Hungary in May, while short-lived, further exacerbated fears of Bolshevism among allied peacemakers.[62] In his memoir of the conference, the American Secretary of State Robert Lansing described Eastern Europe as 'a volcano on the very point of eruption'. Without swift action to ward off revolution, Lansing warned that 'it threatened to spread to other countries and even engulf the very foundations of modern civilization'.[63]

The peace conference was a site of many lofty aspirations, none more so than Wilson's doctrine of self-determination, which inspired hopes in many anti-colonial nationalists and other national groups but was ultimately applied unsatisfactorily – where it was applied at all.[64] Because the conference was a magnet for activists and lobbyists from across the world, many proposals were received which had the intention of reorganizing international intellectual life in different ways, but few were seen as priorities and consequently they went unfulfilled. Many years later, the British classical scholar and internationalist Gilbert Murray argued that the statesmen at Paris 'paid far too little attention to economics and none to education'.[65] Intellectual and cultural issues were, however, treated seriously in discussions about wartime culpability and reparations. Here, national delegations cited the damage done to intellectual capital in wartime, in the process ensuring that the wartime destruction of Europe's high culture was laid bare.

The peace conference was a moment to consider the extent of wartime damage to sites of cultural and intellectual importance as well as being a forum to facilitate their reconstruction. These issues generally emerged at bodies established to deal with other issues, such as the Commission on the Responsibility of the Authors of the War and on Enforcement of Penalties (CRAWEP) and the Commission on the Reparation of Damage (CRD). Both of these commissions were presented with detailed evidence of the cultural destruction of wartime which was submitted by

[62] Gerwarth, *The Vanquished*, pp. 118–52.
[63] Robert Lansing, *The Peace Negotiations: A Personal Narrative* (New York, 1921), p. 111.
[64] Erez Manela, *The Wilsonian Moment*, and Adom Getachew, *Worldmaking after Empire: The Rise and Fall of Self-Determination* (Princeton, 2019), pp. 37–70.
[65] *Education and the United Nations: A Report of a Joint Commission of the Council for Education in World Citizenship and the London International Assembly* (Washington, DC, 1943), p. 4.

Figure 1.1 French Prime Minister Georges Clemenceau addresses a session of the Paris Peace Conference, 1919 (Mondadori Portfolio/Hulton Fine Art Collection/Getty)

states to make the case for criminal prosecution and moral compensation, respectively. The evidence assessed by these commissions detailed instances of damage done to churches, schools, libraries, universities, books, and artworks and cumulatively constituted proof of the enemy's wartime conduct but also amounted to a detailed record of the harm done to the fabric of cultural and intellectual life during the conflict.

The CRAWEP was set up in January 1919 to enquire 'into the responsibilities relating to the war' and breaches of existing international law during the conflict.[66] Its purpose was to ascertain culpability for the war with a view to bringing the perpetrators to trial. The submissions to this commission were all framed by the Hague Conventions of 1899 and 1907, in order to demonstrate where

---

[66] 'Commission on the Responsibility of the Authors of the War and on Enforcement of Penalties', *American Journal of International Law*, 14.1/2 (1920), p. 95.

breaches in international law took place. Article twenty seven of the Hague rules explicitly prohibited war being waged upon buildings dedicated to religion, art, or science, while article fifty-six of the 1907 convention forbade the wilful destruction or seizure of the property of institutions 'dedicated to religion, charity and education, the arts and sciences'.[67] A wide range of evidence of cultural damage of different types was submitted to the commission, including claims by the Belgian, Serbian, and Romanian delegations of deliberate destruction of libraries and educational institutions by invading and occupying forces during the war.[68] The commission concluded that among the crimes that should be prosecuted was 'wanton destruction of religious, charitable, educational, and historic buildings and monuments'.[69] Political disagreements meant that the post-war trials, which began in Leipzig in 1921, fell short of the aspirations of many of the parties at the Paris Peace Conference; criminal prosecution for cultural destruction remained unfulfilled.[70]

It was within the realm of compensation, rather than criminal responsibility, that the cultural excesses of the war became more apparent. The CRD was the primary forum for these discussions.[71] When different national delegations submitted their list of claims in February 1919, they were not bound by the specific language of the Hague conventions and thus cultural damage was elaborated upon in greater detail to make the case for moral redress. The French and British submissions both made reference to artworks as a category of war damage.[72] The Serbian document referenced damage to libraries, museums, theatres, and physics and chemistry

[67] O'Keefe, *The Protection of Cultural Property in Armed Conflict*, p. 24. ihl-databases.icrc.org/applic/ihl/ihl.nsf/ART/195–200066?OpenDocument [accessed 8 June 2021].

[68] The Belgian, Serbian, and Romanian claims can be found in *La paix de Versailles: responsabilités des auteurs de la guerre et sanctions* (Paris, 1930), pp. 69–85; 110–5; 216–7.

[69] 'Commission on the Responsibility of the Authors of the War an on Enforcement of Penalties', pp. 114–5.

[70] John Horne and Alan Kramer, *German Atrocities 1914: A History of Denial* (New Haven, CT, 2001), pp. 330–55.

[71] Wayne Sandholtz, *Prohibiting Plunder: How Norms Change* (Oxford, 2007), pp. 108–25.

[72] 'Mémoire de la délégation française', *La paix de Versailles: la Commission de Réparations des Dommages*, I (Paris, 1932), p. 190, 'Mémoire de la délégation britannique', p. 206.

laboratories.[73] The Czechoslovak submission discussed 'intellectual and moral damage' while the Belgian document had a separate category for 'science and art', which included universities, observatories, churches, monuments, and pieces of art 'belonging to the state'.[74] The language of cultural damage and reparation reflected the differing national experiences of the war and the relative value of different cultural and intellectual sites and practices within them.

New states also appealed to the peace conference to arrange the restitution of intellectual capital to them not because of wartime damage, but as a consequence of the collapse of empire. The new Kingdom of the Serbs, Croats and Slovenes wrote to the CRD to request that the new Yugoslav state be sent a share of collections of state universities, academies, and scientific institutions in Austria in proportion with the number of inhabitants who were incorporated into the new state from the former Habsburg Empire. It also called for the return of 'archives, books, manuscripts, museum pieces, artworks, removed or taken away, from any period' belonging to the territory now comprising the new Yugoslav state, as well as all 'writings and documents constituting a source of the history of the Serbs, Croats and Slovenes'.[75] In this manner, intellectual capital was portrayed as essential in the creation of new, post-imperial states.

The submissions to both the CRAWEP and the CRD enumerated, in clear and legally informed language, the cultural excesses of wartime violence. The work of the CRD proved protracted and contentious, with the commission itself, as well as the Council of Four (made up of leaders of the major allied states), adding different provisions to the final treaties which meant that they were not consistent in terms of what damage to intellectual property required reparation.[76] The results

[73] 'Projet de la délégation serbe', *La paix de Versailles: La Commission de Réparations des Dommages*, I (Paris, 1932), p. 188.

[74] 'Classement des dommages de guerre de la République tchécoslovaque' and 'Projet de la délégation belge', *La paix de Versailles: La Commission de Réparations des Dommages*, I, pp. 204, 207.

[75] Copies of Yugoslav proposals (dated 17 May 1919), communicated by John C. Shvegel to Sumner, 21 May 1919, The National Archives (United Kingdom, TNA), FO 608/308.

[76] Erik Goldstein, 'Cultural Heritage, British Diplomacy, and the German Peace Settlement of 1919', *Diplomacy & Statecraft*, 30 (2019), pp. 336–57; Andrzej Jakubowski, *State Succession in Cultural Property* (Oxford, 2015);

were mixed but demonstrated a clear Western-centrism whereby damage done to Western sites – as well as damage done by Germany – was held to a higher moral standard and thus required reparation. For this reason, article 247 of the Treaty of Versailles required that Germany restore manuscripts and incunabula to Louvain library in Belgium.[77] At the conference, a disgruntled John Maynard Keynes claimed that the punitive reparation settlement would 'sow the decay of the whole civilized life of Europe'.[78]

Intellectual Reconstruction and the Post-war Settlements

Having visited the peace conference in April 1919, Guglielmo Ferrero wrote that what the world needed to avert the collapse of civilization was 'an Esperanto of the spirit if not of the flesh'.[79] Beyond the formal commissions, a considerable range of petitions and proposals were submitted to the conference for consideration. Some of these came from representatives of national groups, while others came from transnational associations or private individuals. Most were united in the conviction that Paris was the place where the world would be rebuilt for the better.[80] Much as intellectuals were pre-occupied with the issue of reconstruction in 1919 and fostering international intellectual cooperation to build stability, the peace conference was a forum for discussions about how intellectual life might be rebuilt and, in turn, contribute to global stability. However, despite the prevalence of rhetoric regarding civilizational decline and the prominence of scholars in national delegations, the peacemakers did not generally address

---

Ana Filipa Vrdoljak, 'Enforcement of Restitution of Cultural Heritage through Peace Agreements', in Francesco Francioni and James Gordley eds., *Enforcing International Cultural Heritage Law* (Oxford, 2013), pp. 22–39; Sandholtz, *Prohibiting Plunder*; Jeremiah J. Garsha, 'Expanding Vergangenheitsbewältigung? German Repatriation of Colonial Artefacts and Human Remains', *Journal of Genocide Research*, 22 (2020), pp. 46–61.

[77] Tomás Irish, 'The "Moral Basis" of Reconstruction? Humanitarianism, Intellectual Relief and the League of Nations', *Modern Intellectual History*, 17.3 (2020), p. 769.

[78] Keynes, *The Economic Consequences of the Peace*, p. 225.

[79] Guglielmo Ferrero, 'The Crisis of Western Civilization', *The Atlantic Monthly*, 125.5 (1920), p. 710.

[80] Thomas R. Davies, 'The Roles of Transnational Associations in the 1919 Paris Peace Settlement: A Comparative Assessment of Proposals and Their Influence', *Contemporary European History*, 31.3 (2022), pp. 353–67.

intellectual or cultural matters in the treaties beyond the category of reparations.[81]

Ideas for intellectual reconstruction abounded in Paris. The American educator Fannie Fern Andrews was appointed to represent the American Bureau of Education at the conference. Andrews had travelled to The Hague in 1915 to attend a meeting of political activists working for peace and one of the key ideas that she developed called for the establishment of an international bureau of education as part of a post-war settlement. In Paris in 1919, she drafted an article for the Covenant of the League of Nations to establish an educational institution but this was not adopted in the final settlement. While unsuccessful in Paris, Andrews' proposal was influential in the creation of the International Bureau of Education at Geneva in 1925.[82]

A similar initiative was proposed by the Belgian internationalist and peace activist Paul Otlet. Before 1914, Otlet and his collaborator Henri La Fontaine were involved in many schemes that sought to categorize international knowledge. This began with international bibliographical projects and ultimately led to the establishment of the Union of International Associations (UIA) in 1910.[83] In February 1919, the UIA proposed the creation of a 'Charter of Intellectual and Moral Interests'. This advocated for the inclusion of a 'charter of intelligence' alongside a labour and economic charter to guide the League of Nations and made the case that any exercise in world government would need to take account of intellectual matters.[84]

---

[81] On expert membership of national delegations see: Tomás Irish, 'Scholarly Identities in War and Peace: the Paris Peace Conference and the Mobilization of Intellect', *Journal of Global History*, 11.3 (2016), pp. 365–86; Volker Prott, 'Tying up the Loose Ends of National Self-determination: British, French and American Experts in Peace Planning, 1917-1919', *Historical Journal*, 57.3 (2014), pp. 727–50.

[82] Fannie Fern Andrews, *Memory Pages of My Life* (Boston, MA, 1948), pp. 112–8; Jan Stöckmann, *The Architects of International Relations: Building a Discipline, Designing the World, 1914–1940* (Cambridge, 2022), pp. 1–3.

[83] W. Boyd Rayward, 'Creating the UIA: Henri La Fontaine, Cyrille van Overbergh and Paul Otlet', in Daniel Laqua, Christophe Verbruggen and Wouter van Acker, eds., *International Organizations and Global Civil Society: Histories of the Union of International Associations* (London, 2019), pp. 17–35; Alex Wright, *Cataloguing the World: Paul Otlet and the Birth of the Information* Age (New York, 2014).

[84] Daniel Laqua, Christophe Verbruggen, and Wouter Van Acker, 'Introduction: Reconstructing the Identities of an International Non-Governmental Intelligence Agency', in *International Organizations and Global Civil Society*,

Otlet further developed on these ideas later in 1919, calling for the creation of a Global Intellectual Centre to serve the League of Nations. He argued that the League would need to be equipped with political, economic, and intellectual organs, with all three 'forming the framework of the civilization of tomorrow'.[85] 'Our generation must call upon intelligence', Otlet claimed, to address the problems of the future, and this required the establishment of a centre to bring together national representatives from around the globe to exchange information and conduct, conserve, and disseminate research.[86] Otlet's proposal built upon much internationalist work which had taken place in the world of science and letters over the preceding half century and, more specifically, the efforts which the UIA had been making since 1910. The Belgian foreign minister Paul Hymans argued that international intellectual relations should be included in the Covenant of the League of Nations, a proposal that was, in the words of one account, received 'coldly'.[87] These proposals later became influential in the establishment of the League's International Committee on Intellectual Cooperation (ICIC) in 1922.[88] Otlet's proposal demonstrated that intellectuals and intelligence were seen as potentially important in helping to restore order to the world.

The American historian James Shotwell took a different approach. He felt that intellectual life might contribute to post-war stability through the writing of history. As a member of Woodrow Wilson's team of experts at the peace conference, Shotwell worked on the establishment of the International Labour Organization.[89] He also developed a project to make official war documentation accessible to researchers. During the war, Shotwell had become convinced of the idea that historical research should be directly applicable to the modern world, with its influence on public opinion being a key measure of its

p. 1; Daniel Laqua, *The Age of Internationalism and Belgium: Peace, Progress and Prestige* (Manchester, 2015), p. 194.

[85] Paul Otlet, 'Centre intellectuel mondial au service de la Société des Nations', LNA/R1027/13B/4675/4646, p. 5.

[86] Otlet, 'Centre intellectuel mondial', p. 6.

[87] Gwilym Davies, *Intellectual Cooperation between the Two Wars* (London, 1943), Gwilym Davies Papers, National Library of Wales (NLW), Aberystwyth, V/8/21, p. 4.

[88] League of Nations, *Ten Years of World Co-operation* (Geneva, 1930), p. 313.

[89] Lawrence E. Gelfand, *The Inquiry: American Preparations for Peace, 1917–1919* (New Haven, CT, 1963).

success.[90] Raising the ominous spectre of civilizational decline, he claimed in 1918 that 'unless a systematic effort is made to deal with the problem of preserving the records of the present, our age will leave no more record than that which saw the fall of Rome'.[91] In Paris, Shotwell advocated for 'all existing official papers and documents of Germany' to be accessible to researchers, authorized by the League of Nations.[92] He also urged the British government to make its war archives available to researchers.[93] 'Without documents', he argued in a lecture at the Sorbonne in May 1919, 'there can be no history'.[94]

While Shotwell's project was ultimately unsuccessful, archives did appear in a number of the post-war treaties. The collapse of empires presented difficulties as new states made claims upon archival records formerly held centrally by imperial governments, as was the case with the Habsburgs in Vienna. In the years following the peace conference, Austria signed a series of agreements for the return of archives with Czechoslovakia and Romania, before a general convention was agreed between Austria, Italy, Poland, Romania, Czechoslovakia, and the Kingdom of Serbs, Croats and Slovenes in 1922.[95] These agreements were a measure of the present-day administrative importance of archives as well as their value in providing historical substance to claims of national difference. They did not seek to foster international understanding of the conflict as Shotwell's proposal had envisaged and this meant that, as he wrote in 1924, 'vast masses of source material essential for the historian were effectively placed beyond his reach'.[96] The American instead turned his attention to working with individuals who had direct experience of war government.[97] He was appointed editor of the Carnegie Endowment for International Peace's (CEIP) *Economic and Social History of the World War* project while in Paris and used his time there to recruit contributors, with the series eventually running to

[90] Josephson, *James T. Shotwell and the Rise of Internationalism in America*, p. 105.
[91] 'Favors trade research', *New York Times*, 29 June 1918, p. 7.
[92] Shotwell, *At the Paris Peace Conference*, p. 300.
[93] Shotwell, *At the Paris Peace Conference*, p. 357.
[94] Shotwell, 'The Social History of the War: Preliminary Considerations', p. 292. He repeated this line in the preface to Hubert Hall's Carnegie volume on *British Archives and Sources for the History of the World War* (London, 1925), ix.
[95] Jakubowski, *State Succession in Cultural Property*, p. 78.
[96] Shotwell, 'Preface', p. x.   [97] Josephson, *James T. Shotwell*, pp. 106–7.

152 volumes.[98] In a speech in Belgrade in 1925, Shotwell justified his vast project because it would 'preserve for future generations all documents that relate to the late war'.[99]

Shotwell's initiative was part of a wider concern to preserve war documents. In 1917, the French government announced the creation of a Library and Museum of the War. Building upon a private initiative, its purpose was to bring together and catalogue war documents and to make them available to researchers to 'later write the history of current events'.[100] Herbert Hoover, too, felt a keen desire that the war should be documented in full. In 1918, he put up $50,000 for the creation of a war library at Stanford University, and paid for a team of researchers led by E.D. Adams to gather documents in Paris.[101] At the peace conference, Hoover made an unsuccessful request that Adams be allowed to read and make copies of 'documents of historical interest to the Peace Conference', with a view to them being sent to Stanford.[102] Another of Hoover's scholars, Frank A. Golder, was a member of the Inquiry and was later appointed to a 'special mission' by Hoover to collect documents for Stanford while working with the American Relief Administration in Russia.[103] Archibald Cary Coolidge, a historian and director of the Harvard University Library, also served on Wilson's Inquiry and later worked with the ARA in Russia; he used his time in Europe to buy up books for his institution's new Widener Memorial Library.[104]

[98] Katharina Rietzler, 'The War as History: Writing the Economic and Social History of the First World War', *Diplomatic History*, 38. 4 (2014), pp. 826–39.
[99] James Shotwell, 'The Effects of the War', 9 October 1925, CURBML, Shotwell Papers, Box 280, Economic & Social History of WW I, Reviews, General, Part II.
[100] 'Notice sommaire', c1919, CURBML, Carnegie Endowment for International Peace (CEIP) Centre Européen, Box 144, Folder 1; Camille Bloch, 'Centres d'études et de documentation pour l'histoire de la guerre: bibliothèque et musée français de la guerre', *Révue de synthèse historique*, 33.7 (1921), pp. 37–44.
[101] *Hoover Institution on War, Revolution, and Peace* (Stanford, CA, 1963), pp. 1–2.
[102] Minutes of the daily meetings of commissioners plenipotentiary, Tuesday, 24 June 1919, *Papers Relating to the Foreign Relations of the United States: The Paris Peace Conference, 1919*, vol. 11 (Washington, DC, 1945), pp. 245–6.
[103] Golder to Bowden, 2 October 1920, HILA, Frank A. Golder Papers (FGP), Box 22, Folder 5, Reel 28.
[104] Gerald M. Rosberg, 'Leon Trotsky's Personal Papers', *Harvard Crimson*, 3 July 1967.

The peace conference was a magnet for myriad ideas about how to build a stable post-war order. Drawing on wider discourses of civilizational decline, intellectual life featured in many proposals to the conference but, as the peacemakers prioritized other issues, few of these proposals made their way into post-war treaties or the Covenant of the League of Nations. While there was a widely articulated desire among intellectuals to rebuild Europe's cultural life following the war, this was generally considered in abstract and intangible terms that related to the resumption, reorganization, or reconceptualization of intellectual activities. While the peace conference was sitting, a more tangible threat to intellectual life emerged which linked fears about the spread of Bolshevism, the decline of civilization, and the wellbeing of those involved in intellectual pursuits. This new crisis became a major preoccupation of the politicians and diplomats assembled in the French capital and was the spur for the reconstruction of intellectual life to begin in earnest.

The Post-war Humanitarian Crisis

Having toured Europe in October 1919, Sir William Goode, the British Director of Relief, reported back to his government on the conditions in Central Europe, paying particular attention to the deprivation in Vienna. 'For the first time in my life', he wrote, 'I found a whole nation, or what was left of it, in utter, hopeless despair'.[105] Central Europe had experienced extreme hunger in wartime but this became acute in 1919 and was not helped by the decision of the allied powers to continue their blockade of the Central Powers until the signing of the Treaty of Versailles in June 1919.[106] The peace conference was inundated with reports of famine in Central and Eastern Europe, which became more graphic and more insistent as the year progressed.

The imperative of providing food aid to those who were starving was connected to wider perceived fears regarding the advance of Bolshevism after the war and the salvaging of civilization. At the peace conference, Robert Lansing, the American Secretary of State, famously remarked that 'full stomachs mean no Bolsheviks', and

[105] Dispatch from Sir William Goode, 1 January 1920, *Miscellaneous Series No. 1 (1920). Economic Conditions in Central Europe* (London, 1920), p. 9.
[106] Nicholas Mulder, *The Economic Weapon: The Rise of Sanctions as a Tool of Modern War* (New Haven, CT, 2022), pp. 88–108.

many allied politicians held similar views.[107] Goode argued that 'it is inconceivable that the conditions I have witnessed over half of Europe ... can be allowed to continue without a daily risk of political conflagration such as that which now isolates Russia from the civilized world'.[108] And while many believed that the post-war settlement was a means of salvaging civilization, critics argued that it could achieve the opposite. 'To aim deliberately at the impoverishment of Central Europe', claimed Keynes in his critique of the allied reparations policy, would lead to a 'final confrontation' between reaction and revolution, which would destroy 'the civilization and the progress of our generation'.[109]

Nineteen nineteen saw both the creation of new humanitarian organizations and the reconfiguration of more longstanding entities, both in order to address Europe's post-war crises. These actions were rooted in a desire to counter Bolshevism as well as a general sense of moral responsibility to feed Central Europe, motivations which sat uncomfortably alongside a reticence among some to help former Central Power states.[110] The American Relief Administration (ARA) was established in February 1919 following an executive order by Woodrow Wilson. Armed with a $100 million appropriation from Congress, it began food distribution in April 1919.[111] Under the leadership of Herbert Hoover, the ARA would become the key relief organization in Europe in the years that followed, although its federal mandate expired in June 1919 meaning that it then became a private body rather than a state-led one.[112] The ARA was, in the words of Tammy M. Proctor, an experiment in 'the exportation of American values through food aid to most of Europe by the 1920s'.[113] Staffed by well-educated young Americans, many of whom were themselves veterans of the war, the ARA's network would prove important not just in its own rights but as a vessel through which smaller humanitarian initiatives could function.[114]

---

[107] John M. Thompson, *Russia, Bolshevism and the Versailles Peace* (Princeton, NJ, 1966), p. 222.

[108] *Economic Conditions in Central Europe*, p. 14.

[109] Keynes, *The Economic Consequences of the Peace*, p. 268.

[110] Irwin, *Making the World Safe*, p. 142.

[111] Cabanes, *The Great War and the Origins of Humanitarianism*, pp. 189–239.

[112] Irwin, 'Taming Total War', pp. 771–2.

[113] Proctor, 'An American Enterprise', p. 30.

[114] Bertrand Patenaude, *The Big Show in Bololand: The American Relief Expedition to Soviet Russia in the Famine of 1921* (Stanford, CA, 2002), p. 7.

At the same time as the ARA was coming into being, many organizations which had been active in relief during the war, such as the American Red Cross (ARC), the Young Men's Christian Association (YMCA), the Jewish Joint Distribution Committee (JDC), and Near East Relief (NER), began to transition out of their wartime activities in order to address the post-war crises.[115] The reconfiguration of relief activities after the war sometimes took on distinct intellectual contours. The work of the Commission for Relief in Belgium (CRB) left a balance of 150 million francs outstanding by the time its work came to an end in September 1919. Herbert Hoover proposed that a proportion of this surplus be used to establish an educational foundation managed by Belgians and Americans. Accordingly, the Fondation Universitaire was established and given fifty-five million francs with a mission statement to fund travelling scholarships for needy scholars and support the endowment of libraries and laboratories.[116]

As post-war humanitarianism took shape in 1919, Austria and Poland, and their child populations, were the focus of significant efforts.[117] However, it was not until early 1920 that intellectual life was identified as a distinct and important problem amidst the wider humanitarian crisis. The work of the British Friends in Vienna formed an important precedent in the development of intellectual relief and ultimately led to the establishment of bespoke organizations that aimed at providing aid to the educated middle classes. The Quakers had been active in humanitarian aid during the First World War through distinct British and American organizations. The British Friends' relief mission had workers in Vienna by the summer of 1919.[118] Unlike the ARA, the Quakers, for whom pacifism was a core belief, saw no issues in engaging with ex-enemy states such as Germany.[119]

[115] Julia F. Irwin, 'Taming Total War: Great War-Era American Humanitarianism and its Legacies', *Diplomatic History*, 38.4 (2014), p. 772.

[116] Walter Montgomery, *Educational Reconstruction in Belgium: Department of the Interior Bureau of Education, Bulletin, 1921*, no. 39 (Washington, DC, 1921), pp. 9–11. Kenneth Bertrams, 'The Domestic Uses of Belgian–American "Mutual Understanding": The Commission for Relief in Belgium Educational Foundation, 1920–1940', *Journal of Transatlantic Studies*, 13.4 (2015), pp. 326–43.

[117] Rodogno, *Night on Earth*, pp. 38–9; Jaclyn Granick, *International Jewish Humanitarianism in the Age of the Great War* (Cambridge, 2021), pp. 80–8.

[118] Proctor, 'An American Enterprise', pp. 34–5.

[119] Proctor, 'An American Enterprise', p. 31; Guy Aiken, 'Feeding Germany: American Quakers in the Weimar Republic', *Diplomatic History*, 43.4 (2019), pp. 597–617.

By the spring of 1920, the Friends' Emergency and War Victims' Relief Committee began providing breakfasts for 'the most necessitous students', a task in which they were assisted by the Student Christian Movement.[120] The mission in Vienna distributed aid to students and professors that had been raised by a committee in Oxford; Agnes Murray, daughter of Gilbert Murray, was a crucial figure in this initiative. In a contemporary report, the British Quakers claimed that the wider humanitarian crisis now had a more specific intellectual focus: 'the hunger and poverty which is now spread wide over Central Europe threatens to overwhelm the Universities, which have been such important centres of learning for the Western World'.[121] Another account claimed that 'students have gone to bed from hunger and exhaustion and have been found dead some days later'.[122] The work of the British Friends was the first alarm bell that highlighted the impact of the hunger crisis on Europe's intellectual communities.

While the British Quakers highlighted and oversaw early intellectual relief in Vienna, they expressed some reluctance about maintaining a permanent institution with this focus. In the spring of 1920, the Friends issued an appeal calling on British universities to help their suffering colleagues elsewhere; it argued that 'we believe that in the interests of humanity and learning alike, the Universities of the more fortunate countries should come to the rescue of those in Central Europe'.[123] The appeal stated that 'one of the hardest hit sections in Vienna is found amongst the members of the university'.[124] In July 1920, a Universities' Committee was set up under the umbrella of the Imperial War Relief Fund, centralizing the work that had been initiated in Vienna by both the Friends' mission and the Student Christian Movement.[125] Chaired by Sir William Beveridge, the committee stated its aims as being to 'deal with distress among university

---

[120] The SCM had been active in Vienna since February 1920. 'Outlines of a scheme for assisting the universities of Central Europe', cMarch 1920, LSF/YM/MfS/ FEWVRC/4/3/8/1. Ruth Rouse, *Rebuilding Europe: The Student Chapter in Post-War Reconstruction* (London, 1925), pp. 14–22.

[121] 'Outlines of a scheme for assisting the universities of Central Europe', March 1920, LSF/YM/MfS/FEWVRC/4/3/8/1.

[122] 'Appeal for the Universities', 4 March 1920, LSF/YM/MfS/FEWVRC/4/3/8/1.

[123] 'Outlines of a scheme for assisting the universities of Central Europe'.

[124] 'Appeal for the Universities'.

[125] Georgina Brewis, *A Social History of Student Volunteering: Britain and Beyond, 1880–1980* (New York, 2014), pp. 51–2.

and secondary teachers and students in Central Europe'; accordingly, it sought to raise money for those in need through appeals to the British academic community.[126] The Universities' Committee worked closely with the secretary of the World Student Christian Federation (WSCF), Ruth Rouse, and its student relief programme.[127] Much like the Friends' mission or that of the WSCF, the Universities' Committee provided aid to ex-enemy states such as Germany and Austria.[128] Meanwhile, the WSCF itself formalized its commitment to intellectual relief in August 1920 by establishing European Student Relief (ESR).[129]

Across the Atlantic, the spring of 1920 also saw the emergence of intellectual relief as a discrete and organized element of wider humanitarian programmes with the backing of philanthropic foundations. These foundations were united in their belief in the cause of liberal internationalism and American global leadership.[130] The years that followed the end of the First World War provided many instances for American investment of this nature; the philanthropist Anson Phelps Stokes remarked that there were considerable opportunities available for 'philanthropically disposed Americans with large means to invest money [. . .] in the educational reconstruction of Europe'.[131]

A major American funder of intellectual relief was the Commonwealth Fund (CF). Founded in October 1918 following a bequest from Anna M. Harkness, its broad mission was to do 'something for the welfare of mankind'. In its first year of operation, the fund articulated a desire to contribute to a 'specific piece of reconstruction

---

[126] 'Universities Committee: The Work of the Past Year and the Future Outlook', October 1921, LNA/R1032/13C/25541/14297; IWRF, Inter-University Conference, 7 July 1920. LSEASC/BEVERIDGE/VII/90/66.

[127] Tara Windsor, '"The Domain of the Young as the Generation of the Future": Student agency and Anglo-German exchange after the Great War', in Marie-Eve Chagnon and Tomás Irish, eds., *The Academic World in the Era of the Great War* (London, 2018), p. 166.

[128] IWRF, Inter-University Conference, 7 July 1920. LSEASC/BEVERIDGE/VII/90/66.

[129] Brewis, *A Social History of Student Volunteering*, p. 53; Benjamin L. Hartley, 'Saving Students: European Student Relief in the Aftermath of World War I', *International Bulletin of Mission Research*, 42.1 (2018), pp. 295–315.

[130] Inderjeet Parmar, *Foundations of the American Century: The Ford, Carnegie and Rockefeller Foundations in the Rise of American Power* (New York, 2012), pp. 58–68.

[131] Anson Phelps Stokes to Wickliffe Rose, 7 May 1923, Rockefeller Archive Center (RAC), Sleepy Hollow, New York, International Education Board (IEB), FA062, Series 1, Subseries 1 (hereafter 1.1), Box 1, Folder 17.

work' in Europe.[132] On the recommendation of the ARA, the CF decided that this special focus would be Europe's intellectuals. Being a foundation rather than a humanitarian organization, the Commonwealth Fund made an appropriation of $500,000 in 1920 with specific instructions that the money be used for 'food drafts for intellectuals'.[133] The administration of this money was put in the hands of the ARA. The story of how this money was spent will be taken up in Chapter 2.

Conclusion

In 1920, Herbert Hoover spoke of the terrible material situation facing over 100,000 students and professors, which would, without immediate action, lead to 'decadence in the intellectual fibre of Europe'. Hoover justified aid to universities facing difficulties by arguing that 'to allow these institutions to disintegrate would be a disaster not only to their own nations, but to the whole civilised world'.[134] In the aftermath of the First World War, civilization was a malleable term which could be utilized as a shorthand for a variety of ills threatening Europe. In this case, it simultaneously encapsulated fears about Europe's intellectual and cultural traditions, the destructiveness of modern warfare, and the desire for stability in Central and Eastern Europe in the face of the Bolshevik threat.

Nineteen nineteen is a hinge from one period of crisis to another; it was in this period that politicians, diplomats, and intellectuals sought to take stock of the destruction of wartime, enumerating the losses of gifted scholars and destruction of sites of cultural importance in order to cumulatively assess the consequences of these tribulations for Western civilization. The Paris Peace Conference was a microcosm of this

---

[132] Max Farrand report, 7 October 1919, *The Commonwealth Fund: First Annual Report of the General Director for the Year 1918–1919* (New York, 1920), pp. 5–11.

[133] Max Farrand, No 364. American Relief Administration – Food Drafts for the Intellectual Class in Central Europe, 10 June 1920, RAC, Commonwealth Fund Records (CF), FA290, SG 1, Series 18, Subseries 1 (hereafter 18.1) Box 12, Folder 119. Report by Max Farrand, *The Commonwealth Fund: Second Annual Report of the General Director for the year 1919–1920* (New York, 1921), p. 8.

[134] 'Chain of Expert Testimony on the Federation European Relief Scheme', LSF/ YM/MfS/FEWVRC/MISSIONS/10/5/2/3.

process, with issues of intellectual decline and cultural destruction appearing in plenary sessions and discussions ostensibly focused on other matters, such as reparations. Everywhere, journalists, politicians, diplomats, and intellectuals cited the fragility of civilization to explain the great convulsions being experienced across Europe. At the same time, as 1919 moved into 1920, the humanitarian crisis facing Central and Eastern Europe became a central concern for politicians and intellectuals. Framed against the backdrop of advancing Bolshevism, the new crisis threatened intellectual communities too, but was prospective rather than retrospective; here, aid could be organized, and disaster could, theoretically, be mitigated. Whereas Valéry's 'crisis of the mind' largely described a cultural, or imagined, decline, in that it related to the corruption of modes of thought and its implications for Western civilization, Europe's post-war humanitarian crisis was tangible and very real.

By the middle of 1920, a distinct thread of post-war reconstruction and humanitarian relief had emerged which placed Europe's intellectual communities at its core. However, the material conditions that underpinned intellectual relief were not fixed at this point; they would evolve in the months and years that followed, as a consequence of the Volga famine in Russia of 1921–22, hyperinflation in Germany in 1922, the ongoing displacement of people as a result of the Russian Civil War, and deportations by the Bolshevik government. The chapters that follow will explore the discrete dimensions of this intellectual relief, showing how European intellectual life was rebuilt as a distinct humanitarian project.

2 | Feeding Bodies

Food Relief and 'The Most Deplorable Victims of the War'

In late 1920 Vienna, an old café basement, recently used as a storeroom for coal, was transformed; long tables were covered in white linen and decorated with flowers and up to 250 people dined there daily. This was the scene at the 'intellectual kitchen' of the University of Vienna; a site where, in the midst of famine conditions where one scholar described feeling like 'a worm crawling round a dung heap', academics dined with their peers exclusively, with no places set for spouses, children, or siblings.[1] Funded by American philanthropy, the kitchen allowed 'grizzly-bearded, spectacled gentlemen' and 'clean-shaven, keen-eyed young lecturers' to come together to receive culinary and intellectual sustenance in a city ravaged by the effects of war and blockade.[2] One recipient of this aid spoke of his delight that the former enemy had acknowledged that, following the bitterness of wartime, they were again considered 'among the carriers of civilization'.[3] In many cities across Central and Eastern Europe, such scenes were common. Tables were laid for intellectuals alone, who were singled out for support by a range of humanitarian agencies, at a time of ubiquitous need – but why?

This chapter is about people. It focuses on the intellectuals who fell into poverty during and after the First World War and found themselves facing disease and starvation in its wake. One Austrian newspaper claimed in 1921 that these impoverished intellectuals were 'the most deplorable victims of the war'.[4] A range of philanthropists, politicians, and

---

[1] 'The University of Vienna, 1920', LSF/YM/MfS/FEWVRC/MISSIONS/4/3/8/9.

[2] 'Ivan', 'The Professors' Mess', Rockefeller Foundation Records, SG. 1.1, Series 100, Box 77, Folder 728.

[3] Clemens von Pirquet, 'Memorandum for Dr. Williams', 30 November 1920, RAC, Rockefeller Foundation Records (RF), SG 1.1, Series 100, Box 77, Folder 728.

[4] 'Die Rettungsaktion für die geistigen Arbeiter Osterreichen', *Neue Freie Presse*, 15 January 1921, p. 2. 'Relief Work for the Brain-Workers of Austria', 15 January 1921 LSF/YM/MfS/FEWVRC/MISSIONS/4/3/8/5.

Figure 2.1 Attendees at the intellectual kitchen of the University of Vienna, c1920 (© Rockefeller Archive Center)

humanitarian workers agreed with this assessment and asserted that intellectuals – distinct from their wider communities – needed to be kept alive as a discrete group of people. The emphasis on selective and elitist aid is especially pertinent in this period because it occurred against the backdrop of an evolving humanitarianism that was increasingly characterized by the principle that 'need, not identity', should shape the distribution of aid.[5] Focusing on those who both distributed and received intellectual relief highlights how multiple humanitarianisms co-existed in this transitional period, where older forms of elitist aid coexisted alongside newer approaches that emphasized the suffering brought on by total war and its aftermath. Intellectual relief cuts to the core of a key issue in humanitarianism, both historically and in the present day; its claims to universalism which sit, often uncomfortably, alongside its practice of difference.[6]

---

[5] Barnett, *Empire of Humanity*, p. 82.
[6] Didier Fassin, 'Inequality of Lives, Hierarchies of Humanity: Moral Commitments and Ethical Dilemmas of Humanitarianism', in Ilana Feldman and Miriam Ticktin eds., *In the Name of Humanity: The Government of Threat and Care* (Durham, NC, 2010), p. 239.

Intellectual relief presupposed that certain individuals needed to be kept alive not necessarily because of the severity of the conditions which they encountered – which were often also experienced among the wider populations in which they lived – but because of who they were and what they represented. The post-First World War humanitarian moment saw the targeting of social groups for distinct reasons. In the case of children, for example, humanitarian discourses emphasized their innocence, as well as their importance to the future reconstruction of their states and the international community more generally.[7] Intellectual feeding in the aftermath of the First World War highlights how discourses of humanitarian solidarity were created while also illuminating the social standing of intellectuals across Europe and the role which they were expected to play in post-war stabilization and reconstruction.[8]

Following the First World War, a common humanitarian concern with the fate of intellectuals emerged which emphasized the imperative of acting to save the lives of individuals facing starvation and disease. This process was led in the main by American philanthropy and saw the emergence of a discourse of suffering that was framed by afflicted intellectuals in Central and Eastern Europe, British and American aid workers, as well as the international community of scholars. This discourse mirrored wider humanitarian narratives of the period in its depictions of acute need, hunger, and death. It also emphasized difference by asserting that intellectuals, irrespective of whether they were in Austria, Germany, Poland, Hungary, or Russia, constituted a discrete group whose cultural and social standing rendered their suffering especially troubling. Edgar Rickard, Director General of the American Relief Administration, claimed that intellectuals needed to know that they were 'entitled to be treated just a little bit differently and better than the mass of people'.[9] The emphasis on difference and the elevation of the suffering of middle-class intellectuals makes this

---

[7] Ellen Boucher, 'Cultivating Internationalism: Save the Children Fund, Public Opinion and the Meaning of Child Relief, 1919-24', in Laura Beers and Geraint Thomas, eds., *Brave New World: Imperial and Democratic Nation-Building in Britain between the Wars* in (London, 2011), pp. 176–82; Baughan, '"Every Citizen of Empire Implored to Save the Children!"' pp. 130–32.

[8] On solidarity, see Jeffrey Flynn, 'Human Rights, Transnational Solidarity, and Duties to the Global Poor', *Constellations*, 16.1 (2009), pp. 59–77.

[9] Draft letter from Edgar Rickard to Barry C. Smith, February 1922, HILA, American Relief Administration Russian Operational Records (ARAROR), Box 326, Folder 8, Reel 403.

relief part of the 'recasting' of bourgeois Europe and a means of providing stability to societies that were threatened by war, mass politics, economic disruption, and the threat of revolutionary Bolshevism.[10] Viewed through the lenses of both class and gender, intellectual relief was not simply about saving individuals who were synonymous with branches of learning, but also about reaffirming middle-class interests across Central and Eastern Europe in the face of the Bolshevik threat.[11]

Post-war intellectual feeding addressed two distinct crises. The first was the starvation experienced as a consequence of the First World War. This was especially pronounced in Germany and Austria given the extension of the allied blockade into the armistice period. This initially came to a head in 1919 and 1920 but was also experienced across large swathes of Eastern Europe in the same period. The second crisis was the Volga famine which gripped Russia from the summer of 1921. These overlapping crises mobilized a wide range of humanitarian organizations and actors – both national and international – and demonstrated a common concern with the fate of intellectuals among the wider suffering populations. Across the early 1920s, the provision of aid to intellectuals emerged as a distinct component of humanitarian responses to mass hunger.

This chapter draws primarily upon the work of humanitarian organizations in Austria and Russia, not on the basis that the two countries had a great deal in common in terms of the origins and specific manifestations of their respective hunger crises, but because organizations working in these regions deployed similar humanitarian initiatives to save middle-class intellectuals and thus demonstrated continuities in humanitarian discourses and practices. The cases of Austria and Russia reveal much about how intellectual relief was conceptualized and organized; in both instances, much was made of the social status of those in need of assistance and, in each case, aid served to reinforce their sense of social difference within their wider populations. Intellectual need was justified to wider audiences, be they philanthropists or members of the public, by emphasizing both the extent of suffering itself and the eminence of those experiencing it. The

[10] Maier, *Recasting Bourgeois Europe*.
[11] Horne and Gerwarth, 'Bolshevism as Fantasy', pp. 40–51; Emily Baughan, 'International Adoption and Anglo-American Internationalism', p. 185.

distribution of this aid was structured in a manner which served to perpetuate the sense of social difference of those who received it.

Europe's Intellectuals and the Humanitarian Crisis

While news of the humanitarian catastrophe facing Central and Eastern Europe reached allied states by the end of the First World War, it was not until late 1919 and early 1920, once humanitarian work had commenced in countries such as Poland and Austria, that the crisis facing Europe's intellectuals began to receive considerable attention. Information made its way west in a variety of ways. Travellers who had visited Austria, Germany, Poland, or Russia wrote of their experiences and drew attention to the deteriorating situation. Concurrently, writers, artists, scholars, and students who were experiencing famine and disease appealed to those who they thought could help, from their peers in Europe and North America to international bodies like the newly-established League of Nations. While the majority of money for intellectual relief came from private philanthropy, humanitarian organizations, such as the Friends' Emergency and War Victims' Relief Committee and the Imperial War Relief Fund, issued public appeals in order to raise money and awareness for the plight of Europe's intellectuals.[12] Cumulatively, these descriptions painted a graphic picture of suffering, making plain the ravages of hunger and disease as well as the omnipotence of death. Unlike the mass media campaigns of organizations such as the Save the Children Fund (SCF) which sought to mobilize a wide public, appeals for intellectuals tended to be directed towards members of the international community of learning or groups felt to have much in common with those in need.[13] Invocations of intellectual suffering sought to create solidarity with a specific coterie of learned people to ensure that they were marked out as different and deserving of bespoke aid within the wider humanitarian landscape.

---

[12] On the work of British Quakers, see Proctor, 'An American Enterprise', pp. 29–42 and the 1926 account of Ruth Fry, *A Quaker Adventure: The Story of Nine Years' Relief and Reconstruction* (London, 1926). For more on the IWRF see Emily Baughan, 'The Imperial War Relief Fund and the All British Appeal: Commonwealth, Conflict and Conservatism within the British Humanitarian Movement, 1920–25', *The Journal of Imperial and Commonwealth History*, 40.5 (2012), pp. 845–61.

[13] Rouse, *Rebuilding Europe*, p. 42.

The Austrian capital Vienna occupied a central place in the genesis of post-war intellectual relief as it was there that many influential initiatives originated. Austria suffered from food shortages during the First World War but this became acute in the aftermath of the armistice with the continuation of the allied blockade of ex-enemy states and the onset of rapid inflation.[14] By 1919, Austria was in the grip of *die Hungerkatastrophe*.[15] While Germany also suffered from acute hunger in this period it was intentionally omitted from many relief schemes because of the stigmatization of Germany in the allied imagination following its role in the outbreak of war in 1914 and the atrocities committed in Belgium.[16] Austria was less associated with wartime atrocities among former allies and was thus viewed differently from Germany, meaning that its status as a former enemy state did not preclude widespread humanitarian mobilization from 1919. The SCF focused much of its early feeding work on Vienna in 1919, as did the FEWVRC, the IWRF, and the ARA.[17]

Accounts of intellectual life in post-war Austria, and Vienna in particular, described suffering in graphic terms. Linsly R. Williams of the Rockefeller Foundation (RF) reported from the Austrian capital in April 1920 that eighty per cent of the city's physicians were 'in poverty or in distress'. He described meeting one professor at the university, 'formerly a stout thick-set man', who had been reduced to 'practically nothing but skin and bones' by hunger.[18] Marjorie Vernon, who was part of the FEWVRC in Vienna, reported that 'doctors, lawyers, university professors, under-graduates, artists and higher grade civil servants', comfortably off before 1914, were now 'fantastically poor'.[19] Vernon's report outlined hunger, illness, and widespread homelessness

---

[14] Maureen Healy, *Vienna and the Fall of the Habsburg Empire: Total War and Everyday Life in World War I* (Cambridge, 2004), pp. 31–86.

[15] Patricia Clavin, 'The Austrian Hunger Crisis and the Genesis of International Organization after the First World War', *International Affairs*, 90.2 (2014), p. 267.

[16] Aiken, 'Feeding Germany: American Quakers in the Weimar Republic', pp. 597–617.

[17] Cabanes, *The Great War and the Origins of Humanitarianism 1918–1924*, p. 284; Baughan, '"Every Citizen of Empire Implored to Save the Children!"', pp. 116–37.

[18] Linsly R. Williams, 'Report on the Situation in Vienna: Special Report on Condition of Medical Teachers and Doctors', 15 April 1920, RAC/RF, SG 1.1, Series 100, Box 77, Folder 728, pp. 13–4.

[19] Report by M. Vernon, 29 June 1920, LSF/YM/MfS/FEWVRC/4/3/7/2, p. 1.

among Viennese intellectuals, to such an extent that rabbits and guinea pigs – essential for some scientific research – were being eaten in quantities to make them 'almost worth their weight in gold'.[20] One account from a Viennese intellectual, cited in a British Friends' document, stated that 'no Englishman can imagine in what a state of dirt we have to live'.[21] Against growing reports of widespread hardship, speculation abounded. In the summer of 1920, Sigmund Freud became aware of a rumour, current in the United States, that he had committed suicide during the war owing to the severity of conditions in Vienna.[22]

Given its reputation as a centre for high culture, the fate of Vienna and its intellectuals dominated international attention in 1920. Beyond the Austrian capital, the situation facing intellectuals across Europe was also grave. An ARA worker reported from Poland in 1920 that there was 'no practical limit' to the quantity of food that should be used to feel intellectuals there.[23] In the same year, it was reported that intellectual life in Germany was imperilled because 'wages do not rise with the fall of the mark, as do those of organised labour'.[24] The plight of intellectuals in Russia also received considerable attention in the period following the Bolshevik takeover; the British author H.G. Wells visited Russia in 1920 and wrote of 'science and art starving and the comforts and many of the decencies of life gone'.[25] The situation of Russian intellectuals became a greater source of interest to Western philanthropists and scholars following the beginning of the Volga famine in 1921. News of this famine began to reach Western Europe and the United States by the summer of 1921, by which time it was estimated that up to 25 million people were threatened with starvation.[26]

Unlike the situation in Austria, the Russian famine began in the midst of a civil war on which the fate of the Bolshevik regime rested.[27]

[20] Report by M. Vernon, 29 June 1920, LSF/YM/MfS/FEWVRC/4/3/7/2, p. 15.
[21] 'The University of Vienna, 1920', LSF/YM/MfS/FEWVRC/MISSIONS/4/3/8/9.
[22] Ernest Jones, *Sigmund Freud: Life and Work, Volume Three: The Last Phase, 1919–1939* (London: The Hogarth Press, 1957), p. 26.
[23] W. M. Gwynn, 'A Relief Worker's Account of Work in Galicia', *ARA Bulletin*, 2.3 (1920), p. 26.
[24] 'A Capital Offense', LSF/YM/MfS/FEWVRC/MISSIONS/10/5/2/3
[25] H. G. Wells, *Russia in the Shadows* (London, 1920), p. 87.
[26] Cabanes, *The Great War and the Origins of Humanitarianism*, p. 189.
[27] Tehila Sasson, 'From Empire to Humanity: The Russian Famine and the Imperial Origins of International Humanitarianism', *Journal of British Studies*, 55.3 (2016), pp. 519–37.

Moreover, since the Bolshevik takeover in 1917, intellectuals occupied a difficult space in Russia; many had fled and allied themselves with the anti-Bolshevik whites, while others within Russia were viewed with suspicion, tried, and deported or even executed.[28] Assistance to Russia was divisive, with opponents claiming that it constituted aid to an enemy state and querying the rectitude of action that could be construed as support for the Bolshevik government.[29] In June 1921, the Russian intellectual Maxim Gorky made an appeal to Western intellectuals calling on them to raise awareness of the scale of the famine and the disaster facing Russia.[30] Thereafter, organizations such as the American Relief Administration, the Quakers, and Save the Children all signed agreements with the Soviet government to distribute aid in Russia.[31] American philanthropic interests gave significant sums of money to the ARA, which in turn resumed the interest in assisting intellectuals that it had evidenced in Central and Eastern Europe in the preceding years.

Descriptions of the conditions facing Russian intellectuals were unflinchingly visceral. One professor in Saratov, located on the Volga river, claimed that 'for six months we had to live as beasts and I could no longer think of myself as a man'.[32] Pitirim Sorokin, a sociologist at the University of Petrograd who was forced to leave Russia in 1922 because of his anti-Bolshevik outlook, claimed that faculty meetings in Petrograd generally began with a roll call of the dead and had become a means of determining who was still alive.[33] The faculty, in which five scholars had already died from starvation, disease, compulsory labour, or suicide, had become a sort of

---

[28] Finkel, *On the Ideological Front*, pp. 13–38; Lesley Chamberlain, *Lenin's Private War: The Voyage of the Philosophy Seamer and the Exile of the Intelligentsia* (New York, 2006).

[29] Linda Mahmood and Vic Satzewich, 'The Save the Children Fund and the Russian Famine of 1921–23: Claims and Counter-Claims about Feeding "Bolshevik" Children', *Journal of Historical Sociology*, 22.1 (2009), pp. 55–83; Carl-Emil Vogt, 'Fridtjof Nansen et l'aide alimentaire européenne à la Russie et à l'Ukraine bolchéviques en 1921-1923', *La contemporaine*, 3.95 (2009), pp. 5–12.

[30] Patenaude, *The Big Show in Bololand*, p. 27.

[31] Vogt, 'Fridtjof Nansen et l'aide alimentaire européenne', pp. 7–10.

[32] 'The Professors in Saratov', 2 May 1922, Beveridge Papers, LSEASC/ BEVERIDGE/VII/90/218.

[33] Petrograd was renamed Leningrad in 1924 and has been known as Saint Petersburg since 1991.

'undertaker's bureau'.[34] Harrowing accounts were not restricted to private correspondence. A British organization called the Committee for the Relief of Russian Intellectuals (CRRI) published a public appeal in 1922 which described the suffering of Russian academics in unvarnished terms, where one couple 'sleep on the bare floor awaiting death from starvation' while another scholar had 'become thin and transparent like a ghost'.[35] The CRRI's appeal recounted an example of a 'famous electrical engineer' in Yalta who had been placed in an asylum owing to his 'constant worry about how to feed his family' and where he later took his own life.[36] In this way, descriptions of the physical manifestations of intellectual suffering differed little from established humanitarian tropes.[37]

American humanitarian workers who were involved in the distribution of aid corroborated these accounts of desperation in correspondence with their funders in the United States. The YMCA worker Edgar MacNaughten wrote of how one junior professor in Russia 'took poison and hung himself', as he was 'driven to despair by adversity'.[38] In October 1923, O.J. Frederiksen, based in Odesa with the YMCA, reported with macabre humour to a colleague that 'when I wrote you a few days ago that I was afraid of being eaten up by the students it [was] a joke, but in the last couple of days it has been more of a serious possibility'.[39] Appeals issued by universities themselves wrote of starvation and death in similar terms. In November 1922, the University of the Crimea at Simferopol, founded in 1918, claimed that seventy-five per cent of its students were affected by famine and 'there were cases of death and suicide from

---

[34] Sorokin, 'Academic Life in Soviet Russia, RAC, Laura Spelman Rockefeller Memorial Records (LSRM), (FA061), Series 3, Subseries 3 (hereafter 3.3), Box 9, Folder 105, p. 4.

[35] 'Committee for the Relief of Russian Intellectuals', p. 1. Parliamentary Archives (PA), Stow-Hill papers, STH/DS/2/1/u, p. 2.

[36] 'Committee for the Relief of Russian Intellectuals', p. 1. PA/STH/DS/2/1/u, pp. 2–3.

[37] James Vernon, *Hunger: A Modern History* (London, 2007), pp. 29–40.

[38] Edgar MacNaughten, 'Children a curse and not a blessing', RAC/LSRM, 3.3, Box 10, Folder 115.

[39] O. J. Frederiksen to Marcia Dunham, 5 October 1923, RAC/LSRM, 3.3, Box 9, Folder 105. *American Relief Administration, Annual Report of the Executive Committee. Meeting of Trustees and Members, 4 April 1923* (New York, 1923), p. 22.

hunger'.[40] An appeal from the University of Rostov in 1922 claimed that a number of professors had died from 'intolerable life conditions'.[41] These graphic accounts made it clear that Russian intellectuals were experiencing almost incomprehensible circumstances in their day-to-day lives; they sought to create solidarity in the most basic way possible, by appealing to common humanity.[42]

Despite the severe conditions experienced by these learned communities, advocates of intellectual relief were acutely aware that the claims of need from intellectuals could seem less deserving when compared to those of starving children. Writing from Poland in 1920 where they were working with the ARA, K. Wyganowska noted that 'needy people of the inferior classes would not understand why the American mission is offering gifts exclusively to the needy "intelligentsia"'.[43] In the early days of the Russian famine, Mowatt Mitchell of the ARA admitted that publicizing their work on behalf of intellectuals might cause 'a great deal of criticism of our interest in this special class of "non-producing parasites" while millions of babies starve'.[44] An ARA report written in 1922 noted that when they started their work the previous year 'the call for the universities could not be heard for the cries of dying children' but emphasized that Russia's reconstruction depended upon intellectual relief.[45] J.J. Schokking, a representative of European Student Relief, argued that assistance to children would not succeed if aid to 'those capable of guiding social life' – the intellectuals – was neglected.[46] While there was a conviction among those engaged in intellectual relief regarding its necessity, there was an understanding that it could be perceived as less worthy in the wider humanitarian landscape in which organizations like Save the Children had effectively mobilized graphic images

[40] Prof. L. Vishnovsky to Gibson, 6 November 1922. LNA/R1049/13C/24805/23815.
[41] 'To the mission of Dr. Nansen. About the state of Rostov University', LNA/R1049/13C/24805/23815.
[42] Fassin 'Inequalities of Life, Hierarchies of Humanity', p. 254.
[43] K. Wyganowska to Louis Mamroth and Jan Wyganowska, 7 December 1920, HILA/ARAEOR, Box 94, Folder 2, Reel 143.
[44] Mowatt M. Mitchell to George Barr Baker, 15 November 1921, HILA/ARAROR Box 515, Folder 4, Reel 613.
[45] 'The Plight of Higher Education in Russia', 1922, HILA/FGP Box 25, Folder 5, Reel 31.
[46] Schokking to Paul Appell, 15 February 1922, Archives nationales (AN), Paris, France. AJ/16/6995.

of starving children in their appeals.[47] Crucially, intellectual relief benefited from philanthropic foundations for substantial donations, obviating the need for public appeals in the mass media in the manner of SCF.

In the early 1920s, international awareness was drawn to the fact that intellectuals were suffering as a distinct group within Europe's wider humanitarian crises. Descriptions of the conditions facing them were similar to wider narratives of the period in that they described terrible suffering in unflinching terms. Intellectual communities undoubtedly benefited from their traditional international connectedness, which meant that descriptions of the plight of Vienna, for example, shocked middle-class audiences in France, Britain, and North America. This connectedness and traditional prestige meant that scholars in famine-stricken countries could access an international audience of like-minded and influential people that listened to their accounts, felt a sense of solidarity, and were moved to action by them.

The Meanings of Intellectual Suffering

While the conditions facing many intellectuals across Central and Eastern Europe had much in common with the wider populations which they inhabited, these individuals were portrayed as different – by humanitarian organizations, politicians, and by themselves – because of their learning. This, too, was part of the discourse surrounding intellectual humanitarianism, which emphasized difference and the idea that the scholarly esteem of many of the individuals in question made their suffering especially worthy of aid. This was often linked to the reputation of a particular city or institution, to the distinction of an individual scholar, and sometimes to the discipline in which they worked. Fundamentally, intellectual relief relied upon a pre-existing transnational solidarity which was closely linked to the old Republic of Letters.

Much of the discourse surrounding intellectual relief hinted at – but did not always explicitly address – the important function that intellectuals could play in their respective states, many of which, such as Austria or Poland, were emerging from the embers of

---

[47] Ellen Boucher, 'Cultivating Internationalism: Save the Children Fund, Public Opinion and the Meaning of Child Relief, 1919-24', pp. 169–88.

empire.[48] Alonzo Taylor, a director of the American Relief Administration, wrote in late 1920 that the futures of the new states of Poland, Czechoslovakia, Austria, and Hungary depended upon 'the brains of this intellectual class'.[49] In late 1921, a pamphlet published by European Student Relief claimed that the new states of Central and Eastern Europe were suffering from a dearth of 'professional men to meet the rapidly developing demands of the new order'.[50] While directors of humanitarian organizations spoke in sometimes grand terms about the importance of intellectuals to democratic societies (and as a bulwark against Bolshevism), the practice of distributing aid demonstrated much ambiguity about who this might include, as will be elucidated below.

Vienna was the symbolic epicentre for immediate post-war humanitarian aid to intellectuals. Of all of the sites that suffered from hunger and disease, Vienna occupied an elevated place in the imagination of the world's scholars as an ancient seat of learning. Ruth Rouse of ESR described pre-war Vienna as 'the queen city, the intellectual, artistic and commercial centre of Middle Europe'.[51] The British ambassador to Austria, Francis Lindley, remarked in late 1919 that 'it is a tragic thing to see a great centre of culture and decent civilization on the brink of complete ruin'.[52] Vienna's plight was, then, the crisis of civilization writ large. Austrian scholars leveraged this reputation in appealing for help; a group of Viennese physicians wrote to their counterparts in the United States, urging them to come to the aid of the 'old seat of medical science in Vienna'.[53] Pertinently, because Germany was perceived as the ex-enemy most responsible for the excesses of wartime by allied states, few German cities were portrayed

---

[48] For more on how universities emerged following the collapse of the Habsburg Empire, see Jan Surman, *Universities in Imperial Austria 1848–1918: A Social History of a Multilingual Space* (West Lafayette, IN, 2018), pp. 243–66.

[49] 'The Situation of the Intellectual Class in Central Europe', RAC/CF, SG 1, 18.1, Box 12, Folder 119. This was also published in the *ARA Bulletin*, 2.3 (1920), p. 36.

[50] 'Why do they go on studying?' LSF/YM/MfS/FEWVRC/MISSIONS/10/5/2/3.

[51] Rouse, *Rebuilding Europe*, p. 14.

[52] F.O. Lindley to Lord Curzon, 27 November 1919, British Library (BL), Curzon papers, MSS Eur F.112/212(b)/185.

[53] Prof. Freih. V. Eiselsberg, 'Misery of Vienna Physicians', 1 March 1920, RAC/RF, SG 1.1, Serise 100, Box 77, Folder 728.

in the same way as Vienna. In his presidential address to the British Academy in 1920, Sir Frederic Kenyon remarked that 'appeals are being made from Germany and Austria for direct assistance from England for the intellectual life of those countries' needed to acknowledge the fact that Britain and other allies had 'legitimate grounds for resentment'.[54] Wartime resentments were more apparent in France, which had been invaded during the conflict. When the historian Louis Eisenmann urged the Sorbonne to support Viennese scholars in late 1921, he was keen to distinguish Austria from Germany. Austrian culture, Eisenmann wrote privately, 'is not German culture. It is a special culture, whose German background is tinged with international influences to the point that it has taken on its own colour.'[55] In the context of discourses on aid, Vienna managed to generally sidestep the lingering bitterness that influenced many allied attitudes towards Germany and German scholars and which meant that the ARA formally excluded Germany from its activities.[56]

Requests for intellectual aid frequently spoke the language of civilizational decline. This was generally applied to territories rather than individuals. An appeal initiated by the Friends' Emergency and War Victims' Relief Committee in 1921 stated that 'a blight such as has not threatened civilization since Rome declined and Europe entered the dark ages hangs over the world today' and warned that a 'noble and splendid civilization' could pass away.[57] The FEWVRC's appeal for universities argued that 'Europe's debt to Vienna is great' and asked that people contribute to the public appeal 'in the name of learning and of art'.[58] Speaking in 1924, Herbert Hoover argued that it was in the 'interest of civilization' that intellectuals in Russia

---

[54] 'International Scholarship' – Presidential Address by Sir Frederic Kenyon, 21 July 1920, *Proceedings of the British Academy 1919–1920*, vol. 9 (London, 1920), pp. 26–7.

[55] Eisenmann to Paul Appell, 3 December 1921, AN/AJ/16/6962.

[56] For more on the post-war intellectual 'blockade' of Germany, see: Elisabeth Piller, '"Can the Science of the World Allow This?": German Academic Distress, Foreign Aid and the Cultural Demobilization of the Academic World, 1919-1925', in *The Academic World in the Era of the Great War*, pp. 189–212; Marie-Eve Chagnon, 'American Scientists and the Process of Reconciliation in the International Scientific Community, 1917-1925', in *The Academic World in the Era of the Great War*, pp. 213–32.

[57] *Hidden Tragedy in Vienna*, LSF/YM/MfS/FEWBRC/4/3/7/4, pp. 26–7.

[58] 'Appeal for the Universities', 4 April 1920, LSF/YM/MfS/FEWVRC/MISSIONS/4/3/8/9.

should be aided.[59] The emphasis on civilization served multiple purposes in this context. Civilization was widely presented as synonymous with high culture and so intellectual relief was a tangible means through which civilizational collapse might be forestalled. Civilization was also seen as a universal entity that transcended national borders and created bonds of commonality between those who were deemed to be 'civilized'. By presenting intellectual issues as a matter of universal importance, those advocating for aid to intellectuals could, in many cases, circumvent difficult issues of national difference and wartime resentment towards ex-enemies. This strategy resembled the manner in which Save the Children mobilized the image of the 'universal child' in order to overcome lingering wartime enmities.[60]

In contrast to appeals that emphasized the universal nature of suffering, such as those relating to starving children, many appeals on behalf of intellectuals emphasized difference by referring to their subjects' esteem and fame. In drawing up one appeal, F.R. Hoare of the British Quakers fretted over which famous names ought to be included as 'great names to the Western world', noting the 'startling omissions' of figures including Sigmund Freud from a working draft.[61] One of the British Friends' public appeals of 1920 on behalf of Vienna noted that 'many of these men who are now starving led the thought of Europe in the years before the war'.[62] Another recounted the case of 'one world famous professor' who had 'been subsisting for three months on tea and soup alone'.[63] Public renown was also mobilized to raise awareness of the plight of intellectuals elsewhere; in Russia, a report reached the American Relief Administration of 'very well-known professors and practice physicians with renowned names' who had 'reached absolute impoverishment'.[64] The pre-war esteem of individual writers and

---

[59] Hoover to Laura Spelman Rockefeller Memorial, 9 October 1924, RAC/LSRM, 3.3, Box 10, Folder 112.

[60] Cabanes, *The Great War and the Origins of Humanitarianism*, p. 273.

[61] F.R. Hoare to Donald Grant, 15 June 1920, LSF/YM/MfS/FEWVRC/ MISSIONS/4/3/8/3.

[62] 'Appeal for the Universities', 4 April 1920, LSF/YM/MfS/FEWVRC/ MISSIONS/4/3/8/9.

[63] Notes from the Friends Emergency and War Victims' Relief Committee, 26 March 1920, LSF/YM/MfS/FEWVRC/MISSIONS/4/3/8/9.

[64] 'The position of physicians in Russia in the year of Revolutions and the work of the ARA', in Yale University Divinity Library Special Collections (YUDLSC),

scholars was frequently invoked with the expectation that this would mobilize sympathy for their suffering. It assumed that a learned, middle-class audience would feel solidarity with their kin elsewhere. In a similar manner, the plight of Russian intellectuals was often presented as an issue for the whole world; Fridtjof Nansen, the League of Nations High Commissioner for Refugees who oversaw the response of European non-governmental organizations to the famine, wrote in 1922 that if learned Russians succumbed to conditions, 'the intellectual patrimony of humanity will be diminished'.[65] Nansen operated a special fund for 'relief to Russian intellectuals' which operated via the International Committee of the Red Cross (ICRC) and had sent food parcels to 2,000 Russians by April 1922.[66]

With accounts of well-known leaders of European thought confronting starvation and illness, tales of their ability to *continue* their scholarly work against the odds often took on heroic overtones. Stories of continuity were frequently cited as evidence of the importance of intellectual relief, with accounts of intellectuals eking out research while facing unimaginable hardship portrayed as evidence of a damaged civilization on its last legs. In 1922, the well-connected American archaeologist Thomas Whittemore described impoverished academics in Russia as 'heroic men [who] stand in their laboratories struggling on through their last days for the science of their country and of humanity'.[67] Mowatt Mitchell, working with the ARA in Russia, wrote of his amazement that intellectuals could 'live and continue mental activities under present conditions' and warned that it was 'morally impossible' for the world not to act.[68] A committee in Czechoslovakia invested Russian intellectuals with martial qualities by labelling them 'soldiers of civilization' because they were continuing 'the cultural and scientific tradition of Russia'.[69] This framing was not

World Student Christian Federation Records (WSCF), RG46, Series 24, Box 297, Folder 2709.

[65] 'Les événements de Russie', *Le Temps*, 7 June 1922, p. 2. Vogt, 'Fridtjof Nansen et l'aide alimentaire européenne.'

[66] 'Action de secours aux intellectuels russes', AN/AJ/16/6995.

[67] Unsigned report c1922, The Committee for the Rescue and Education of Russian Youth in Exile, RAC/LSRM, 3.3, Box 8, Folder 94, p. 6.

[68] Walter Lyman Brown to Edgar Rickard, 7 March 1922, HILA/ARAROR, Box 515, Folder 4, Reel 613.

[69] 'Report on the sending of help to Russian intellectuals from a Czecho Slovak committee', 2 March 1922, HILA/ARAROR, Box 424, Folder 14, Reel 500.

restricted to Russia; a report from 1922 wrote of German scholars making 'desperate efforts to keep the lamp of knowledge burning'.[70] Against all the odds, the continuation of intellectual work was itself a metaphor for a weakened civilization staving off the imagined onset of barbarism and invested intellectuals themselves with heroic, martial, and often traditionally masculine qualities.

The Practice of Intellectual Relief

The practice of intellectual relief was backed substantially by American money. The New York-based Commonwealth Fund appropriated over a million dollars for intellectual humanitarianism in Central and Eastern Europe between 1920 and 1922.[71] This money was used to feed and clothe intellectuals in four targeted areas: Austria, Poland, Czechoslovakia, and Hungary, with the majority of these funds expended in Austria and with Germany – pointedly – overlooked. The Jewish Joint Distribution Committee also awarded significant sums to intellectual relief, with both the JDC and CF working through the American Relief Administration to provide food, medicine, and clothing to those in need. The Commonwealth Fund took over distribution of food following the ARA withdrawal in 1923 and ultimately ended its intellectual feeding programme in Austria in 1924 when the crisis had passed.[72]

American philanthropy coexisted and cooperated with domestic relief initiatives. The Mittelstandshilfe, a statistical bureau, was set up to keep a record of all the needy members of the Austrian middle classes; it held details of 140,000 such people, of whom 80,000 had received some sort of assistance by January 1921.[73] The Austrian suffragist and former opera singer Helène Granitsch directed Zegam, a cooperative which purchased food for intellectuals and the middle

---

[70] Abel Jones, 'A Menace to Learning', *Welsh Outlook*, 10.4 (1923), p. 107.

[71] This is equivalent to around $15 million in 2023. *The Commonwealth Fund: Second Annual Report of the General Director for the Year 1919–1920* (New York, 1921), p. 8; *The Commonwealth Fund: Fourth Annual Report, for the Year 1921–1922* (New York, 1923), p. 38.

[72] *The Commonwealth Fund: Fifth Annual Report for the Year 1922–1923* (New York, 1924), pp. 48–9.

[73] 'Relief Work for the Brain-Workers of Austria', 15 January 1921, LSF/YM/MfS/FEWVRC/MISSIONS/4/3/8/5.

classes in Austria.[74] Zegam was also designated as a central agency to coordinate the many international relief efforts in Austria, ensuring that they worked in harmony with each other as well as those already active, and Granitsch highlighted to the ARA especially 'needy cases' who they might assist.[75] In common with other relief organizations such as European Student Relief, Granitsch endorsed the idea of self-help and collective cooperative action rather than outright charity, and felt that 'people must be physically maintained so that they can be intellectually productive'.[76]

Perhaps the most striking manifestation of this type of intellectual relief was the phenomenon of the 'intellectual kitchen', where scholars, writers, artists, poets, students, and others from creative professions were fed collectively.[77] Intellectual kitchens also exemplified the coming together of international, national, and local initiatives. These kitchens often existed alongside (but separate from) other feeding sites in the cities in which they were based, suggesting that upkeep of intellectuals necessitated distinct, bespoke treatment. Kitchens such as this became relatively widespread in Central and Eastern European cities in the early 1920s, operating in different ways depending on their location, and sometimes permitting family members to attend and sometimes not.[78] The Commonwealth Fund maintained kitchens for professors in the cities of Vienna, Graz, Leoben, and Innsbruck.[79] By 1922, the CF was running 106 relief kitchens in Austria, of which

---

[74] Its full title was Zentraleinkauf für die Verbände der geistige Arbeiter und des Mittelstandes. A brief discussion of Granitsch's wartime activities can be found in Megan Brandow-Faller, 'The Mobilization of Vienna's Women Artists and the Interwar Splintering of Austrian Frauenkunst', *Austrian Studies*, 21 (2013), pp. 142–62.

[75] 'Die Mittelstandsvertretung beim Bundespräsidenten Dr Hainisch', *Neue Freie Presse*, 21 January 1921, p. 5; Unsigned cable, 6 May 1921, HILA/ARAEOR, Box 510, Folder 9, Reel 609.

[76] Helène Granitsch to Oskar Halecki, 4 October 1922, LNA/R1030/13C/21087/14297; 'Quinze jours en Autriche Hongrie: Vienne survivante', *Les Annales: Politiques et littéraires*, 12 November 1922. Brewis, *A Social History of Student Volunteering*, p. 55.

[77] Tom Scott-Smith has shown how communal kitchens were typical of nineteenth-century humanitarianism. *On an Empty Stomach: Two Hundred Years of Hunger Relief* (Ithaca, NY, 2020), pp. 4–5.

[78] They are variously referred to as intelligentsia kitchens, professors' messes, and intellectual kitchens.

[79] Statement by Professor Clemens von Pirquet, 30 December 1921, RAC/CF, SG 1, 18.1, Box 12, Folder 120.

six were for professors and thirteen were for students.[80] The CF reported that it had provided over one million meals to intellectuals in Austria in 1920–21.[81]

Towards the end of 1920, an intellectual kitchen was created for the academic staff at the University of Vienna. The kitchen was funded initially by gifts from the Rochester and Commonwealth funds, with a local committee using the money to purchase American Relief Administration food drafts. It was situated in the basement of the Arcaden Café in Vienna, which had previously been both a meeting place for billiard players and a storeroom for coal.[82] Hilda Clark, an aid worker with the British Friends in Vienna, reported that the kitchen was 'cheerful and pleasant and clean, and the meal is beautifully cooked and served'.[83] The Vienna kitchen supplied subsidized meals, rather than free food; diners purchased an iron coin at the beginning of the week and, in turn, exchanged this for individual paper meal tickets.[84] Meals were prepared using the nem system, developed by the Austrian physician Clemens von Pirquet to calculate nutritional content. Perhaps best-remembered for coining the term 'allergy', Pirquet designed his nem system – based on the nutritional value of milk – as a replacement for the calorie.[85]

The intellectual kitchen at the University of Vienna fed 250 people daily by 1921 and was designed to create a sense of difference, not only by separating out intellectuals from the wider population, but by distinguishing the kitchen from other feeding stations in the city. Tables were covered with white linen and decorated with flowers. One observer claimed that one could be fooled into thinking they were attending 'a banquet to celebrate some distinguished scientist or at some aristocratic club – and this, indeed, was the aim aspired to'.

---

[80] *The Commonwealth Fund: Fifth Annual Report. For the year 1922–1923*, p. 49.
[81] *The Commonwealth Fund: Third Annual Report. For the Year 1920–1921* (New York, 1922), p. 27.
[82] The organizing committee included the rector and prorector of the university, the Argentine ambassador Dr. Fernandez Perez, as well as the Austrian physician Clemens von Pirquet. 'Ivan', 'The Professors' Mess', RAC/RF, SG 1.1, Series 100, Box 77, Folder 728.
[83] Clark, November 1920, LSF/YM/MfS/FEWVRC/4/3/7/2.
[84] 'Ivan', 'The Professors' Mess', RAC/RF, SG 1.1, Series 100, Box 77, Folder 728.
[85] Richard Wagner, *Clemens von Pirquet: His Life and Work* (Baltimore, MD, 1968), pp. 44, 138–139. On the emergence of the calorie, see Nick Cullather, 'The Foreign Policy of the Calorie', *American Historical Review*, 112.2 (2007), pp. 337–64.

Figure 2.2 The intellectual kitchen at the University of Vienna, c1920
(© Rockefeller Archive Center)

The hope was that diners should 'feel comfortable and at home'.[86]
A French journalist, visiting an intellectual kitchen in Vienna in
November 1922, commented on the white tablecloth and the 'fresh
autumnal flower in a vase on every table' which seemed to 'pay
homage to the quality of the clientèle'.[87] In this way, the intellectual
kitchen drew on longstanding trends in collective feeding that saw it
as a means of creating – or reinforcing – civility and solidarity.[88]

   While the intellectual kitchen seemed, superficially, to restore
a semblance of bourgeois, pre-war order, things were not always as
they seemed. When Sir William Goode, who was by then the British
representative on the Austrian Section of the Reparation Commission,
visited the University of Vienna intellectual kitchen, he sat opposite
a man who was 'the great authority on Caesar's campaigns' and was
wearing an Austrian Army officer's uniform. Somewhat perplexed by
this, Goode asked the university's rector why, '"if the famous

[86] 'Ivan', 'The Professors' Mess', RAC/RF, SG 1.1, Series 100, Box 77, Folder 728.
[87] 'Quinze jours en Autriche Hongrie: Vienne survivante'.
[88] Vernon, *Hunger*, p. 166.

gentleman opposite is not in the Army, does he wear [an] officer's uniform?" "Because" – the Rector Magnificus lowered his voice – "he has no other clothes to wear."[89]

Intellectual kitchens were intentionally designed as sites of scholarly exchange in order to mitigate the perception that attendees were benefiting from beneficence. One American observer of the University of Vienna intellectual kitchen reported that it was 'all arranged very tactfully so as not to give the impression of a charity'.[90] An anonymous account of the same kitchen stated that there was 'a constant mental interchange', with the 'leaders of the intellectuals and guardians of science' seen 'wandering from seat to seat, from table to table'.[91] The organizers of this work were generally pleased with its effect; the Commonwealth Fund reported in 1923 that one of its successes was in enabling 'men of the highest standing to meet under pleasant circumstances', the importance of which could 'hardly be overstated'.[92]

Intellectual kitchens were set up across Europe in this period but not all were created on the pattern seen in Austria. The case of Poland, site of a major humanitarian intervention from 1919, forms a useful contrast.[93] Poland had sites for intellectual feeding in Warsaw, Kraków, Lwów, and Wilna.[94] There is some evidence to suggest that the refined atmosphere created in Vienna was not achieved in Polish intellectual kitchens, with one account stating that intellectuals were 'not pleased with the menu' and were too 'accustomed to fine cooking'.[95] And, whereas Vienna received much international attention in 1920 owing to its being seen as one of Europe's centres of civilization, intellectual relief in Poland started at the same time but was less well-publicized.

[89] William Goode, 'Austria', *Journal of the British Institute of International Affairs*, 1.2 (1922), p. 51.

[90] Stephen Duggan to Herbert Hoover, 28 December 1920, HILA/ARAEOR, Box 555, Folder 2, Reel 656.

[91] 'Ivan', 'The Professors' Mess', RAC/RF, SG 1.1, Series 100, Box 77, Folder 728.

[92] *The Commonwealth Fund: Fourth Annual Report, For the Year 1921–1922*, pp. 37–38.

[93] Christopher Blackburn, 'The Rebirth of Poland: American Humanitarianism after the Great War', *Studia Historyczne*, 4.228 (2014), pp. 522–539.

[94] Lwów is now known as Lviv and is part of modern Ukraine while Wilna is now called Vilinus and part of modern Lithuania. 'Extension of Assistance to the Intellectual Classes', *ARA Bulletin*, 2.12 (1921), p. 29.

[95] J. Baudouin de Courtenay, 'Delicate benefactors and haughty and insolent beggars', HILA/ARAEOR, Box 94, Folder 2, Reel 143.

In most cases, intellectual relief was organized and conceptualized in terms of nation states, the salvation of which was presented as contributing to a greater universal civilization. Intellectual feeding in Poland differed as it explicitly identified three different intellectual groups for assistance: Poles, Russians, and Jews. Post-revolutionary violence in Russia meant that a large number of Russians were displaced in Poland, among whom Jews fleeing anti-Semitic violence were prominent. This movement of people added to a significant Jewish population in Poland of around four million in 1920.[96] Meanwhile, the new Polish state was involved in multiple conflicts with its neighbours between 1918 and 1921, which meant that its borders remained in flux.[97] Both the American Relief Administration and the Jewish Joint Distribution Committee saw aid to Poland as a major priority in 1919, with the JDC – which focused on aiding Jewish people specifically – contributing $6 million by the end of 1920.[98] The JDC and CF both contributed significant sums towards intellectual relief in Poland which was administered by the ARA; they in turn served over two million meals in intellectual kitchens between November 1920 and June 1922.[99] Intellectual relief in Poland demonstrated the challenges of viewing those contained within the borders of nation states solely in terms of nationality, as many intellectuals had been educated in German or Russian prior to Polish independence and often did not characterize themselves in terms of fixed national identities.[100]

In many parts of Poland, kitchens were organized separately for intellectuals depending on whether they could be categorized as Jews, Poles, or Russians.[101] Separate kitchens for Jewish intellectuals, serving kosher rations, were run in Wilna and Warsaw. The feeding of Jewish intellectuals faced the specific challenge of widespread anti-Semitism. One report submitted to the ARA noted the difficulty encountered in

[96] Granick, *International Jewish Humanitarianism*, p. 81.
[97] Jochen Böhler, *Civil War in Central Europe, 1918–1921: The Reconstruction of Poland* (Oxford, 2018), pp. 59–66.
[98] Granick, *International Jewish Humanitarianism*, p. 91.
[99] 'Statement Showing the Number of Meals Served in Intelligentsia Kitchens Through Poland', HILA/ARAEOR, Box 551, Folder 7, Reel 652.
[100] Marci Shore, *Caviar and Ashes: A Warsaw Generation's Life and Death in Marxism, 1918–1968* (New Haven, CT, 2006), pp. 2–5.
[101] 'Subject: Student & Intelligentsia Feeding', 28 June 1922, HILA/ARAEOR Box 706, Folder 3, Reel 816; 'American Service to the Intellectual Classes', *ARA Bulletin*, 2.9 (1921), p. 32.

securing a site for Jewish intellectual kitchens in Warsaw, Lwów, and Kraków, all of which were cities with recent histories of pogroms.[102] Anti-Jewish violence occurred elsewhere; in Vienna, where both city and university had a reputation for anti-Semitism in this period, Jewish students were attacked by German nationalists at a mensa in April 1920.[103] A report issued by the British Quakers a few months later claimed that their chief challenge was managing 'a clash of races and religions' and noted that an 'excessive proportion of Jews' were obtaining breakfasts at some sites.[104]

Following the post-war assistance to Central and Eastern Europe, the Russian famine of 1921–23 occasioned a second wave of intellectual feeding. The ARA reached an agreement with the Soviet government to operate in Russia in August 1921 and, backed by over a million dollars from the Laura Spelman Rockefeller Memorial (LSRM), the upkeep of Russian intellectuals became part of its mission.[105] Relief in Russia was more politically challenging than its preceding schemes in Central Europe; in 1922, the Commonwealth Fund offered to provide assistance to Russian intellectuals on the basis of need but this was rebuffed by the Soviet government.[106] American aid to Russian intellectuals sometimes operated with, and sometimes without, the official sanction of the Soviet government, and also ran alongside a number of Russian relief initiatives.[107] When the ARA pulled out of Russia in July 1923, its work was continued by the Student Friendship Fund (SFF) with continued backing from the LSRM as well as its own fundraising activities.[108]

[102] John C. Miller, 'Present Status Third Commonwealth Fund Gift', 9 May 1921, HILA/ARAEOR, Box 706, Folder 3, Reel 816.

[103] Norah E. Warner to Eleanora Iredale, 28 April 1920, LSF/YM/MfS/FEWVRC/4/3/8/1.

[104] Unsigned letter to 'The Secretary of the Polish Unit', 18 June 1920. LSF/YM/MfS/FEWVRC/MISSIONS/12/5/9.

[105] Patenaude, *The Big Show in Bololand*, p. 179; *The Laura Spelman Rockefeller Memorial: Report for 1923* (New York, 1924), pp. 8–9; *The Laura Spelman Rockefeller Memorial: Report for 1924* (New York, 1925), p. 16.

[106] H. H. Fisher, *The Famine in Soviet Russia, 1919–1923* (New York, 1927), p. 387.

[107] Kendall E. Bailes, 'Natural Scientists and the Soviet System', in Diane P. Koenker, William G. Rosenberg, and Ronald Grigor Suny, *Party, State and Society in the Russian Civil War* (Bloomington and Indianapolis, IN, 1989), pp. 284–92.

[108] Ruml to Hibbard, 16 November 1923, RAC/LSRM, 3.3, Box 10, Folder 112; 'International Goodwill in Action', HILA/ARAEOR, Box 555, Folder 1, Reel 656.

Intellectual kitchens were also used to feed victims of the Russian famine. One student likened the opening of ARA kitchens in Petrograd in 1922 to 'a ray of light in bad weather. This kitchen, with its clean white table cloth and flowers, seemed like paradise to us.'[109] Ukraine was badly affected by the famine and became a particular focus for the SFF's intellectual relief in this period. In 1923, it was reported that the intellectual kitchen at Odesa was serving 526 meals a day and commented that 'it is pathetic that some of the old and world-known professors, especially of theoretical subjects, cannot pay' the subsidized rate, such was their poverty.[110] In Kyiv, the LSRM-supported intellectual kitchen provided 240 intellectuals with their daily meal as late as April 1926, while the same body also funded a rest home for professors as well as medical aid.[111] In the Ukrainian intellectual kitchens, professors were allowed to bring family members, which was not the case in other instances.[112]

In 1923, the philosopher Walter Benjamin wrote that 'anyone who does serious intellectual work in Germany is threatened with grievous hunger', yet many of the feeding schemes described so far deliberately excluded Germany.[113] One notable exception to this can be seen in the realm of student feeding, for which the key organization was European Student Relief, formed in October 1920 when it took over the student feeding activities which had been overseen by the British and American Quakers in Vienna.[114] Between 1920 and 1924, ESR raised $1.9 million in thirty-seven countries through a series of public appeals to students, with aid, primarily in the form of food, given to tens of

---

[109] Report of A. Mordovskaya, European reports – Russia, letter no. 21, YUDLSC/ WSCF/RG46, Series 24.D (aa), Box 297, Folder 2717.

[110] O.J. Frederiksen to Marcia Dunham, 5 October 1923, RAC/LSRM, 3.3, Box 9, Folder 105.

[111] 'Professors' Kitchen', YUDLSC/WSCF/RG46, Series 24.D (aa), Box 298, Folder 2721.

[112] O.J. Frederiksen, 'Feeding of Professors in the Ukraine', RAC/LSRM, 3.3, Box 10, Folder 112.

[113] Wolfram Eilenberger, *Time of the Magicians: The Invention of Modern Thought, 1919–1929* (London, 2020), p. 194.

[114] Rouse, *Rebuilding Europe*, pp. 14–8. See Brewis, *A Social History of Student Volunteering*, pp. 53–8; Isabella Löhr, *Globale Bildungsmobilität 1850–1930: Von der Bekehrung der Welt zur globalen studentischen Gemeinschaft* (Göttingen, 2021); Löhr, 'Coping With a Post-War World: Protestant Student Internationalism and Humanitarian Work in Central and Eastern Europe during the 1920s', *Social History*, 48.1 (2023), pp. 43–64.

thousands of students in nineteen countries, including 7.6 million meals to Russian students following the famine.[115] ESR became the International Student Service (ISS) in 1925.[116] In Germany, the ESR worked with the Wirtschaftshilfe der Deutschen Studentenschaft, which operated on the principle of self-help, with students expected to perform manual labour of different kinds for portions of the year in addition to their studies. Reinhold Schairer, one of the leaders of the Wirtschaftshilfe, aspired for the German university to become self-sufficient, and within a few years it was a national organization that found jobs for students, managed a network of subsidized cafeteria, and provided loans.[117] By 1923, Schairer and Paul Rohrbach estimated that almost two thirds of the entire German student body were involved in manual labour of some variety, such as work in factories, mines, or construction.[118] The development of the German 'work-student' was a consequence of acute economic suffering but allowed students to exercise a degree of agency without feeling beholden to external assistance; it was down to the 'conscious will of the students themselves' allied to generous aid from overseas.[119] An ESR report of 1923 reported proudly that 'the "work student" is a reality, and no longer scoffed at or persecuted'.[120]

While the feeding of students and professors seemed superficially to be separate endeavours, one presupposed the other; if students were to be kept alive and nurtured, they would need teachers.[121] Materials produced by the Wirtschaftshilfe to encourage overseas assistance urged would-be supporters to 'save the seed'. 'Even in the sorest famine', it urged, 'pains are taken before all else to save and preserve

---

[115] Rouse, *Rebuilding Europe*, p. 37; *Report on European Student Relief 1920–1923* (Geneva, 1923), LNA/R1031/13/22761/14297, p. 46.

[116] Hartley, 'Saving Students: European Student Relief in the Aftermath of World War I', pp. 295–315.

[117] Malcolm L. Richardson, 'The Political Odyssey of Reinhold Schairer, 1933-1955', *German History* 39.3 (2021), p. 380; Rouse, *Rebuilding Europe*, p. 96.

[118] Reinhold Schairer and Paul Rohrbach, 'The "Wirtschaftshilfe der Deutschen Studentenschaft" at Dresden', in Rohrbach ed., *The German Work-Student* (Dresden, 1924), p. 91.

[119] Schairer and Rohrbach, 'The "Wirtschaftshilfe der Deutschen Studentenschaft" at Dresden', pp. 88–90.

[120] *Report on European Student Relief 1920–1923*, p. 48.

[121] Michael Hainisch, 'Official Statements on Relief Benefits: President Hainisch of Austria', *ARA Bulletin*, 2.14 (1921), p. 13.

sowing-seed for the next harvest. The sowing seed for the spiritual future of Germany is the young generation at the universities, the students.'[122] This metaphor was utilized widely. Nitobe Inazō, one of the undersecretaries-general of the League of Nations, wrote in 1923 that 'students are the seed, and universities the seed-bed of the new intellectual harvest that shall feed, renew and make grow the knowledge and moral forces of mankind'.[123] The relationship between the relief of intellectuals and aid to students was not always clearly demarcated. ESR, for example, aided not only students but a range of other intellectuals, as did organizations like the Student Friendship Fund. Some initiatives that prioritized intellectual relief included students in that categorization while others did not. For the most part, a distinction tended to be drawn between aid to older intellectuals with established professional positions and younger students.[124]

The practice of intellectual relief shows that not only were intellectuals assisted because of a sense of categorical difference, but the manner in which this aid was delivered was also different. The use of neatly decorated communal kitchens provides one striking example of this and was intended to replicate pre-war life for these eminent scholars. This sense of difference could also be seen in the way in which intellectual suffering was portrayed which frequently placed a strong emphasis on social class, as will be demonstrated in the following section.

The Social Dynamics of Intellectual Aid

'Without exaggeration, those belonging to the middle class may be said to be most cruelly wronged, amongst them the intellectual workers', wrote an Austrian professor to the ARA in 1921.[125] While intellectual relief was a matter of ideas, it was also a class issue, and it was often

---

[122] 'Save the Seed!' in Rohrbach ed., *The German Work-Student*, p. 93.

[123] *Report on European Student Relief 1920–1923*, p. 3.

[124] On student relief see Windsor, '"The Domain of the Young as the Generation of the Future": Student Agency and Anglo-German Exchange after the Great War'; Johanna M. Selles, *The World Student Christian Federation 1895–1925: Motives, Methods and Influential Women* (Eugene, OR, 2011); pp. 93–116; Brewis, *A Social History of Student Volunteering* and Hartley, 'Saving Students: European Student Relief in the Aftermath of World War'.

[125] Charles N. Leach, 'American Physicians Relief Committees for Vienna', *ARA Bulletin*, 2.9 (1921), p. 27.

categorized under the wider umbrella of aid to the middle classes (or *Mittelstandshilfe* as it was called in Austria).[126] The middle classes, and university professors among them, were widely seen to be suffering disproportionately in the early 1920s as many were in receipt of state salaries which could not keep pace with inflation.[127] Accounts often claimed that middle-class workers did not have the same protections that organized labour provided for the working classes.[128]

Class issues pervade accounts from the period. Inflation, starvation, and disease had a profound impact upon the privileged positions that intellectuals held in their societies before the war. Hitherto representatives of bourgeois Europe, their societal position had been threatened by war as well as the rise of mass politics and socialist revolution. An ARA director stated in 1920 that 'the intellectual class is neither radical at the left nor reactionary at the right, but represents the sanest viewpoint and capacity' in Central and Eastern Europe.[129] Seeing intellectuals according to their social standing is a means of understanding the process of bourgeois 'recasting' in the face of the Bolshevik threat, as well as explaining why it was deemed important by British and American organizations.[130] Emphasis on the material decline of intellectuals in Central and Eastern Europe helped create a sense of solidarity with their equivalents in other, more fortunate parts of the world.

Accounts of intellectual suffering frequently referred to a decline in their standard of living which was evidenced through material sacrifices, such as the sale of items which may have seemed luxurious to others. Harold Gibson of ESR described how certain Russian professors had sold 'jewellery, trinkets, ornaments, unnecessary furniture' and 'all spare clothing, the "superfluous" part of a suit, and even all

---

[126] In a German context, Mittelstand referred to those workers between the ruling classes and the proletariat. Jürgen Kocka, 'The First World War and the "Mittelstand": German Artisans and White-Collar Workers', *Journal of Contemporary History*, 8.1 (1973), p. 101.

[127] Mary E. Cox has shown that middle- and upper-class children in Germany were worse off after the war. Mary Elisabeth Cox, *Hunger in War and Peace: Women and Children in Germany, 1914–1924* (Oxford, 2019), p. 334.

[128] 'Extension of Assistance to the Intellectual Classes', *ARA Bulletin*, 2.12, (1921), p. 29; 'Notes on Relief Operations', *ARA Bulletin*, 2.21 (1922), p. 36.

[129] 'The Relief of the Intellectual Classes in Central Europe', *ARA Bulletin*, 2.3, (1920), p. 36.

[130] Maier, *Recasting Bourgeois Europe*, pp. 3–9.

books which are not absolutely essential for their work'.[131] One Viennese intellectual exclaimed in the summer of 1920 that 'we have spent our capital, we have sold our furniture and jewellery' and asked 'how shall we live now?'[132] This language appeared in public appeals such as that issued by the Committee for the Relief of Russian Intellectuals in 1922. It described a professor and his wife who had 'sold even their bed and bedstead for food. They sleep on the bare floor awaiting death from starvation.'[133]

The idea that intellectuals inhabited a different social class can also be seen in the frequent accounts of their physical appearance, which, it was frequently implied, challenged their traditional dignity.[134] One account submitted to the Laura Spelman Rockefeller Memorial recalled a meeting with a professor at the University of Perm in Russia dressed 'in a torn and dirty overcoat, with an old and torn cap and with boots from which his feet covered with filthy cloth socks' who was 'immeasurably far removed from the ordinary picture of a college professor'.[135] The perception of a connection between the physical appearance of intellectuals and both their social standing and sense of dignity was widespread. A report on the needs of Russian intellectuals in 1924 stated that 'some of the most sensitive men of science remained away from gatherings rather than expose the glaring delinquencies of their clothes'.[136] The availability of shoes was another indication of intellectual deprivation. An account of life in Vienna written in late 1920 described a professor whose wife and daughter were never seen in public together 'because of the impossibility of both simultaneously wearing their only pair of shoes'.[137] An account from Germany reported that a professor stripped the leather from his sofa in order to make shoes for his children.[138] The Quaker humanitarian Hilda Clark

---

[131] Harold Gibson, 'The Position of University Professors and Teachers in Russia Today', LNA/R1049/13C/24805/23815, p. 1.
[132] Report by M. Vernon, 29 June 1920, LSF/YM/MfS/FEWVRC/4/3/7/2, p. 1.
[133] 'Committee for the Relief of Russian Intellectuals', p. 1. PA/STH/DS/2/1/u, p. 2.
[134] Jeffrey Flynn, 'On the Relatively Recent Rise of Human Dignity', *Anthropological Quarterly*, 89.3 (2016), pp. 895–905.
[135] Zensinov, 'Education in Russia under the Bolshevist Regime', RAC/LSRM, 3.3, Box 9, Folder 105, p. 6.
[136] Elisabeth Bredin, 'Distribution of New Clothing to Russian Professors, 1924', RAC/LSRM, 3.3, Box 10, Folder 112.
[137] 'Unhappy Vienna', Dec 1920, LSF/YM/MfS/FEWVRC/4/3/7/2.
[138] 'A Menace to Learning', p. 107.

noted that many members of the Austrian middle classes were 'not seen in the streets when their decent clothing is worn out' but noted that an 'educated person' sometimes had a different estimation of what this entailed compared to others.[139] In this way, the physical appearance of intellectuals was a manifestation of their impoverished state and gave appeals for their assistance more urgency.

Many humanitarian organizations agreed that beyond feeding intellectuals, an attempt should be made to reinforce their pre-war sense of social difference by ensuring that they were well-dressed. Accordingly, the provision of clothes became a widespread part of intellectual relief. A 1921 Commonwealth Fund grant to Central European intellectuals provided clothes to men and women in Hungary, Poland, and Austria, cumulatively constituting expenditure of $150,000.[140] The provision of clothes for intellectuals revealed difficult social dynamics. The American Section of European Student Relief (ASESR) provided clothing relief to almost 2,000 people in Moscow, Odesa, Ekaterinoslav, and newly renamed Leningrad in 1924.[141] These clothes were designed for professors so that they could be differentiated from the general ARA relief suit. Elisabeth Bredin, who oversaw its distribution, stated that 'familiarity with the ARA clothing package suit which appears on young and old, fat and thin, determined us not to brand the man of science with a "relief" costume'.[142] It was not enough to merely clothe intellectuals; they needed to maintain their sense of social difference, a decision which was based upon the experience of humanitarian activities over the preceding years.

Many reports also referred to the fact that intellectuals were often 'too proud' to ask for assistance. While a stigma regarding the acceptance of aid is common in other humanitarian settings, advocates of intellectual relief maintained that it was specific to the class that they sought to assist.[143] Edgar Rickard of the ARA claimed that during the

---

[139] Hilda Clark's notes on Austria, November 1920, LSF/YM/MfS/FEWVRC/4/3/7/2.

[140] *The Commonwealth Fund: Third Annual Report. For the Year 1920–1921*, p. 27.

[141] Situated in modern Ukraine, Ekaterinoslav has been known as Dnipro since 2016.

[142] Elisabeth Bredin, 'Distribution of New Clothing to Russian Professors, 1924', RAC/LSRM, 3.3, Box 10, Folder 112.

[143] Vernon, *Hunger*, p. 180.

Figure 2.3 Intellectuals in Vienna try on shoes provided by the Commonwealth Fund, c1921 (Hoover Institution Library and Archives)

First World War, American humanitarian workers in Belgium learned that 'intelligentsia will skate on the thin edge of starvation before taking their families into a public soup kitchen' and tailored their post-war aid on this basis.[144] An account published in the *ARA Bulletin* in 1920 stated that 'it is as true of the Vienna "intellectual" as of any other than he prefers starvation to beggary'.[145] In Poland it was claimed that many intellectuals initially refused to attend intellectual kitchens because they felt that it was 'a kind of gift'.[146] The idea that intellectuals were too proud or ashamed to make people publicly aware of their privations was widespread; it further reinforced the sense of social difference and the affront to intellectual dignity which underpinned intellectual relief.

[144] Rickard to Smith (draft), February 1922, HILA/ARAROR, Box 326, Folder 8, Reel 403.

[145] 'The Relief of the Intellectual Classes in Central Europe', p. 40.

[146] Baudouin de Courtenay, 'Delicate benefactors and haughty and insolent beggars'.

The practice of intellectual relief often revealed striking gender dynamics. Intellectuals were overwhelmingly assumed to be male and descriptions of their need frequently referred to their inability to feed their families. In many cases, the ability of men to provide for their wives and daughters was a further symbol of their impoverishment. Some accounts referred not only to the poverty of the individual scholar but also their wider family, in order to emphasize their perilous status and justify assistance. One Viennese scholar's case was described as 'specially tragic' with a report stating that they had 'never seen more starved-looking people than he and his family'.[147] In Hungary, the former minister of education Count Albert Apponyi wrote that 'it is very difficult for a man to put forth his whole intellectual powers when he is faced with the incessant struggle to obtain daily bread for himself and his family'.[148] Being classified as an intellectual and thus eligible for bespoke aid could benefit other family members. Clemens von Pirquet wrote that those who were most visible in their gratitude for relief in Vienna were the families of intellectuals, urging his colleagues to 'witness the triumphant joy of wife and children' at the receipt of food parcels.[149]

While intellectual relief was often premised upon difference from wider society, this sat uneasily alongside familial responsibilities. One Russian professor, the recipient of a new suit from the Maxim Gorky Committee, felt that it was 'a little distressing to have a good suit yourself when your wife and children are shivering with cold'.[150] Some feeding programmes *only* fed intellectuals and not their dependents. At the aforementioned University of Vienna intellectual kitchen, for example, wives and children were not allowed entry, and admission was reserved for the university's faculty members, who were overwhelmingly male.[151] The most prominent women in the Viennese intellectual kitchen were the 'white-clad girls' who served the male

---

147 Undated report on Austrian docents, LSF/YM/MfS/FEWVRC/MISSIONS/10/5/2/3.

148 Oskar Halecki, *Enquiry into the Conditions of Intellectual Life: General Situation* (Geneva, 1923), p. 5. LNA/R1057/13C/31949/29604.

149 Pirquet, 'Memorandum for Dr. Williams', 30 November 1920, RAC/RF, SG. 1.1, Series 100, Box 77, Folder 728.

150 Harold Gibson, 'The Position of University Professors and Teachers in Russia Today', LNA/R1049/13C/24805/23815, p. 1.

151 'Ivan', 'The Professors' Mess' RAC/RF, SG. 1.1, Series 100, Box 77, Folder 728.

diners 'under the supervision of a vigilant manageress'.[152] Moreover, this and other Commonwealth Fund intellectual kitchens seemed to provide *better* rations to their recipients, with the average cost per person a full ten dollars higher for intellectual feeding when compared to general feeding programmes in Austria.[153] And, while some research into the most appropriate diets for 'brain work' appeared in the early 1920s, the CF pattern does not appear to have been replicated in other intellectual kitchens.[154]

Intellectual relief was gendered in other ways; many large organizations, such as the Friends Emergency War Relief Victims' Committee and European Student Relief, had senior female leadership, and women were prominent in the organization and distribution of aid to scholars on the ground in places like Vienna. Indeed, Ruth Rouse, one of the leading figures in the establishment of the ESR, stated that a key event in the gestation of that entity was a meeting of women students' societies at the University of Vienna in 1920 to draw up a memorandum on the economic position of women students.[155] Hélène Granitsch played a key role in organizing relief for intellectuals and middle classes in Austria and in soliciting aid from international organizations. She used her renown as a suffragist and feminist to mobilize international opinion to help Vienna. In November 1922, Granitsch went to Paris, where she organized the sale of items made by middle-class Viennese women to raise money for Austrian intellectuals.[156] *Le Petit Parisien* hailed her as a true feminist for whom practical actions were more important than words and someone who had 'boundless devotion' to her task.[157] Granitsch was prominent in the international women's movement in her later life.

Intellectual relief was bound up in wider issues of class and gender. In order to emphasize their social difference within their wider societies and to ensure this was maintained, aid took the form of superficial status symbols, such as clothes and shoes. The descriptions of the tattered clothes of many intellectuals – especially in Russia – often

[152] 'Ivan', 'The Professors' Mess', RAC/RF, SG. 1.1, Series 100, Box 77, Folder 728.
[153] *The Commonwealth Fund: Fourth Annual Report. For the Year 1921–1922*, p. 38.
[154] 'Food for Brain Workers', *Scientific American*, 128.4 (1923), p. 239.
[155] Rouse, *Rebuilding Europe*, p. 17.
[156] 'Autriche', *Le Temps*, 25 November 1922, p. 2.
[157] 'Nos Échos', *Le Petit Parisien*, 17 November 1922, p. 2.

implied that these people had been used to better living standards and thus deserved better, in order to differentiate them from recipients of 'ordinary' aid. An implicit comparison was drawn to the pre-war living standards of intellectuals in Europe and their subsequent decline, which cut to the core of their sense of dignity. Intellectual relief was also highly gendered; a focus on intellectuals, who were, overwhelmingly male, meant that aid, too, was often limited to husbands and not their wives or children.

Identifying the Intellectuals

Many descriptions of the terrible conditions encountered by Europe's intellectuals reached the offices of philanthropists and humanitarian organizations and emphasized that, while their material suffering was similar to that of millions of people across the continent, their social status was not. Most of the general correspondence produced by humanitarian organizations tended to portray intellectuals as a collective and categorized intellectual relief either as relief to 'intellectuals', 'intelligentsia', or 'intellectual workers', without necessarily providing further clarification as to what sort of profession or vocation this included.[158] This was complicated by the fact that to be an intellectual, or member of the intelligentsia, meant different things in different countries. These were heterogeneous terms that were contested and could encompass a disparate set of people.[159] The distribution of aid, however, required that organizations take practical decisions about precisely who would – and would not – be helped. In other words, it made them determine which intellectuals counted.

---

[158] For an overview of the interwar debate on the status of intellectual workers, see Christophe Verbruggen, '"Intellectual Workers" and Their Search for a Place Within the ILO During the Interwar Period', in Jasmien van Daele, Magaly Rodriguez García and Geert van Goethem, eds., *ILO Histories: Essays on the International Labour Organization and Its Impact on the World during the Twentieth Century* (Berne, 2010), pp. 271–92.

[159] Peter Kenez, 'Introduction: The Bolsheviks and the Intelligentsia', in Diane P. Koenker, William G. Rosenberg, and Ronald Grigor Suny, eds., *Party, State and Society in the Russian Civil War* (Bloomington, IN, 1989), p. 239; Janek Wasserman, 'The Austro-Marxist Struggle for "Intellectual Workers": The Lost Debate on the Question of Intellectuals in Interwar Vienna', *Modern Intellectual History*, 9.2 (2012), pp. 361–88.

Some funders mandated that a particular disciplinary focus be taken. The Rockefeller Foundation, for example, had a stated remit to support medical sciences and invested substantially in medical education across Europe in the 1920s.[160] They aided physicians in Vienna in 1920 where it was estimated that eighty per cent of doctors were 'in poverty or in distress'.[161] An Amerikanische Ärzte Hilfsaktion was set up to distribute aid under the direction of Clemens von Pirquet.[162] Similarly, in 1922 and 1923 the ARA paid particular attention to the relief of medical doctors as part of its wider aid to Russia.[163] For the most part, however, intellectual relief did not focus on specific disciplines or professions as with the relief to medical doctors.

Harold Fisher of the ARA acknowledged in 1922 that much assistance was being given to those 'whom we describe as the intellectuals' and it is clear that this labelling was seen as subjective in many cases.[164] Humanitarian workers in the field often found themselves having to interpret vague instructions as to whom they should be assisting. Having decided in 1922 to vote an appropriation 'exclusively for the relief of the intelligentsia classes of Austria', the Commonwealth Fund then had to decide exactly who these 'intelligentsia classes' were, deciding to 'take a rather liberal view regarding the professional categories coming within the limits of this action'.[165] In late 1923, S.M Keeny was charged with distributing Laura Spelman Rockefeller Memorial money to intellectuals in Russia via the ASESR. He wrote to the donors to ask whether he should prioritize 'old men who have made their reputations', 'men of middle age who are in the midst of their work', or 'young men of promise'.[166] The request caused some confusion among the LSRM leadership, where it was determined that the workers on the ground 'should be the very best judge as to what

---

[160] Raymond B. Fosdick, *The Story of the Rockefeller Foundation* (New York, 1952), pp. 108–19.

[161] Williams, 'Report on the Situation in Vienna', p. 13.

[162] Williams, 'Report on the Situation in Vienna', pp. 15–6.

[163] 'The position of physicians in Russia in the year of Revolutions and the work of the ARA', in YUDLSC/WSCF/RG46, Series 24, Box 297, Folder 2709.

[164] Fisher to Rickard, 27 November 1922, HILA/ARAROR, Box 502, Folder 2, Reel 589.

[165] Eva Lutyens, 'Intelligentsia Progress Report #1', 4 April 1922, RAC/CF, SG 1, 18.1, Box 12, Folder 121.

[166] Extract from letter by S.M. Keeny to E.T. Colton under date of December 6, 1923', RAC/LSRM, 3.3, Box 10, Folder 112.

should be done and what should not be done'.[167] Determining exactly who was and was not a member of the intelligentsia clearly posed challenges.

While generally invoking the imperative of assisting intellectuals, funders often left it to the aid workers themselves to exercise judgement about where it would be best spent. In exceptional cases, individual aid workers drove the process. Edgar MacNaughten of the Student Friendship Fund sought and obtained a succession of small grants from the LSRM in order to cater to specific problems affecting scholars in Ukraine. He personally selected fourteen scholars in Kyiv and nineteen in Odesa who were 'reputed to be the most active in original research' who were given monthly aid so that they might be 'reduced from household worries for more significant things before them'.[168] The SFF was 'kicked out' of Russia in 1925 by the Soviet government, but, as MacNaughten was trusted by all parties, he continued to facilitate small-scale intellectual relief programmes in Ukraine well into the late 1920s, at a time when Ukrainian intellectual life was being increasingly repressed by the Soviet state.[169] Aid workers with expert knowledge of conditions in a given area could make a compelling and specific case, but these instances were relatively isolated.

Some organizations kept detailed inventories of which professions were aided, but this was far from a widespread or consistent practice. The ARA maintained lists of which professions in Hungary were sent food packages, with professors, actors, painters, physicians, and lawyers all receiving aid but 'state officials' being most represented in the summer of 1921 and 'pensioners and widows' topping the list in December 1921.[170] The Student Friendship Fund did likewise in Russia, keeping accounts of the disciplines of the just over three

---

[167] Chorley to Woods, 17 January 1924, Extract from letter by S.M. Keeny to E.T. Colton under date of December 6, 1923', RAC/LSRM, 3.3, Box 10, Folder 112.
[168] 'Report on $5,000 distributed by Mr. Edgar MacNaughten to the Men of Science and the intelligentsia in the Ukraine', 10 July 1925, RAC/LSRM, 3.3, Box 10, Folder 115.
[169] Fosdick to Ruml, 3 July 1925, RAC/LSRM, 3.3, Box 10, Folder 113; Halyna Hryn, 'The Executed Renaissance Paradigm Revisited', *Harvard Ukrainian Studies*, 27.1–4 (2004/5), pp. 67–96.
[170] J. N. Laurvik, 'American Aid for the Hungarian Intellectual Middle-Class', *ARA Bulletin*, 2.14, (1921), p. 23; 'Third Distribution of Food Packages Donated by the Commonwealth Fund to the Intelligentsia of Hungary', *ARA Bulletin*, 2.19, (1921), p. 40.

thousand intellectuals who were fed in selected cities in 1924. In Leningrad, Moscow, and Kyiv, the category that was most represented on each list was physicians, although historians, natural scientists, and engineers were also prominent.[171] In other instances, less exact definitions were utilized by those involved in the distribution of aid. The ARA decided to prioritize educators in Poland before moving on to 'other intelligentsia', which included doctors, lawyers, musicians, painters, engineers, and writers.[172] While invocations of 'intellectuals' or 'intelligentsia' were common in appeals to and from humanitarian organizations, the ultimate decision about who would or would not receive aid was sometimes arbitrary, often dictated by local conditions and needs and the expertise of aid workers in situ, or mediated by the terms under which the funder in question operated.

Conclusion

The need for intellectual aid began to lessen in Central Europe by 1923 and in Russia a year or two later. In a retrospective account, the ARA claimed grandly that 'in the blood-stained country of Lenin and Trotsky', its action had 'saved the Russia of Pushkine and Tolstoy'.[173] The impact of feeding programmes is, however, difficult to measure. The archives of humanitarian organizations are full of letters of gratitude from recipients to their benefactors which often mirror the motivations of the humanitarians and therefore need to be treated with some caution. Letters criticizing or complaining about the nature of food or clothes received tend not to be filed alongside more laudatory responses.[174] The Commonwealth Fund, for example, received thousands of letters from individual scholars, politicians, and learned societies which were then written up approvingly in the fund's annual report.[175] The ARA, too, was sent hundreds of messages

---

[171] See reports on Leningrad, Moscow, and Kyiv in RAC/LSRM, 3.3, Box 10, Folder 112.

[172] John C. Miller, 'Present Status Third Commonwealth Fund Gift', 9 May 1921, HILA/ARAEOR, Box 706, Folder 3, Reel 816.

[173] 'Russia and the ARA', HILA/FGP, Box 24, Folder 3, Reel 30, p. 8.

[174] For example, students in Ukraine complained that they were sent non-matching pairs of shoes from a public appeal in the US. Barinsky, 'An open letter to American students', c1923, HILA/ARAROR Reel 180.

[175] *The Commonwealth Fund: Second Annual Report of the General Director for the year 1919–1920*, p. 9.

of gratitude from Russian intellectuals following its LSRM-funded work. Some are undoubtedly moving. One Russian woman wrote that 'you have reached those who will not go and beg, who suffer in silence and die, but you should have seen the joy and tears when your parcel reached them'.[176]

Letters of gratitude frequently praised the American source of food aid. A Viennese doctor who received Rockefeller Foundation aid in 1920 wrote that his children and grandchildren would remember 'the time when American doctors saved him from bitter wants'.[177] Another Austrian professor, the beneficiary of Quaker-organized assistance, wrote of his gratitude towards 'English and American friends'.[178] Some Russian recipients wrote that the appearance of ARA food packages 'seemed like a miraculous manifestation of Providence'.[179] In common with much American humanitarian work elsewhere in this period, intellectual relief was benevolent as well as a means of extending American influence abroad and effecting what Frank Costigliola called the United States' 'economic and cultural penetration of Europe'.[180]

Responses to the receipt of aid sometimes moved past superficial platitudes to deeper political commentary. The Viennese economist Eugen Schwiedland viewed 'the noble relief of the United States in the reconstruction of Europe' in racial terms because the continent was 'for Anglosaxonry the road to Asia, whose command seems to be the great task she has to assume'.[181] Meanwhile, the historian Oscar Mitlis claimed, possibly in reference to the Paris Peace Conference, that intellectual relief would 'last in all times to come better than a treaty confirmed with hundred seals'.[182] These responses suggest that,

---

[176] Quoted in Edward G. Sabine to Director, ARA, 19 May 1923, RAC/LSRM, 3.3, Box 9, Folder 105.

[177] Pirquet, 'Memorandum for Dr. Williams', 30 November 1920, RAC/RF, SG. 1.1, Series 100, Box 77, Folder 728.

[178] Appeal for the Universities', 4 March 1920, LSF/YM/MfS/FEWVRC/4/3/8/1.

[179] Benois to Renshaw, June 1923, RAC/LSRM, 3.3, Box 9, Folder 105.

[180] Frank Costigliola, *Awkward Dominion: American Political, Economic, and Cultural Relations with Europe, 1919–1933* (Ithaca, NY, 1984), p. 39.

[181] Schwiedland to Commonwealth Fund, 14 February 1922, HILA/ARAEOR, Box 475, Folder 2, Reel 570.

[182] Mitlis to Commonwealth Fund, 25 February 1922, HILA/ARAEOR, Box 475, Folder 2, Reel 570.

unsurprisingly, intellectuals could identify the political realities that framed aid.

The impact of feeding on intellectual work is difficult to determine. For some humanitarian workers like Edgar MacNaughten, who spent years based in the same communities, it was possible to see the results of their labours. He wrote in 1924 that aid meant that one Russian intellectual could 'turn his attention from hunting for wood to the valuable work of searching for the unknown in his chosen field'.[183] This was more than a metaphor. One of the professors who was a recipient of aid in Ukraine sent MacNaughten copies of his subsequent publications, while another told him that 'we shall endeavour to work as intensively as the actual conditions of life will permit in order to give our gift to the world culture'.[184] The personalized work of MacNaughten in Ukraine was exceptional; he could speak with authority of individual cases having come to know people personally over a period of time. Of course, feeding the bodies of these individuals was only one half of the conundrum in the salvation of their intellectual lives; their minds, too, would need sustenance in the form of scientific literature to replace that which was not received since 1914 or had been destroyed in the conflicts that followed. This is discussed in Chapter 3.

While the results may be difficult to quantify, these feeding programmes demonstrate that across Europe and North America, there was a growing recognition that intellectuals constituted a distinct sector of society which would have a particular role to play in the post-war stabilization of Central and Eastern Europe. Their plight was deemed to require special treatment because they had fallen so far from their bourgeois pre-war standing. There was a widespread acceptance in the affected countries, from Austria to Poland, Germany to Russia, that the plight of intellectuals was a specific problem, essential for but separate from their wider populations. This conviction was shared by philanthropists in North America who were willing to award substantial sums to support intellectuals, although wartime alliances precluded the inclusion of certain ex-enemy states. And while much of the discourse, and the repeated invocation of 'intellectuals' as a collective, suggested a consensus about precisely who was included in this

---

[183] MacNaughten to Colton, 12 February 1924, YUDLSC/WSCF/RG46, Series 24, Box 297, Folder 2710.
[184] L. Karovitsky to MacNaughten, April 1925, and Sinelnikov to MacNaughten, 10 April 1925, RAC/LSRM, 3.3, Box 10, Folder 115.

categorization, the practice of humanitarianism revealed much ambiguity about the allocation of aid. Intellectual relief was premised upon difference, be it for reasons of learning, class, gender, or a combination of these things, and humanitarianism consciously aimed to perpetuate this sense of social differentiation in the process of recasting bourgeois Europe.

3 | Feeding the Mind
The Post-war Book Crisis

'If we regard the professors only as needy individuals', wrote Ethan Colton at the end of 1924, 'we must, of course, give first thought to food and clothing. But dealing with them also as scientists, we are unable to resist their repeated appeals for scientific literature.' Colton, by then recently returned to the United States, had been stationed in Russia with the Student Friendship Fund, an organization that provided assistance to students and professors. He wrote to the Laura Spelman Rockefeller Memorial to seek further funding not for food, but for books and laboratory equipment.[1] 'Men of this type', Colton continued, 'endure ruinous privation before they will accept food or clothing. But, as active scientists, they will accept further aids to work with profound appreciation, and in giving these aids we are helping those who mean most for the future of Russia.' Colton argued that this book aid was necessary as part of a wider project to bring about the 'preservation and recuperation of the scientific and cultural life of the Russian nation', in the aftermath of the Volga famine and amidst severe grain shortages.[2]

Colton's request was not unusual in the early 1920s; across Central and Eastern Europe, from Germany to Poland, Austria to Russia, specialist literature, especially that from other countries, had been in short supply since the beginning of the First World War in 1914. For many humanitarian operations, aid to intellectuals meant feeding their minds as well as their bodies. This was not always an approach that was initiated by aid workers but rather one that emerged from the practical experience of dealing with impoverished intellectual populations. Long bibliographies of desired publications frequently appear

[1] 'Talks on Russia', *Evening Star*, 13 December 1924, p. 12.
[2] In this letter Colton was paraphrasing a longer unsigned report about the activities of the SFF, mostly likely authored by Edgar MacNaughten, and which used some of the same terminology. E. T. Colton to Beardsley Ruml, 31 December 1924, RAC/LSRM, 3.3, Box 10, Folder 112.

among the files of humanitarian organizations which were presented in good faith when inquiries were made among communities about their needs. This meant that books and periodicals, as well as food, medicine, and clothing, would be selected based on need and specialism and sent to intellectuals so that they could continue with their cerebral work. In this way, intellectual achievement and specialism shaped the type of aid being sent to learned communities.

Book aid emerged at the end of the war alongside humanitarian feeding programmes for intellectuals. It was widespread in many of the vanquished states of Central and Eastern Europe where wartime deprivation was compounded by post-war inflation and economic crisis. The earliest book relief initiatives responded to a sense of profound emergency about conditions in these states around 1920 and hinged on scholars' inability to purchase up-to-date scholarly literature from other countries. However, book relief differed from other forms of emergency aid because it was, at its heart, premised upon international exchange. While emergency assistance in the early 1920s could plug perceived gaps in knowledge through the one-off provision of books, the long-term solution to the problem required the creation – or restoration – of a system of international exchange to ensure that essential publications could reach those who needed them on an ongoing basis, whether they were situated in Vienna, Budapest, Munich, Moscow, or Kyiv. While book relief came to prominence in the context of the wider post-war humanitarian crisis, its ultimate resolution lay in the creation of an international order based on friendly engagement between states that had been enemies in wartime and which amounted to the resolution of the difficult legacy of the war itself.[3] In the elegant words of the German librarian Fritz Milkau, it was a matter of tying 'together again the thousand broken threads' from the war.[4]

Book relief was, in its early stages at least, understood and justified by donors and recipients alike as a humanitarian issue, where literature was as essential to the wellbeing of recipients as food or medicine. It constituted another way in which European intellectuals were identified as a group requiring bespoke aid in the post-war period.

[3] Horne, 'Demobilizing the Mind: France and the Legacy of the Great War, 1919-1939', pp. 101–19.
[4] Milkau to Ruml, 20 October 1924, RAC/LSRM, 3.6, Box 62, Folder 662.

The historian James Shotwell claimed that by providing 'a stimulus to productive scholarship', intellectuals in vanquished states might be less likely to feel that they had 'suffered an injustice'.[5] This suggested that, in keeping them active and content, intellectuals might be a stabilizing force in the successor states of Central and Eastern Europe. While book relief was frequently earmarked for individual intellectuals, the recipients of this aid tended to be universities, research institutes, and specialist libraries where these individuals worked.

Unlike food or medical aid, however, intellectual sustenance did not literally save lives. Intellectual needs, and the provision of often specialist literature, were highly subjective, which meant that states could simultaneously give and receive. This was not a one-way process dominated by donors giving to passive recipients.[6] Vanquished states like Germany, Hungary, and Austria were vocal in highlighting their postwar intellectual deprivation so as to articulate a sense of grievance emanating from post-war treaties, while sometimes also supplying books to other nations in order to lessen their respective post-war isolation. Book relief was a powerful means through which states, victors and vanquished alike, could pursue cultural diplomacy; it blurred the lines between donors and recipients and exhibited myriad competing and intersecting motivations.[7]

The post-war book crisis first emerged as an international issue in 1920; it reached its nadir in Germany in 1922 and 1923, in tandem with hyperinflation, but the immediate sense of emergency had passed by the mid-1920s with the stabilization provided by the Dawes Plan and the international goodwill engendered by the Locarno Treaties of 1925. Book relief tells us much about how humanitarian initiatives developed beyond the immediate period of crisis that necessitated intervention; the relationships that were developed at the start of the decade to address an emergency continued into the late 1920s, by which time they had been reshaped into research collaborations by

---

[5] Shotwell to Fosdick, 17 January 1924, RAC/LSRM, 3.6, Box 52, Folder 558.
[6] Susan Gross Solomon '"The Power of Dichotomies": The Rockefeller Foundation's Division of Medical Education, Medical Literature, and Russia', in Giuliana Gemelli and Roy MacLeod eds., *American Foundations in Europe: Grant-Giving Policies, Cultural Diplomacy and Trans-Atlantic Relations, 1920–1980* (Brussels, 2003), pp. 31–52.
[7] Benjamin G. Martin and Elisabeth Piller, 'Cultural Diplomacy and Europe's Twenty Years' Crisis, 1919–1939: Introduction', *Contemporary European History*, 30.2 (2021), pp. 149–63.

the relative stability of the period, much as was the case with other humanitarian initiatives.[8]

The Origins of the Book Crisis

In 1920, Austrian newspapers began discussing the existence of a *Büchernot*, or book emergency.[9] This crisis was the result of several interconnected factors. The international circulation of publications had been disrupted by the outbreak of war in 1914 for many countries in Central and Eastern Europe. Wartime animosities, blockade, and the logistical difficulties presented by the conflict meant that gaps developed in the collections of many specialist libraries which had been unable to acquire recently published work from overseas.[10] A further compounding factor was the severe inflation of the immediate post-war years, which meant that the purchase of literature from abroad was often prohibitively expensive, such that missing material could not easily be replaced.[11] The adoption of protectionist policies by many states, and the continuation of violence across parts of Europe in the early 1920s, exacerbated the matter.[12]

Across Europe, inflation led to great difficulties for those wishing to purchase books from other countries. In Vienna, a pamphlet which might cost a couple of cents in the USA could not be bought for under one hundred crowns in 1920.[13] By November 1922, hyperinflation meant that a book valued at forty-five shillings in England would cost 80,000 marks in Germany.[14] The result of the increasing cost of acquiring material was that the collections of significant European libraries suffered. The Bavarian State Library in Munich, one of Germany's leading repositories, could afford subscriptions to one

---

[8] Rodogno, *Night on Earth*, pp. 289–94.

[9] 'Aktion zur Behebung der Büchernot geistiger Arbeiter Osterreichs', *Neues Wiener Journal*, 4 April 1920, p. 19; 'Die Büchernot', *Arbeiter Zeitung*, 2 July 1920, p. 4; 'Die Büchernot', *Neues Wiener Tagblatt*, 5 July 1920, p. 7.

[10] Fox, *Science Without Frontiers*, pp. 50–2; Irish, *The University at War*, pp. 24–7.

[11] Steiner, *The Lights that Failed*, pp. 191–215; 272–9.

[12] Ivan T. Berend, *Decades of Crisis: Central and Eastern Europe before World War II* (Berkeley, CA, 1998), pp. 234–9; on the continuation of violence see the essays in Gerwarth and Horne eds., *War in Peace*.

[13] 'To all Friends of Brain-work', c1920, LSF/YM/MfS/FEWVRC/4/3/8/1.

[14] Gonzague de Reynold, 'Enquête sur les conditions du travail intellectuel: Allemagne', LNA/R1057/13C/29762/29604, p. 5.

thousand periodicals in 1914 but only fifty by 1923, and many German libraries reported similar difficulties.[15] Cumulatively, the economic situation meant that Central and Eastern European states struggled to buy specialist literature from overseas.

Inflation also meant that the publication of new material became excessively expensive. The cost of paper and printing all increased in this period. In 1920, a report reached the Quakers in London that the famous German theologian Adolf von Harnack could no longer afford to publish his works and would instead be depositing the manuscripts in a library in Berlin.[16] By September 1922, the cost of printing a work in Germany had increased by 17,200 per cent compared to the pre-1914 period.[17] In France, the cost of printing in 1921 was reported to have risen by 300 per cent in comparison to pre-war costs.[18] Post-war economic difficulties manifested in other ways. The Jagiellonian University in Kraków announced its intention to award Woodrow Wilson an honorary degree in February 1919 but could not do so because of the scarcity of parchment. The degree was ultimately awarded in 1921.[19] For many European intellectuals, this was all further evidence of the imminent collapse of civilization, with the production and dissemination of knowledge itself, and their deep-rooted belief in the inevitability of progress, coming under threat.

The demand for books became apparent through the earliest humanitarian interventions on behalf of European intellectuals. The activities of the Quakers in Austria in 1919 and 1920 soon revealed that, in addition to food and medical supplies, intellectuals sought up-to-date specialist literature and scientific equipment.[20] Stefan Meyer, an internationally renowned physicist and director of the Institute for Radium Research in Vienna, reported in May 1920 that inflation

---

[15] Memorandum, 'Bavarian State Library, Munich', 22 March 1924, RAC/LSRM, 3.6, Box 61, Folder 657.

[16] Account of Professor Schucking, 21 May 1920. LSF/YM/MfS/FEWVRC/MISSIONS/10/5/2/3.

[17] *Bericht der Notgemeinschaft der deutschen Wissenschaft über ihre Tätigkeit bis zum 31. Marz 1922* (Wittenberg: Herrosé & Ziemsen Gmbh, 1922), p. 24.

[18] 'Demande présenté par la Société d'études de presses universitaires de France', c1921, CURBML/CEIP Centre Européen, Box 113.

[19] Larry Wolff, *Woodrow Wilson and the Reimagining of Eastern Europe* (Stanford, CA, 2020), p. 243.

[20] Responses to questionnaire May and July 1920, LSF/YM/MfS/FEWVRC/MISSIONS/4/3/8/9.

meant his institute could not afford essential scientific journals like *Nature* and *Philosophical Magazine*.[21] Writing from Graz in June 1920, the Quaker aid worker Agnes Murray reported that professors there sought 'pamphlets, leaflets or papers on learned subjects since the beginning of the war'.[22] The reports that emerged from Austria in this period were mirrored elsewhere. In May 1920, Millicent Taylor, who was part of the Friends' Poland Unit, was presented with a long list of books and periodicals by the librarian at the University of Warsaw which covered a vast range of fields and had not been received by the university since 1914.[23] Taylor's experience was replicated across Central and Eastern Europe.

Discourse on intellectual need was frequently articulated using the language of humanitarianism. The scholar Didier Fassin has argued that this framing generates support and fosters compassion; in this way, contemporaries sought to draw on wider humanitarian rhetoric in order to draw attention to – and sympathy for – cerebral deprivation.[24] The metaphor of intellectual starvation was not new in this period. It had been deployed during the First World War to generate support for schemes to send specialist literature to prisoners of war. The utilization of this language continued, and was significantly expanded, in the post-war period.

The metaphor of hunger was deployed in a number of ways. The absence of specialist books was frequently presented in the same terms as acute food shortages meaning that hunger and starvation could be portrayed as intellectual phenomena. In 1921, Donald Grant, who was based in Russia with the Quakers, reported 'an absolute famine in all books and laboratory supplies'.[25] During the hyperinflation of 1922, the socialist Karl Kautsky wrote that German artists and writers were 'starving not only physically' but were 'finding it more and more impossible to satisfy their intellectual hunger'.[26] In the same year, Harold Gibson of ESR invoked a 'famine of the intellect' to describe

---

[21] Meyer to Lindemann, 9 May 1920, LSF/YM/MfS/FEWVRC/MISSIONS/4/3/8/9.

[22] Agnes Murray to F.R. Hoare, 2 June 1920, in LSF/YM/MfS/FEWVRC/MISSIONS/4/3/8/3.

[23] Millicent Taylor to Ruth Fry, 31 May 1920. LSF/YM/MfS/FEWVRC/MISSIONS/13/3/2/6.

[24] Fassin, *Humanitarian Reason*, pp. 2–3.

[25] Rouse, *Rebuilding Europe*, p. 179.

[26] Karl Kautsky, 'Germany Since the War', *Foreign Affairs*, 1.2 (1922), p. 113.

conditions in Russia and claimed that normal conditions would not be restored 'until this famine is also relieved'.[27]

The hunger metaphor also informed how solutions to the absence of specialist literature were framed by equating the provision of books with the provision of food. Max Farrand, director of the Commonwealth Fund in New York, observed that the European 'intellectual class' were as 'concerned over the shortage of material and facilities for their work as they are over the scarcity of food'.[28] Following his visit to Russia in 1920, H.G. Wells reported that Russian scientists 'value knowledge more than bread'.[29] Intellectuals in Ukraine claimed that 'although we hunger for food, our craving for books is even more acute'.[30] The Kyiv-born but US-based historian Manya Gordon argued that 'once hunger is conquered, a nation still needs hope and faith and knowledge if it is ever to come back to normal health', urging that books and laboratory equipment be provided for Russia in addition to food relief.[31] The mobilization of the language of humanitarianism sought to generate sympathy and to position book aid as a humanitarian issue.

Reports urging action to address the book crisis frequently referred to international isolation. The majority of those countries in need were those for whom warfare had disrupted the importing of literature, as was the case in the Central Powers during the Great War and Russia during the civil war. In its international appeal issued in 1920, the Arbeitsmittel-Beschaffungs-Ausschuss (AMBA) stated that 'Austria has been entirely cut off from the greater part of the world for the last five years'.[32] The American Committee to Aid Russian Scientists with Scientific Literature made a public plea in 1922 which began with the assertion that 'Russian scientists have been almost completely cut off from access to western European and American literature since 1914'.[33] Lingering wartime

[27] 'The Famine of the Intellect', *Student Service Bulletin*, 12 (1922), p. 2. HILA/ARAROR, Box 502, Folder 2, Reel 589.

[28] Max Farrand, 10 June 1920, RAC/CF, SG 1, 18.1, Box 12, Folder 119.

[29] Wells, *Russia in the Shadows*, p. 41.

[30] MacNaughten to Ruml, 30 September 1926, RAC/LSRM, 3.3, Box 10, Folder 113.

[31] Manya Gordon, 'Czechoslovakia and the Future of Russia', RAC/LSRM, 3.3, Box 9, Folder 105, p. 6.

[32] YM/MfS/FEWVRC/4/3/8/1.

[33] 'American Committee to aid Russian Scientists with Scientific Literature', *Science*, 55.1434 (1922), pp. 667–8.

resentments meant that this continued after the guns had fallen silent for some ex-enemy states. In 1924, the German-born American anthropologist Franz Boas argued that Germany was 'cut off from all knowledge of the advance of science'.[34]

References to intellectual isolation were similarly apparent elsewhere; on visiting Budapest in 1920, Edwin Embree, an officer for the Rockefeller Foundation, wrote of his surprise that 'medical men who had been in England had not yet heard of the death of Sir William Osler'.[35] Osler – a Canadian physician of international repute – had been dead for seven months by the time that Embree visited Hungary. International disconnectedness worked in multiple ways; London's Royal Society admitted that it had stopped sending official publications to Russia during the civil war owing to the 'uncertainty regarding the existence or continuance of the various academies'.[36] The repeated invocation of this sense of disconnection within reports and appeals at the time demonstrated that the issue of international order and the normalization of international relations would need to be part of the ultimate resolution of the book crisis.

Emergency Aid in Post-war Europe

The first book relief organizations emerged around 1920 as a response to news of the publication crisis in Central and Eastern Europe. Typically small-scale and temporary operations, they were usually initiated and overseen by scholars and intended to function for as long as emergency conditions prevailed. The literature that was often deemed to necessitate 'emergency' action was that within the pure, applied, or medical sciences, in which knowledge was understood to develop rapidly and where the absence of recent publications could be damaging to the research and teaching work of individuals or institutions. There was considerable crossover in respect of the membership of these different operational groups, many of which had connections to larger humanitarian organizations who were engaged in food and medical relief at the time.

[34] Boas to Vincent, 21 January 1924, RAC/LSRM, 3.6, Box 61, Folder 657.
[35] RAC/RF, Officers Diaries, RG12, A-E, Edwin R. Embree, Family Journal no. 5, p. 2.
[36] Edwin Deller to Joseph Thomson, 30 July 1920, Royal Society Archives (RSA), NLB/59/243.

The trip of writer and socialist H.G. Wells to Russia in September 1920 was a key moment in drawing attention to conditions and spurring the establishment of relief initiatives in Britain.[37] Wells wrote to both the Royal Society and the British Academy in October 1920, attaching lists of publications requested by Russian scholars.[38] This led to the establishment of the British Committee for Aiding Men of Letters and Science in Russia, which was populated by leading figures from both learned societies. The committee compiled a list of books in 'pure and applied science' needed by Russian intellectuals and appealed to British scientists to send them to Russia via the committee to save the 'flower of mental life'.[39] The committee operated until 1922, by which point it had raised £448 and sent ten cases of books to the House of Savants in Petrograd.[40]

Similar initiatives emerged in the United States. The American Committee to Aid Russian Scientists was established in 1922 to furnish scholars with scientific literature that had been published since 1914.[41] The committee was chaired by Vernon Kellogg, an entomologist and evolutionary biologist at Stanford University who served with Herbert Hoover's Commission for Relief in Belgium during the war and was later involved in ARA relief operations in Poland and Russia. The committee took book donations and shipped them to Russia using the American Relief Administration's distribution network.[42] By December 1922, the committee had sent eleven tons of specialist literature to intellectuals in Russia and Ukraine.[43] As a mark of gratitude, the Astronomical Observatory in Kyiv sent a small number of their recent

[37] Wells wrote an account of his experiences in *Russia in the Shadows* (London, 1920).

[38] Council meeting of 24 November 1920, BAA/Minutebook of the British Academy, 1919–24, 76; Jeans to Israel Gollancz, 29 October 1920, RSA/NLB/59/653; Jeans to Wells, 5 November 1920, RSA/NLB/59/712.

[39] Ernest Barker, E. P. Cathcart, and A. S. Eddington et al., 'The British Committee for Aiding Men of Letters and Science in Russia', *The Athenaeum*, 7 January 1921, p. 25.

[40] 'Scientific books for Russia', *The Scotsman*, 16 February 1922, p. 9.

[41] 'American Committee to aid Russian Scientists with Scientific Literature', pp. 667–8.

[42] By August 1922, forty universities, twenty-three learned societies, and 120 private individuals had contributed. 'Aid to Russian Scientists', *Science*, 56.1453 (1922), 504–5, ARA Bulletin, 2.21 (1922), p. 35.

[43] Vernon Kellogg, 'Russian Scientific Aid', *Science*, 56.1460 (1922), p. 717

publications via the ARA to observatories in the United States in 1923.[44]

The provision of emergency aid from North America and Western Europe to Russia was generally viewed positively and was complicated only by logistical issues. The situation was more complicated in the case of ex-enemy states. While knowledge of the suffering experienced in countries such as Austria and Germany was becoming well-established in the USA and Western Europe by 1920, wartime hostilities remained close to the surface. On his fact-finding mission to Germany in 1920, Edwin Embree wrote that 'it was no pleasant thing to go into the land of the Boche'.[45] Book relief required the passage of time and reconciliation in order for institutions in ex-enemy states to be fully integrated into the international mainstream.

Some book relief organizations saw the exchange of publications as a means of fostering better relations between countries and thus made reconciliation between former enemies an explicit part of their wider mission. Established in 1920, the Anglo-American University Library for Central Europe (AAULCE) claimed that its work offered a 'unique opportunity of reconciling the intellectual world'.[46] The AAULCE operated on the premise that book relief required the resolution of two related problems; the first being the immediate provision of scholarly literature and the second being the restoration of international exchanges. The AAULCE set out to provide English-language material for the intellectual communities of Central Europe. It established library centres in Berlin, Budapest, Frankfurt, Göttingen, Kraków, Munich, Prague, and Vienna from which individuals or institutions could borrow relevant material. The AAULCE had two main offices, one at London School of Economics where the librarian B.M. Headicar oversaw operations, and the other at the newly established Institute of International Education (IIE) in New York, where Stephen Duggan was in charge. Its base at the London School of Economics meant that AAULCE was connected to the Imperial War Relief Fund's Universities' Committee and its chair, William Beveridge, who was also the director of the London School of Economics. By 1922, with

[44] William N. Haskell to ARA, 12 July 1923, HILA/ARAROR, Box 488, Folder 15, Reel 569.
[45] RAC/RF, Embree, Family Journal no. 8, pp. 1–3.
[46] 'The Anglo-American University Library for Central Europe', October 1920, LSEASC/BEVERIDGE/VII/90/96/1–4.

the conflict receding into the distance, the AAULCE dropped references to wartime alliance in its title and operated simply as the University Library for Central Europe.

On the other side of the Atlantic, Franz Boas was an AAULCE collaborator in New York. Boas was educated at Heidelberg, Bonn, Berlin, and Kiel before moving to the United States and holding teaching positions at Clark and Columbia universities.[47] In December 1920, he established the Emergency Society of German Science and Art, which set itself the goal of 'providing funds for the continuation of intellectual, and in particular, of scientific activities in Germany and Austria'.[48] Boas was also the secretary of the Germanistic Society of America, first established in 1904, which began providing German and Austrian libraries and scientific institutions with American literature 'which under present conditions cannot otherwise be obtained'. In the year 1925, 1,370 subscriptions to current editions of 161 American journals were sent to ninety-seven German and Austrian institutions, with the Hamburg America Line providing free shipping.[49]

American foundations funded much of the cultural reconstruction of Europe and were especially receptive to projects involving book relief. In an era during which the United States had formally withdrawn from the European scene following the decision of its senate not to ratify the Treaty of Versailles, the investment of foundations was a means through which American interests were propounded on the international stage and a 'stable and peaceful world order' was built on American terms.[50] The support of US-based foundations was usually in keeping with the specific focus of the fund in question and offered a means of spreading American knowledge across the world. The Carnegie Endowment for International Peace funded the creation of

---

[47] Stephen J. Whitfield, 'Franz Boas: The Anthropologist as Public Intellectual', *Society*, 47.5 (2010), p. 431.

[48] American Philosophical Society Archives (APSA), Philadelphia, Franz Boas Papers, MSS B.B61, Boas, Draft of circular letter, December 1920; Georg Schreiber, *Die Not der deutschen Wissenschaft und der geistigen Arbeiter* (Leipzig, 1923), p. 102; Piller, '"Can the Science of the World Allow This?"', p. 197.

[49] *Germanistic Society of America: Report for the Year 1925* (New York, 1925), p. 1; Piller, *Selling Weimar*, p. 60.

[50] Katharina Rietzler, 'Before the Cultural Cold Wars: American Philanthropy and Cultural Diplomacy in the Inter-war years', *Historical Research*, 84.223 (2011), p. 152; Parmar, *Foundations of the American Century*, p. 58.

an American Library in Paris, which was intended as a hub for American ideas in Europe.[51] The Rockefeller Foundation, established in 1913, had a specific medical focus and thus spent over $100,000 between 1921 and 1925 on its Division of Medical Education programme to provide medical literature to European countries.[52] The Laura Spelman Rockefeller Memorial was founded in 1918 and, from 1922, took a special interest in the social sciences, which informed how it engaged with book relief schemes.[53]

Book relief was challenging in a variety of ways. Committees had to source specialist literature and then arrange for its transportation over long distances to those who had requested it. Given the specificity of the form of aid being sought, not every organization was regarded as successful in meeting its aims. The Swiss author Gonzague de Reynold, who was a member of the League of Nations' International Committee on Intellectual Cooperation, dismissed much of this relief work as 'haphazard' and 'inadequate' in 1922.[54] As late as 1924, W. Dawson Johnston, librarian at the American Library in Paris, criticized relief efforts because 'too many books are being sent to points where they are simply kept in storage, or if unpacked, are uncatalogued, shelved in inaccessible rooms, or made so little use of that the object of the gift is defeated'.[55] Conceived in response to a perceived scholarly emergency, book relief presented distinct organizational challenges.

Book Relief and National Needs

The resonant metaphor of intellectual hunger framed scholarly need in humanitarian terms and gave impetus to book relief schemes. The practice of this relief demonstrated that it differed, often in fundamental ways, from other types of aid. As literature cannot alleviate literal, bodily hunger, definitions of need were deeply subjective; books could be deemed essential in some contexts and less so in others. This meant

---

[51] Rietzler, 'Before the Cultural Cold Wars', pp. 157–8.

[52] Solomon, 'The Power of Dichotomies', pp. 31–2.

[53] Ron Chernow, *Titan: The Life of John D. Rockefeller, Sr* (New York, 1999), p. 596.

[54] Gonzague de Reynold, 'Statement by M. de Reynold on the Condition of Intellectual Life in Austria', LNA/R1046/13C/23024/23024, p. 5.

[55] W. Dawson Johnston to John J. Coss, 14 March 1924, RAC/LSRM, 3.6, Box 61, Folder 657.

that, unlike with food aid, the boundary between donors and recipients was fluid and it was often possible to occupy both roles simultaneously.[56] Organizations were formed in what Anglo-American humanitarians deemed 'recipient' countries such as Germany, Austria, Hungary, and Russia. Many of these national organizations were established to serve a number of interconnected purposes, within which the acquisition of periodical literature from overseas sat alongside cultural diplomatic aims and the long-term development of international research collaborations. Some of these organizations also themselves provided other countries with specialist literature, demonstrating that the states, institutions, and individuals at the heart of the post-war crisis also exerted considerable agency.

National organizations frequently mobilized the language of scientific universalism in order to seek assistance and frame it as an international imperative. In the summer of 1920, the Austrian organization AMBA issued an international appeal addressed to 'brain-workers' of the world, calling on them to send spare copies of books and periodicals published since 1914 to Austria and to exchange books and periodicals 'on the basis of their intrinsic value and not on that of the publisher's price'. The AMBA appeal argued that international action would not only benefit Austria but 'the whole scientific world'.[57] Established in 1920, AMBA's committee was composed of eminent figures at the University of Vienna, including the neurosurgeon Anton Eiselsberg and the neurologist Sigmund Freud. AMBA's appeal was received relatively positively by its international audience and by the summer of 1920 it was working with committees in England, the Netherlands, Switzerland, and Germany to secure books.[58] It collaborated with the Anglo-American University Library for Central Europe on the acquisition of English-language literature with all books acquired through this mechanism marked with an AMBA stamp so that they were 'not to be sent out of Austria without permission'.[59]

---

[56] Nikolai Krementsov and Susan Gross Solomon, 'Giving and Taking Across Borders: The Rockefeller Foundation in Russia, 1919-1928', *Minerva*, 39.3 (2001), p. 265.

[57] The appeal was received by both the Society of Friends in London and the Rockefeller Foundation in New York. LSF/YM/MfS/FEWVRC/4/3/8/1. RAC/RF, SG. 1.1, Series 100, Box 77, Folder 728.

[58] 'Die Büchernot', *Arbeiter Zeitung*, 3 July 1920, p. 4.

[59] Annex to von Pflügl letter, 1 August 1922, LNA/R1031/13/22254/14297.

AMBA also sent representatives to Germany to acquire books from booksellers in Leipzig and Berlin.[60]

In late 1922, the League of Nations' International Committee on Intellectual Cooperation issued an appeal calling on libraries and intellectuals around the world to send scholarly literature to Austria. While the appeal sought to provide books and not food for Austrian intellectuals, it utilized the same type of language that was apparent in the schemes to feed Viennese scholars in 1920 by arguing that Europe could not afford to see 'one of the main centres of its intellectual life and of its culture fall into decay'.[61] The ICIC's appeal was published in November 1922, mirroring the League's simultaneous commitment to the financial reconstruction of Austria at the same time.[62] In response, the ICIC received letters from institutions around the world with details of available books and, following consultation with Alfons Dopsch of the University of Vienna, decided which of these should be sent to Austria.[63] Both the ICIC appeal and its AMBA precursor emphasized the universal importance of aiding Austria, an ex-enemy state but, crucially, one that was not associated in the allied imagination with the worst excesses of wartime.

Germany's position and status on the international stage differed from that of Austria. It was, in the imagination of Western allies, the primary enemy in the recently ended war and was typically perceived as being more complicit in both the outbreak of the war and the worst excesses committed during it, such as the destruction of Louvain university library in August 1914. While Austria was the beneficiary of much sympathy, both in 1920 and with the League of Nations appeal in 1922, the position of Germany was more complex.

The Notgemeinschaft der Deutschen Wissenschaft (Emergency Committee for German Science) was established in October 1920 with the backing of Germany's scientific academies, technical schools, research institutes, and universities.[64] It drew inspiration from a submission by Adolf von Harnack to the Weimar Assembly in

---

[60] 'Verbilligung wissenschaftlicher Bücher', *Reichspost*, 18 January 1921, p. 3.

[61] De Reynold, 'Statement by M. de Reynold on the Condition of Intellectual Life in Austria', LNA/R1046/13C/23024/23024, p. 5.

[62] Clavin, 'The Austrian Hunger Crisis and the Genesis of International Organization after the First World War', pp. 265–78.

[63] Irish, 'The "Moral Basis" of Reconstruction?' p. 791.

[64] Ulrich Marsch, *Notgemeinschaft der Deutschen Wissenschaft: Gründung und frühe Geschichte 1920–1925* (Frankfurt-am-Main, 1994), p. 78.

February 1920 which argued that the preservation of German *Wissenschaft* would be essential to solidifying Germany's 'reputation and global position'.[65] Led by former Prussian education minister Friedrich Schmidt-Ott, the Notgemeinschaft sought to secure funding for German research in order to avert 'the complete collapse of German science posed by the current economic emergency'.[66] It was successful in acquiring financial support from both state and private sources. The Notgemeinschaft was organized into sub-committees representing various disciplines and provided funding towards activities such as the publication of work, the purchase of laboratory equipment and materials, animals for experiments, scholarships for international travel, and much else.[67] Its establishment overlapped with the adoption by the Weimar government of a policy of public diplomacy which increasingly emphasized Germany's cultural achievement to inter-national audiences.[68] Schmidt-Ott argued, following Harnack, that *Wissenschaft* was 'today perhaps the only thing left for which the world still envies Germany'.[69]

The Notgemeinschaft found a receptive audience for its work in the United States. While the USA had been an associated power during the war, it had not experienced invasion or cultural mobilization to the same extent as France or Belgium, and was therefore generally less hostile towards ex-enemy states. American foundations were broadly opposed to the allied 'boycott' of German academics and sought to prevent the emergence of two opposed camps in international scholarship.[70] The Franco-Belgian occupation of the Ruhr in 1923

[65] Notker Hammerstein, *Die Deutsche Forschungsgemeinschaft in der Weimarer Republik und im Dritten Reich: Wissenschaftspolitik in Republik und Diktatur, 1920–1945* (Munich, 1999), p. 33.
[66] *Bericht der Notgemeinschaft der Deutschen Wissenschaft*, p. 5; Gerald Feldman, 'The Politics of Wissenschaftspolitik in Weimar Germany: A Prelude to the Dilemmas of Twentieth-Century Science Policy', in Charles S. Maier ed., *Changing Boundaries of the Political: Essays on the Evolving Balance between the State and Society, Public and Private in Europe* (Cambridge, 1987), p. 269.
[67] Marsch, *Notgemeinschaft der Deutschen Wissenschaft*, pp. 81–2; De Reynold 'Enquête sur les conditions du travail intellectuel: Allemagne', pp. 8–12.
[68] Hammerstein, *Die Deutsche Forschungsgemeinschaft in der Weimarer Republik und im Dritten Reich*, p. 49; Piller, *Selling Weimar*, pp. 110–5.
[69] Feldman, 'The Politics of Wissenschaftspolitik in Weimar Germany', p. 267.
[70] Katharina Rietzler, 'Philanthropy, Peace Research, and Revisionist Politics Rockefeller and Carnegie Support for the Study of International Relations in Weimar Germany', *GHI Bulletin Supplement*, 5 (2008), p. 65.

exacerbated a breach between the former wartime allies and generated further international sympathy for Germany.[71] The USA's sizable ethnic German population was a contributing factor, as was the fact that many leading American scholars had been educated in Germany before the war.[72] For its part, Germany had identified the cultivation of American opinion in order to facilitate its own post-war reconstruction.[73]

In January 1924 Franz Boas encouraged the Laura Spelman Rockefeller Memorial to work with the Notgemeinschaft to help address the gaps in German specialist libraries.[74] In May 1924, Beardsley Ruml of the LSRM announced that it had approved the 'general policy of aid to foreign libraries in connection with the books and periodicals in the social sciences'.[75] On hearing news of the Memorial's scheme, the American ambassador to Germany, Alanson Houghton, stated that it was 'pure gold' and would 'be received most cordially'.[76] The LSRM took a twin-track approach to book relief: it assisted the state libraries at Berlin and Munich directly but also contributed funding to the Notgemeinschaft to assist German university libraries, starting with a grant of $52,000 in late 1924.[77] The Memorial made grants totalling $27,500 to the Bavarian State Library and $41,000 to the Prussian State Library between 1925 and 1927.[78] In keeping with its own mission, the LSRM's funding facilitated the purchase of books in the social sciences which often, although not always, concerned either American themes or were penned by American authors.[79]

[71] Steiner, *The Lights that Failed*, pp. 221–3.
[72] Daniel T. Rodgers, *Atlantic Crossings: Social Politics in a Progressive Age* (Cambridge, MA, 1998), pp. 76–89.
[73] Piller, *Selling Weimar*, p. 55.
[74] Boas to Ruml, 7 February 1924; Boas to George Vincent, 21 January 1924. RAC/LSRM, 3.6, Box 61, Folder 657.
[75] Ruml to Ford, 29 May 1924, RAC/LSRM, 3.6, Box 61, Folder 657.
[76] Woods to Ruml, 11 July 1924, RAC/LSRM, 3.6, Box 61, Folder 657.
[77] Ruml to Schmidt-Ott, 23 September 1924, Ruml to Schmidt-Ott, 12 January 1925, Schmidt-Ott to Ruml, 27 October 1924 RAC/LSRM, 3.6, Box 61, Folder 657.
[78] Ruml to Schnorr von Carolsfeld, 12 January 1925; Ruml to Schnorr von Caroslfeld, 2 June 1927, Schnorr Von Carolsfeld to Ruml, 10 November 1924, RAC/LSRM, 3.6, Box 49, Folder 516. Ruml to Milkau, 12 January 1925, and Ruml to Fehling, 2 June 1927, RAC/LSRM, 3.6, Box 62, Folder 662.
[79] A.W. Fehling, 'Report on the Bayrische Staatsbibliothek, Munich, RAC/LSRM, 3.6, Box 49, Folder 516.

In a European context, the Notgemeinschaft faced a complex challenge as Germany was frozen out of much international scholarly activity.[80] In its first annual report, published in 1922, the Notgemeinschaft detailed activities in North America, South America, Switzerland, and Scandinavia, while the major European allies were conspicuous by their absence.[81] By 1924, Hans Schnorr von Carolsfeld, director-general of the Bavarian State Library, reported that while some overseas exchanges had resumed, no French scientific societies (and only certain English institutions) were sending their publications.[82] Exclusion of this type, a continuation of wartime belligerence, was one of several factors which led to the Bavarian State Library and others seeking funding from the LSRM to fill gaps in their collections.

While both Germany and Russia had become major recipients of medical literature from the Rockefeller Foundation in the early 1920s, during the same period Germany was also a significant provider of medical publications going to Russia, via the Notgemeinschaft, in the same period.[83] By 1930, Adolf Jürgens, who worked for the organization's library committee, reported that the connection with Russia was its 'most active' exchange.[84] At the same time, the close connections were built with institutions in Hungary, a fellow vanquished state.[85] In spite of Germany's formal exclusion from many international organizations, the Notgemeinschaft was able to utilize book relief as a means of consolidating links with other countries in the same period.

---

[80] Brigitte Schroeder-Gudehus, 'Challenge to Transnational Loyalties: International Scientific Organizations after the First World War', *Science Studies*, 3.2 (1973), pp. 93–118.

[81] *Bericht der Notgemeinschaft der Deutschen Wissenschaft*, pp. 32–3.

[82] Schnorr Von Carolsfeld to Ruml, 10 November 1924, RAC/LSRM, 3.6, Box 49, Folder 516.

[83] *Fünfter Bericht der Notgemeinschaft der Deutschen Wissenschaft*, p. 127; Solomon, 'The Power of Dichotomies', pp. 47–50; Susan Gross Solomon, 'Introduction: Germany, Russia, and Medical Cooperation Between the Wars', in Solomon ed., *Doing Medicine Together: Germany and Russia between the Wars* (Toronto, 2006), pp. 3–9.

[84] Adolf Jürgens, 'Un office central des bibliothèques allemandes', *La coopération intellectuelle*, 2 (1930), p. 473, 483.

[85] *Vierter Bericht der Notgemeinschaft der Deutschen Wissenschaft*, p. 105; H. A. Krüss, 'The Prussian State Library and Its Relations to Other German and Foreign Libraries', *Bulletin of the American Library Association*, 20.10 (1926), p. 207.

Hungary established a Committee to Ensure the Scientific Work of Hungarian Universities in 1922 under the leadership of Albert Apponyi. By that time, Hungarian intellectual life was suffering from the acute economic situation: scholars were unable to purchase scientific literature from abroad, laboratories could not afford essential overseas apparatus, and authors could not afford to publish their work.[86] As with the Notgemeinschaft, the Hungarian committee viewed culture as a useful tool through which to project a positive image of Hungary abroad.[87] Emile de Grósz, professor at the Royal Hungarian University of Budapest, argued that Hungarian culture was 'our sole weapon and source of strength' and 'the only safeguard of our future'.[88] The committee issued an international appeal and worked with a range of scholarly associations while also appealing to the Hungarian government and domestic industry for direct funding. It was dissolved in 1925 with its task 'fulfilled', by which point it had raised a sum equivalent to 40,000 Swiss Francs.[89]

Hungary was never subject to the same prolonged bitterness as Germany in the imagination of the ex-allied states of Western Europe and was welcomed back into the international fold relatively quickly in the early 1920s. As was the case for Germany, Hungary was initially excluded from the League of Nations but was later admitted as a member in September 1922.[90] Hungarian institutions received books from a range of international organizations in the 1920s. The library of the University of Budapest received donations from the French Foreign Ministry, the Carnegie Endowment for International Peace, and the Rockefeller Foundation, as well as the Notgemeinschaft.[91] While Hungary received books from organizations based in ex-allied states, it encountered problems among the successor states to the Habsburg

[86] Oskar Halecki, 'Enquiry into the Conditions of Intellectual Life. Second Series. Intellectual Life in Various Countries: Hungary, General Situation', LNA/R1057/13C/31949/29604, p. 5.

[87] Zsolt Nagy, *Great Expectations and Interwar Realities: Hungarian Cultural Diplomacy, 1918–1941* (Budapest and New York, 2017), p. 8.

[88] Emile de Grósz, 'Report on the Three Years' Activities of the Committee Founded to Ensure the Scientific Work of the Hungarian Universities (July 1922-June 1925)', LNA/R1075/13C/41427/38975, p. 1.

[89] De Grósz, 'Report on the Three Years' Activities', pp. 2–3.

[90] Nagy, *Great Expectations and Interwar Realities*, p. 49.

[91] Gyula Bisztray, 'La bibliothèque de l'université de Budapest et le bureau central bibliographique des bibliothèques publiques de Hongrie', *Revue des bibliothèques*, 40 (1930), p. 268.

Empire; the Hungarian government alleged in 1923 that a number of these, in particular Czechoslovakia, refused to engage in 'intellectual relations'.[92]

Further east, Russian institutions had found it difficult to source publications since the outbreak of war, while the Bolshevik takeover and ensuing civil war served only to further complicate the matter. The issue was raised as early as July 1918 by Sergei Oldenburg, the permanent secretary of the Academy of Sciences, who wrote to the People's Commissariat for Education (Narkompros) to stress the importance of international contacts. In the summer of 1921 Narkompros established an agency for the purchase and distribution of foreign literature. The Russian Academy of Sciences created its own body for the international exchange of books and periodicals in 1922.[93] As was the case in Austria, Germany, or Hungary, the ultimate resolution of the Russian situation depended upon the re-establishment and normalization of international relations. For ex-enemy states, it was the war itself that had severed these connections but in the case of Russia it was instead the fact that many Western states did not establish diplomatic relations with the new Bolshevik government until the mid-1920s.

There were two main rationales for book relief becoming a forum through which states could articulate political grievances to an international audience. First, book relief was itself international in nature, as the crisis could not be addressed solely by the provision of aid from one country. Rather, the full resolution of the book famine required the reactivation of international exchanges that had been well-established prior to the First World War, underscoring the present isolation of the states in question. Second, the need for books continued beyond the resolution of the acute hunger crisis that affected Central Europe in the early 1920s; gaps remained in major collections by the late 1920s, and countries continued to use their intellectual need to generate symbolic capital on the international stage. All of this was part of the wider 'explosive development' of cultural diplomacy in interwar Europe, which emerged, in the words of Benjamin Martin and Elisabeth Piller, as a consequence of the period's crises.[94]

---

[92] Temporary Mixed Commission for the Reduction of Armaments, 3 August 1923, LNA/R219/8/24366/20397, p. 4.
[93] Krementsov and Solomon, 'Giving and Taking Across Borders', pp. 275–6.
[94] Martin and Piller, 'Cultural Diplomacy and Europe's Twenty Years' Crisis', pp. 150–1.

In vanquished states such as Germany, Austria, or Hungary, appeals for intellectual assistance played upon the same discourses of civilizational decline that were invoked by the victorious allies. The AMBA appeal of spring 1920 claimed that Austria's isolation from European intellectual life could threaten 'the unity of civilization' because 'culture and civilization are the property of all nations alike'.[95] The German philosopher and Nobel prize winner Rudolf Eucken argued that the 'paralysis' which threatened Germany's mental life was damaging to Germany's 'high position in the civilization of the world'.[96] Many appeals issued in the name of national intellectual life or scholarship in different nations consciously spoke of the universal claims of civilization, simultaneously affirming nineteenth-century liberal internationalist themes while invoking post-war pessimism.

Vanquished states often articulated a deep sense of grievance in how book aid was framed by the post-war settlement. In 1920, the historian Carl Ferdinand Lehmann-Haupt of the University of Innsbruck warned the Quaker relief mission that Austrian nationalists who advocated the unification of Germany and Austria and resented the treaties of Versailles and Saint-Germain could refuse aid outright. Lehmann-Haupt claimed that if intellectual aid were to be given to Austria but not Germany 'there might be the suspicion that it is not altogether philanthropic, but that England wants to point out that it considers Germany the real enemy'.[97] Differences in approaches to, and treatment of, ex-enemy states were viewed critically by those who were in receipt of assistance. Notably, the Quakers did not exclude ex-enemy states from their humanitarian work, on the basis of their pacifism.[98]

Appeals for assistance were often explicit in linking intellectual relief to treaty revision. In 1923, with hyperinflation at its peak, the German politician Georg Schreiber argued that reparation demands needed to be lessened because 'the fate of German science and the fate of the

---

[95] AMBA appeal, LSF/YM/MfS/FEWVRC/4/3/8/1.

[96] Rudolf Eucken, 'The Troubles of Intellectual Life in Germany', in Paul Rohrbach ed., *The German Work-Student* (Dresden, 1924), pp. 5–6. Georg Schreiber made a similar argument. Schreiber, *Die Not der deutschen Wissenschaft*, p. 101.

[97] 'Extracts from Professors Lehman-Haupt's letter to Agnes Murray', LSF/YM/MfS/FEWVRC/4/3/8/2.

[98] Proctor, 'An American Enterprise', pp. 29–42; Aiken, 'Feeding Germany: American Quakers in the Weimar Republic', pp. 597–617.

reparations issue is inextricably linked'.[99] In the same year, the left-liberal German student leader Reinhold Schairer further developed this idea. Schairer had been present at Versailles in 1919 as part of the German delegation and in the post-war period led the German student self-help organization Wirtschaftshilfe der Deutschen Studentenschaft.[100] In 1923 he wrote an extensive report for the World Student Christian Federation in which he rejected historic parallels that likened modern Germany to ancient Greece or Rome. 'The fall of a nation from a high position in modern civilization to one of more or less ruin is without precedent in history', he argued. Instead, 'the scientific life of the intellectual classes and the whole fabric of modern industrial civilization' was being destroyed by 'the pressure brought to bear upon it by Versailles'. The only way to save German intellectual life, Schairer argued, was through 'a change in the demands put upon Germany by the Versailles Court'.[101] In this reading, treaty revision was a means of averting civilizational collapse.

The universal claims of intellectual relief were another means of making the case for treaty revision in Hungary. An appeal launched by the Committee to Ensure the Scientific Work of Hungarian Universities in August 1922 stated that 'the war, the revolutions, and the Trianon peace treaty have dealt the scientific labours of the universities of Hungary serious, almost intolerable, blows'.[102] The emphasis on cultural loss as a consequence of the treaty of Trianon mirrored wider efforts by the Hungarian state to cultivate an international image of itself as an outpost of Western civilization in Central Europe which was suffering under the post-treaty conditions.[103] Apponyi wrote to Henri Bergson, president of the ICIC, in 1924 urging that his committee publish an appeal on behalf of Hungarian intellectual life and

[99] Schreiber, *Die Not der Deutschen Wissenschaft*, p. 106.
[100] Richardson, 'The Political Odyssey of Reinhold Schairer, 1933–1955', p. 380.
[101] Reinhold Schairer, 'The Collapse of the Intellectual Life of Germany', c1923, YUDLSC/WSCF/RG46, Series 31. D (c), Box 132, Folder 1010.
[102] Appeal of Committee to Ensure the Scientific Work of Hungarian Universities, 1 August 1922. LNA/S402/ 2/13.
[103] Steven Seegel, *Map Men: Transnational Lives and Deaths of Geographers in the Making of East Central Europe* (Chicago, IL, 2018), pp. 84–8; Pál Teleki, *The Evolution of Hungary and its Place in European History* (New York, 1923), pp. 51–3; Zsolt Nagy, 'The Race for Revision and Recognition: Interwar Hungarian Cultural Diplomacy in Context', *Contemporary European History*, 30.2 (2021), pp. 234–7.

argued at length that Hungary had always 'followed western civilization in its convulsions, its struggles, and also in its rebirths'.[104] The
ICIC issued an international appeal on behalf of Hungarian intellectual
life later that year.

As book relief was a matter of metaphorical rather than literal life and
death, it could also be mobilized in the furtherance of wider arguments
about international politics. The power of the metaphor of intellectual
and cultural death mirrored allied fears about the crisis of civilization
and thus was an effective means of making subtle claims about the
urgency of treaty revision and the lessening of reparations. Because the
ultimate resolution of the book crisis required the restoration of international knowledge flows, it underlined the isolation of some ex-enemy
states in the early 1920s and demonstrated the importance of normalizing international relations. Premised as it was upon metaphorical starvation, the book famine demonstrated that distinctions between the donor
and the recipient entity were not always clear and that states like
Germany could fulfil both functions simultaneously.

Intellectual Relief and the Problem of International Order

Book relief had two distinct manifestations; it was an emergency, short-
term measure, intended to address an immediate economic and
humanitarian crisis through the provision of literature published
since 1914. It was also a problem of international order and the difficulty faced by crisis-stricken countries in securing regular access to
scholarly material from other nations. There were many reasons for
this, ranging from prohibitive exchange rates caused by inflation and
currency depreciation to ongoing enmity between institutions and
states following the war.[105] Viewed from this perspective, the ultimate
resolution of the book crisis was not the provision of humanitarian aid
as such but rather the restoration of normal international relations
between states and their cultural institutions to their pre-war state.[106]
While book relief began as a result of an acute humanitarian urge to
feed the minds of starving individuals, the final resolution of the crisis
could only be achieved through international reconciliation between

[104] Apponyi to Bergson, 22 September 1924, LNA/R1075/13C/39204/38975.
[105] Berend, *Decades of Crisis*, pp. 224–7.
[106] Peter Burke, *A Social History of Knowledge, Volume II: From the Encyclopédie
to Wikipedia* (Cambridge, 2012), pp. 165–7.

states and institutions. This was a problem that extended far beyond the physical exchange of publications.

The restoration of severed international connections was one of the key issues confronting fractured European cultural life in the early 1920s. Some international organizations had redefined themselves in wartime as inter-allied and continued this stance into the post-war period while other inter-allied organizations, such as veterans' groups, came into existence at the war's end. In both cases, this positive articulation of exclusionary policies can be seen as emblematic of a wider culture of victory which gave meaning to wartime sacrifice.[107]

Such exclusion can also be viewed negatively, with ex-enemy states omitted from post-war international organizations as 'moral' punishment for their wartime behaviour.[108] For example, there were also gaps in the collections of many allied countries which were missing some scholarly literature produced in ex-enemy states during wartime. France, Italy, and Serbia used the reparations provisions of the Treaty of Versailles to arrange for the delivery of periodicals published in Germany between 1914 and 1919 to their intellectual institutions as a payment-in-kind; this was an act based not on reconciliation and reciprocal exchange, but on wartime alliance and narratives of German culpability.[109] This punitive conceptualization of exclusion was premised upon a hierarchy of ex-enemies within the allied imagination, with Germany at its top. States which featured lower in said hierarchy, such as Austria, Hungary, and Bulgaria, were reintegrated into the international fold more readily. The problem of post-war order and exclusion was further complicated by the non-recognition of the Bolshevik government in Russia by many Western states.

The post-war isolation of ex-enemies from international activities was a complex phenomenon. Germans were formally excluded from many scientific organizations such as the International Research Council, sporting events including the Olympic games, and

---

[107] John Horne, 'Beyond Cultures of Victory and Cultures of Defeat? Inter-war Veterans' Internationalism', in Julia Eichenberg and John Paul Newman eds., *The Great War and Veterans' Internationalism* (Basingstoke, 2013), pp. 213–6.

[108] Schroeder-Gudehus, 'Challenge to Transnational Loyalties' p. 102.

[109] 'Fourniture de publications périodique Allemande en vertu du paragraphe 19, annexe II, partie VII du traité', AN/AJ/6/1826.

international organizations such as the League of Nations.[110] In the case of scholarly organizations, the non-inclusion or 'boycott' of German science was often followed by a counter-boycott.[111] The persistence of wartime belligerence into the 1920s varied from country to country, much of which was premised upon wartime experience; attitudes in France and Belgium, both of which were invaded in war-time, tended to be harder than was the case in Britain or the United States.[112] Unsurprisingly, pacifist organizations had few issues in including representatives of former enemy states. Beyond institutions, individual relationships between erstwhile colleagues in former belligerent states often picked up by the early 1920s but, again, this was often contingent on wartime experience and individual attitudes.

The issue of international order quickly became a preoccupation for the League of Nations' International Committee on Intellectual Cooperation.[113] Following its creation in 1922, the committee was inundated with correspondence from across Europe detailing the suffering of intellectuals; the ICIC accordingly decided that this should become its focus.[114] The committee was neither well-financed nor did it have the staff to support major relief efforts, so the most effective direct action it could take to address the book crisis was to issue international appeals encouraging intellectual communities to send literature to Austria (1922) and Hungary (1924). As it did not have resources to address the crisis of intellectual life in a humanitarian sense, the ICIC decided instead to diagnose what lay at its roots. In 1922, it was asked by the League's Council to investigate the 'urgent needs of scholars and

---

[110] Schroeder-Gudehus, 'Challenge to Transnational Loyalties', pp. 93–102; Fox, *Science Without Frontiers*, pp. 57–64; Piller, '"Can the Science of the World Allow This?"', pp. 189–92; Cock, 'Chauvinism and Internationalism in Science', pp. 249–88; Matthew P. Llewellyn, 'Chariots of Discord: Great Britain, Nationalism and the "Doomed" 1924 Paris Olympic Games', *Contemporary British History*, 24.1 (2010), p. 79; Christoph M. Kimmich, *Germany and the League of Nations* (Chicago, IL, 1976), pp. 23–48.

[111] Piller, *Selling Weimar*, pp. 134, 216.

[112] On American attitudes see Chagnon, 'American Scientists and the Process of Reconciliation in the International Scientific Community, 1917-1925', pp. 213–32.

[113] Daniel Laqua, 'Transnational Intellectual Cooperation, the League of Nations, and the Problem of Order', *Journal of Global History*, 6 (2011), pp. 223–47; Jean-Jacques Renoliet, *L'UNESCO oubliée: la Société des nations et la coopération intellectuelle, 1919–1946* (Paris, 1999).

[114] Conrad Hoffmann to Nitobe Inazō, 12 October 1922; Grete Ebel to Nitobe, 16 November 1922, LNA/R1049 13C/24805/23815.

scientific institutions, more especially as regards the exchange of books and instruments of research'.[115] Accordingly, the ICIC commissioned a series of reports on the state of European intellectual life.

The results of the inquiries pursued by the ICIC showed that the exchange of publications remained a major problem across Europe. In November 1923, the League's secretariat produced a report on international intellectual assistance which noted that many Central and Eastern European states were 'cut off from Western countries owing to their geographical situation and the depreciation of their exchange'.[116] It also noted that one-off donations and emergency relief were an inadequate response and that a 'more systematic organization for intellectual assistance' was required.[117] Book relief was somewhat ill-defined and the report claimed that institutions who appealed for publications were 'not always fully informed as to all the really essential publications which have appeared in other countries'.[118] Another League report from the same period claimed that states sought not financial aid but assistance 'to emerge from their intellectual isolation'.[119] In response, the League's fifth assembly called on states to adhere to the 1886 Brussels Convention for the Exchange of Official Documents, Scientific or Literary Publications, to which sixteen countries had signed up by 1921.[120] It also proposed the creation of national committees on intellectual cooperation to identify national needs, encourage direct liaison between members, and facilitate international exchanges without the ICIC's involvement.[121]

---

[115] Report by M. Viviani adopted by the Council 30 January 1923. LNA/R1050/13C/25986/23815; Irish, 'The "Moral Basis" of Reconstruction?' p. 788.

[116] 'Rapport du Secrétariat sur l'organisation de l'entr'aide intellectuelle internationale', LNA/R1033/13C/32294/14297, p. 4.

[117] 'Rapport du Secrétariat sur l'organisation de l'entr'aide intellectuelle internationale', pp. 1, 7.

[118] 'Rapport du Secrétariat sur l'organisation de l'entr'aide intellectuelle internationale', p. 5.

[119] Commission de cooperation intellecutelle, 'Les premiers résultats de l'enquête dans des pays de l'Europe centrale et orientale', LNA/R1057/13C/29752/29604, p. 5.

[120] League of Nations. Thirteenth Session of the Council. Minutes of the seventeenth meeting, held on Tuesday, 30 September 1924. LNA/R1075/13C/39515/38975.

[121] 'Conclusions of the report by M. Jacques Bardoux', August 1923, LNA/R1033/13C/14297/30801; Irish, 'The "Moral Basis" of Reconstruction?' p. 798.

The many reports into myriad aspects of intellectual life produced by the League between 1922 and 1924 demonstrated that international order was fundamental to intellectual reconstruction. The ICIC's analysis of the situation in Central and Eastern Europe asserted that intellectual cooperation could be 'an exceptionally powerful factor for pacification and union' but that this was complicated by wider issues of order and exclusion in which the League, through its non-inclusion of Germany and Russia, was complicit.[122] Lingering wartime bitterness also impacted the work of the ICIC. It refused, in the same period, to issue an international appeal on behalf of German intellectual life, which led to the resignation of Albert Einstein, the German representative on the committee, in March 1923. And, when overtures were made towards Friedrich Schmidt-Ott of the Notgemeinschaft to form a German national committee on intellectual cooperation, he declined, citing belligerent statements made by members of the ICIC.[123]

Locarno and After

The challenge of readmitting Germany into the international mainstream continued to linger over Europe until the start of 1925. By that point, with the Ruhr occupation having generated greater compassion for Germany, there was evidence that relations were very tentatively being resumed. In January of 1925, almost a year before the Locarno treaties were signed, the University of Hamburg approached the Sorbonne in Paris about the exchange of publications. Acting as an intermediary, the French consul in Hamburg assured the rector of the French university that its German counterpart had 'always demonstrated liberal and democratic tendencies' and that the teaching staff did not engage in political polemics.[124] Previously frosty relations were beginning to thaw.

Improving international relations were accompanied by a growing sense that the worst of the intellectual crisis was over. Conrad Hoffman of European Student Relief wrote in 1925 that 'the emergency relief, as such, is to cease', to be replaced by 'growing constructive aspects of our

---

[122] 'Les premiers résultats de l'enquête dans les pays de l'Europe centrale et orientale', 20 July 1923, LNA/R1057/13C/29752/29604, p. 2.
[123] Irish, 'The "Moral Basis" of Reconstruction?' p. 792.
[124] A. Tinayre to Paul Appell, 14 January 1925, AN/AJ/16/6958.

activities', such as student exchanges and self-help activities.[125] This conclusion was also reached by the Hungarian Committee to Ensure the Scientific Work of Hungarian Universities in 1925; Emile de Grósz wrote that they were hopeful that 'Hungary has now passed through the stage of relief and henceforth needs but practical and constant nursing back to its pristine vigour'.[126] The establishment of formal diplomatic relations between many European states and the Soviet government in late 1924 meant that when the Academy of Sciences in Leningrad celebrated its two hundredth birthday in 1925, eminent delegations from around the world participated in the ceremonies. Soviet Russia became increasingly visible at international congresses.[127]

The symbolism of the Locarno treaties of 1925 was critical to international reconciliation; the foreign ministers of Germany, France, and Britain fraternized together in public at the negotiations and the agreements themselves seemed to guarantee peace in Western Europe as Germany agreed to accept its border with France. The 'spirit of Locarno', with ex-enemy states working together in the pursuit of stability, facilitated what John Horne has called the 'cultural demobilization' of former belligerents, or the winding down of hostile wartime attitudes in word and deed.[128] Locarno brought Germany back into the international mainstream; it joined the League of Nations as a council member the following year, and a number of other international organizations subsequently invited ex-enemy states to join.[129] The International Research Council did so in 1926 but only Hungary, of the former Central Power states, accepted the invitation.[130] In 1926 the British internationalist Alfred Zimmern wrote excitedly to Stephen Duggan in New York of the possibilities afforded by what he called the 'academic Locarno'.[131] In a similar manner, the French philosopher Jean Cavaillès spoke of a '*Locarno de l'intelligence*'.[132]

[125]   Conrad Hoffmann to Beardsley Ruml, 10 July 1925, RAC/LSRM, 3.3, Box 10, Folder 113.
[126]   De Grósz, 'Report on the Three Years' Activities', p. 4.
[127]   Solomon and Krementsov, 'Giving and Taking Across Borders', p. 286.
[128]   Horne, 'Demobilizing the Mind', pp. 101–19.
[129]   Irish, *The University at War*, pp. 189–90.
[130]   Fox, *Science without Frontiers*, pp. 80–1.
[131]   Zimmern to Duggan, 28 May 1926, UNESCO Archives, A.XI.10. Zimmern also used this term elsewhere. See Laqua, 'Transnational Intellectual Cooperation', p. 234.
[132]   Sirinelli, *Génération intellectuelle*, pp. 539–61.

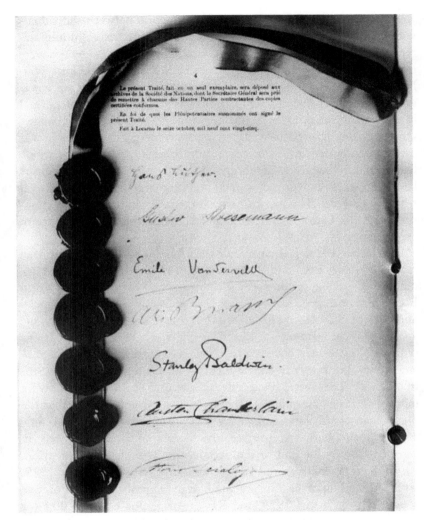

Figure 3.1 Signatures of the French, German, and British foreign ministers on the Locarno Treaties, October 1925 (AFP/Stringer/Getty)

The process of cultural demobilization was complex and progressed on multiple trajectories and at different speeds, depending on the national, institutional, and personal experiences of wartime.[133] In the

133 Horne, 'Beyond Cultures of Victory and Cultures of Defeat?' pp. 207–22; Piller, *Selling Weimar*, pp. 234–73.

years prior to 1925, there was much interaction between individuals within formerly belligerent states, as well as the provision of humanitarian assistance to former enemies, although not all ex-enemies were treated the same by states that had been allied during the Great War. Prior to 1925, much book aid was viewed through the lens of emergency assistance, but its culmination was the restoration of normal international relations and the creation of permanent exchanges. Once book relief had moved beyond its 'emergency' phase, it was often reconfigured into something more lasting; relationships which had been built between funders and national organizations against the backdrop of crisis evolved to facilitate ongoing support for general research projects. The work of the Notgemeinschaft and its relationship with the Laura Spelman Rockefeller Memorial is an important example of this.

In October 1925, just days after the Locarno agreements had been reached, Friedrich Schmidt-Ott wrote to Beardsley Ruml in New York requesting funding for three research institutes, the Institute for World Economics and Sea Traffic at Kiel University, the Institute for Social and Political Sciences at Heidelberg University, and the State Economic and Historical Seminar at the University of Berlin. Schmidt-Ott requested the money not because these institutions were in a state of emergency, but rather to enable them to 'do the highest kind of scientific work'. They were awarded a grant of $16,500 the following month.[134] From the mid-1920s there was a growing desire that the Notgemeinschaft, an emergency organization, should become a permanent body to oversee the development of research in Germany.[135] By the end of the decade, the Rockefeller Foundation, which had taken over the responsibilities of the LSRM in 1929, awarded funding to the Notgemeinschaft for a number of collaborative research projects. In 1929, the RF gave a grant of $125,000 (or $25,000 each year for five years) to the Notgemeinschaft for a collaborative anthropological research project, while in 1931, the Foundation voted an appropriation of $25,000 for the formation of

---

[134] Schmidt-Ott to Ruml, 19 October 1925, Schmidt-Ott to Ruml,
        27 October 1925, Ruml to Schmidt-Ott, 19 November 1925 RAC/LSRM, 3.6,
        Box 61, Folder 658.
[135] Feldman, 'The Politics of Wissenschaftspolitik in Weimar Germany', p. 273;
        Hammerstein, *Die Deutsche Forschungsgemeinschaft in der Weimarer
        Republik und im Dritten Reich*, p. 64.

a committee for the scientific study of problems in the field of international relations.[136] A relationship born out of acute need had developed into something durable and long-lasting.

By the end of the 1920s, the Notgemeinschaft had ceased to be an emergency body. In the words of Adolf Jürgens it had become a 'servant of science and an organization that protects the most important new German research'.[137] By then it had been officially renamed the Deutsche Gemeinschaft zur Erhaltung und Förderung der Forschung (German Foundation for the Preservation and Promotion of Research), explicitly reflecting the transformation in its function.[138] By this time, the body was viewed with some jealousy by Germany's former enemies. Speaking in the French chamber of deputies in 1930 Edouard Herriot noted that in the midst of an economic crisis 'the German government safeguarded the rights and the interests of science' because it was essential for the 'reconstruction and ultimate defence of the country'. This was an example, Herriot argued, for France to follow, as he urged greater spending on science.[139]

While the situation in large parts of Central and Eastern Europe had stabilized by the late 1920s, widespread book aid continued in the Soviet Union but bore different characteristics. The head of the Rockefeller Foundation, Alan Gregg, visited Russia in 1927 and thereafter the RF increasingly dealt directly with the Soviet government rather than acting through intermediaries. Between 1928 and 1933, the foundation appropriated $50,000 to send scientific literature to Russia.[140] While it would not enter the League of Nations until 1934, the Soviet government began to work with the League's International Institute of Intellectual Cooperation (IIIC) in Paris, receiving its official

---

[136] 'Notgemeinschaft der Deutschen Wissenschaft Anthropological Study', 13 November 1929, RAC/RF, SG 1.1, Series 300, Box 20, Folder 187; Minute of the Rockefeller Foundation, 16 December 1931, RAC/RF, SG 1.1, Series 300, Box 20, Folder 188; Rietzler, 'Philanthropy, Peace Research, and Revisionist Politics', p. 72.

[137] Jürgens, 'Un office central des bibliothèques allemandes', *La coopération intellectuelle*, 2 (1930), p. 473.

[138] Feldman, 'The Politics of Wissenschaftspolitik in Weimar Germany', p. 278.

[139] Edouard Herriot, *Journal official de la République française, Débats parlementaires. Chambre des deputés*, 11 July 1930, p. 3114.

[140] Solomon and Krementsov, 'Giving and Taking Across Borders', pp. 292, 297.

publications, including its published reports on European intellectual life and international bibliography.[141]

The creation of new links between international organizations and the Soviet government meant that older approaches to aid practices were side-lined as was the case for individual aid workers such as Edgar MacNaughten who had knowledge of certain local contexts and therefore exerted considerable agency before the thawing of relations with Russia. MacNaughten began work in Russia during the First World War with the Young Men's Christian Association and by the mid-1920s was working with the Student Friendship Fund in Ukraine.[142] The SFF had been in operation since the early 1920s and the provision of books was a key element of its assistance. While the book crisis had largely passed by the mid-1920s elsewhere in Europe, MacNaughten saw that many of the smaller university centres of Ukraine and southern Russia still had acute needs and noted that he was receiving 'repeated and insistent inquiries' for scientific literature.[143] In response, the SFF supplied 18,000 textbooks for institutions and 657 scientific texts and 292 periodicals for specialist libraries or individual professors in 1924–25 alone.[144] The SFF was financially supported through public appeals but also received significant funding via the Laura Spelman Rockefeller Memorial in New York.

MacNaughten's local connections and the trust which the Soviet authorities placed in him were critical to much of this work. When the Soviet government decided that it would not approve further SFF activity in Russia in 1925, MacNaughten continued to operate as an individual with the financial support of the LSRM.[145] But from 1927, with the Rockefeller Foundation dealing directly with the Soviet government, MacNaughten found that he was rebuffed in his approaches to Rockefeller philanthropies for funding to supply books to Ukrainian

[141] L. Levinson to Georges Lackhevitch, 6 February 1929, UNESCO/A.I.68.
[142] The SFF also operated under the title American Section European Student Relief and was administered through the World Student Christian Federation.
[143] MacNaughten to Ruml, 30 September 1926, RAC/LSRM, 3.3, Box 10, Folder 113; 'List of journals and periodicals requested for the bureau section scientific workers', YUDLSC/WSCF/RG46, Series 24, Box 297, Folder 2719.
[144] 'Summary of Operations of the Student Friendship Fund in Russia, 1924-25' RAC/LSRM, 3.3, Box 10, Folder 115.
[145] 'The attitude of the Soviet government towards relief', RAC/LSRM, 3.3, Box 10, Folder 115; Solomon and Krementsov, 'Giving and Taking across Borders', p. 281.

intellectuals.[146] In 1929, he was informed that it was the Rockefeller Foundation's policy to deal with recipients directly – not via intermediaries.[147] The carefully organized network that MacNaughten had built up over years of work in Ukraine had become an impediment to the successful funding of this project. Having devoted much of his life to various humanitarian activities in Russia, MacNaughten claimed in 1929 that he had 'never been reconciled to the failure in securing funds for scientific books for the professors'.[148]

By the late 1920s, Europe's post-war intellectual crisis had receded. The acute post-war inflation that gripped much of Central and Eastern Europe and which made the acquisition of scholarly material from other countries so challenging had been resolved by the mid-decade. The attendant issue of normalizing international relations in order to revive the international exchange of publications also eased with the passage of time, distance from the war, and the tentative reestablishment of exchange networks. The Locarno treaties of 1925 were both a symbol of reconciliation and a spur to further international cooperation. That was, of course, all prior to the Wall Street crash in the autumn of 1929.

Conclusion

'The relationship of humanity to the humanities', wrote Ruth Rouse of European Student Relief in 1925, was 'the basis of all relief of intellectual famine'.[149] Although this neat turn of phrase overlooked the vast work undertaken in the sciences, by the mid-1920s Rouse, and those involved in other organizations engaged in intellectual relief, could reflect on five years of work which meant that the immediate post-war emergency had been overcome. In Rouse's words, this humanitarian work 'saved the seed of intellectual life' with signs of 'the harvest to come'.[150]

---

[146] MacNaughten to Ruml, 7 November 1927, RAC/LSRM, 3.3, Box 10, Folder 116; Edmund E. Day to MacNaughten, 11 January 1928, MacNaughten to Ruml, 7 November 1927, RAC/LSRM, 3.3, Box 10, Folder 116.

[147] MacNaughten to Max Mason, 19 May 1929, MacNaughten to Ruml, 7 November 1927, RAC/LSRM, 3.3, Box 10, Folder 116; George E. Vincent to MacNaughten, 23 May 1929, RAC/LSRM, 3.3, Box 10, Folder 116.

[148] MacNaughten to Ruml, 21 January 1929, RAC/LSRM, 3.3, Box 10, Folder 116.

[149] Rouse, *Rebuilding Europe*, p. 175.

[150] Rouse, *Rebuilding Europe*, pp. 183–4.

Book relief was a core component of the wider process of intellectual reconstruction after the First World War. It highlighted the ways in which the figure of the intellectual was regarded as deserving bespoke humanitarian assistance to ensure that they were not only kept alive physically but were also intellectually productive. The language of humanitarianism was mobilized by donors and recipients alike to emphasize the imperative of providing specialist literature, often framing it in terms of life and death. While barriers to accessing recent scholarship were a significant inconvenience to those involved in intellectual pursuits, the book famine did not, of course, lead to literal death. Intellectual needs were subjective, varied from case to case, and complicated the neat distinction between donor and recipient. The power of the intellectual starvation metaphor made it a resonant means of engaging with themes in international relations and so it was used by committees in vanquished states to articulate critiques of the peace settlements. Taken together, this demonstrated that those in receipt of aid could exercise a considerable degree of agency.

The ultimate resolution of the *Büchernot* was not to be found in emergency aid; rather, it would be achieved through the restoration of international order. Friedrich Schmidt-Ott noted in 1924 'that innumerable old exchange connections are still broken'; thus, it was only through the restoration of international exchanges that ongoing gaps in library collections could be avoided.[151] For many, this was the reconstruction of the transnational community of knowledge that had existed prior to 1914, based as it was upon the flow of people and ideas across Europe and the world. The full resumption of international exchange required the reintegration of former belligerent states into the international mainstream and the surmounting of wartime animosities. This was a complex process which played out at different paces depending on the context; the Rockefeller philanthropies were quick to initiate contact with German scholars in the early 1920s whereas others, especially in France, were more hesitant. The symbolism of the 1925 Locarno treaties was crucial in facilitating this process. Having overcome the period of emergency relief, some of the relationships between donor and recipient were refashioned as ongoing research

---

[151] Schmidt-Ott to Ruml, 27 October 1924, RAC/LSRM, 3.6, Box 61, Folder 657.

collaborations, a transformation that other humanitarian organizations confronted by the mid-1920s.[152]

The post-Locarno normalization was relatively short-lived. The 'hinge years' of 1929–33, beginning with the Wall Street crash in 1929 and concluding with the withdrawal of Hitler's Germany from the League of Nations in 1933, undermined much of the internationalist progress that followed Locarno.[153] Unsurprisingly, Europe's totalitarian turn had consequences for the many agencies and international connections that had been forged over the preceding decade and a half. In 1933, the Soviet Politburo forbade Russian scientists from participating in Rockefeller Foundation programmes.[154] Friedrich Schmidt-Ott, the architect of the work of the Notgemeinschaft, was replaced as its head by the Nazi government.[155] Meanwhile, a new international crisis emerged in Europe which would lead to the widespread displacement of scholars from Germany and, ultimately, the outbreak of another world war in 1939.

---

[152] Löhr, *Globale Bildungsmobilität 1850–1930*, pp. 331–4.
[153] Steiner, *The Lights that Failed*, pp. 800–16.
[154] Solomon and Krementsov, 'Giving and Taking Across Borders', p. 297.
[155] Feldman, 'The Politics of Wissenschaftspolitik in Weimar Germany', p. 279.

4 | *Knowledge Displaced*

In May 1920, Thomas Whittemore sent an urgent cable from Constantinople, epicentre for many Russian refugees during and after the civil war, to his colleague Seth Gano in Boston.[1] Whittemore was a well-travelled and well-connected American archaeologist who had conducted pre-war excavations in Egypt, spent much of the First World War undertaking humanitarian work in Russia, and counted Gertrude Stein and Henri Matisse among his friends.[2] In his message, Whittemore described how 'intellectual families' from across Russia were constantly arriving in the Ottoman capital and its vicinity. He proposed educating young Russians among them using 'internationally known Russian professors', themselves refugees, in order to preserve Russian 'national life in exile'.[3]

Whittemore had witnessed the terrible suffering of Russian refugees in Constantinople at first hand; he described a situation in which many refugees faced starvation and malnourishment and led to some 'losing their teeth, others [...] going blind, and some more becoming insane'.[4] Yet, in the years following 1920, he personally oversaw a scheme to select only the most intellectually able displaced Russian students in order to place them at elite schools and universities across Europe. They were then given clear instructions that the ongoing support of their studies was dependent on them being high achievers.[5]

---

[1] Constantinople was renamed Istanbul in 1930.

[2] Tomás Irish, 'Educating Those Who Matter: Thomas Whittemore, Russian Refugees and the Transnational Organisation of Elite Humanitarianism after the First World War', *European Review of History/Revue européenne d'histoire* 28.3 (2021), pp. 441–62.

[3] Whittemore to Gano, 13 May 1920, CURBML/BAR Ms Coll/CERYE, IX.1, Box 95, Folder 17.

[4] Whittemore memorandum, c1922, CURBML/BAR Ms Coll/CERYE, IX.4, Box 99, Folder 11.

[5] Account of Whittemore work, YUDLSC/WSCF/RG46, Series 24.D (aa), Box 298, Folder 2723.

Whittemore's project sought to maintain and nurture displaced Russian intellectual life in exile until the anticipated fall of the Bolshevik regime, at which point these high-performing scholars would return home to assist the project of national reconstruction. Far from being an isolated initiative, Whittemore's project was one of many that took root in post-war Europe which sought to help a displaced intellectual elite. Herbert Hoover, who oversaw the wartime work of the Commission for Relief in Belgium and the post-war American Relief Administration, stated that keeping displaced Russian intellectuals alive in body and mind was 'one of the greatest services to humanity I can conceive'.[6]

***

Intellectual displacement was a widespread issue which affected both individuals and institutions in the aftermath of the First World War. It was the consequence of a number of key wartime and post-war developments. The shifting fronts of total war created vast numbers of refugees across Europe. The war also led to the collapse of empires, which uprooted millions of people and made minorities of millions more. The creation of new states from the embers of empire meant that many people found themselves situated within states with which they no longer identified.[7] Within this context of the widespread movement of people, the suffering of intellectuals was seen by many national governments and humanitarian organizations as a distinct problem that required a focused response.

Intellectual displacement was presented as a humanitarian problem with its own distinct past. Ruth Rouse of European Student Relief likened post-war intellectual displacement to the forced migration of the Jewish diaspora in the first century AD.[8] In 1923, the Swiss writer Gonzague de Reynold claimed, with reference to Russian intellectual displacement, that there had not been 'such an uprooting of intellectual life of a people' since the flight of the Israelites.[9] Both Rouse and de

---

[6] Memorandum regarding talk of Mr. Whittemore, 1 January 1921, CURBML/ BAR Ms Coll/CERYE, IX.4, Box 99, Folder 10.

[7] Mira L. Siegelberg, *Statelessness: A Modern History* (Cambridge, MA, 2020), p. 59.

[8] Rouse, *Rebuilding Europe*, p. 157.

[9] Gonzague de Reynold, *La vie intellectuelle dans les divers pays: Russie. Rapport sur la situation et l'organisation des intellectuels russes hors de Russie* (Geneva, c1923), p. 5.

Reynold spoke of civilization and used the metaphor of light and darkness to explain the importance of the situation. De Reynold felt that refugee scholars needed aid in order to 'maintain that flame' of civilization.[10] Rouse claimed that displaced intellectuals 'will bring light and life to the world'.[11] The historic dimension to the problem of displacement added weight to fears about the collapse of civilization, itself seen in historic terms, with the examples of Greece and Rome referenced with ominous regularity.

'Intellectual life' was often invoked by politicians, humanitarians, and intellectuals and was a term used to encompass and denote a wide range of ideas. It could refer to the cultural potential of entire national populations but also encompassed the institutional infrastructure that made national cultural production possible, such as libraries, laboratories, museums, and universities, many of which found themselves in new states following the peace settlements. To many observers, the idea of intellectual life underpinned claims to both national difference and civilizational advancement, both of which were important to states that were being reconstituted following the end of the war.

Relief to refugees was a political and cultural issue in which displaced intellectuals were presented as symbols of national life in exile. This was true, for example, of Belgian scholars among the million refugees who fled following the German invasion in 1914. As cultural representatives of displaced national communities, the ultimate goal of humanitarian aid was to ensure that intellectuals continued their work before they could return home and the restoration of national life itself could be effected. In this way, intellectual relief was both a cultural and political issue which cut to the core of debates about the post-war (re)establishment of states. Eric D. Weitz has defined the post-war order as being characterized by the rise of population politics 'and an ideal of state sovereignty rooted in national homogeneity'.[12] In the post-war impulse to create homogenous states, displaced intellectuals (and institutions), took on great symbolic value as the embodiments of their national life and a key vector in its restoration. In 1919, the Belgian scholar A.J. Carnoy, who had himself been exiled in Britain and the

[10] De Reynold, *La vie intellectuelle dans les divers pays*, p. 24.
[11] Rouse, *Rebuilding Europe*, p. 157.
[12] Eric D. Weitz, 'From the Vienna to the Paris System: International Politics and the Entangled Histories of Human Rights, Forced Deportations, and Civilizing Missions', *American Historical Review*, 113.5 (2008) p. 1314.

United States during the war, argued that the collapse of empire and establishment of new states would lead to a rise in the number of 'autonomous centres of culture', with each 'racial and linguistic group' developing 'its own characteristics in art and literature'.[13] The collapse of empires that followed the First World War ushered in the age of national self-determination and meant that intellectual life in Europe was generally equated with nations, rather than being viewed through the lenses of ethnicity, race, or religion.

While intellectual migration is primarily associated with the twentieth century, creators of knowledge have been forced to migrate – for a whole host of reasons, from natural disaster to political, religious, and racial persecution – for centuries.[14] The most prominent example of twentieth-century intellectual dislocation concerns the exodus of scholars from Nazi Germany which commenced in 1933.[15] This migration, discussed further in the Epilogue, dominates the scholarship due to the fame of many of the individuals involved and the tremendous impact which they had upon their disciplines and recipient societies following their arrival.[16] The issue of intellectual displacement was, however, long-standing in Europe. Thousands of intellectuals were among the millions of Jews to flee pogroms in Russia in the late nineteenth and early twentieth centuries.[17] The outbreak of the First World War led to a decade of displacement with first Belgian, then

[13] A.J. Carnoy, 'The Restoration of Belgium and Her Future', *University of California Chronicle*, 21.1 (1919) p. 61.

[14] Stephen Duggan and Betty Drury, *The Rescue of Science and Learning: The Story of the Emergency Committee in Aid of Displaced Foreign Scholars* (New York, 1948), pp. 1–2; Burke, *A Social History of Knowledge II*, pp. 208–209; Lewis Coser, 'Refugee Intellectuals', *Society*, 22.1 (1984), p. 61.

[15] Duggan and Drury, *The Rescue of Science and Learning*; Jean-Michel Palmier, *Weimar in Exile: The Antifascist Emigration in Europe and America* (London, 2006).

[16] Burke, *A Social History of Knowledge II,* p. 140; Renato Camurri, 'The Exile Experience Reconsidered: A Comparative Perspective in European Cultural Migration during the Interwar Period', *Transatlantica: Revue d'études américaines. American Studies Journal*, 1 (2014) pp. 1–3.

[17] Steven Cassedy, *To The Other Shore: The Russian Jewish Intellectuals who Came to America* (Princeton, NJ: Princeton University Press, 1997); François Guesnet, 'Russian-Jewish Cultural Retention in Early Twentieth Century Western Europe: Contexts and Theoretical Implications', in Jörg Schulte, Olga Tabachnikova and Peter Wagstaff eds., *The Russian Jewish Diaspora and European Culture, 1917–1937* (Leiden, 2012), pp. 1–8.

Serbian, and finally Russian scholars, writers, and students forced to flee their homes, primarily because of conflict.[18]

Post-1933 intellectual migration was notable for the absence of humanitarian discourse; agencies found jobs for scholars in need based on intellectual excellence and institutional need.[19] This had not been the case with the preceding mass migration across Europe. The displacement of Belgian and Serbian scholars during the First World War, and Russian intellectuals in the time of the civil war, was all part of a wider humanitarian crisis, through which millions of people were dislocated, starving, suffering from disease, or – in some cases – all three. Institutions that had been damaged or destroyed in conflict also needed to be rebuilt.[20] In this context, aid to scholars, students, and writers was part of a wider humanitarian effort that explicitly stated its intention to save lives. Because much of this humanitarianism came at the conclusion of one great conflict, it was often forward-facing, with an emphasis on the preservation or education of those with specific skills in order to assist with the future reconstruction of their home country.

By the end of the First World War there were many humanitarian organizations operating in the field of refugee relief, from large bodies such as the League of Nations' High Commission for Refugees to well-funded and small-scale amateur operations often with very specific aims.[21] While they were sometimes underpinned by multiple (and

---

[18]   Catherine Gousseff, *L'exil russe: La fabrique du réfugié apatride (1920–1939)* (Paris, 2008); Chamberlain, *Lenin's Private War*; Catherine Andreyev and Ivan Savický, *Russia Abroad: Prague and the Russian Diaspora* (New Haven, CT, 2004); Marc Raeff, *Russia Abroad: A Cultural History of the Russian Emigration, 1919–1939* (Oxford, 1990); Robert C. Williams, *Culture in Exile: Russian Emigrés in Germany, 1881–1941* (Ithaca, NY, 1972).

[19]   Simone Lässig, 'Strategies and Mechanisms of Scholar Rescue: The Intellectual Migration of the 1930s Reconsidered', *Social Research*, 84.4 (2017), p. 782.

[20]   On displacement in the First World War, see: Peter Gatrell, *A Whole Empire Walking: Refugees in Russia During World War I* (Bloomington, IN, 2005); Alex Dowdall, *Communities Under Fire: Urban Life at the Western Front, 1914–1918* (Oxford, 2020); Tony Kushner, 'Local Heroes: Belgian Refugees in Britain during the First World War', *Immigrants & Minorities*, 18.1 (1999), pp. 1–28; Matteo Ermacora, 'Assistance and Surveillance. War Refugees in Italy, 1914-1918', *Contemporary European History* 16.4, (2007), pp. 445–59.

[21]   Most attention has been paid to the work of the League and Fridtjof Nansen rather than the smaller initiatives. Cabanes, *The Great War and the Origins of Humanitarianism 1918–1924,* pp. 133–88; Martyn Housden, 'White Russians Crossing the Black Sea: Fridtjof Nansen, Constantinople and the First Modern

even competing) motivations, they were united by the emphasis on their intended subjects. Refugee intellectuals were particularly well-placed to avail themselves of humanitarian assistance because they were literate, highly educated, and as such could gain access to assistance by deploying the vocabulary of civilizational decline and national reconstruction which was also being propounded by many organizations. Intellectuals, with their pre-existing connections to the international world of scholarship and their knowledge of multiple languages, proved adept at effectively navigating the international humanitarian landscape of the early 1920s.[22]

Intellectual displacement and issues of national sovereignty were closely linked by the end of the First World War, meaning that this is a story not only of individuals and groups of people but also of institutions such as universities, libraries, and laboratories. Many of these institutions were displaced by virtue of finding themselves situated in a new country following the redrawing of national boundaries at the end of the conflict. Displacement will be discussed here in a broad, occasionally metaphorical sense, to refer not only to the experiences of people such as anti-Bolshevik Russians who physically moved location, but also to institutions which had *not* themselves changed location, but whose encompassing borders had been redrawn. This was the case with the universities lost by the Hungarian state due to the territorial changes demanded by 1920's Treaty of Trianon, which were frequently invoked to make wider claims about national difference and

Repatriation of Refugees Displaced by Civil Conflict, 1922-23', *Slavonic and East European Review*, 88.3 (2010), pp. 495–524; Katy Long, 'Early Repatriation Policy: Russian Refugee Return, 1922-1924', *Journal of Refugee Studies*, 22 (2009), pp. 133–54; John F.L. Ross, 'Fridtjof Nansen and the Aegean Population Exchange', *Scandinavian Journal of History*, 40.2 (2015), pp. 133–58; Keith David Watenpaugh, 'Between Communal Survival and National Aspiration: Armenian Genocide Refugees, the League of Nations, and Practices of Interwar Humanitarianism', *Humanity*, 5.2 (2014), pp. 159–81; Elizabeth White, 'A Category "Easy to Liquidate"': The League of Nations, Russian Refugee Children in the 1920s and the History of Humanitarianism', in Magaly Rodríguez García, Davide Rodogno, and Liat Kozma eds., *The League of Nations' Work on Social Issues* (Geneva, 2016), pp. 201–16.

22 On the international connectedness of the world of scholarship, see Irish and Chagnon eds., *The Academic World in the Era of the Great War*; Tamson Pietsch, *Empire of Scholars: Universities, Networks and the British Academic World, 1850–1939* (Manchester, 2014); Heather Ellis and Simone M. Müller, 'Editorial: Educational Networks, Educational Identities: Connecting National and Global Perspectives', *Journal of Global History*, 11.3 (2016), pp. 313–9.

civilizational advancement. In many cases, intellectuals and institutions that had been displaced were presented as representatives of national life itself and were therefore viewed as key to the process of reconstruction.

Intellectual displacement in the early 1920s needs to be understood in the context of the events of the First World War. The experiences of Belgium and Serbia led to the emergence of humanitarian norms which remained prominent in the years that followed and which firmly established the idea that intellectuals and their institutions were representatives of national life in temporary exile. From the work of large organizations with state backing, to smaller, amateur committees, the refugee intellectual became established as a distinct figure within the humanitarian landscape. While intellectuals and institutions were frequently portrayed as emblems of nations in exile, the 'restoration' of national life through their return did not always come to pass; as many European governments began to establish diplomatic relations with the Bolshevik regime in Russia by the mid-1920s, the possibility for return receded and, accordingly, many refugees became permanent exiles.

Intellectual Displacement during the First World War

The issue of intellectual displacement came to the fore during the First World War and established practices and discourses that would influence events in the early 1920s. The two key wartime examples of intellectual displacement concerned Belgian refugees who fled the German invasion of 1914 and Serbians who did likewise following their country's occupation by the Central Powers in late 1915. In both cases, the provision of assistance to displaced intellectuals was deemed a symbolic means of nurturing national life in exile for the duration of the occupation. Intellectuals, be they university scholars, writers, or students, were cast as representatives of national cultural life, and it was the task of allied countries to ensure that this life could continue until such point as occupation finished and culture could return home again, whereupon the nation would be restored.

Germany's invasion of Belgium in the autumn of 1914 led to the displacement of over one million people.[23] Belgium's plight quickly

---

[23] Michaël Amara, 'Belgian Refugees during the First World War (France, Britain, Netherlands)' in Gatrell and Zhvanko eds., *Europe on the Move*, pp. 197–214.

became a cause célèbre in allied and many neutral countries and secured an elevated position in the allied imagination as the supreme instance of German wartime barbarism. Many humanitarian initiatives soon emerged to provide aid to Belgian refugees.[24] The suffering of Belgium's intellectual community constituted a distinct manifestation of this; the German invasion and the destruction of the university library at Louvain created global outrage in August 1914 and, by October 1914, all four Belgian universities (Louvain, Ghent, Brussels, and Liège) had been closed and would remain so until January 1919.[25] Given the centrality of intellectual life to events following the German invasion of Belgium, the rehousing of displaced scholars quickly emerged as a humanitarian aspiration and soon became an international endeavour.

Intellectual aid of this type was facilitated by the fact that many belligerent countries had partially empty university buildings in wartime, meaning that specialist facilities were often readily available to house scholars in need. A number of British universities allowed Belgian students to enrol free of charge and instituted courses in which they were taught by Belgian professors.[26] French universities similarly allowed Belgian students to study at their institutions without fees, while refugee professors taught at the universities of Bordeaux, Dijon, and Poitiers.[27] In the neutral United States, Harvard University allocated a fund of $100,000 to enable Belgian scholars to teach within the institution in 1915, while the Rockefeller Foundation provided stipends to displaced Belgian scientists so that they could continue their research work.[28] In Britain and France, which found themselves with large numbers of both students and professors, an emphasis was

---

[24] Kushner, 'Local Heroes: Belgian Refugees in Britain during the First World War', pp. 1–28.

[25] Léon Leclère, 'Les universités Belges de 1914 à 1919', *Revue internationale de l'enseignement*, 73 (1919), pp. 356–62.

[26] Irish, *The University at War*, pp. 21–2; Charles Dejace, 'The Belgian University at Cambridge', in *A Book of Belgium's Gratitude*, pp. 294–7; 'University and Educational News', *Science*, New Series, 40.1039 (1914), p. 782; 'University and Educational News', *Science*, New Series, 40.1040 (1914), pp. 813–4

[27] Tomás Irish, 'National Survival and International Expansion: French Universities and the First World War', in Charlotte Lerg and Heike Bungert eds., *Jahrbuch für Universitätsgeschichte*, vol. 18 (Stuttgart, 2017), pp. 143–62.

[28] 'Lady Osler and Louvain Professors', *New York Times*, 21 October 1914. *The Rockefeller Foundation, Annual Report 1913–14* (New York, 1915), p. 29; *The Rockefeller Foundation, Annual Report 1917* (New York, 1917), p. 297.

placed on ensuring that Belgians were being taught by Belgians, replicating, as far as was possible, intellectual life at home.

Similar policies were also applied to Serbian scholars and students from late 1915, following the beginning of the second major campaign of the Central Powers against Serbia.[29] The French government agreed to allow Serbian schoolchildren and university students to study free of charge at French institutions.[30] A total of 690 Serbian students studied at French universities through this scheme.[31] The same policy was followed in Britain, although in fewer numbers. In total, around 5,500 Serbian student refugees studied in Europe during the First World War.[32] As with its Belgian counterpart, the Serbian relief campaign was a temporary measure which sought to ensure continuity of intellectual life in exile.

The reception given to Belgian and Serbian scholars and students was framed by wartime alliances and was notable for the discourse which emphasized the imperative of the continuation of intellectual life. Assistance to displaced scholars was understood as a temporary wartime imperative and established the idea of holding national intellectual life in trust, 'without a breach in continuity', until such time as normal conditions were resumed.[33] In October 1914, with the German army having advanced worryingly close to the French capital, University College London offered to facilitate the temporary transfer of the Sorbonne to England for the duration of the conflict in the event of the occupation of Paris. The proposal was firmly rejected; French intellectual life would continue, and the state would fight the war metaphorically as well as militarily.[34] In a conflict portrayed as a confrontation between civilization and barbarism, and where national cultures were mobilized alongside armies, the death of national intellectual life equated to defeat for the nation itself.

The guardianship of intellectual life was an idea explored by a number of thinkers in the United States at the end of the war. In his

---

[29] Paunović, Igrutinovic, Zec, et al, *Exile in the Classroom*, p. 59.
[30] Paunović, Igrutinovic, Zec, et al., *Exile in the Classroom*, p. 63; Report of the University of Paris for 1915–16, AN/F17/13698, p. 12.
[31] Paunović, Igrutinovic, Zec, et al, *Exile in the Classroom*, p. 73.
[32] Paunović, Igrutinovic, Zec, et al, *Exile in the Classroom*, p. 89.
[33] 'University and Educational News', *Science*, New Series, 40.1034 (1914) p. 592.
[34] Louis Liard to T. Gregory Foster, 6 October 1914, AN/61/AJ/85.

1918 book *The Higher Learning in America*, the economist Thorstein Veblen bemoaned the damage caused by the war to international intellectual life.[35] He argued that as a consequence of the 'insolvency' of European intellectual life the United States had taken on a new position 'of trust and guardianship'.[36] This meant that when crisis befell Europe, the United States, in a position of 'strategic reserve', could 'retrieve so much as may be of those assets of scholarly equipment and personnel that make the substantial code of Western Civilization'. Veblen envisaged this as an interim solution, in which the USA acted as 'keepers of the ways and means whereby the republic of learning is to retrieve its fortunes'.[37] Veblen's position was shared by others. Max Farrand, the American historian and general director of the Commonwealth Fund, noted in 1919 'the obligation which rests upon this country to take over certain tools of scholarship which have formerly been prepared by scholars of other countries'.[38] While both Farrand and Veblen undoubtedly saw the dislocations of wartime as part of a wider crisis through which the United States could benefit, they also invoked a sense of grave obligation to maintain the republic of letters through temporary assistance.[39]

Russian Intellectuals and Post-war Intellectual Dislocation

The collapse of empires as a consequence of the First World War meant that millions of people were left without states to call home. This was complicated by the consequences of over four years of warfare through which civilians, prisoners of war, and demobilized soldiers were dislocated.[40] The end of the war also created further population problems; the redrawing of national borders at the Paris Peace Conference, and the limited application of Woodrow Wilson's doctrine of self-determination, meant that many successor states contained significant minority populations. The post-war settlements gave states to sixty

---

[35] Thorstein Veblen, *The Higher Learning in America: A Memorandum on the Conduct of Universities by Business Men* (New York, 1918), p. 49.
[36] Veblen, *The Higher Learning*, p. 48.
[37] Veblen, *The Higher Learning*, pp. 52–53.
[38] Farrand to Commonwealth Fund Executive Committee of Directors, 20 February 1919, RAC/CF, SG 1, 2.4, Box 23, Folder 197.
[39] Peter Burke, *What is the History of Knowledge?* (Cambridge, 2016), p. 86.
[40] Peter Gatrell, *The Making of the Modern Refugee* (Oxford, 2015), p. 15.

million Europeans but left a further twenty-five million people as minorities in new countries.[41]

This situation was exacerbated by the mass displacement of people caused by the conflicts that cumulatively constitute the Russian Civil War. By the start of 1920, the Red Army was in the ascendency over the anti-Bolshevik forces who had been pushed back to southern Ukraine and Crimea.[42] Waves of refugees were forced to leave Ukraine between 1919 and 1920, with 10,000 fleeing from Odesa and crossing the Black Sea to Constantinople in the spring of 1919, followed by a further 150,000 who left after General Wrangel's defeat in November 1920.[43] The latter evacuation was substantially assisted by the Allies: France, Britain, and the United States.[44] There was a further movement of people due to pogroms perpetrated by Polish and Ukrainian armies, as well as the Bolshevik and anti-Bolshevik forces in the former Russian Empire, all of which killed up to 200,000 people by 1920.[45]

It has been estimated that in the early 1920s there were between 750,000 and two million displaced Russians around Constantinople, Athens, or the Polish-German border.[46] Constantinople soon became, in the words of historian Martyn Housden, 'a bottleneck for desperate people', and a series of refugee settlements emerged on the shores of the Bosporus, the Gallipoli peninsula, as well as across the Balkans and the eastern Mediterranean.[47] The Autumn of 1922 gave rise to a further factor in Russian displacement, when the Bolshevik government commenced the forced expulsion of intellectuals that it deemed to be potentially subversive.[48] Cumulatively,

---

[41] Siegelberg, *Statelessness*, p. 59.   [42] Gerwarth, *The Vanquished*, pp. 92–3.

[43] Cabanes, *The Great War and the Origins of Humanitarianism*, 141.

[44] Raeff, *Russia Abroad*, p. 17.

[45] Oleg Budnistskii, *Russian Jews Between the Reds and the Whites, 1917–1920* (Philadelphia, PA, 2011), pp. 216–8; Gerwarth, *The Vanquished*, pp. 89–90; Cabanes, *The Great War and the Origins of Humanitarianism*, p. 143; Lisa Silverman, *Becoming Austrians: Jews and Culture Between the World Wars* (Oxford, 2012), p. 12.

[46] Cabanes, *The Great War and the Origins of Humanitarianism*, p. 14.

[47] Housden, 'White Russians Crossing the Black Sea', pp. 497–8.

[48] Stuart Finkel, 'Purging the Public Intellectual: The 1922 Expulsions from Soviet Russia', *The Russian Review*, 62.4 (2003), p. 592; Sheila Fitzpatrick, *The Cultural Front: Power and Culture in Revolutionary Russia* (Ithaca, NY, 1992), pp. 37–51; Finkel, *On the Ideological Front*, pp. 13–38.

there were up to fifteen million refugees scattered across Europe by the start of the 1920s.[49]

Intellectual displacement soon came to be seen as a specific issue that necessitated special treatment. Writing from Poland in September 1920 where she worked with the Russian Red Cross, Ludmilla Lubimoff described how 'many persons of the well-educated class came to us being deprived of all means of sustenance, and often having neither linen nor shoes', including an 'old man clad in rags' who had been a professor at the University of Kyiv.[50] Such descriptions, highlighting the fall from middle- or upper-class comforts caused by revolution and dislocation, were common in the correspondence of humanitarian workers. Appeals for aid, too, often emphasized difference based on the learning and social status of refugees. In May 1923, a group of leading British legal figures, led by Lord Phillimore, wrote an appeal to the *Times* newspaper which stated that among the around 20,000 Russians still stranded in Constantinople were twenty-five Russian lawyers and their families. In his appeal, Phillimore encouraged British lawyers to gift financial aid to help these 'highly educated and gently brought up' refugees to escape Constantinople.[51]

Concern for the plight of displaced Russian intellectuals was shared by Fridtjof Nansen, the High Commissioner for Refugees at the League of Nations. At a crucial meeting in Geneva in August 1921 to determine the League's policy towards refugees, one of the resolutions stated that it was of particular importance to ensure 'special protection and employment for Russian intellectuals who are refugees in foreign lands'.[52] In practice, the underfunded League did little to specifically aid displaced intellectuals beyond raising awareness of their conditions and encouraging national governments to act.[53]

---

[49] Peter Gatrell, 'Introduction', in Gatrell and Liubov Zhvanko eds., *Europe on the Move: Refugees in the Era of the Great War* (Manchester, 2017), p. 3.

[50] Lubimoff to Cantacuzène, 8 September 1920, RAC, Office of the Messrs. Rockefeller (OMR), Series Q, Box 42, Folder 368.

[51] Lord Phillimore, Robert Younger, Douglas McGarel Hogg, et al., 'Russian Refugee Barristers', *The Times*, 3 May 1923, p. 5.

[52] 'Conference on the Question of Russian Refugees', 24 August 1921, LNA/C.277.M.203.1921.VII.

[53] League of Nations, Russian Refugees. General Report on the Work Accomplished up to 15 March 1922, by Dr. Fridtjof Nansen, High Commissioner of the League of Nations. 15 March 1922. LNA/C.124.M.7411.

By 1921, Russian intellectual refugee groups had been established in sixteen different countries, with Paris, Berlin, and Prague
emerging as key centres.[54] The movement of refugee intellectuals
was funded and facilitated by a wide range of actors, including
national governments, international non-governmental organizations, and of small-scale, amateur initiatives. By the early 1920s,
Western Europe had become, in the words of one observer, 'an
alma mater for the Russian Refugees' in a process that integrated
the work of national governments, humanitarian organizations of
different sizes, American philanthropists, and the agency of intellectual refugees themselves.[55]

National Relief and Cultural Diplomacy

The assistance provided to refugee intellectuals across Europe was
often the result of government policy and a means of conducting
cultural diplomacy.[56] Among the many national governments that
supported the upkeep of refugee intellectuals in their countries, the
successor state of Czechoslovakia was the most comprehensive in its
approach.[57] In the spring of 1923 the *Czechoslovak Review* reported
that 'Prague has become the focus of constructive Russian life
abroad'.[58] The post-war Czechoslovak president Tomáš G.
Masaryk, himself a sociologist and philosopher, was keen to portray
the new state as democratic, Western-facing, and European.[59] The
Czechoslovak prime minister Edvard Beneš argued in 1922 that the
state's support for Russian intellectuals should be seen in the context
of wishing to portray itself as an outward-looking and culturally

---

[54] Robert H. Johnston, *New Mecca, New Babylon: Paris and the Russian Exiles,
1920–1945* (Montreal, 1988); Elena Chinyaeva, 'Russian Émigrés:
Czechoslovak Refugee Policy and the Development of the International Refugee
Regime Between the Two World Wars', *Journal of Refugee Studies*, 8.2 (1995),
pp. 142–62; I. Souworkoff, 'Etranger. Un congrès des professeurs russes',
L'Information universitaire, 9 November 1921, p. 1.

[55] Manya Gordon, 'Czechoslovakia and the Future of Russia', p. 4.

[56] Martin and Piller, 'Cultural Diplomacy and Europe's Twenty Years' Crisis,
1919-1939', pp. 149–63.

[57] Chinyaeva, 'Russian Émigrés', p. 143.

[58] 'Prague Welcomes Russian Students', *The Czechoslovak Review*, 7.4 (1923).
p. 93.

[59] Andrea Orzoff, *Battle for the Castle: The Myth of Czechoslovakia in Europe,
1914–1948* (Oxford, 2009), pp. 9–11.

European.[60] Masaryk and Beneš were also motivated by anti-Bolshevism; they hoped that their support for displaced democratic Russian forces would put pressure on the Bolshevik government and lead to the emergence of a democratic Russia in the future.[61] By 1925, there were around 25,000 displaced Russians in Czechoslovakia.[62]

Czechoslovakia welcomed Russian students and professors in large numbers. In the autumn of 1921, a group of around 1,500 Russian students made their way to the country from Constantinople to complete their studies, having been selected and vetted by displaced Russian professors with assistance from European Student Relief.[63] By 1923, it was reported that there was a total of 30,000 student refugees in Europe, of whom 12,000 were Russian; Czechoslovakia supported one-third of these students.[64] One Russian student journal claimed that Prague had been 'converted into a big foreign Russian intellectual centre' where students and professors 'found in the dark night of emigrant life a flash of culture and hope'.[65] These students were often taught by refugee Russian professors, meaning that, in the words of one observer, they were 'in almost native soil'.[66] The welcome extended to students came with attendant conditions, as Beneš explained in a speech in 1922. For example, there was a strict ban on political action; one Russian student who arrived from Serbia began 'making agitation among his colleagues' and was immediately deprived of his financial assistance and made to leave the country.[67] And despite the enthusiasm of the state in accommodating Russian scholars, linguistic differences and divergences of scholarly approach meant that the process of acclimatizing to their new intellectual surrounds was not always straightforward.[68]

Czechoslovakia's Russian Action policy featured two threads which were evident in other examples of intellectual relief in the period. First,

[60] 'Discours de M. Beneš', *Recueil de documents étrangers*, 109 (1922), p. 136.
[61] Andreyev and Savický, *Russia Abroad*, p. 25.
[62] Chinyaeva, 'Russian Émigrés', p. 143. [63] Rouse, *Rebuilding Europe*, p. 74.
[64] *Report on European Student Relief 1920–1923* (Geneva, 1923), p. 41. LNA/ R1031/13/22761/14297.
[65] 'Students life: Russian students in Czechoslovakia', YUDLSC/WSCF/RG46, Series 24.D (aa), Box 298, Folder 2723.
[66] Unsigned report c1922, The Committee for the Education of Russian Youth in Exile, RAC/LSRM, 3.3, Box 8, Folder 94, p. 1.
[67] 'Discours de M. Beneš', p. 135.
[68] Andreyev and Savický, *Russia Abroad*, pp. 84–87.

it aimed to train refugees for their future return to Russia so that they could assist in the task of reconstruction.[69] Second, as was the case with assistance to Belgian universities during the First World War, Czechoslovak policy aimed to preserve the life of Russian institutions whose cultural importance simultaneously provided prestige to the host state. Institutions such as a Russian Law Faculty, a Russian People's University, and a Russian Historical Archive were established in Prague.[70] The Russian émigré community was supported throughout the interwar years by the Czechoslovak government and this programme of support was placed directly under the control of the foreign minister.[71] The Czechoslovak government also supported the publication of work by Russian intellectuals in Russia, which was deemed important in maintaining continuity in Russian intellectual life.[72]

Other states, often working closely with European Student Relief, also provided support to displaced Russian intellectuals and students in this period. Around 1,400 to 1,500 Russian students settled in the Kingdom of Serbs, Croats and Slovenes and entered universities in Belgrade, Zagreb, and Ljubljana. The Yugoslav government subsidized the study of refugee students but was unable to fully cover living and study costs, resulting in many taking on additional paid work.[73] Russian cultural organizations and publishing houses were established in Germany.[74] Russian institutions, such as the Turgenev Library and the Russian Popular University, also appeared in France, where the government underwrote the study of refugee students and professors at the Sorbonne.[75] Russian students were also welcomed to universities in Britain where their fees were often waived but, as university education was not centralized in the UK, this was an institutional decision rather than a top-down state policy.[76]

---

[69] John Hope Simpson, *The Refugee Question. Oxford Pamphlets on World Affairs* (Oxford, 1939), p. 10; Gousseff, *L'exil russe*, p. 93.

[70] Andreyev and Savický, *Russia Abroad*, pp. 80–116.

[71] Chinyaeva, 'Russian Émigrés', p. 143

[72] Andreyev and Savický, *Russia Abroad*, p. 115.

[73] Ray H. Legate, 'Russian Refugee Students in Jugoslavia', September 1923, YUDLSC/WSCF/RG46, Series 24.D (aa), Box 298, Folder 2723.

[74] Williams, *Culture in Exile*, pp. 130–3.

[75] Johnston, *New Mecca, New Babylon*, pp. 38, 52–53.

[76] Elina Hannele Multanen, 'British Policy Towards Russian Refugees in the Aftermath of the Bolshevik Revolution', PhD dissertation, School of Slavonic and East European Studies, University College London, 2000, p. 248.

While support for intellectual exiles could be a useful tool of cultural diplomacy, in some new states it was incompatible with an increasingly exclusionary vision of the nation.[77] Most state-led support for Russian refugees originated from an anti-Bolshevik conviction and a belief that the Soviet government in Russia would be short-lived. This position was far from straightforward; anti-Bolshevism and anti-Semitism sometimes went hand-in-hand due to the association of Jewish people with the Bolshevik Revolution within much White Russian propaganda as well as the prominence of Jews in the short-lived soviets that emerged in Europe after the First World War.[78] The conflict itself had rendered the Jews, in Jaclyn Granick's words, 'a whole diaspora walking' and, while precise numbers are difficult to determine, it is clear that Jews were very well-represented among groups of displaced intellectuals such as those coming from Russia.[79] Institutionalized anti-Semitism rose in many successor states in the 1920s, with Hungary introducing quotas for Jewish university students in 1920 while institutions in Poland, Romania, and Austria adopted informal means of excluding Jews in the same decade.[80] Against the backdrop of rising unemployment, the middle classes often turned against Jewish communities as they were seen to be 'over-represented' in certain, frequently intellectual, professions.[81] As the Jewish people had no state of their own, international action presented positive possibilities; in 1924, a proposal emerged for an international university at Danzig under the protection of the League of Nations to cater to Jewish students who were being denied opportunities to study in eastern European countries. It was not adopted.[82]

Having been mistrustful of Bolshevism and fearful of the spread of revolution, many European states were slow to establish diplomatic

---

[77] Berend, *Decades of Crisis,* p. 296.
[78] Gerwarth, *The Vanquished*, pp. 142–45; Éva Forgács, 'In the Vacuum of Exile: the Hungarian Activists in Vienna 1919-1926', in John Neubauer et al. eds., *The Exile and Return of Writers from East-Central Europe: A Compendium* (Berlin, 2009), pp. 109–22.
[79] Granick, *International Jewish Humanitarianism*, p. 6; Brian Horowitz, *Russian Idea-Jewish Presence: Essays on Russian-Jewish Intellectual* Life (Brighton, MA, 2013), p. 124.
[80] Surman, *Universities in Imperial Austria*, p. 249; Silverman, *Becoming Austrians,* pp. 5, 12.
[81] Berend, *Decades of Crisis,* p. 295.
[82] See correspondence in LNA/R1066/13C/32839.

relations with the new Russian state. France did not recognise the Soviet Union until late 1924.[83] This complicated the matter of state-sponsored support of refugee intellectuals. Official recognition of the Soviet government meant that assistance to displaced scholars could be seen as support for political opposition. Accordingly, the French government cut off its financing to displaced Russian intellectuals in France in July 1925. Around the same time, French institutions received requests from scholars and institutions in Soviet Russia seeking to collaborate through book exchanges and reciprocal visits.[84] All of this placed anti-Bolshevik Russian exiles in France in a difficult position. Dismayed by the cessation of their aid from the French state, they wrote to the French government to urge its continuation, claiming that the assistance had 'no political character and pursued only noble goals of scientific culture and civilization – a purely humanitarian task'.[85] For its part, the French government sought to avoid the provision of aid to Russian intellectual exiles directly by funding Thomas Whittemore's refugee relief committee, effectively outsourcing the work.[86] As in many other spheres of intellectual relief, the mid-1920s saw a change in emphasis as the immediate sense of crisis passed, leaving a growing acceptance that some of the radical changes wrought by the war – such as the emergence of Bolshevik rule in Russia – were here to stay.

Humanitarian Organizations and Intellectual Displacement

Beyond actions initiated by national governments, many bespoke organizations were formed in the post-war period which viewed the relief and education of displaced intellectuals and students as key aims. These organizations varied greatly in terms of size and scope, with some, like European Student Relief, having a global reach, and smaller, amateur organizations developing a very specific geographical or intellectual focus. Many of these bodies worked closely with national governments in order to house refugees and enable them to continue their intellectual activities. Most of these initiatives placed considerable emphasis on reconstruction as the ultimate goal of humanitarian

---

[83] Winter, *The Day the Great War Ended*, p. 205.
[84] See correspondence in AN/AJ/16/6994.
[85] Draft petition of Groupe académique russe, c1925, AN/70AJ/146.
[86] Paul Appell, Louis Gentil and Étienne Fournol to the President du Conseil, c July 1924, UNESCO/B.VI.2.

assistance; recipients of aid were an elite grouping who were ultimately expected to return to their country of origin to assist in its rebuilding.

European Student Relief was among the largest supporters of Russian refugee students.[87] By 1922, it had provided relief to 68,000 students, of whom many were Russian refugees. ESR was funded through public appeals and made a virtue of its non-political status, claiming that it existed 'not to further any political aim but to bring relief'.[88] It advocated the idea of self-help, encouraging refugee students to find additional work so that they did not become dependent upon foreign aid; refugee Russian students, based in Germany, were sent to France to assist in the task of reconstruction in the summer of 1922. Ruth Rouse of ESR felt that intellectual relief could be a powerful force for fostering peace and argued that centres like Prague were places where 'experiments of all kinds in international goodwill can be carried on by native and foreign students together'.[89]

Many philanthropic foundations and humanitarian organizations emphasized the idea that education was an important lever for post-war reconstruction. The Carnegie Endowment for International Peace contributed $50,000 to the American Central Committee for Russian Relief because the 'future reconstruction of a Russian republic' would depend upon the contributions of 'teachers, professional men and educated business people'.[90] A Revolving Scholarship Fund defined its activity as assisting Russian students with the qualities 'for reconstruction work' who would return to Russia 'at the first opportunity'.[91] The Russian Zemstvos and Town Relief Committee, or Zemgor, stated its concern for both the physical and 'moral health' of displaced children and argued that education would allow refugees to be 'of assistance to their Motherland, when she will need them'.[92] Led by the

---

[87] Hartley, 'Saving Students: European Student Relief in the Aftermath of World War I', pp. 295–315.

[88] L.W. Halford, "The Torch of Learning", *Russian Life*, 6 (1922), pp. 217–8, in West Glamorgan Archive Service (WGAS), Swansea, Winifred Coombe Tennant Papers (WCTP), D/DT 4012.

[89] Rouse, *Rebuilding Europe*, p. 156; See also Selles, *The World Student Christian Federation, 1895–1925*, pp. 132–6.

[90] This body was chaired by Julia Grant Cantacuzène. *Carnegie Endowment for International Peace, Year Book 1921* (Washington, DC, 1921), 43–4.

[91] 'Summary of the Effort to Aid Russian Students in America', HILA/ARAROR, Box 326, Folder 8, Reel 403.

[92] 'The Children of Russian Refugees in Europe', RAC/OMR, Series Q, Box 42, Folder 366, pp. 11, 20.

Russian aristocrat Georgy Lvov, Zemgor oversaw the running of educational institutions across Europe for displaced Russians, and had
over 5,000 students in its care by 1925.[93] The link between education
and reconstruction was premised on the idea that refugees would
eventually return home, a widespread assumption in the early 1920s.

Beyond large organizations, a range of more modest initiatives were
established during this period. The work of these smaller humanitarian
groups elucidates the practice of intellectual relief in greater detail.
Often backed by private philanthropy, these bodies were targeted in
their selection of intellectuals for assistance and avoided all euphemism
in explaining the elitist rationale for their existence. Smaller humanitarian organizations often placed a distinct emphasis on the importance
of saving intellectuals as national representatives above other displaced
people and advocated the attendant benefits of this approach for
humanity as a whole. They also emphasised the temporary nature of
this aid.

Smaller aid initiatives often came into existence as a consequence of
an inability on the part of larger humanitarian organizations to provide
aid to intellectuals as a group. In 1920, W. E. Haigh, in Poland with the
British Quakers, wrote of 'the terrible position of these representatives
of the Russian intelligentzia' but noted that, under existing arrange-
ments, it was 'impossible' for him to 'advance any materials in any
quantity, or funds, which were destined for Poland' to these refugees
without specific direction from Quaker headquarters in London.[94] In
Poland, Ludmilla Lubimoff claimed that 'intellectual help' was needed
for the 'famous men who have occupied eminent places in science and
literature'.[95] Small, bespoke organizations could address these needs in
a more rigorous manner.

This was the case for the intellectuals who were expelled from Russia
by the Soviet regime in the late summer of 1922. Around one hundred
of them, including the prominent theologian and philosopher Nikolai
Berdyaev, congregated in Berlin. Their plight soon came to the attention of senior figures at the American Relief Administration, which did

---

[93] 'Statement of the educational work of the Russian Zemstvos and Towns Relief
    Committee', 1 April 1925, and Russian Zemstvos and Towns Relief Committee,
    in RAC/OMR, Series Q, Box 42, Folder 366; Gousseff, *L'exil russe*, pp. 271–3.
[94] Haigh to Fry, 8 July 1920, LSF/YM/MfS/FEWVRC/MISSIONS/8/4/4/1.
[95] Lubimoff to Cantacuzène, 14 June 1921, RAC/OMR, Series Q, Box 42, Folder
    368.

not itself operate in Germany; however, senior figures at the ARA were adamant in their desire to help these eminent figures, who they described as 'completely destitute'.[96] As the ARA had no presence in Germany, Vernon Kellogg organized a committee called the Science Relief Fund (SRF) which included representatives of the displaced intellectuals. Kellogg issued appeals for financial support among American academics, funding which was then distributed to the Russian refugees with the help of the YMCA in Germany.[97] Its mission accomplished by the end of 1923, the SRF's concluding report stated that the Russian intellectuals 'saw in this action the appearance of those deep ties which bind the whole of cultural mankind in both hemispheres regardless of nationality'.[98]

Relief to displaced intellectuals was elitist in nature and was premised upon the specific intellectual attainment of the individuals in question. Still, it was relatively rare that this was articulated as the only rationale for this aid; in general, assistance for intellectuals was still framed by the language of humanitarianism with its emphasis on themes such as hunger and risk of death. A notable exception was the Appointments Committee for Russian Scientific and Literary Men, which was established in Britain in 1921 and which aimed to find suitable employment for displaced Russian intellectuals at British institutions. Placements were based upon the specific expertise of refugee intellectuals and motivated by the fear that the wider world was 'losing the benefit of their knowledge and aptitude'.[99] This scheme – which matched intellectuals to jobs according to their expertise – did not meet with great success. One recipient of the appeal commented pessimistically that 'there appears to be an excess of supply over demand of Russian educated men'.[100]

More typically, intellectual relief to displaced individuals sought to save the lives of displaced intellectuals, rather than merely finding them employment. The Committee for the Education of Russian Youth in

---

[96] Benningsen to Mowatt Mitchell, 31 October 1922, HILA/ARAEOR, Box 664, Folder 1, Reel 777.

[97] See correspondence in HILA/ARAEOR, Box 664, Folder 1, Reel 777.

[98] The Science Relief Fund, Berlin 1923, HILA/ARAEOR, Box 664, Folder 1, Reel 777.

[99] Members included Sir Arthur Schuster, Viscount Bryce, Charles Sherrington, Paul Vinogradoff, and Sir Frederic Kenyon. Circular letter of the Appointments Committee for Russian Scientific and Literary Men, c1921, RS/MS/663/4/7.

[100] Deller to Schuster, 10 May 1921, RSA/MS/663/4/7.

Exile (CERYE), which was established by Thomas Whittemore in Constantinople in 1920 and funded by a range of wealthy Americans including John D. Rockefeller, Jr, forms a good example of this. Whittemore's committee aimed to select the most intelligent and intellectually capable students, most of whom were impoverished refugees in Constantinople, before securing placements for them at prestigious schools and universities across Europe. 'Youth' was taken as a very broad category which meant that Whittemore supported those undertaking their first degree or those who were conducting, or seeking to publish, advanced graduate research. Whittemore felt that relief should support 'as many as possible of those who matter', by which he meant those deemed to be the most intellectually able.[101]

Unlike ESR, which was reliant on public appeals to fund its activities, Whittemore counted upon private backing and could thus frame his work in explicitly elitist terms. In keeping with similar initiatives, Whittemore wanted to train young experts in order that they could assist in the project of reconstruction or, as he put it, 'raising seedlings for the scientific reforestation of Russia'.[102] He also invoked the language of civilizational decline, arguing that his work was important 'not only for Russia, but likewise for the civilized world'.[103] In 1922 the CERYE was responsible for the support of 227 advanced students in Europe, who were placed at universities and technical schools in France, Belgium, Switzerland, the Kingdom of Serbs, Croats and Slovenes, Czechoslovakia, Turkey, Germany, Bulgaria, Syria, and Italy.[104] These students were chosen on the basis of academic excellence and were instructed to achieve 'conspicuously high' attainments and to 'distrust all political organizations working outside of Russia'.[105] Whittemore was aware of the cultural diplomatic value to

---

[101] Whittemore to Elisabeth Cram, 23 November 1923, CURBML/BAR Ms Coll/ CERYE, IX.1, Box 94, Folder 35.

[102] Whittemore report, 20 September 1923, 13 October 1922, RAC/OMR, Series Q, Box 42, Folder 369.

[103] Unsigned report c1922, The Committee for the Rescue and Education of Russian Youth in Exile, RAC/LSRM, 3.3, Box 8, Folder 94, p. 5.

[104] 'Mr Thomas Whittemore', in Pratt to Rockefeller, 13 October 1922, RAC/ OMR, Series Q, Box 42, Folder 369. A 1924 report revealed that 'practical' subjects, such as engineering, were dominant in Whittemore's cohort. 'The 'Rhodes Scholars' of Russia's Future', *Boston Transcript*, 5 January 1924, CURBML/BAR Ms Coll/CERYE, IX.1, Box 97, Folder 27.

[105] Account of Whittemore work, Box 298, Folder 2723.

states in supporting Russian refugees and leveraged this during his negotiations with them. For example, when seeking to secure places for students at French institutions, he informed the French Foreign Ministry that he had already received 'flattering offers' from German universities but wished to place the students in France.[106] While self-managed in nature, private initiatives like Whittemore's were part of a wide humanitarian landscape in which state action was also an important factor.

The labelling of refugee groups as 'intellectuals' was sometimes seen as a means of assisting certain political or class interests. The daughter of former American president Ulysses S. Grant and wife of a Russian prince, Julia Dent Grant Cantacuzène, established a Committee for the Relief of Russian Refugees (CRRR) which oversaw a range of initiatives for displaced intellectuals. Elihu Root, the former American Secretary of State, was one of the vice-presidents of the CRRR and urged that special assistance should go to those who 'by intellectual superiority, by education, by energy and enterprise, by capacity for organization or administration in commerce or finance or manufacture or any branch of production or in literature or religion have achieved any success'.[107] While Cantacuzène spoke of 'intellectuals' as a group, some figures expressed their fear that in reality such activity was merely a means of supporting the Russian aristocracy by proxy. Raymond B. Fosdick, a future president of the Rockefeller Foundation, claimed that there was a perception that Cantacuzène was 'carrying on her work exclusively for the aristocrats, and that from the standpoint of preserving the culture of Russia, many of this class are far inferior to the representatives of the middle-class'.[108] The overlap between the preservation of displaced intellectuals and noble interests was considerable; Whittemore's group, too, aided many people from aristocratic backgrounds, but tended to place more emphasis on academic excellence above all else. Fosdick's observations highlight the complexity of the interests at stake within the intellectual relief ecosystem and the intersection between cultural and political interests.

---

[106] Edouard Herriot to Paul Appell, 3 November 1924, AN/70AJ/146.
[107] 'Letter received by Princess Cantacuzène from Mr. Elihu Root and read at the Annual Meeting of the American Central Committee for Russian Relief, Inc'. 7 November 1921, RAC/OMR, Series Q, Box 42, Folder 368.
[108] Raymond Fosdick to Rockefeller, 5 April 1922, RAC/OMR, Series Q, Box 42, Folder 368.

Many of these smaller organizations were backed by American finance and thus enabled a more subtle means of conducting cultural diplomacy than was the case with the state-backed policies of Czechoslovakia or France. Whittemore regarded his work as 'breaking America's spiritual silence in Europe'.[109] An organization called the Russian Student Fund aimed to extend 'American ideals' through the education of one thousand 'carefully selected young men' in the United States in order to create 'a Russian Lincoln, Washington, Roosevelt, or Woodrow Wilson', who would then return to Russia.[110] Knowing of the widespread support of American philanthropists for these initiatives, appeals for help from Europe were sometimes framed in the language of American values. Writing from Poland, Ludmilla Lubimoff appealed to Cantacuzène to 'help us under the American flag – the symbol of culture, freedom and progress to maintain the remainder of the Russian educated and professional men'.[111]

Much of this aid was organized under the umbrella of national identity; refugee intellectuals were generally identified by aid organizations as representatives of a nation. This usually overrode other identifiers, such as religion or ethnicity, and provided a political justification for assistance. These labels were less clearly defined in the case of the many displaced Jewish people who were divided as to whether they wished to constitute a nation state and had no territory to call their own.[112] The Quaker Hilda Clark remarked of Jewish refugees in Austria that their 'sense of nationality and responsibility for any one country is not developed'.[113] In the records of many of these organizations, with the notable exception of the Jewish Joint Distribution

---

[109] Whittemore report, 20 September 1923, 13 October 1922, RAC/OMR, Series Q, Box 42, Folder 369.

[110] Familiar names were on the board of directors: Stephen Duggan (director of the IIE), E.T. Colton (Assistant General Secretary of the International Committee of the YMCA), and John R. Mott (general secretary of the YMCA) 'Russian Students in America: Extending American Ideals', YUDLSC/WSCF/RG46, Series 24.D (aa), Box 297, Folder 2718.

[111] Lubimoff, general appeal, 25 November 1920, RAC/OMR, Series Q, Box 42, Folder 368.

[112] Alexis Hofmeister, 'The Years of 1918–1923 as a Transformative Period of Jewish Politics', in Burkhard Olschowsky, Piotr Juszkiewicz and Jan Rydel eds., *Central and Eastern Europe after the First World War* (Berlin, 2021), pp. 285–9.

[113] Hilda Clark notes on Austria, November 1920, LSF/YM/MfS/FEWVRC/4/3/7/2.

Committee, which focused on Jewish relief, refugee intellectuals tended to be organized by their nationality rather than their religion or ethnicity, although sometimes these groupings could be referenced interchangeably; the Quaker W.E. Haigh compared the respective attitudes of White Russians, Lithuanians, and Jews in Poland in a letter written in 1920.[114] The primacy of nationality is important because it suggests that those without a clear national allegiance faced greater barriers in accessing aid. Organizational archives do not provide clear answers on this matter, but they do tell us much about the strategies employed by refugee intellectuals in appealing to humanitarian organizations.

Refugee Voices

The voices of refugees are often difficult to source in the historical record. Their engagements with humanitarian bodies are frequently shaped by their desire to conform to the perceived expectations of those organizations.[115] Displaced intellectuals had distinct advantages when navigating the aid landscape in the aftermath of the First World War; much like many philanthropists and humanitarians, they too could deploy the language of high culture and civilization in order to justify their need for support above the wider refugee population. Intellectuals, who were frequently multi-lingual and well-educated, could 'write upwards' to those exercising power with great conviction.[116] These interactions tell us much about the ability of refugees to exercise agency in their particular plight; they were not always as helpless as official records might imply.[117]

Displaced intellectuals deployed a number of strategies when appealing for assistance, one of which was to echo dominant narratives regarding the importance of intellectuals for post-conflict reconstruction. In December 1920 a group of Ukrainian refugee students in Czechoslovakia wrote to the Quakers in London to seek material aid. In their appeal they described an assault on the educated life of Ukraine by the Bolsheviks and the Polish government, both of whom were trying to 'kill the nation' by targeting its 'educated people'. They argued that Ukrainian refugee intellectuals deserved particular attention

---

[114] Haigh to Fry, 8 August 1920, LSF/YM/MfS/FEWVRC/MISSIONS/8/4/4/1.
[115] Gatrell et al., 'Reckoning with Refugeedom', p. 71–9.
[116] Gatrell et al., 'Reckoning with Refugeedom', p. 84.
[117] Gatrell, 'Introduction', pp. 5–8; Rodogno, *Night on Earth*, p. 6.

because the 'education and of subsequent supply of intelligent men' would be essential for the recovery of Ukraine and the wider 'restoration of order in Eastern Europe'.[118] In so doing, their appeal mirrored humanitarian discourses that regarded educated experts as integral to national and international reconstruction.

Displaced intellectuals often deployed the elevated language of civilization in order to make their case to organizations who they felt could help them. In 1923, Sofia Roussova, a refugee Ukrainian economist in Czechoslovakia, wrote an appeal to the League of Nations on behalf of the Ukrainian Emigration Committee in Prague. Drawing on discourses which portrayed Bolshevism as the barbaric other to European civilization, Roussova argued that Ukrainian national culture needed to be supported in the face of repressive Bolshevik rule because 'every national culture contributes new riches to the treasury of universal civilization'. Roussova asked the League to provide money so that the committee could continue publishing in Ukrainian while in temporary exile, stating that 'we have lots of intellectual capital but its money that we require'.[119]

Details of the work of humanitarian organizations of all sizes spread quickly across displaced communities in southeastern Europe, generating a growing awareness among refugees that they could ameliorate their own conditions if they could make contact with representatives of these organizations. As Thomas Whittemore personally managed the Committee for the Education of Russian Youth in Exile, educated refugees became aware that if they could just make contact with the American archaeologist, they may be able to secure a funded place to study at an elite European university. One student by the name of Pygov travelled 'without any means' from Gallipoli to Constantinople, a distance of almost 300 kilometres, in search of Whittemore.[120] And, knowing the potential of the CERYE's work to change their lives, some lied about their circumstances in order to meet the exacting intellectual profile demanded. One Russian refugee was turned down when it was discovered that 'his only aim is to get to Germany by some means or others'.[121]

[118] Memorial, 6 December 1920, LSF/YM/MfS/FEWVRC/MISSIONS/12/2/19.
[119] Sofia Roussova to League of Nations, 2 July 1923, LNA/R1057/13C/29433/
       29433.
[120] Unsigned report c1922, RAC/LSRM, 3.3, Box 8, Folder 94, pp. 8–9.
[121] Belash to Whittemore, 27 October 1922, CURBML/BAR Ms Coll/CERYE,
       IX.1, Box 94, Folder 9.

The language of intellectual relief could also be deployed to other ends. In 1922, Alexandre Kolenko found himself a refugee in Tunisia. A veteran of a number of conflicts, Kolenko and his wife fled during the civil war, leaving behind their medical student son in Crimea, but subsequently wished to reunite the family. In September 1922 he wrote a letter to Winifred Coombe Tennant, a Welsh suffrage activist who was representing Britain as a substitute delegate at the League of Nations Assembly in Geneva.[122] Kolenko claimed that his son had 'exceptional intelligence' and that 'his place is in the workspace of a scientist, a laboratory ... but he is stuck in the prison of communism'. Kolenko asked Coombe Tennant whether she could pass details of his request to 'Monsieur Rockfeler'.[123] Kolenko's letter suggests that refugee communities had an awareness of the wider humanitarian landscape and knew that certain figures like Rockefeller might view an appeal that emphasized intellect favourably. As it was, Coombe Tennant was not acquainted with the American philanthropist but did present details of Kolenko's case to Fridtjof Nansen, who was unable to help.[124] While refugees could utilize the elitist and differentiated language of intellectual relief, they were not always successful in their requests for assistance.

Institutions Displaced, Institutions Returned

Beyond individuals, displacement also emerged as an institutional issue in the aftermath of war. The cessation of conflict saw some victors claim the intellectual spoils of their triumph through the occupation of universities. In Central and Eastern Europe, empires collapsed and new states quickly emerged from their ashes, even before the Paris Peace Conference formally confirmed their territorial limits. With the substantial redrawing of the map of Europe, the boundaries encompassing institutions sometimes moved even when physical bricks and mortar did not. The American Relief Administration referred to these institutions as 'refugee-universities'.[125] Intellectual institutions held a

---

122 Robert Laker, 'Geneva in Motion: Winifred Coombe Tennant's Experiences at the Third Assembly of the League of Nations', MA Dissertation, Swansea University, 2020.

123 Alexandre Kolenko to Winifred Coombe Tennant, 6 September 1922, WGAS/WCTP/D/DT 3992.

124 Coombe Tennant to Kolenko, 27 September 1922, WGAS/WCTP D/DT 3998.

125 'The Future Home of the Refugee-universities', *ARA Bulletin*, 2.16, (1921), p. 45.

particular rhetorical power in this context as they connected the issues of territoriality, minority populations, and historic cultural development.[126] The transfer of universities from one country to another under the terms of the post-war treaties was often hailed as a symbolic completion of the reconstruction of national life, as was the case with France and the University of Strasbourg. The opposite was true when vanquished states such as Hungary lost institutions as a consequence of the redrawing of borders under the Treaty of Trianon in 1920.

For the defeated states of the First World War, the loss of cultural institutions in the aftermath of the conflict was evidence that national life itself was incomplete. These issues were especially pronounced in central Europe following the collapse of the Austro-Hungarian Empire. Long-established cultural institutions such as universities, which formerly belonged to a network of Habsburg institutions, became minorities in new self-determined nation states.[127] In some cases, universities were occupied by advancing forces at the end of the war before the occupation was given formal approval in international treaties.

Two Hungarian universities became parts of new states. The Elisabeth University at Pozsony (Bratislava) was occupied by Czechoslovak forces on 1 January 1919 and was, within a week, formally declared to be under the political control of Czechoslovakia. By September 1919 the Czechoslovak forces suppressed the faculties of philosophy and medicine resulting in the professors from these faculties setting themselves up in Budapest.[128] In a similar manner, the University of Kolozsvár (Cluj) was occupied by Romanian forces in May 1919.[129] At Cluj/Kolozsvár, the rector claimed that this constituted a breach of article fifty-one of the Hague Convention and expressed his shock that the Allies at the peace conference who represented 'civilized countries' would not allow Hungary 'to safeguard western science' by maintaining control of the

---

[126] Siegelberg, *Statelessness*, p. 59; Weitz, 'From the Vienna to the Paris System', pp. 1329–33; Mark Mazower, 'Minorities and the League of Nations in Interwar Europe', *Daedalus*, 126.2 (1997), pp. 47–63.

[127] Surman, *Universities in Imperial Austria 1848–1918*, pp. 245–7.

[128] Report by Elisabeth University, Pécs, 6 September 1923, LNA/S402/2/13. pp. 2–3.

[129] *The Case of Hungary: A Brief, Submitted by the Committee on Foreign Relations of the Senate of the United States by the Hungarian American Federation* (Cleveland, OH, 1919), p. 7.

university.[130] The Treaty of Trianon, signed in June 1920, reduced the territory of Hungary by two thirds, leaving the new state significantly reduced in size; importantly, it confirmed that the institutions that found themselves in Romania and Czechoslovakia at the end of the war would remain within those borders. The Romanian claim of the town of Cluj/Kolozsvár, the capital of Transylvania, was especially problematic to Hungary, which asserted that the town was historically Hungarian and for which the university was one of a number of important cultural sites.[131] Cluj/Kolosvár was also symbolically important as the town in which the provincial parliament voted to unite Transylvania with Hungary in 1867.[132]

The universities at both Cluj/Kolozsvár and Pozsony/Bratislava were converted into national institutions by their respective governments. Staff at the University of Kolozsvár were required to take an oath of allegiance to the Romanian king and those who refused to do so were dismissed.[133] As institutions themselves constitute communities of individuals, many of the students and professors returned to Hungary and temporarily settled in a military barracks in Budapest.[134] On visiting Budapest in July 1920, Edwin Embree, an officer for the Rockefeller Foundation, was approached by Count Miklos Bánffy and was urged to encourage the foundation to intervene in respect of Kolozsvár. Embree noted that the issues in Transylvania were 'not medical but political'.[135] The displaced university was formally re-established in Hungary at Szeged in 1921. In a similar manner, the

---

[130] Etienne Schneller, 'La Prise de l'Université des Sciences rle he «François Joseph» à Kolozsvár' in *Mémoire au sujet des violations de droit commises par le régime roumain en Transylvanie contre les minorités nationales, de religion et de race* (Budapest, c1921), pp. 92, 95, LNA/S379/44/1.

[131] *The Case of Hungary*, p. 14. Romanian scholars, similarly, claimed the historically Romanian character of Transylvania. Iorga Nicolae, *Histoire des roumains et de leur civilisation* (Paris, 1920), p. 199–235.

[132] Andreea Dăncilă, 'The Dynamic of Post-War Political Structures in Multi-Ethnic Regions: Transylvania at the End of 1918', in Burkhard Olschowsky, Piotr Juszkiewicz and Jan Rydel eds., *Central and Eastern Europe After the First World War* (Berlin, 2021), p. 223.

[133] *Recueil des griefs de la minorité hongroise: Dérivant de la violation du traité conclu à Paris le 9 déc. 1919 entre les principales puissances alliées et associées et la Roumanie au sujet de la protection des minorités* (Budapest, 1922), p. 48.

[134] 'The future home of the refugee-universities', p. 45.

[135] Edwin Embree, 'Log of Journey to Europe', entry for 30 July 1920. RAC/RF/RG 12, A-E, P. 18.

Hungarian University of Pozsony was set up in the town of Pécs for the 1923/4 academic year.[136]

The re-establishment of these universities in Hungary did not lessen the Hungarian sense of grievance as they were now required to start with a blank slate, lacking both the basic resources with which to equip their new institutions and also their institutional inheritances. The rector of the university of Kolozsvár wrote to the League of Nations in November 1922 describing how they had, following the Romanian occupation, lost 'our university, our still growing library, our scientific institutes, our clinics, in short, all that we possessed'.[137] Oliver Eöttevényi, a prominent advocate of treaty revision, wrote that he 'read with bitterness' how some successor states, beneficiaries of the post-war settlements, 'have boasted to foreigners as if those cultural achievements had been creations of their own'.[138]

The new Romanian university was also a beneficiary of the cultural diplomacy of other states. Romania was a key post-war ally of France and doubled its territory in the post-war settlements. As early as September 1919, France was concerned that the teaching staff at the Romanian University of Cluj were not up to standard and that it might 'lose its reputation'. A number of French scholars were sent to Cluj and other Romanian institutions in the years that followed to bolster its perceived intellectual deficiencies.[139] Following his visit to the University of Cluj in 1920, the French geographer Emmanuel de Martonne compared it to the University of Strasbourg, which France had recently reclaimed from Germany. De Martonne argued that the institution would become a 'home of high culture shining over the provinces returned from foreign domination'.[140] For victors and vanquished alike, intellectual institutions could be symbols of their cause.

[136] Report by Elisabeth University, Pécs, 6 September 1923. LNA/S402/2/13. pp. 2–3.

[137] Rector of Szeged University to ICIC, November 1922, LNA/R1050/13C/24014/32240.

[138] Oliver Eöttevényi, 'Cultural Effects of the Treaty of Trianon', in Albert Apponyi ed., *Justice for Hungary: Review and Criticism of the Effects of the Treaty of Trianon* (London, 1928), p. 208.

[139] M. de Saint-Aulaire to Stephen Pichon, 13 September 1919, AN/AJ/16/6990.

[140] Emmanuel de Martonne, 'Un semestre d'enseignement géographique à l'université de Cluj (Roumanie)', *Revue internationale de l'enseignement*, 76 (1922), p. 80.

Hungarian appeals for treaty revision frequently pointed to the intellectual and cultural losses which had been brought about by Trianon. As specialist literature was essential to post-war national reconstruction, the loss of institutions could result in a loss of knowledge. Eöttevényi claimed that Trianon resulted in Hungary losing 745 public and scientific libraries, or four million volumes (of a pre-war total of 9.5 million).[141] An international appeal issued by the Hungarian Academy of Letters and Sciences in 1921 decried the alleged desecration of monuments and artworks in the territories lost by Hungary under the terms of the treaty of Trianon. Calling Hungary one of 'the outposts of European civilization', it urged the drafting of international legislation in order to protect objects of art, much as had been done for minorities in successor states.[142] Hungarian claims to represent European civilization were common in this period; one sympathetic British observer wrote in 1923 that Hungarian universities, specifically the university of Budapest, were 'the barrier between Western culture and Balkan barbarity'.[143]

In 1923, the Hungarian government responded to a League of Nations inquiry by claiming that its intellectual life had been directly damaged by Trianon. Hungary had been 'deprived of the intellectual force of 3.5 million Hungarians', they argued in reference to the territorial losses of Trianon.[144] In the same year, the former minister of education Baron Jules Wlassics also wrote to the League to highlight the fact that the Hungarian minority in successor states were being denied access to 'Hungarian culture', referring not only to the daily press and political publications, but also to 'scientific and literary works'. Wlassics called on the League's International Committee on Intellectual Cooperation to provide stronger protections to minority populations so that Hungarian culture itself could be saved among the millions of former Hungarian subjects cut off by the Treaty of

---

[141] Eöttevényi, 'Cultural Effects of the Treaty of Trianon', p. 240.

[142] Hungarian Academy of Letters and Sciences, 'Address to the Academies of the World', 28 November 1921, BAA/SEC/2/1/1. On Hungarian invocations of 'civilization', see Teleki, *The Evolution of Hungary and its Place in European History*, pp. 51–3; Nagy 'The Race for Revision and Recognition', pp. 231–2; Seegel, *Map Men*, pp. 84–90.

[143] F.G. Montfort Bebb, 'The Universities of Central Europe', *The Contemporary Review*, 123 (1923), p. 773.

[144] *La situation du travail intellectuel en Hongrie: réponse à la commission de coopération intellectuelle de la société des nations* (Budapest, 1923), p. 19.

Trianon.[145] For vanquished nations such as Hungary, these intellectual institutions were symbols displaced from the new state; in contrast to the cases of Belgium or Serbia during the First World War, in which the situation was understood to be temporary, Hungary's post-war losses had been rendered permanent by an international treaty.

States that emerged triumphant from the war were able to welcome home hitherto exiled institutions. For France, the return of the University of Strasbourg, situated in the province of Alsace, provided great symbolic importance in asserting its sense of victory. Following its triumph in the Franco-Prussian War of 1870–71, Germany had taken over the University of Strasbourg, renaming it the Kaiser-Wilhelms-Universität. During the First World War, the Paris government made plans to reconstitute the university as a French institution and in November 1918, a delegation of French scholars went to Strasbourg to initiate this process.[146] On 7 December 1918, French troops closed the university and German scholars were, it was alleged, given twenty-four hours' notice to leave.[147] While there was some anger regarding the circumstances surrounding the French occupation of the University of Strasbourg, the transfer of the institution was uncontroversial; the restoration of Alsace and Lorraine was one of Woodrow Wilson's fourteen points and was commonly accepted as a key war aim for France.[148] The University of Strasbourg was formally ceded to France as part of the territories of Alsace and Lorraine under the terms of the Treaty of Versailles in 1919.

The restoration of the University of Strasbourg to France was portrayed as integral to national life itself. Speaking at a ceremony to inaugurate the re-established university in November 1919, the French president Raymond Poincaré called the university 'France's intellectual lighthouse on the eastern border', which suggested that Germany was still seen as occupying barbaric darkness.[149]

145 Jules Wlassics, 'Culture nationale et droits minoritaire' *Revue de Hongrie*, LNA/R1047/13C/25920/23024, pp. 4, 6.
146 John E. Craig, *Scholarship and Nation Building: The Universities of Strasbourg and Alsatian Society, 1870–1939* (Chicago, IL, 1984), pp. 204–24.
147 Supplement to the *Columbia Alumni News*, 10.26 (1919). Columbia University Archives (CUA), Columbia University, New York, World War One (WWI) Collection, Box 17, Folder 3.
148 Irish, *The University at War*, pp. 173–4.
149 'Inauguration de l'université de Strasbourg 21–23 novembre 1919', *Revue internationale de l'enseignement*, 73 (1919), p. 416.

The French historian Christian Pfister claimed that 'France did not cease to be present' at the university in the decades that it spent under German rule, even following the departure of French scholars in 1871.[150] In 1920, the newly formed Friends of the University of Strasbourg wrote of the importance of the acquisition of cultural capital to the French nation. Addressing the entire French nation, they argued that 'Alsace and Lorraine bring to you an inestimable treasure; great buildings, precious collections, remarkably well-equipped laboratories, a magnificent tradition of learning and labour which has been undertaken at Strasbourg for three centuries in spite of the vicissitudes of history'. It would be, the group argued, a 'home for Latin civilization'.[151] In this way, the cultural assets of the formerly displaced institution were seen as strengthening the nation itself – and completing victory.

In contrast to the individual cases discussed above, the resolution to institutional displacement was political rather than humanitarian. Refugee intellectuals could aspire to physically return home, even if that did not always ultimately come to pass. Brick–and–mortar institutions, on the other hand, usually needed home to return to them to bring their period of displacement to an end. This was accomplished through post-war treaties but as these favoured victor states, the vanquished would have to hope for revision of these settlements in the future. The return of displaced institutions, or the appeals in favour of those now exiled, demonstrated the important link between organized intellect and national life at the end of the First World War and mirrored the rhetoric surrounding refugee intellectuals in the same period.

Conclusion

In 1926, Thomas Whittemore's Committee for the Education of Russian Youth in Exile began to wind down its activities and announced that it would not support any new students.[152] By that point, the archaeologist had to confront the possibility that 'not a single youth of the emigration' might ever make it back to Russia.[153] A key

---

[150] 'Inauguration de l'université de Strasbourg 21–23 novembre 1919', p. 401.
[151] 'Société des amis de l'université de Strasbourg, 1920', AN/AJ/9/6177.
[152] Memorandum, Office of John D. Rockefeller Jr, November 17, 1926, RAC/OMR, Series Q, Box 42, Folder 369.
[153] Whittemore to Brent, 26 May 1926, CURBML/BAR Ms Coll/CERYE, IX.1, Box 94, Folder 21.

goal of the CERYE was to ensure the educational continuity of an intellectual elite ahead of their return to Russia where they would play a key role in its post-war, and post-Bolshevik, reconstruction. In this way, it constituted a modest contribution to holding Russian intellectual life in trust against the backdrop of civil war, famine, and growing state oppression. Despite the realization of his organization's ultimate aspiration being cast into doubt, Whittemore argued that his work, and that of similar initiatives, 'will be justified and not in vain' because they had 'trained for intellectual work in other countries a strong Russian contribution to the advancement of universal culture'.[154] By the time the committee concluded its work in 1931, one thousand Russians had been assisted in this manner.

The crisis of intellectual displacement had lessened by the mid-1920s, by which time many organizations, such as Whittemore's CERYE, found that their work was mostly complete. The establishment of relations between many European states and Bolshevik Russia from 1924 was a key development which meant that continued support for political opponents outside of Russia became difficult for many countries to sustain. Moreover, the stability of the Soviet regime meant that it was less likely that educated refugees would return home to aid in a reconstruction project as many Western humanitarians had initially hoped.[155] Simultaneously, awareness of the persecution of perceived enemy intellectuals by the Soviet government had become more widespread and meant that the repatriation of refugees came to be regarded as a dangerous policy.[156] In 1924, the League of Nation's ICIC was sent accounts of the persecution of nineteen Ukrainian intellectuals within the Soviet Union but it determined that it could not intervene on their behalf.[157] In many cases, the aspirations of Western humanitarians to hold Russian intellectual life in trust ahead of its ultimate return – as had been the case with Belgium during the First World War – proved misplaced.

While many humanitarian initiatives concluded in this period, the experience of displacement did not. Thousands of dislocated Russian intellectuals, unable to return home, had to come to terms with their existence not as refugees but as exiles in Europe and North America.

---

[154] Whittemore to Brent, 26 May 1926, CURBML/BAR Ms Coll/CERYE, IX.1, Box 94, Folder 21.
[155] Raeff, *Russia Abroad*, p.16.   [156] Chinyaeva, 'Russian Émigrés', p. 156.
[157] Henri Bergson to Nitobe Inazō, 5 April 1924, LNA/R1068/13C/35146; 'Red Persecution of Intelligentsia', *The Times*, 4 March 1924, p. 13.

They inhabited a space that was, in Edward Said's words, a 'median state, neither completely at one with the new setting nor fully disencumbered of the old'.[158] Subsequent crises meant that many of these exiles would continue to be itinerant. The Great Depression led to many Russian scholars who had settled across Europe needing to seek work elsewhere; the New York-based Institute of International Education took a lead in trying to find placements for these scholars, many of whom first left Russia during the Civil War, in North American institutions.[159] Exile could last a lifetime.

The post-war experience of displacement, and the manner in which it was addressed by national governments and humanitarian organizations, shows the powerful rhetorical link between national life and intellectual culture. Intellectual elites were frequently treated differently to the wider body of refugees. In many cases, they were seen as representatives of national life in exile that needed to be temporarily sustained – or held in trust – in order to restore or rebuild the nation itself. This pattern was established with Belgian and Serbian scholars during the First World War and repeated with anti-Bolshevik Russians in the early 1920s. In this context, refugee intellectuals were well-equipped to make their voices heard through their transnational connectedness, education, and linguistic skills. The same emphasis on nations can be seen with intellectual institutions; their displacement was presented as a symbolic reconstitution of the nation itself, but one that required the force of international treaties – or their revision – to ultimately be resolved. The humanitarian response to intellectual displacement, while couched in the familiar language of civilization, often included references to national values, whether to describe the displaced intellectuals being assisted, or to justify assistance from American funders or European governments. From the perspective of those assisting intellectual refugees, their work was rationalized by the idea that national intellectual life could not cease and must be held in trust until such time as it could return home again.

Post-war displacement was a further way in which the identities and activities of Europe's intellectuals were highlighted. Against the backdrop of hunger, disease, inflation, and dislocation, they were treated as

---

[158] Edward Said, 'Intellectual Exile: Expatriates and Marginals', *Grand Street*, 47 (1993), p. 114.

[159] Rockefeller Archive Center (RAC), Institute of International Education Records (IIE) RG 1, Series 3, 8 HF 1.12.

a discrete group that required urgent aid to be kept alive, productive, and, in the case of refugees, ready to participate in national reconstruction efforts when the time arose. While much of the rhetoric urging assistance to refugee intellectuals emphasized their role as representatives of national communities, the frequent invocation of intellectuals by humanitarian organizations suggested a growing transnational understanding of their wider societal importance.

5 | Books and Buildings
The Reconstruction of Libraries after the First World War

On 26 August 1918, a ceremony was held at the French port town of Le Havre, wartime seat of the Belgian government, to mark the fourth anniversary of the burning of the university library of Louvain in 1914.[1] The commemoration recalled a shocking event which was used to mobilize international sympathy at the beginning of the First World War and which became synonymous with German 'barbarism' and the excesses of the conflict that followed. The burning of Louvain library, with the destruction of over 300,000 volumes, 1,000 manuscripts, and 900 incunabula, was portrayed as an especially egregious and visceral example of modern warfare, with cultural and educational sites rendered military targets and knowledge itself subsumed by the flames.[2]

The 1918 ceremony was choreographed to mirror the wider political configuration of the world in the final months of the Great War. Representatives of universities from allied and neutral countries such as France, the United States, Spain, and Switzerland all spoke to show solidarity with the plight of Belgium.[3] Letters were read out from the allied generals Douglas Haig, Ferdinand Foch, and John Pershing, while government ministers from Italy and Britain were also present.[4] The memory of Louvain was intimately linked to the allied cause as the war reached its conclusion. Speeches were unstinting in their assertion of German culpability and its wider implications for the war: the Allies represented the values of civilization; the Germans those of barbarism. One French newspaper reported that 'this unforgettable day will endure as a display of solidarity among civilized people; for the

[1] Œuvre internationale de Louvain, *La nouvelle bibliothèque de l'université* (Louvain, 1929), p. 2.
[2] Kramer, *Dynamic of Destruction,* p. 6.
[3] Arthur Raffalovich, 'La commémoration de la destruction de Louvain', *Journal des Débats*, 3 September 1918, p. 2.
[4] 'La commémoration de Louvain', *L'Attaque*, 26 August 1918, p. 1.

Germans it is a great moral defeat and the beginning of their atonement for their crimes'.[5]

Among the speakers that day was Étienne Lamy, permanent secretary of the Académie Française, and a key figure in coordinating French efforts to collect books to restore the collections of Louvain in order to ensure that the damage caused by the German army did not endure. The burning of books was a shocking act, Lamy argued, even when considered alongside the vast loss of life in wartime, because the written word was the bequest of one generation to the next and the means by which societies communicated 'the secret of their genius, the story of their efforts and the confession of their mistakes'. Lamy asserted that the destruction of books amounted to the revocation of 'the gift of the dead' because the printed word held historic importance in the onward march of civilization. While books were sacred, so too were libraries, which he termed 'sanctuaries' for intelligence, a meeting place for ideas, teachers, and students in their pursuit of truth. Thus, the greatest crime of the Germans in August 1914 was not to have destroyed hundreds of thousands of volumes and rare manuscripts, but to have 'destroyed the sanctuary where intellects could be in communion' and where 'generations enriched themselves from truth'.[6]

***

This chapter explores how knowledge was rebuilt in the aftermath of the war and argues that it constituted a symbolically important component of the wider process of reconstruction. It takes the example of three university libraries (Louvain, Belgrade, and Tokyo) which were destroyed either during the conflict or in its immediate aftermath and analyses how and why they were rebuilt. University libraries held a particular resonance during and after the First World War as symbolic embodiments of civilization. The destruction of university libraries during the war shocked observers due to the contents of these buildings: books and manuscripts, the physical manifestations of knowledge itself. In a conflict that was defined by the Allies as a fight for the preservation of civilization, damaged university libraries

---

[5] 'Une cérémonie expiatoire commémore l'anniversaire du sac de Louvain', *Excelsior*, 27 August 1918, p. 2; *Le Figaro* also described the ceremony as a 'moral defeat.' 'Une expiation', *Le Figaro*, 26 August 1918, p. 1.

[6] Étienne Lamy, 'L'université de Louvain', *Revue des Deux Mondes*, 47.6 (1918) p. 6.

became resonant symbols of European culture assailed. Their reconstruction following the war took on significant urgency against a backdrop of widespread prognostication relating to the collapse of civilization. The discourse surrounding destroyed libraries, as was the case with that relating to the post-war humanitarian crisis, demonstrated that while the crisis of civilization was in many respects an imagined phenomenon, it was also tangible. This can be seen clearly in the outrage regarding the wartime destruction of books and through the establishment of the many international initiatives that sought to replace them.

While we know very little about the formal reconstruction of knowledge, this phenomenon tells us much about the ways in which politicians, intellectuals, and humanitarian actors regarded the replacement of books and manuscripts destroyed in the war as a key element of post-war reconstruction. The destruction of libraries has a long history that predates August 1914.[7] In the years immediately preceding the First World War, knowledge was consumed by flames on a number of occasions and often for innocent reasons; in 1904, the collections of Turin university library were incinerated because of an electrical fire, while the new library at Stanford University was destroyed by the 1906 San Francisco earthquake.[8] Contemporaries looked to the more distant past in order to establish points of comparison for the destruction of Louvain library. Étienne Lamy was not alone by placing it in a longer historical lineage alongside the destruction of the great library of Alexandria during the occupation of Julius Caesar in 48BC (and again in 643AD) or the 'bonfire of the vanities' led by the supporters of the friar Girolamo Savonarola in fifteenth-century Florence. Postwar discourses of cultural decline frequently made reference to the disappearance of ancient civilizations as a means of drawing urgent attention to the immediate crisis facing Europe. What better an example of the recession of civilization than the disappearance of the buildings that housed its treasures and gave it substance? The reconstruction of libraries and their collections after the war constituted a symbolic attempt to ward off the collapse of civilization, replace

---

[7] Burke, *A Social History of Knowledge II*, pp. 139–47; Richard Ovenden, *Burning the Books: A History of Knowledge Under Attack* (London, 2020).

[8] 'Many Precious Volumes Destroyed in Turin Fire', *New York Times*, 30 January 1904, p. 1; 'New Library, Stanford University', *The Indianapolis News*, 26 April 1906, p. 8.

lost knowledge, and to ensure that Europe did not go the way of the lost civilization of Byzantium.[9]

The destruction of Louvain library was a shocking moment at the outset of the First World War that outraged international opinion and retained a long cultural memory. It was, however, not the only instance of cultural violence that took place during an increasingly total war. Almost a month after Louvain, the thirteenth-century Reims Cathedral was shelled by the German army, again shocking a wide audience, albeit for other reasons given the cathedral's Christian symbolism. While the outcry that followed these events led Germany to appoint experts to ensure that cultural sites were protected in Belgium, there was considerable evidence of cultural violence on other fronts.[10] The Austrian bombardment of Belgrade at the beginning of the war, which preceded the events at Louvain, led to the destruction of the University of Belgrade and the Serbian national museum.[11] It was later claimed that the Bulgarian occupation of Serbia had led to the widespread removal of books from specialist libraries.[12] After the war, Romania claimed that both the German and Bulgarian forces were responsible for the deliberate destruction and pillage of libraries, archives, museums, and historic documents during the conflict.[13] Cultural violence in Eastern Europe received less attention compared to that which took place in Belgium and France; the latter occupied an elevated place in the international imagination both during and after the war, and reflected the biases of international elites towards Western Europe's position as a centre of 'civilization'.[14]

The reconstruction of knowledge was an international phenomenon that connected actors across Europe and the world in the procurement of books, manuscripts, incunabula, and artworks for rebuilt libraries. It was a transnational process through which actors spanning the globe

---

[9] Burke, *A Social History of Knowledge II*, pp. 139–40.

[10] Sandholtz, *Prohibiting Plunder*, pp. 106–7.

[11] R. A. Reiss, *Rapport sur les atrocités commises par les troupes austrohongroises pendant la première invasion de la Serbie* (Paris, 1919), p. 24.

[12] 'Bulgarian rule in Serbia: the confiscation of private property', Appeal of the Central Serbian Committee for the Relief of the Serbian People, c.1917, CURBML/CEIP, VII.Q, Box 298, Folder 3.

[13] 'Mémoire de la délégation roumaine: déposé le 8 mars 1919', in *La paix de Versailles: responsabilités des auteurs de la guerre et sanctions*, pp. 216–7.

[14] Jan Ifversen, 'Europe and the Concept of Margin', in Tessa Hauswedell, Axel Körner and Ulrich Tiedau eds., *Re-Mapping Centre and Periphery: Asymmetrical Encounters in European and Global Contexts* (London, 2020), pp. 27–43.

Figure 5.1 Ruins of Louvain University library, c1915 (Universal History Archive/Getty)

were mobilized in a common cause to symbolically rebuild what was seen to be a universal intellectual patrimony. The three examples explored here – Louvain library, the university library at Belgrade, and the library of Tokyo Imperial University (TIU) – were all linked by similar actors and by preoccupations with the fate of civilization and wartime alliances. The latter example, destroyed by the Great Kantō earthquake of 1923, is featured here due to the resulting mobilization of an international (primarily Euro-American) network of scholars, philanthropists, and politicians who were moved to act to rebuild a library whose reconstruction was articulated as a universal imperative. This owed much to Japan fighting the recently ended war on the allied side and also because of the sympathy evinced by damage done following a natural disaster, rather than in war.[15] The reconstruction

---

[15]   Julia F. Irwin and Jenny Leigh Smith, 'Introduction: On Disaster', in *Isis*, Focus: Disasters, Science, and History, 1.111 (2020), pp. 98–103.

of TIU library (completed in 1928) had much in common with that undertaken at Belgrade (which ended in 1926) and Louvain (completed in 1928); the rebuilding of all three libraries was presented to European and North American audiences as essential to the strengthening and spread of civilization, the promulgation of peaceful international relations, and also the inter-allied hierarchies that had emerged during the Great War.

Libraries and Post-war Reconstruction

Post-First World War reconstruction can be understood in multiple ways. John Horne has shown that while it entailed the repair of material damage on various wartime fronts, it also encompassed phenomena such as political, social, and cultural reconstruction.[16] In this way, post-war rebuilding can be understood as both a literal, tangible endeavour to reconstruct property which had been the victim of wartime fighting, as well as a metaphorical, intangible process in which political and cultural discourse shifted to emphasize the peaceful interaction of states and, later, engagement between former enemies.[17] It might, in Horne's reading, include buildings that literally replaced those damaged during the war, as well as those which were built as allegorical representations of reconstruction such as the Palais des Nations in Geneva, constructed to house the League of Nations.[18]

Reconstruction was a complex process that constituted a key feature of people's experience of war and its aftermath. It linked, as Pierre Purseigle has shown, local and transnational actors, such as humanitarians and town planners; it also had its own temporalities which extended long into the 1920s and 1930s.[19] For local populations, delays to the completion of reconstruction could cause anger, while for their part, politicians were often eager to declare a formal 'end' to reconstruction.[20] The issue of temporalities is key, given that the

---

[16] John Horne, 'Reconstruction, Reform and Peace in Europe after the First World War', in *Revival after the Great War*, p. 297.

[17] Horne, 'Demobilizing the Mind: France and the Legacy of the Great War, 1919-1939', pp. 101–19.

[18] Horne, 'Reconstruction, Reform and Peace in Europe after the First World War', p. 311.

[19] Pierre Purseigle, 'Catastrophe and Reconstruction in Western Europe: The Urban Aftermath of the First World War', in *Revival after the Great War*, p. 39.

[20] Purseigle, 'Catastrophe and Reconstruction in Western Europe', pp. 44–7.

reconstruction of war damage often overlapped with destruction which was not caused by the war, but which took place in the same period and was governed by the same transnational drive to rebuild. This was the case with the destruction of Tokyo Imperial University library in September 1923.

Damage done to cultural sites such as libraries during and after the war was frequently portrayed as constituting a loss not to one particular nation but to civilized humanity as a whole. In late August 1914, Emmanuel Havenith, the Belgian envoy to the then-neutral United States, declared the destruction of Louvain an 'outrage on the rights of humanity and civilization which is unprecedented in history'.[21] From its earliest days, the First World War was understood and articulated (in allied and some neutral states) as being a war in defence of civilization against German *Kultur*. This proved an effective means of mobilizing publics to support the conflict while it was ongoing. The aftermath of the war left ruins across the various fighting fronts in Europe, including wrecked libraries whose contents – the books and manuscripts which embodied their claims to universal importance – were destroyed.

The rebuilding of these university libraries should be understood as constituting an attempt to symbolically rebuild 'civilization' itself through the exemplary reconstruction of cultural sites. This demonstrated the resilience of civilization following a vastly destructive conflict and in the face of post-war violence, humanitarian crises across Europe, and the rise of Bolshevism. The language of civilization was frequently invoked to explain the imperative of library reconstruction. The Danish scholar Kristoffer Nyrop, who played a key role in organizing Denmark's contribution to Louvain's reconstruction, wrote in 1917 that the destruction of the University of Louvain 'was possibly intended as a death-blow to Belgian civilization, but the result will certainly be just the opposite'.[22] Leo Capser, who oversaw the Carnegie Endowment for International Peace's reconstruction of the university library in Belgrade, stated that the project was intended to consolidate the process of extending Western civilization to the Balkans that had begun during the war.[23] Representatives of Tokyo

---

[21] 'In Grief over Louvain', *Washington Post*, 29 August 1914, p. 3.
[22] Kristoffer Nyrop, *Is War Civilization?* (London, 1917), p. 54.
[23] 'Carnegie Gift to Belgrade', *New York Times*, 30 Oct 1921, CURBML/CEIP, VII.Z, Box 320, Folder 21.

Imperial University stated their hope that the reconstruction of their library following international appeals would be a monument to 'the amity of civilized nations'.[24] The task of rebuilding university libraries and replacing the destroyed books on their shelves was a hugely ambitious transnational endeavour and the language framing reconstruction placed an emphasis on the universal importance of each of these institutions.

While each of the library reconstruction initiatives under consideration here was described using universal terms such as 'civilization', the projects themselves bore the imprint of wartime politics. All three of the major reconstruction initiatives that followed the war took place in countries that had been on the allied side in the conflict: Belgium, Serbia, and Japan.[25] At the start of the First World War, the international world of intellectuals and culture, which had traditionally made grand claims to its universalism, saw belligerents on opposing sides divided. During the conflict, the international was superseded by the inter-allied, with the United States, France, and Britain overseeing the creation of new international connections which excluded enemy states such as Germany and emphasized the shared wartime cause of the Allies.[26] This inter-allied configuration continued well into the 1920s. The money for each of the three libraries in question came from the United States and constituted, as Tammy Proctor has argued in the case of Louvain, a means by which American philanthropists could demonstrate their appreciation for European culture.[27] Britain and France also played prominent roles in these projects, as will be shown. Beyond the reconstruction of buildings, the participation of states in schemes to restock the shelves of these libraries also constituted a form of cultural diplomacy that owed much to wartime alliance, placing permanent stocks of knowledge relating to the cultural attainment of a given state on the shelves of these rebuilt libraries. In many cases, national committees explicitly stated their desire to provide the

---

[24] Anesaki Masaharu and Yamada Tamaki, 'First Report on the Reconstruction of the Tokyo Imperial University Library', *First Report on the Reconstruction of the Tokyo Imperial University Library* (Tokyo, 1926), RAC/OMR, Series G, Box 130, Folder 994, pp. 2–3.

[25] Serbia was part of the Kingdom of Serbs, Croats and Slovenes following the First World War, which was known as Yugoslavia from 1929 until 1992.

[26] Irish, 'From International to Inter-Allied', pp. 311–25.

[27] Proctor, 'The Louvain Library and US Ambition in Interwar Belgium', pp. 147–8.

'best of' their national learning in a given field. As such, participation in the reconstruction of the library collections constituted a global performance of inter-allied politics and ensured the primacy of inter-allied thought on the shelves of these rebuilt institutions.

While civilization was widely invoked in this period, it did not apply equally – or mean the same thing – in Belgium, Serbia, or Japan. The label of 'civilized' was applied by Euro-America to order the wider world and its political, legal, and cultural development, while also excluding other populations on the basis of their racial characteristics.[28] The University of Louvain was established in the fifteenth century and thus considered one of Europe's 'ancient' universities. Belgium's physical location in the west of Europe, its Catholicism, and its recent colonial history, as well as its wartime experience of German invasion and occupation, meant that its claims to embody civilization were historic and uncontested. Japan's trajectory was different; it had isolated itself from the wider world until the nineteenth century and consciously adopted a process of Westernization in the late nineteenth and early twentieth centuries such that it could now be regarded as part of the wider community of 'civilized' nations.[29] University education was an important component of Japan's Westernization. In the aftermath of the 1923 earthquake, the legal scholar Takayanagi Kenzō appealed for American aid and claimed that TIU was 'responsible for whatever strength and shortcoming[s] modern Japan, as is known to the whole world, stands for'.[30] Similarly, at the time of the First World War, the Balkans were perceived in Western Europe as being at the periphery of European civilization and thus requiring greater work to attain Western standards.[31]

The reconstruction of university library collections at Louvain, Belgrade, and Tokyo was therefore an affirmation of their respective civilizations as they were understood by Western intellectuals and

---

[28] Ada Dialla and Alexis Heraclides, *Humanitarian Intervention in the Long Nineteenth Century: Setting the Precedent* (Manchester, 2015), pp. 31–3.

[29] Dialla and Heraclides, *Humanitarian Intervention in the Long Nineteenth Century*, pp. 42–3; Iida Yumiko, 'Fleeing the West, Making Asia Home: Transpositions of Otherness in Japanese PanAsianism, 1905-1930', *Alternatives: Global, Local, Political*, 22.3 (1997), pp. 409–32.

[30] Takayanagi Kenzō to Arthur Woods, 16 January 1924, RAC/OMR, Series G, Box 130, Folder 995.

[31] Maria Nikolaeva Todorova, *Imagining the Balkans* (Oxford, 2009), pp. 130–3.

philanthropists. Furthermore, it spoke to the perceived importance of universities as agents of civilization in this period. Each of these reconstruction projects cumulatively sought to push back against narratives of civilizational decline, as well as embodying the spirit of the age, with its emphasis on building durable peace and strong inter-allied relationships. The projects to rebuild the university libraries at Louvain, Belgrade, and Tokyo were exemplary and sought to ensure that they would not be regarded in the same way as the ancient library at Alexandria.[32]

The rebuilding of libraries posed important questions about knowledge and the future of the world. In each case, the direct reproduction of destroyed collections proved impossible; the literal replacement of lost knowledge was neither practical nor necessarily desirable. Consequently, many of the relief committees, formed to rebuild and restock these libraries, had to determine what sort of knowledge should be included in them. As these libraries were symbols of the resilience and persistence of civilization, these were significant questions that went to the core of understandings about the function of knowledge in stable societies and the peaceful interrelation of states. In most cases, it was decided that modern collections emphasizing scientific subjects would be an important keystone of these libraries, rather than the replication of historic collections.

There is a final reason why the destruction and reconstruction of libraries held a symbolic importance in the post-First World War period. Wartime photos of ruined buildings often acted as metaphors for human suffering.[33] Depictions of ruined libraries acted as representations of something larger: the crisis of civilization itself. Images of destroyed buildings were used to generate public sympathy and convey a sense of outrage in ways that the written word could not, and depictions of destroyed buildings were published and reached wide audiences during and after the First World War. Moreover, images of ruined libraries and their reconstruction could be used to depict progress and, ultimately, the completion of the project; the literal filling of a library with books indicated the successful conclusion of an initiative.

[32] Jon Thiem, 'The Great Library of Alexandria Burnt: Towards the History of a Symbol', *Journal of the History of Ideas*, 40.4 (1979), pp. 507–26.
[33] Nicole Hudgins, 'Art and Death in French Photographs of Ruins, 1914-1918', *Historical Reflections / Réflexions Historiques: Special Issue: Rethinking World War I: Occupation, Liberation, and Reconstruction*, 42.3 (2016), p. 60.

The visual nature of the damage and reconstruction process undoubtedly explains why these projects appealed to philanthropists and politicians, who could clearly track their beginnings and eventual culmination in a meaning-laden opening ceremony; images thus presented them with a standard against which they could measure their aspirations to rebuild intellectual life.

The Reconstruction of Belgrade University Library

Despite the centrality of the destruction of Louvain to allied narratives of wartime barbarism, it was not the first university library to be damaged in the conflict. The Austrian army bombarded Belgrade from the beginning of the war on 28 July 1914 and, in the words of the rector of the University of Belgrade, Djordje Stanojević, the institution constituted a 'good target'. The national museum, national library, and university suffered extensive damage as a result of the shelling.[34] The University of Belgrade never received the same attention in the allied imagination as its counterpart at Louvain did; for one, the university was relatively new, being formally founded as a university as recently as 1905.[35] It was not an 'ancient university' like Louvain but a 'younger sister' to longer-established institutions in Western Europe.[36] From 1914, the aggression of Germany and the victimhood of Belgium took primacy in the international mind when discussing the excesses of wartime. Unlike Belgium, which was taken by the advancing German army in August 1914, Belgrade was not occupied by the Habsburg forces until the end of 1915.

Despite the dominance of Louvain in many narratives of cultural destruction that appeared at the start of the war, the damage to Belgrade university and its library was also widely reported in allied countries.[37] The American journalist John Reed's account of *The Eastern Front*, published in 1916, claimed that the university was a deliberate target for the Austro-Hungarians because of the

---

[34] Djorje Stanojević, 'Avant-propos', in *Le bombardement de l'université de Belgrade* (Paris, 1915), p. 7.
[35] Stanojević, *Le bombardement de l'université de Belgrade*, pp. 15–7.
[36] Lucien Poincaré, 'Préface', *Le bombardement de l'université de Belgrade*, p. 6.
[37] Nadine Akhund, 'The World of the Carnegie Endowment in the Balkans after World War One: The University Library of Belgrade, 1919-1926', *INFOtheca*, 12.1 (2011), p. 4.

association between pan-Serb nationalist students and the assassination of Archduke Franz Ferdinand in 1914.[38] There was also widespread reporting of the looting of books and manuscripts from Serbian libraries as well as the 'systematic spoliation' of collections by Austrian and Bulgarian forces.[39] One particularly graphic newspaper report from February 1918 claimed that in Belgrade 'war has shown itself in

Figure 5.2 Damage sustained by the University of Belgrade following Austrian bombardment, 1914 (Djorje Stanojević, *Le bombardement de l'université de Belgrade* [Paris, 1915])

[38] John Reed, *The War in Eastern Europe* (New York, 1916), pp. 65–6.
[39] 'Serbian Libraries Sacked', *The Mail*, 18 February 1916, p. 3; 'La presse allemande et la résistance serbe', *Bulletin Yougoslave*, 15 December 1915, p. 3; 'The Looting of Libraries: Prof. Firth on Restitution by Treaty', *The Times*, 13 December 1917, p. 5.

its most odious form' and that certain public buildings had been looted to the extent that 'only the bare walls are left'.[40]

Representatives of Serbian education and culture were prominent in raising awareness of the fate of educational institutions in wartime. In December 1914, an appeal by the Archbishop of Belgrade gained considerable coverage in British newspapers. It described how the Austrian army had destroyed 'educational and humanitarian institutions' in Belgrade.[41] In March 1915 the Archbishop issued an appeal in a similar vein which was widely covered in American newspapers.[42] In the same year, Stanojević published a photographic account of the damage inflicted upon his institution, which included jarring photographs of shell holes perforating lecture theatres and offices as well as smashed items in science laboratories; one depicted books sitting serenely and almost implausibly on a shelf surrounded by rubble.[43] The Geneva-based Serbian Central Committee for the relief of the Serbian People issued an international appeal noting how 'the war has not spared even the institutions of high intellectual culture and religious objects'.[44] The same body also sought to raise awareness in the United States of Bulgarian cultural vandalism in Serbia and the destruction of 'Serbian progress in civilization'.[45]

By the war's end, a number of initiatives emerged which sought to replace the destroyed books of Belgrade's university library. In January 1919, the Royal Society of Literature in London formed a committee to reconstruct Belgrade's libraries. In a letter to *The Times* publicizing the body's work, Lord Crewe wrote that libraries, including that of Belgrade University, had been 'systematically dispersed or destroyed' and called on members of the public to provide books, in history, belles-lettres, poetry, travel, philosophy, science, and

[40] 'German Plunder: Systematic Looting of Belgrade', *Newcastle Daily Chronicle*, 15 February 1918, p. 4.

[41] 'Serbian Need of Help', *The Mail*, 26 December 1914, p. 3.

[42] 'Serbia Appeals to America for Aid', *Nashville Tennessean*, 28 March 1915, p. 30; 'Appeal from Serbia', *Dayton Daily News*, 23 March 1915, p. 6; 'Serbian Bishop Makes Pathetic Appeal for Help', *Bridgeport Times and Evening Farmer*, 24 March 1915, p. 12.

[43] Djordjević, *Le bombardement de l'université de Belgrade*.

[44] Appeal of the Central Serbian Committee for the relief of the Serbian People, CURBML/CEIP, VII.Q, Box 298, Folder 3.

[45] 'Serbia Devastated' and 'Bulgarian Rule in Serbia: the confiscation of private property', CURBML/CEIP, VII.Q: Box 298, Folder 3.

education.[46] In a version of the appeal published in the *Fortnightly Review*, Crewe stated that 'the Austro-Hungarians and the Bulgarians were at special pains to remove all means of education and culture in Serbia, and they destroyed her libraries after taking from them all that they themselves wanted'.[47] By 1923, when the committee completed its work, over 18,000 volumes had been collected and sent to Belgrade.[48]

The reconstruction of the library building was an American initiative. During the war, the Carnegie Endowment for International Peace's Division of Intercourse and Education announced that an appropriation of $500,000 would be set aside for reconstruction in the devastated areas of Belgium, France, Serbia, and Russia. This money was used to fund symbolic relief projects and libraries emerged as a major focus of the CEIP's efforts. The money was ultimately used to fund (partially or in full) the rebuilding of Louvain university library, the construction of a new library in Reims, the reconstruction of the village of Fargniers in France, restoration work at Westminster Abbey, and some relief for Russian refugees.[49] The Carnegie Endowment's project to rebuild a select number of European libraries must be understood in the context of Andrew Carnegie's historic mission to build libraries and promote literacy as part of his philanthropy.[50] The reconstruction of two university libraries among these projects spoke to the cultural violence of the First World War, the suffering of allied civilian populations, and reasserted faith in education and knowledge as essential to healthy post-war societies.

The decision to rebuild the university library at Belgrade was taken in 1920 with the CEIP committing to physically rebuild the library as well as equipping it with two thousand books on American history and institutions.[51] The library in Belgrade differed from its counterpart in

---

[46] 'The Serbian Libraries', *The Times*, 18 January 1919, p. 4.

[47] 'Books for Serbia', *Fortnightly Review*, 105.629 (1919), pp. 815–6. Another appeal was issued in April 1920. 'Serbian National Libraries', *The Times*, 10 April 1920, p. 8.

[48] 'Reconstruction of Serbian Libraries', *Yorkshire Post*, 16 August 1923, p. 2.

[49] *Carnegie Endowment for International Peace, Year Book 1921* (Washington, DC, 1921), 35–42. Akhund, 'The World of the Carnegie Endowment in the Balkans after World War One', p. 7.

[50] Akhund, 'The World of the Carnegie Endowment in the Balkans after World War One', p. 6.

[51] M. R. Vesnitch to Butler, 20 April 1920; Haskell to Dodge, 22 June 1920, CURBML/CEIP, VII.Z, Box 320, Folder 21.

Louvain because, while extensive damage had been caused to the University of Belgrade by Austrian bombardment during the war, the proposed building was to be brand new, built as part of a new university campus planned by the Yugoslav government.

The Belgrade project was framed by its American backers as being part of the restoration and spread of civilization. Leo Capser, the CEIP representative who spent nine months in the Kingdom of Serbs, Croats and Slovenes in 1921, stated that the complex would mark 'an epoch in the cultural advancement of these people', meaning that 'technical and professional men' would no longer need to leave the country for an education.[52] In an interview with the *New York Times* in October 1921, Capser explained that he regarded the project as both a means of restoring Serbian intellectual life after the convulsions of the war, and of completing the spread of Euro-American civilization to the Balkans following the war.[53] Whereas the reconstruction of Louvain was framed as a reassertion of Europe's centuries-old civilization, the work at Belgrade university library was articulated as an endeavour of another nature.

While it was cloaked in the language of civilization, there was a strong element of American cultural diplomacy in the reconstruction of the library and the ceremonies surrounding it. The foundation stone for the new library was laid by Prince Alexander, the prince regent of the Kingdom of the Serbs, Croats and Slovenes, on 23 June 1921.[54] Busts of both Woodrow Wilson ('as he appeared during the Paris peace conference') and Andrew Carnegie were commissioned to take 'place of honour' in the new library building.[55] A few weeks after the foundation stone had been laid, the Yugoslav prime minister, Nikola Pasič, wrote to Capser to state that the gift of the library by the Endowment demonstrated 'the spirit of sympathy and interest so clearly indicated in this period of reconstruction [which] strengthens the bonds of a true friendship between our peoples'.[56] Both the Serbian and American national anthems were sung at the foundation stone laying ceremony. The library, which had capacity for 200,000 books, was finally

[52] Capser, 'A Report on the Library to be Erected at Belgrade', CURBML/CEIP, VII.Z: Box 320, Folder 21.

[53] Todorova, *Imagining the Balkans*, p. 130.

[54] Capser to CEIP, 24 June 1921, CURBML/CEIP, VII.Z: Box 320, Folder 21.

[55] 'Will Adorn Belgrade Hall of Study', *The Anaconda Standard*, 23 April 1922, p. 28; Akhund, 'The Work of the Carnegie Endowment in the Balkans after World War One', p. 7.

[56] Pasič to Capser, 30 July 1921, CURBML/CEIP, VII.Z: Box 320, Folder 21.

completed and opened in 1926.[57] Part of the collections to be held in the new library were those taken by occupying forces during the war and later returned to the new state.

The reconstruction of Belgrade university library encapsulated many of the themes of wartime. It reaffirmed Serbia's place in the hierarchy of allied states and reinforced the Serbian-American relationship. The new building, and its contents, were the result of Euro-American revulsion at cultural destruction which took place during the conflict. Baron Paul d'Estournelles de Constant, president of the CEIP's European office, wrote in 1921 that the reconstruction was 'a protest against the destructive vandalism of the Austro-German armies'.[58] However, unlike Louvain, the library at Belgrade was a means through which civilization's spread to the new Yugoslav state could be overseen by the steadying hand of the United States of America and the Carnegie Endowment for International Peace.

Louvain: Rebuilding an 'Ancient' Site of Learning

The destruction of the university library at Louvain by the German army in late August 1914 shocked the world of learning. It was cited by allied propagandists as evidence of the barbarism of the enemy and became a key way in which they sought to secure neutral opinion to their side.[59] The University of Louvain was founded in 1425 with its library building added in the seventeenth century. It housed important manuscript and incunabula collections which were, in the words of the librarian Paul Delannoy, 'priceless treasures' whose destruction had stunned the 'entire world'.[60] Images of the library, often presented in a 'before and after' form, were widely published in newspapers and periodicals around the world. *The Times* reported that the arson at Louvain was 'without a parallel even in the Dark Ages' and noted that books, too, 'were committed to the flames'.[61] Another newspaper

[57] Akhund, 'The Work of the Carnegie Endowment in the Balkans after World War One', p. 20.

[58] Paul d'Estournelles de Constant, 'Préface' to Justin Godart, *L'Albanie en 1921* (Paris, 1922), p. 18.

[59] Proctor 'The Louvain Library and US Ambition in Interwar Belgium', p. 150.

[60] Paul Delannoy, *L'Université de Louvain: conférences données au Collège de France en février 1915* (Paris, 1915), p. vii.

[61] 'Without a Parallel Even in the Dark Ages', *The Scotsman*, 29 August 1914, p. 5.

remarked that the destruction of Louvain marked a 'return to the barbarities of the Middle Ages'.[62]

The replacement of books, either with equivalent or similar items, was a means of demonstrating solidarity with Belgium and the wider allied cause. Attempts to rebuild the collections of the library emerged almost as soon as their destruction became known. A French committee, led by the historian Pierre Imbart de la Tour and based at the Institut de France, was organized as early as September 1914. In January 1915, the committee issued an international appeal for contributors.[63] By December 1914, Henry Guppy, the librarian at John Rylands Library in Manchester, had overseen a donation of 200 books to A.J. Carnoy of Louvain, who was temporarily based in Cambridge, while other learned societies issued public appeals for books.[64] The reconstruction of Louvain's collections soon became an internationally coordinated effort; in March 1915, the British Academy agreed to work with their counterparts at the Institut de France, so long as it did not 'weaken in any way the responsibility of the Germans in respect of the destruction of the Library'.[65] The academy formed two committees. One was a British committee with the mission of gathering books and which was led by former British ambassador to the USA, Viscount Bryce. A second committee was established to work closely with its French counterpart.[66] In 1915, a committee was formed in the United States to raise funds for the physical reconstruction of the library. Chaired by Nicholas Murray Butler, president of Columbia University, the committee only began raising funds formally after the armistice in 1918.[67]

---

[62] 'Another Great Library Gone', *The Indianapolis Star*, 22 June 1919, p. 64.
[63] Léon Mirot, 'France', *Œuvre Internationale de Louvain: Bulletin publié par le commissariat général*, 19–20 (1928), pp. 512–3.
[64] These included the Classical Association, the British Museum, the Bodleian Library, the Signet Library, the National Library of Wales, Victoria University of Manchester, and the universities of Aberdeen, Cambridge, Durham, and Oxford. Henry Guppy, 'The Reconstruction of the Library of the University of Louvain', *Bulletin of the John Rylands Library*, Manchester, 5.1–2 (August 1918-July March 1919, London, Manchester University Press, 1918–1920), p. 14.
[65] British Academy Council Meeting, 10 March 1915, BAA, Minutebook of the British Academy, 1912–1919, p. 66.
[66] British Academy Council Meeting, 5 May 1915, BAA, Minutebook of the British Academy, 1912–1919, p. 69; Council Meeting of 3 June 1915, BAA, Minutebook of the British Academy, 1912–1919, p. 74.
[67] Proctor, 'The Louvain Library and US Ambition in Interwar Belgium', p. 151.

The replacement of the collections of Louvain library led to the establishment of a more permanent international organization following the end of the conflict with the founding of the Œuvre internationale de Louvain in 1919. Directed by an international committee of scientists, artists, and writers, it was connected to a network of national committees who were charged with collecting books. A General Commissariat was set up at Louvain to coordinate the efforts of the national committees, and a regular bulletin was published detailing their efforts.[68] Committees were formed across Europe and the world, in neutral and allied countries alike. Denmark, Spain, France, Britain, Italy, Greece, Poland, Russia, Sweden, Switzerland, Czechoslovakia, Canada, the United States, Japan, and Belgium all formed bodies to rebuild Louvain's collections. Books were also sent from Brazil and Uruguay.[69] Support did not only come through national committees. Among the items destroyed in the fire of 1914 was the Papal Bull issued by Pope Martin V in 1425 which established the university. Following an appeal by the university to Pope Benedict XV in April 1915, the Vatican Library also pledged its backing.[70]

These committees all faced a similar dilemma: what books and manuscripts should furnish a new university library? The reconstruction of a library required reflection upon the type of knowledge it ought to house and how this material might be acquired. Reconstruction was not merely a manner of filling the shelves with books of any variety; rather, they had to be carefully selected, a process which looked both to the past and to the future. Looking back, valuable older manuscripts had been destroyed and needed to be replaced as manifestations of Belgian and universal heritage. Looking forward, consideration was given to what students might need to learn, what lecturers might need to teach, and what researchers might need to investigate. The reconstruction of Louvain library's collections posed fundamental questions about the hierarchy of importance in respect of knowledge within the symbolic reconstruction of a post-war state.

[68] *Œuvre Internationale de Louvain: Bulletin publié par le commissariat général*, 19–20 (1928), p. i.

[69] Committee Meeting, 3 December 1918, CURBML/CEIP, VII.AA, Box 321, Folder 3; 'Un comité russe pour la reconstitution de la bibliothèque de Louvain', *Le Matin*, 26 August 1916, p. 2. More information on French committees to restock Louvain can be found at AN/AJ/6962.

[70] Auguste Pelzer, 'Le Saint-Siège', *Œuvre Internationale de Louvain*, 19–20, pp. 506–9.

The Louvain library collections destroyed in 1914 had been accrued over centuries and included hundreds of manuscripts, incunabula, as well as large printed collections on medicine, law, and theology. Of the latter, the Jansenist collection, assembled between the sixteenth and eighteenth centuries, was especially notable. The issue of how these materials would be replaced – if indeed they should be directly replaced at all – preoccupied committees around the world and posed questions as to the way in which relief should be organized. Herbert Putnam, the Librarian of Congress in the United States who was a key figure in the American committee to rebuild Louvain library, argued that if the aim was to replace specific, expert collections, committees should seek cash rather than book donations, so that they could in turn make targeted purchases on the open market.[71] This presented particular problems for the United States, which hoped to take a symbolic role in overseeing the reconstruction of Louvain, as many of the rarer items such as incunabula were easier to source in Europe than the USA.[72] Putnam was experienced in the matter of building libraries quickly, having overseen the creation and stocking of War Camp libraries for the United States Army during the recently ended conflict.[73]

The logistical issues surrounding the acquisition of books posed a second question for these committees: what function should the new Louvain library serve? In England, Henry Guppy argued that despite the institution's history, the new library should be 'a live, up-to-date collection of books ... in which provision is made for the study of everything useful in the development of mind and matter'.[74] Across the Atlantic Ocean, Nicholas Murray Butler claimed that Louvain needed to decide whether it wanted a 'theological and philosophical library' which typified the library's history, or a collection with broader representation to serve 'a modern body of scholars'.[75] Herbert Putnam remarked that Louvain was not a library for instruction, but a research library, where completeness could never be attained.[76] In the spring of

---

[71] Committee Meeting, 3 December 1918, CURBML/CEIP, VII.AA, Box 321, Folder 3.

[72] Putnam, 4 December 1918, CURBML/CEIP, VII.AA, Box 321, Folder 3.

[73] RAC/RF, SG 1.1, Series 100, Box 78, Folder 731.

[74] Guppy, 'The Reconstruction of the Library of the University of Louvain', p. 4.

[75] Committee Meeting, 3 December 1918, CURBML/CEIP, VII.AA, Box 321, Folder 3.

[76] Committee Meeting, 3 December 1918, CURBML/CEIP, VII.AA, Box 321, Folder 3.

1919, the university's rector, Paulin Ladeuze, stated that he wanted a library that was 'satisfactory to modern scholars', in addition to original incunabula and manuscripts to replace those that had been destroyed.[77] Thus, the decision was taken not to fully replicate the old library's collections, but to complement older materials with more modern acquisitions.

The process of constituting a committee and then identifying, gathering, and sending books to Louvain provided a mechanism through which intellectuals could perform their membership of the wider world of learning. National committees approached the challenge in various ways but generally provided collections of books that were representative of their own 'national' achievement. In this way, the reconstruction of Louvain's collections became a tool of cultural diplomacy, a reminder of wartime alliances, and a means through which national committees could emphasize their contribution to European civilization. The British committee specifically asked that publications be 'representative of English scholarship' and sought contributions from particular learned institutions such as the British Academy and the Royal Historical Society.[78] The Swedish committee sent 'a rich and varied choice of Swedish scientific literature' in two shipments, one in 1923 and a second in 1928.[79] The Czechoslovak committee, established in 1921, sent 2,600 volumes including Czech vocabularies and dictionaries, reproductions of the works of Czech painters, as well as scientific, theological, philosophical, historical, and philological reviews.[80] Kristoffer Nyrop, the chair of the Danish committee, wrote that 'the library of Louvain now possesses the richest collection of Danish scientific books which exists outside of the borders of Denmark'.[81] The American committee provided 27,086 books for

---

[77] 'Memorandum on the Restoration of the University of Louvain', 29 March 1919, CURBML/CEIP, VII.AA, Box 321, Folder 3. See Wolfgang Schivelbusch, *Die Bibliothek von Löwen: eine Episode aus der Zeit der Weltkriege* (Munich, 1988), p. 58.

[78] By the time the library reopened in 1928, the committee had provided 55,193 volumes. Guppy, 'The Reconstruction of the Library of the University of Louvain', pp. 17–8. Henry Guppy, 'Grande-Bretagne', *Œuvre Internationale de Louvain*, 19–20, p. 518.

[79] Axel Nelson, 'Suède', *Œuvre Internationale de Louvain*, 19–20, p. 526.

[80] F. Bous, 'Tchécoslovaquie', *Œuvre Internationale de Louvain*, 19–20, pp. 527–8.

[81] Kristoffer Nyrop, 'Danemark', *Œuvre Internationale de Louvain*, 19–20, p. 510.

Louvain by 1928, with publications drawn from the government, learned societies, universities, and publishers, covering a wide range of disciplines. Putnam described the American contribution as constituting 'an abundant range of material for a working library'.[82]

Perhaps unsurprisingly, the French committee also strongly emphasized the national composition of its donations to Louvain. It took a slightly broader approach than other committees; Léon Mirot, the committee's secretary, stated that it aimed to provide books, to decorate the reconstructed university halls, and to offer teaching and courses in Louvain to equip Belgians with a knowledge of 'French thought and science'. The French committee provided over 80,000 volumes, with books mostly sourced from government departments, learned societies and academies, and universities. A national appeal for funds was circulated in educational institutions, resulting in the collection of 250,000 francs to purchase collections for Louvain. Mirot claimed that cash donations were particularly numerous in Alsace and Lorraine. For their part, Belgian children reciprocated this gesture by donating 232,431 francs to French libraries which had been damaged or destroyed in the war.[83]

Beyond books that embodied the current state of national learning, national committees also attempted to contribute to historic collections. The French committee, for example, oversaw the transfer of specific collections to Louvain, such as the Jansenist library that formerly belonged to the historian Augustin Gazier, who had died in March 1922.[84] The Greek committee donated 700 volumes mainly from learned societies, 30,000 drachmas (from the Greek government), and a collection of 148 castings mostly from the Alexandrian and Roman periods.[85] In Poland, a committee was formed in the summer of 1920 which sent over a thousand books, including a 1716 edition by the seventeenth-century Portuguese legal scholar Agostinho Barbosa in sixteen folio volumes.[86] The Japanese committee collected 15,000 books which emphasized 'the development of Japanese civilization' as

---

[82] Herbert Putnam, 'États Unis d'Amérique', *Œuvre Internationale de Louvain*, 19–20, p. 532.

[83] Mirot, 'France', pp. 513–6.

[84] 'Le dernier Janséniste' *Le Gaulois*, 3 December 1922, p. 1. Mirot, 'France', p. 515.

[85] A. Andréadès, 'Grèce', Léon Mirot, 'France', pp. 522–3.

[86] E. Majkowski, 'Pologne', *Œuvre Internationale de Louvain*, 19–20, pp. 525–6.

well as older items which it hoped could be used to replace Louvain's destroyed incunabula. Among these donations, the rarest was the Jakushitsuroku, a collection edited by Buddhists under the name Gozan in the fourteenth century, as well as Buddhist manuscript fragments from the ninth and tenth centuries, and other editions from the seventeenth century.[87]

The formation of national committees to rebuild Louvain's collections constituted, in many cases, a reaffirmation of wartime alliances. The involvement of Germany in this process was complicated because the ex-enemy state was not allowed to participate on its own terms. In 1915, the librarian Fritz Milkau proposed collecting books in Germany to restore Louvain library, but the project was dropped for fear that it would be rejected by Belgium.[88] Similarly, in 1918, the French newspaper *L'Illustration* claimed that German Benedictines had offered, via the Vatican, to pay for the reconstruction of Louvain library but that the offer was rejected.[89]

The issue of German participation in the restoration of Louvain was an emotive one. From the allied point of view, Germany needed to be involved in replacing the works in an expiatory sense, but without exercising any agency over the process. This was achieved through the inclusion of article 247 in the Treaty of Versailles. The Belgian government petitioned the Paris Peace Conference in April 1919 to require Germany to restore some of the contents of Louvain library as an 'equitable compensation' for wartime damage.[90] The resulting article required Germany to furnish 'the University of Louvain [with] manuscripts, incunabula, printed books, maps and objects of collection corresponding in number and value to those destroyed in the burning by Germany of the Library of Louvain', all as part of its reparation commitments. Article 247 also named two works of art, the triptych of the Mystic Lamb by the Van Eyck brothers and the triptych of the Last Supper by Dierick Bouts, both of which were acquired legitimately by German museums, as requiring return to Belgium, as restitution-in-kind for cultural loss more generally.[91]

---

[87] 'Japon', *Œuvre Internationale de Louvain*, 19–20, p. 532–3.
[88] Schivelbusch, *Die Bibliothek von Löwen*, p. 56.
[89] 'Le crime allemand de Louvain,' *l'Illustration*, 14 September 1918, p. 262.
[90] Hymans to Clemenceau, 22 April 1919, TNA/FO 608/2.
[91] Article 247, The Treaty of Versailles, avalon.law.yale.edu/subject_menus/ versailles_menu.asp [accessed 1 August 2022]; Horne and Kramer, *German Atrocities 1914*, p. 387; Sandholtz, *Prohibiting Plunder*, p. 114, 117.

The vagueness of article 247 led some German librarians to fear – incorrectly – that their collections could be pillaged to compensate Belgium.[92] The restitution of books, manuscripts, and incunabula was a difficult task; a committee at Louvain liaised with German representatives over twelve months to establish the value of destroyed items and to identify suitable replacements. The Louvain committee presented lists of desired books to their German counterparts, while the latter issued circulars to libraries across Germany to identify duplicates in collections. Books were also sourced from the personal collections of recently deceased German professors. The Belgian committee, led by Louis Stainier, used some of the cash reparations due to them to purchase libraries on the open market. In total, private purchases (around 250,000 books in total) constituted the bulk of the books which Germany provided to Louvain.[93] By April 1922, Germany had made reparation to the value of 816,276.01 gold marks under the terms of article 247.[94] The two other items named in article 247, the Van Eyck and Bouts pieces respectively, were both returned to Belgium quickly; Van Eyck's Mystical Lamb was part of a touring exhibition which began in Brussels in August 1920 and concluded in Ghent. An account published in a French periodical claimed that the return of this item caused joy not only to art experts but also to the crowd who saw in it 'the symbol of the justice of their cause [and] a homage to their suffering and their energy'.[95]

By the time it formally opened on 4 July 1928, the library had received 750,000 volumes from around the world.[96] The collection of books for Louvain was a smoother process than the physical reconstruction of the buildings. Nicholas Murray Butler headed the American committee to rebuild Louvain and initial funding was provided by the Carnegie Endowment for International Peace, but, by the early 1920s, it proved difficult to raise the requisite funds to begin the reconstruction of the library buildings. It was not until 1925, with

[92] Schivelbush, *Die Bibliothek von Löwen*, pp. 61–2; 'À Louvain: une lettre de Mgr. Ladeuze', *Revue des deux mondes*, 46 (1928), p. 695.

[93] Schivelbusch, *Die Bibliothek von Löwen*, pp. 62–70.

[94] *Reparation Commission. Statement of Germany's Obligations: Under the Heading of Reparations, etc., at April 30th, 1922* (London, 1922), p. 16.

[95] E. Michel, 'Correspondence de Belgique', *La Chronique des Arts*, 15 October 1920, p. 136.

[96] Frank Pierrepont Graves, 'Report on the Dedication of the Library Building at the University of Louvain', CURBML/CEIP, VII.AA, Box 321, Folder 3, p. 22.

belated contributions coming from John D. Rockefeller, Jr, that funds had been gathered which enabled construction of the new building – led by the American architect Whitney Warren – to begin.[97]

At the outset of his project, Butler had noted that any project that sought to raise money for Louvain would by definition need to reopen wartime issues. This meant reviving feelings of 'dismay, of indignation and of rage at the character and extent of the loss'.[98] This issue became more pronounced as the library neared completion in 1926, when discourse surrounding the proposed inscription for the balustrade, '*Furore Teutonico Diruta, Dono Americano Restituta*' ('destroyed by German fury; restored by American gift'), turned bitterly divisive. Initially proposed by Cardinal Mercier and enthusiastically adopted by Warren, the inscription reflected wartime antipathies that seemed out of keeping with the spirit of reconciliation that followed the Locarno treaties of 1925.[99] It meant that when the library was formally reopened in July 1928, the controversy about the inscription attracted much attention, with Warren refusing to budge on the inscription and the rector Ladeuze seeking a conciliatory middle-ground position; ultimately, the university authorities erected a 'blank' balustrade and prevented Warren from constructing a version bearing his inscription.[100]

Beyond the much-publicized controversy over the inscription, the speeches given at the inauguration of the new library used the language of intellectual reconstruction, international cooperation, and humanitarianism. The American representative Frank Pierrepont Graves spoke of the challenges of restoring a site of 'intellectual and spiritual riches'. Graves, who was the commissioner of the New York State Education Department, suggested that the reconstruction of Louvain was an affirmation of civilization which had been dealt a critical, but not fatal, blow during the war; he claimed that 'restoring these walls and furnishing anew this treasure house of civilization' was the greatest

---

[97] Proctor, 'The Louvain Library and US Ambition in Interwar Belgium', pp. 152–8.

[98] 'Conference with Dr. Butler in his office, April 11, 1919', CURBML/CEIP, VII. AA, Box 321, Folder 3.

[99] Horne, 'Demobilizing the Mind: France and the Legacy of the Great War, 1919-1939', pp. 101–19.

[100] Proctor, 'The Louvain Library and US Ambition in Interwar Belgium', pp. 160–4.

opportunity which had ever presented itself to service 'humanity and progress'.[101]

Cardinal van Roey, president of the board of trustees of Louvain, argued that the new library would be guarded as a 'sacred trust' for the 'civilized world' and a 'the symbol of the spiritual solidarity of the nations'. Van Roey also spoke of intellectual relief, arguing that feeding the mind was as important as keeping people's bodies alive. 'Man does not live by bread alone', he claimed, and the reconstruction of Louvain library was a humanitarian act to 'restore our intellectual life by giving to the University of Louvain a library worthy of its glorious past and worthy of its martyrdom'.[102]

'The Sympathy of the World': Tokyo Imperial University Library

On 1 September 1923 a major earthquake struck Japan, which destroyed ninety per cent of the city of Yokohama, forty-five per cent of the city of Tokyo, and killed 100,000 people.[103] Among the casualties of the earthquake was Tokyo Imperial University, which was widely regarded as Japan's leading university and described by British Foreign Minister Lord Curzon as 'the training ground of almost all the future officials of the Japanese Government'.[104] The library of Tokyo Imperial University and its 700,000 volumes were destroyed in the earthquake and ensuing fire.[105] Whole collections of books on subjects such as history, law, languages, and religion were destroyed, alongside rare manuscripts, picture scrolls, and old prints.[106] In Europe and

---

[101] Graves, 'Report on the Dedication of the Library Building at the University of Louvain', pp. 12–4.

[102] Graves, 'Report on the Dedication of the Library Building at the University of Louvain', pp. 13–4.

[103] J. Charles Schencking, 'Giving Most and Giving Differently': Humanitarianism as Diplomacy Following Japan's 1923 Earthquake', *Diplomatic History*, 43.4 (2019), p. 733.

[104] Curzon to Balfour, 20 October 1923, BAA, Minutebook of the British Academy 1919–1924, pp. 187–8.

[105] The library of Meiji University and its 60,000 volumes was also destroyed by the earthquake.

[106] 'The Reconstruction of the Tokyo Imperial University Library', *The International Supplement of the Imperial University News*, 1 November 1926, in RAC/OMR, Series G, Box 130, Folder 994, p.12.

North America, the swift reconstruction of this library was regarded as an imperative in much the same way as Louvain library had been.

The rebuilding of knowledge in the wake of the First World War was a global phenomenon, albeit one that saw 'civilized' Europe at its heart. The timeframes for reconstruction extended far beyond the war itself and thus came to encompass events that followed in its wake, such as the Great Kantō earthquake. The reconstitution of knowledge was not only about sites of particular importance; the establishment of committees, publication of appeals, and accumulation of replacement books by these committees were all ways through which Euro-American civilization was performed and civilizational values were reaffirmed. The reconstruction of sites outside of Europe and North America reveals much about attitudes towards knowledge in those places. Moreover, it means that initiatives which took place in the immediate post-war period, when civilization seemed to be encountering an existential threat, are essential to this discussion, albeit they took place after the end of the war itself.

The stories of Louvain and Tokyo are closely connected. The destruction of the library at Louvain was seen as an attack on civilization that emanated from the barbarism of wartime. Japanese participation in the reconstruction of Louvain library was framed as a means through which Japan could perform its own role as a 'civilized' state. An account of Japanese contributions to Louvain's reconstruction stated that the reforms of the Meiji period meant that it was in a position to help its Belgian counterpart because 'for a quarter of a century bibliomania has developed considerably in Japanese high society and among Japanese intellectuals'.[107] Japan also participated in post-war intellectual reconstruction by establishing a chair in Japanese Civilization at the Sorbonne in 1920. Libraries such as that of Tokyo Imperial University were much newer than those in Europe's 'ancient universities'; their construction in the late nineteenth century was viewed by European intellectuals, as was the case with Serbia, as evidence that Japan 'belonged' to the civilized world. Japanese appeals issued following the 1923 earthquake also emphasized not 'selfish motive[s]', but 'the future civilization of Japan'.[108]

---

[107] 'Japon', *Œuvre Internationale de Louvain*, 19–20, p. 533.
[108] T. Fujimori to 'President of Oxford University', 24 December 1923, BAA/DWP/3/2/1/3/4.

As J. Charles Schencking has shown, Japan was the recipient of an unprecedented American humanitarian outpouring in which it was given unusual agency to shape the manner in which aid was distributed and used. Schencking calls this 'humanitarianism as diplomacy', in which aid was deployed to promote a state's interest.[109] Intellectual relief to Japan did not deviate significantly from the pattern which had been established during and following the First World War; in certain cases, committees which had been set up to rebuild Louvain library were simply reconstituted with the same membership and procedures to rebuild Tokyo Imperial University library. The British Academy, for example, decided to follow the precedent it had set through how it dealt with Louvain. Former prime minister Arthur Balfour was chosen to chair the committee but remarked that while 'I appear to have been mixed up in the Louvain scheme, I have very little recollection of it'.[110]

Following the earthquake, accounts of the destruction of Tokyo quickly made their way around the world and began to reach intellectual audiences; descriptions of the damage done to TIU's library were, however, less widespread than those dedicated to Louvain during and after the war. In Britain, discussions of the losses to the university library appeared around December 1923, when the British Academy held a meeting to discuss its response to the crisis.[111] In the United States, newspapers began to discuss the matter only once representatives of Tokyo Imperial University arrived in the United States to seek intellectual aid.[112] In France, Serge Eliséev wrote an article about earthquake damage for *L'Europe Nouvelle* in which he speculated about the potential damage to university and library buildings without providing specific details.[113]

---

[109] Schenking, 'Giving most and giving differently', pp. 729–31.

[110] Balfour to Israel Gollancz, 24 October 1923, BAA, Minutebook of the British Academy 1919–1924, p. 190.

[111] 'Books for Japan', *Sheffield Daily Telegraph*, 11 December 1923, p. 8; 'Books for Tokyo University', *The Scotsman*, 10 December 1923, p. 7.

[112] 'Japan Appeals to US to Aid Her Libraries Burned in Disaster', *San Pedro Daily Pilot*, 1 January 1924, p. 8; 'Japan Wants US to Aid Libraries', *The Plain Speaker*, 24 January 1924, p. 6.

[113] Eliséev was a Russian scholar who had been educated in Germany and Japan before taking up a teaching post in St Petersburg, which he was forced to flee, before ultimately settling in Paris. Serge Eliséev, 'Tokyo et Yokohama en ruines', *L'Europe Nouvelle*, 8 September 1923, p. 1139.

The reconstruction of TIU library did not require the same mobilization of public support as that for Louvain library, which was understandable given its post-war timeframe. Much of the communication regarding the extent of damage was undertaken through personal correspondence and individual networks. The organization of intellectual relief to Japan targeted individuals who had previously been engaged in similar projects or who might prove sympathetic to them. Japanese embassies across the world were asked to request that universities, learned societies, and

Figure 5.3 Anesaki Masaharu, librarian at Tokyo Imperial University, sits amidst the ruins of the library in the aftermath of the Great Kantō earthquake (© Rockefeller Archive Center)

individuals provide assistance.[114] The visual nature of the destruction of the library was an important means of illustrating Tokyo's plight and photographs of the flattened site that had once housed the library were sent to potentially sympathetic benefactors overseas.

At a meeting of the Assembly of the League of Nations on 27 September 1923, the League's Committee on Intellectual Cooperation was asked to explore how international assistance might be garnered to support the reconstruction of TIU library.[115] In November 1923, Nitobe Inazō, an under-secretary-general to the League of Nations and a Japanese national, submitted an official appeal to the ICIC on behalf of the Tokyo Imperial University library. The appeal argued that because Tokyo was Japan's capital city, its reconstruction was 'not merely that of a town or a city, but of the capital of the whole nation'; its libraries, museums, and educational institutions were therefore imbued with a particular importance. Nitobe specifically highlighted the needs of Tokyo Imperial University.[116] Nitobe knew well that while the ICIC did not have vast budgets to pursue intellectual reconstruction of this nature, it did have moral authority given the eminence of some of its members, and had, in November 1922, published an international appeal to request that books be sent to Austria, under the coordination of the League. Nitobe himself had been a key figure in the organization of this effort.[117] The president of Tokyo Imperial University, Kozai Yoshinao, also wrote to the secretary general of the League, Eric Drummond, seeking institutional support.[118] In February 1924, the ICIC issued an international appeal which called on 'the spirit of solidarity of the whole world' and asked them to send books to Japanese embassies and legations.[119]

As their Belgian counterparts had done in 1914 and 1915, Japan sent representatives to North America and Europe to raise awareness of the needs of its libraries. In November 1923 Takayanagi Kenzō, professor

[114] Request on behalf of the University Library of Tokyo, 29 November 1923. LNA/R1059/13/32411/31006.
[115] Henri Bergson letter, 6 February 1924, LNA/R1059/13/32411/31006.
[116] Request on behalf of the University Library of Tokyo, 29 November 1923. LNA/R1059/13/32411/31006.
[117] Irish, 'The "Moral Basis" of Reconstruction?' pp. 791–2.
[118] Kozai to Drummond, 8 November 1923, LNA/R1059/13/32411/31006.
[119] Appeal of ICIC, 6 February 1924, LNA/R1059/13/32411/31006.

of law at Tokyo Imperial University, arrived in the United States for this purpose.[120] He met with General William Verbeck, who had formed a committee to provide relief for TIU not long after the earthquake. Verbeck felt that the example of the then-stalled project to fund the reconstruction of Louvain library, in large part by public appeal, suggested that Tokyo should try a different approach; rather than trying to raise money from a range of American institutions and donors, he encouraged Takayanagi to approach one very well-resourced donor: John D. Rockefeller, Jr.[121] Verbeck put Takayanagi in contact with Kenneth Chorley, a close associate of Rockefeller.

By February 1924, a long report on the needs of Tokyo Imperial University sat on Rockefeller's desk.[122] The report proposed two potential routes which cut to the core of issues relating to philanthropy and intellectual relief in the early 1920s. One suggested course of action was to replace the books for the library. The report cited expert opinions of librarians at Yale and Michigan universities who felt that 'too high a value has been placed on the loss of the books'.[123] Andrew Keogh, the librarian at Yale University, stated that Rockefeller should provide the books because the 'the function of a library in a university is, first, to provide books; second, to provide service; and third, to provide an appropriate building'.[124] The report acknowledged that while provision of books would be more in the interests of the university, reconstruction of the building would be 'more effective politically' because 'a building designed by American architects, built to be earthquake proof and fireproof, by American builders, along the best American library lines' would be a 'standing monument' in Tokyo.[125] The latter course of action was selected and Rockefeller awarded a grant of four million yen towards the reconstruction of the library building.[126] The American philanthropist made a number of other donations to libraries in the inter-war period. In 1925 Rockefeller

---

[120]   Frederick F. Russell to Kenneth Chorley, 14 August 1924, RAC/OMR, Series G, Box 130, Folder 995.
[121]   Verbeck to Chorley, 17 April 1924, RAC/OMR, Series G, Box 130, Folder 995.
[122]   'Library of the Imperial University of Tokyo', 8 February 1924, RAC/OMR, Series G, Box 130, Folder 995.
[123]   'Library of the Imperial University of Tokyo', p 5.
[124]   'Library of the Imperial University of Tokyo', p. 10.
[125]   'Library of the Imperial University of Tokyo', p 9.
[126]   Anesaki and Yamada, 'First Report on the Reconstruction of the Tokyo Imperial University Library', pp. 2–3.

pledged $100,000 to the reconstruction of Louvain library and in 1927 he agreed to give $2 million towards the construction of a library for the League of Nations in Geneva.[127] He also funded the reconstruction of Reims Cathedral.[128] Excavation of the new Tokyo site began in 1926 and building was completed by 1928.

Rockefeller's philanthropic approach left the library in need of books and, as was the case with the University of Louvain, committees quickly formed around the world to source appropriate materials. In France, a committee was established at the Musée Guimet in Paris under the stewardship of Charles Maistre, an expert in Japanese culture.[129] Committees were also set up in Belgium, Netherlands, Sweden, Switzerland, Spain, Italy, Greece, China, Siam, and the Vatican.[130] Unlike Louvain or Belgrade libraries, ex-enemy universities had more autonomy in contributing to the international appeal; the University of Vienna and twelve German universities did so.[131] Some German reparation money was paid in books to the Japanese government, and in turn sent to the Imperial University in Tokyo. Anesaki Masaharu, the TIU librarian, reported in 1928 that 'we have recently acquired three remarkable libraries collected by German professors'.[132] By February 1926, the Imperial University had acquired 409,000 volumes as donations and purchased an additional 552,500.[133] In total, 77,000 books came from the United States, with Britain (27,300), Germany (22,800), China (20,000), and France (15,300) all contributing substantially.[134]

---

[127] 'Contributions to Libraries', RAC/OMR, Series E, Box 3, Folder 20.

[128] James Allen Smith, 'An Internationalism of Beauty: The Rockefeller Restorations in France after the Great War', *The Tocqueville Review/La Revue Tocqueville*, 38.2 (2017), pp. 241–51.

[129] 'Dans les ruines d'une ville d'art', *Bulletin de la vie artistique*, 15 September 1923, p. 392.

[130] 'The Reconstruction of the Tokyo Imperial University Library', p.12.

[131] The full list of German universities was: Berlin, Breslau, Bonn, Frankfurt, Göttingen, Greifswald, Halle, Kiel, Königsberg (modern-day Kaliningrad), Marburg, Münster, as well as the Academy of Music in Berlin. Appendix I, List of Donors from Abroad, in *First Report on the Reconstruction of the Tokyo Imperial University Library* pp. 16–29.

[132] Anesaki to John D. Rockefeller Jr, 20 May 1928, RAC/OMR, Series G, Box 130, Folder 996.

[133] Anesaki and Yamada, 'First Report on the Reconstruction of the Tokyo Imperial University Library', p. 11.

[134] 'The Reconstruction of the Tokyo Imperial University Library', p.12.

While there was a global response to Tokyo's need, the United States was widely seen as taking a leading role. The journalist K.K. Kawakami wrote that 'the American government, American Universities, libraries, and various institutions of learning are literally pouring out books in an endeavour to help rehabilitate the Japanese libraries destroyed in the recent holocaust'. Recycling the intellectual sustenance metaphor which appeared in post-war Austria and Russia, Kawakami stated that 'America, which has sent to the earthquake-stricken country food and clothes with unparalleled generosity, is now sending "intellectual food" with equal generosity'.[135] Anesaki wrote in 1926 that the USA led the way and 'later on, help came from Europe and Asia'.[136]

American responses to the calamity were numerous. David Starr Jordan, the former president of Stanford University, circulated an appeal to colleges and libraries across the United States, as did Nicholas Murray Butler, in his capacity as president of the Division of Intercourse and Education of the CEIP.[137] The Library of Congress gathered 1,358 volumes, including three sets of the publications of the Library of Congress itself. The Smithsonian Institution at Washington agreed to ship all government publications to New York, where Japanese vessels arranged their onward transportation to Japan. Of the country's universities, Yale, Minnesota, Pennsylvania, Iowa, Wisconsin, Missouri, and Chicago provided books. Donations were also made in cash, including $5,000 from J.P. Morgan for the purchase of books on English literature and $1,000 from the Seattle Chamber of Commerce for the purchase of law books.[138]

While the United States took the lead in rebuilding TIU's library, Britain also sought to conduct cultural diplomacy through its humanitarian response. The British committee, organized through the British Academy, explicitly stated that it existed 'to evince our sympathy with Japan by means of this tribute to its intellectual life'. The same document noted anxiety regarding international rivalry in aiding Japan, and argued that it was of the 'utmost importance' not to 'fall behind other

---

[135] K. K. Kawakami, 'American Books to Rehabilitate Japan's Lost Libraries', no date, CURBML/CEIP, VII.Z: Box 320, Folder 12.

[136] 'Professor Anesaki Working to Rebuild Great Library', *The Japan Advertiser*, 10 October 1926, in RAC/OMR, Series G, Box 130, Folder 994.

[137] 'Professor Anesaki Working to Rebuild Great Library'; Henry Haskell to Osawa Yuki, 12 February 1924, CURBML/CEIP, VII.Z: Box 320, Folder 12.

[138] K. K. Kawakami, 'American Books to Rehabilitate Japan's Lost Libraries', no date, CURBML/CEIP, VII.Z: Box 320, Folder 12.

countries in maintaining a strong position for English books in all department of literature and learning in Japan'.[139] The BA worked closely with the British Foreign Office; Balfour chaired a body called the Government Fund Committee which connected the learned society to government. This meant that the BA's committee was linked to the British Embassy in Tokyo and could identify and purchase books for the library.

The British committee faced the same dilemmas as had the Louvain committees in determining which books were essential to a modern library. The committee purchased books identified as necessary by the Japanese university, assessed donations provided by the general public, but otherwise decided to purchase volumes 'representative of British scholarship, particularly in the domains of humanities'.[140] The British government also contributed £25,000 towards the purchase of books for Japan, including 'a really representative collection of English literature'.[141] Before the British books were shipped to Japan, an exhibition was held on 9 May 1929 at the Foreign Office to illustrate the history of English printing.[142] By the end of the scheme, a total of 35,639 books had been sent from Britain in 296 cases.[143]

The new library building opened in 1928, in the same year as did Louvain library. In his speech at the dedication, Onozuka Kiheiji, acting president of the university, stated his hope that the event would strengthen American-Japanese relations, but argued that the entire scheme exemplified the 'mutual cooperation among the civilized nations in matters concerning science and education'.[144] A similar tone was struck in a statement read on behalf of the American ambassador to Japan, which stated that the international response to Japan's misfortune was evidence that 'scholarship is international'.[145] The British

---

[139] Israel Gollancz circular, c1924, BAA/DWP/3/2/1/3/4.

[140] 'The Reconstruction of the Tokyo Imperial University Library', p.12.

[141] D. W. Pearson to the Foreign Office, 21 December 1933, in Japan no. 1 (1934). *Report on the British Gift of Books to the Tokyo Imperial University Library, 1923–1933* (London: His Majesty's Stationery Office, 1934), p. 4.

[142] *Report on the British Gift of Books to the Tokyo Imperial University Library*, p. 7.

[143] *Report on the British Gift of Books to the Tokyo Imperial University Library*, p. 8.

[144] 'Address by Professor Kiheiji Onozuka', RAC/OMR, Series G, Box 130, Folder 996.

[145] 'Address by Mr. Neville', RAC/OMR, Series G, Box 130, Folder 996.

Figure 5.4 Book stacks at the new library of Tokyo Imperial University (© Rockefeller Archive Center)

ambassador to Japan spoke of world peace and his hope that the library would be 'a powerful influence in promoting the welfare of humanity'.[146] Cumulatively, the speeches emphasized themes of international cooperation and peace while also reaffirming the USA's leading role in the project of reconstruction.

The response to the Japanese disaster was framed in the same language as that for Louvain relief and ultimately mobilized many of the same actors. As with Louvain, in addition to symbolically reinforcing the status of a 'civilized' state, the donations sought to strengthen bilateral relations between different states and to emphasize the strong diplomatic links binding them. The difference, of course, was that TIU had not been destroyed by war, but by natural disaster, and so its

---

[146] 'Address by the British Ambassador', RAC/OMR, Series G, Box 130, Folder 996.

restoration was not a question of expiation. Ex-enemy states participated in reconstruction schemes as equals, without being required to
provide reparation for war damage as in Louvain. At the same time, the
reconstruction of TIU library owed much to the projects that had taken
place in Belgrade and Louvain and the infrastructures that had been put
in place to identify, assemble, and dispatch books to destroyed libraries. More generally, the TIU project was a product of the post-war
anxieties about lost knowledge and its implications for civilization, as
was the case in Europe following the First World War. In this context,
the act of replacing books, undertaken by committees around the
world, was as meaningful a means of performing intellectual reconstruction as was the digging of foundations or the laying of bricks.

Conclusion

'The destruction of a library, large or small', declared an international
appeal in the spring of 1921, 'always appears a crime against humanity,
a violation of the sacred neutrality of the world of letters, art and
scholarship', irrespective of whether it was 'Alexandria, Louvain or
Cork'.[147] The appeal in question sought books for the public library in
Cork, which had been burned to the ground in December 1920 during
the Irish War of Independence. In the Greater War – the continuation of
violence across Europe after the armistice of 1918 – cultural institutions such as libraries would remain at risk, either as intentional targets
or collateral damage in the fighting and unrest that swept across vast
swathes of Europe.[148]

The symbolic reconstruction of the libraries at Louvain, Belgrade,
and Tokyo took place against this backdrop of violence. In 1920 it was
reported that the university at Kamianets-Podilskyi in Ukraine had
been destroyed and the 'library and archives burned' during fighting
in the Russian Civil War.[149] In the same year, Jean Efremoff – who had
been a minister in the Provisional Government before the Bolshevik
takeover – wrote that 'a great number of books had been destroyed in
Russia'. He urged the Carnegie Endowment to purchase the collections

---

[147] 'Cork People Appeal for Books for their Library', *The Scranton Times*, 26 May
1921, p. 24.
[148] See Gerwarth, *The Vanquished*.
[149] 'Progress of Ukrainian Offensive', *Edinburgh Evening News*, 28 September
1920, p. 5.

of impoverished displaced Russian scholars in order to replace collections in their homeland.[150] In the summer of 1922, the Public Record Office of Ireland (PROI), which housed documents up to seven centuries old, was destroyed during the Irish Civil War. Herbert Wood, deputy keeper of the PROI, wrote that the contents were either 'consumed by the intense heat' or 'scattered by the winds of heaven over the city and suburbs', leaving the new Irish state 'like a new country almost without a history'.[151] In the same year, the American College at Smyrna was destroyed by the invading Turkish forces.[152] This was widely reported upon in the United States, with first-hand testimonies provided by survivors; one recalled that 'all the institution buildings were burned and there is no chance of re-establishing the work there'.[153]

The persistence of violence in the early 1920s made the task of symbolic reconstruction all the more urgent while also demonstrating its limits. There were no international appeals on the scale of those for Louvain or Tokyo to rebuild institutions destroyed in post-1918 fighting. As symbolic sites of reconstruction, the power of their message about the resilience of institutions of knowledge lay in the fact that only a few carefully selected institutions were chosen for focus. This selectiveness meant that the reconstruction of these libraries was deeply meaningful and provided a means of articulating ideas about strong bilateral alliances, international cooperation, and peace. Fundamentally, all three reconstruction projects were shaped by narratives of cultural decline and the solidarities engendered by alliance which emerged from the First World War. As intellectuals ruminated about the fate of civilization, the rebuilding of these libraries was a modest but symbolic act intended to arrest cultural collapse and perpetuate alliances of learning engendered in conflict.

---

[150] Jean Efremoff to d'Estournelles de Constant, 13 March 1920, CURBML/CEIP Centre Européen, Box 144, Folder 2.

[151] Herbert Wood, 'The Public Records of Ireland before and after 1922', *Transactions of the Royal Historical Society*, Fourth Series, 13 (1930), pp. 36, 48.

[152] Smyrna is now known as Izmir.

[153] 'Survivors Tell Wierd [sic] Stories', *Greenville Daily News*, 6 December 1922, p. 4.

6 | *Who Were the Intellectuals?*

In September 1922, Winifred Coombe Tennant travelled to Geneva to represent the British Empire at the League of Nations Assembly. A suffrage activist, patron of the arts, and spiritualist, she became the first woman to represent Britain at an international diplomatic gathering. Among the many events that she attended, Coombe Tennant recalled the most 'wonderful sight', a sitting of the League's Council, at which distinguished international statesmen such as Léon Bourgeois, Arthur Balfour, and the League's Secretary General Sir Eric Drummond were present. 'Before them a little old white-haired somewhat Jewish man was sitting, gently and delicately pouring out the most perfect French "discours" I have ever heard.'[1] The man in question was Henri Bergson, the eminent French philosopher who had recently been appointed chair of the newly formed International Committee on Intellectual Cooperation, a body set up by the League to address scientific, educational, and cultural issues.[2] It was Bergson's responsibility to report on the ICIC's activities to the Council for the latter's approval.[3] Bergson spoke to a chamber filled with politicians, journalists, private secretaries, and interpreters. He was, Coombe Tennant recorded, 'pleading for intellectual co-operation', and stated that it was the duty of 'all men and all nations who have at heart the

---

[1] WGAS/WCTP/D/DT 3978, pp. 26–7.

[2] Jo-Anne Pemberton, 'The Changing Shape of Intellectual Co-operation: From the League of Nations to UNESCO', *Australian Journal of Politics and History* 58. 1 (2012), pp. 34–50; Renoliet, *L'UNESCO oubliée*; Laqua, 'Transnational Intellectual Cooperation, the League of Nations, and the Problem of Order', pp. 223–47; Jimena Canales, 'Einstein, Bergson, and the Experiment that Failed: Intellectual Cooperation at the League of Nations', *Modern Language Notes* 120.5 (2005), pp. 1168–91; Corinne A. Pernet, 'Twists, Turns, and Dead Alleys: The League of Nations and Intellectual Cooperation in Times of War', *Journal of Modern European History*, 12.3 (2014), pp. 342–58.

[3] The Committee of Intellectual Cooperation: Report Submitted to the Council by the French Representative. LNA/C-650–1922-XII, pp. 4–6.

development of civilization' to cooperate in giving assistance to those 'who have suffered and are suffering in the work of pure science'.[4]

The session was covered by newspapers around the world, although, perhaps understandably, with different emphases. In England, *The Times* correspondent claimed that Geneva was a 'muddling but fascinating place' and, suggesting a slight disinterest, that Bergson's speech 'took us away from immediate realities'.[5] In Paris, *Le Temps* reported on the French philosopher's speech in a more sober manner, as did the Viennese *Neue Freie Presse*, which presented a detailed account of Bergson's narrative on the suffering of Austrian intellectual workers.[6] The reaction was also positive in Berlin, where the *Berliner Tageblatt* wrote that Bergson gave a 'long but very interesting and well-received speech', noting that in his reply, the British politician Arthur Balfour argued that similar conditions afflicted the intellectual classes in Germany.[7] In the United States, the *New York Tribune* acknowledged Bergson's speech but reported that 'all subjects were dwarfed by the British split over prime minister David Lloyd George's presence' against the backdrop of the Chanak Crisis, which ultimately led to his resignation weeks later.[8] Intellectual cooperation, and the role that intellectuals could perform in the maintenance of international stability, remained a topic of international importance (and contestation) throughout the 1920s and 1930s.

***

This chapter is about intellectuals, both as individuals and as a collective. It will show how two interconnected questions became widely debated in the aftermath of the First World War: who and what was an intellectual? Discussions regarding the wellbeing and social position of intellectuals crossed international borders and took on particular importance as Europe confronted the task of post-war

---

[4] WGAS/WCT/D/DT 3978, p. 27; The Committee of Intellectual Cooperation: Report Submitted to the Council by the French Representative. LNA/C-650–1922-XII, p. 1.

[5] 'Mr. Lloyd George and Geneva', *The Times*, 16 September 1922, p. 7.

[6] 'La coopération intellectuelle', *Le Temps*, 15 September 1922, p. 1; 'Bergson über eine Hilfsaktion für die geistigen Arbeiter Österreichs', *Neue Freie Presse*, 15 September 1922, p. 32.

[7] 'Die Not der geistigen Arbeiter', *Berliner Tageblatt*, 14 September 1922, p. 2.

[8] 'Balfour against Lloyd George's Trip to Geneva', *New York Tribune*, 16 September 1922, p. 2.

reconstruction. Unlike issues discussed elsewhere in this book, the concern to define the social role of the intellectual and, in many cases, to safeguard their position was shared equally by states that had been victors or vanquished, or had been neutrals in the recent war. While intellectuals have often been framed as national actors in traditional historiography, the humanitarian crisis that inaugurated the decade, and the common material challenges that those involved in matters of the mind confronted across Europe, led to the intellectual being regarded as a transnational actor who could shape not only domestic opinion, but international cooperation too.[9]

The concern with the public function of intellectuals was simultaneously a cultural and social matter. Concerning the former, the post-war years saw widespread discussion of the ways in which intellectuals could shape international public opinion through their vocation, learning, and elevated social standing, largely in response to the devastation of the First World War. During that conflict, many intellectuals took partisan positions in support of their respective nations, and this wartime belligerence led to considerable post-conflict reflection and recrimination, which spilled over into heated polemics about the rectitude of intellectual interventions in public affairs. Perhaps the most famous of these polemics was Julien Benda's 1927 publication *La trahison des clercs*, which has, in the words of Stefan Collini, 'entered the lexicon not just of scholarship but of politics and journalism as well'.[10] Benda's famous account was, however, far from isolated in discussing the public function of the intellectual during this period. Somewhat overlooked in the traditional focus on polemics is the role that international organizations envisaged for intellectuals as facilitators of post-war reconstruction and lasting peace.[11] The 1920s were a period of intensive organization of intellectuals along international lines, which was a direct response to both the issues provoked by the war and the social and economic dislocation that followed.

---

[9] Some representative examples of works that treat intellectuals in national contexts are: Bering, *Die Intellektuellen*; Thomas William Heyck, 'Myths and Meanings of Intellectuals in Twentieth-Century British National Identity', *Journal of British Studies*, 37.2 (1998), pp. 192–221; Collini, *Absent Minds*; Sand, *La fin de l'intellectuel français?*; Winock, *Le siècle des intellectuels*; Finkel, *On the Ideological Front*; Pipes ed., *The Russian Intelligentsia*.

[10] Collini, *Absent Minds*, p. 279.

[11] One exception to this is the work of Daniel Laqua. 'Transnational Intellectual Cooperation, the League of Nations, and the Problem of Order', pp. 241–6.

The First World War and its attendant economic crises meant that intellectuals emerged as a distinct focus not only for humanitarian aid, as was the case in Austria, Germany, Russia, and elsewhere, but also for greater international protections as a social group. After 1918, the economic and social position of intellectual workers emerged as a distinct transnational issue, with unions and organizations formed in the early 1920s at both national and international levels that aimed to represent and protect their interests.[12] The economic standing of intellectuals and intellectual workers remained a problem that transcended national borders throughout the 1920s, with issues such as unemployment, rising costs of living, displacement, and overcrowding of intellectual institutions widespread in Europe in the period. And, while the economic problems of the immediate post-war period receded into the distance by the mid-1920s, they recurred with the onset of the Great Depression at the end of the decade as Europe's post-Locarno stability began to break down.[13]

The position of intellectuals in their respective societies may seem an abstract consideration, but for many contemporaries, the post-war decline in their standing was yet another manifestation of the crisis of civilization. In his famous 1893 treatise on *The Division of Labour in Society*, the French sociologist Émile Durkheim argued that the division of labour and the 'intellectual and material development of societies' constituted nothing less than the 'source of civilization'.[14] The post-war decline in intellectual life, evident through unemployment, displacement, and prohibitive publication costs, was thus taken as another marker of civilizational decline. A report in the French newspaper *Le Temps* in 1922 stated that there had been a 'deplorable diminution of the moral force of traditions bequeathed to us by ancient genius' since the war, and linked the position of intellectual workers

---

[12]   Verbruggen, '"Intellectual Workers" and Their Search for a Place Within the ILO During the Interwar Period', pp. 271–92; Alain Chatriot, 'La lutte contre le "chômage intellectuel" : l'action de la Confédération des Travailleurs Intellectuels (CTI) face à la crise des années trente', *Le Mouvement Social*, 214 (2006), pp. 77–91; Gisèle Sapiro, 'L'internationalisation des champs intellectuel dans l'entre-deux-guerres : facteurs professionnels et politiques', in Gisèle Sapiro ed., *L'espace intellectuel en Europe : De la formation des États-nations à la mondialisation XIXe-XXIe siècle* (Paris, 2009), pp. 111–46.

[13]   Steiner, *The Lights that Failed*, pp. 800–16.

[14]   Emile Durkheim, *The Division of Labour in Society*. Introduction by Lewis Coser. Translated by W. D. Halls (Basingstoke, 1984), p. 12.

with the crisis of civilization.[15] The Italian politician Vincenzo Castrilli argued in 1923 that before the war general prosperity suggested that there would be 'an indefinite expansion of the demand for intellectual workers' but that this had not followed after the conflict ended. 'Advance in civilization', he argued, consisted of 'multiplying the higher needs of the individuals and of the community'.[16] The unstable standing of intellectuals was, then, another manifestation of the fragility of civilization itself.

Alongside this sense of civilizational vulnerability was a growing conviction that intellectuals could play an international role in rebuilding and pacifying Europe. This was connected to wider trends in contemporary thinking about war and peace. Advocates of the democratic control of foreign policy came to the fore following the outbreak of war in 1914; for many of them, the creation of educated public opinion was to be a crucial means of upholding peace. Informed public opinion was to be an antidote to the secret diplomacy which many thinkers argued was a key cause of the conflict.[17] Woodrow Wilson's concept of self-determination held that educated individuals operating through liberal states could, in the words of Leonard V. Smith, 'rebuild the world in their image'.[18] In its bid to reshape the post-war world, the 1919 Zurich conference of the Women's International League for Peace and Freedom proposed that 'only those of high moral and intellectual standing can be trusted' with the task of building a 'new human civilization' through education.[19] Wartime plans for a League of Nations, such as the group led by Viscount Bryce in Britain, worked on the basis that the post-war order would be based on an 'educated Europe where the people were sufficiently instructed so that public opinion could prevent war'.[20] Bryce wrote in 1921 that educated public opinion was 'the best safeguard against revolutionary violence' and argued that nations required 'many vigorous minds, constructive and critical', who were 'constantly occupied in the public discussion of the

---

[15] 'Pour l'intelligence', *Le Temps*, 20 February 1922, p. 1.
[16] Vincenzo Castrilli, 'Intellectual Workers and the Labour Market', *International Labour Review*, 8.3 (1923), p. 362.
[17] Jan Stöckmann, 'The First World War and the Democratic Control of Foreign Policy', *Past & Present*, 249.1 (2020), pp. 150–6.
[18] Smith, *Sovereignty at the Paris Peace Conference*, p. 10.
[19] *Rapport du congrès international de femmes*, p. 267.
[20] Kaiga, *Britain and the Intellectual Origins of the League of Nations, 1914–1919*, pp. 60–1.

current problems of statesmanship'.[21] The British classicist Alfred
Zimmern asserted in 1928 that Europe's post-war recovery, and the
wider restoration of civilization itself, depended upon 'the use made in
public affairs of those who know', a group he defined as those with
'expert knowledge and intellectual and moral leadership'.[22]

The idea that the intellectual had a crucial role in both shaping
and articulating public opinion extended beyond Europe. The 1921
London Declaration of the Pan-African Congress highlighted an
important place for intellectuals as representatives of national
populations, arguing that the 'intelligentsia of right ought to be
recognized as the natural leaders of their groups'.[23] In his speech
on the floor of the League of Nations Assembly in 1931, the
Bolivian writer and diplomat Adolfo Costa du Rels defended intellectuals against charges that they did not inhabit the 'real world',
claiming that 'thanks to his independence, his intelligence, and his
sensibility, the intellectual can best sense the aspirations of people
and give them a human sound'.[24]

It was not in the international domain alone that intellectuals were
perceived as having a role to play in post-war reconstruction. The
German Revolution saw the establishment of a short-lived Council of
Intellectual Workers in 1918 by left-wing intellectuals. This body
envisaged a leading role for intellectuals in the moral leadership of
the nation which, in the words of the writer Heinrich Mann, could
help to 'reconcile Germany with the world'.[25] Beyond Germany, specialist national organizations were formed across Europe and North
America to represent the interests of intellectuals, those who worked on
intellectual pursuits, or who were understood to employ intellectual

---

[21] James Bryce, *Modern Democracies*, vol. 1 (London, 1921), p. 182.
[22] Alfred Zimmern, *Learning and Leadership: A Study of the Needs and
      Possibilities of International Intellectual Cooperation* (London, 1928), p. 85.
[23] The London Manifesto, 1921, www.jpanafrican.org/docs/vol8no4/8.4–8-1
      921Pan.pdf [accessed 1 August 2022]; Jake Hodder, 'The Elusive History of
      the Pan-African Congress, 1919–27', *History Workshop Journal*, 91.1
      (2021), pp. 113–31.
[24] Adolfo Costa du Rels, Speech to the League of Nations Assembly, *Bulletin de la
      coopération intellectuelle*, 1 (1931), p. 410.
[25] Heinrich Mann, 'The Meaning and Idea of the Revolution', December 1918 in
      Anton Kaes, Martin Jay, Edward Dimendberg, eds., *The Weimar Republic
      Sourcebook* (Berkeley, CA, 1994), p. 40; Walter Laqueur, *Weimar: A Cultural
      History* (London, 1974), pp. 66–7.

skills in their work.[26] The emergence of these bodies demonstrated that a discrete strata of educated society emerged from the First World War which was in need of organization and collective protection. The proliferation of these national groupings to address conditions that traversed national borders soon led to the creation of international bodies to coordinate their work.

While the material conditions affecting intellectuals had much in common across Europe, the language used to describe and categorize these groups in question differed depending on the national setting. This category of people were frequently referred to as 'intellectuals' or 'intellectual workers' in English, but, despite the proliferation of these similar (and sometimes interchangeable) terms, this did not constitute a consensus. In Britain, people sometimes spoke of 'black coats' rather than 'intellectual workers'; in the United States, the terms 'brain workers' or 'white collars' were frequently used; while in Germany, the term *Intellektuelle* – a literal translation of the English 'intellectual' or French *intellectuel* – was generally eschewed in favour of *Geistesarbeiter*.[27] In Austria, class politics were a key determinant in how people viewed both the term *Intellektuelle* and intellectual worker.[28] In Russia, the term 'intelligentsia' was widespread and carried with it distinct ideological – and often oppositional – connotations, which in turn changed following the Bolshevik Revolution of 1917.[29] In France, people spoke of *intellectuels* and *travailleurs intellectuels*, but the legacy of the Dreyfus Affair meant that while there was sympathy with the plight of middle-class educated professionals, there was also resistance to the proliferation of a term (*intellectuel*) that came to prominence in the specific political context of *dreyfusisme*. As the

---

[26] A good overview of this was provided by William MacDonald in his 1923 publication *The Intellectual Worker and His Work* (London, 1923).

[27] Bering, *Die Intellektuellen*, pp. 86–93; Habermas, 'Heinrich Heine and the Role of the Intellectual in Germany', p. 76. As Anthony Phelan has noted, 'Geist' has a number of different English equivalents. Anthony Phelan, 'The Theme of the Intellectual', in Phelan ed., *The Weimar Dilemma: Intellectuals in the Weimar Republic* (Manchester, 1985), pp. 1–8; Bernd Widdig, *Culture and Inflation in Weimar Germany* (Berkeley, CA, 2001), p. 178.

[28] Wasserman, 'The Austro-Marxist Struggle for "Intellectual Workers"', p. 371.

[29] Martin Malia, 'What is the Intelligentsia?' in Pipes ed., *The Russian Intelligentsia*, pp. 1–4; Cassedy, *To the Other Shore*, p. 7. The term 'intelligentsia' had slightly different connotations in Poland. Aleksander Gella, 'The Life and Death of the Old Polish Intelligentsia', *Slavic Review*, 30.1 (1971), pp. 1–27.

Dreyfus Affair centred on the guilt of a Jew and given the prominence of Jewish people among the intellectual supporters of Captain Dreyfus, those on the political right came to associate the term 'intellectual' with 'Jew' in a pejorative sense. This right-wing association would proliferate beyond France in the interwar years, notably with the ascent of the Nazis in Germany.[30] As intellectuals were defined in varying ways across nations, anti-intellectualism, too, asserted itself in different forms but was especially pronounced in Germany.[31] Despite the varying nomenclature, across Europe institutions were created at the level of nation states and international organizations to protect intellectuals and harness their learning for the cause of stability and order.

The 1920s was a crucial period for the conceptualization of the intellectual as an international figure through publications as well as the creation of institutions. Much of this activity took place around Geneva, seat of the League of Nations and home to myriad international organizations and gatherings. Quite aside from lofty and idealistic invocations of a 'spirit of Geneva' that permeated many official League publications, the Swiss city became a major centre for intellectual activity of a bureaucratic, if not creative, type in the interwar period.[32] While the League's International Committee on Intellectual Cooperation was not imbued with resources with which to implement ambitious plans, it carried a considerable moral authority – based in part on the eminence of its members – which meant that the ICIC became a magnet for petitions and appeals that concerned intellectuals and intellectual matters, from many parts of the world. Many national organizations in turn affiliated to international bodies that were based in Geneva and which were part of the League's machinery, such as the International Labour Organization (ILO). For these reasons, Geneva became a key site in the interwar intellectual imagination, not only in terms of the practical outputs of committees and organizations, but also as it was a vibrant centre of activity and represented a site to which intellectual communities around the world could appeal when threatened by economic crisis,

---

[30] Sander L. Gilman, *Smart Jews: The Construction of the Image of Jewish Superior Intelligence* (Lincoln NE, 1996), pp. 25, 83–4; Ruth Harris has shown how this binary and exclusivist distinction between dreyfusards and anti-dreyfusards is inaccurate and that there were many anti-Semitic supporters of Dreyfus. *The Man on Devil's Island*, p. 7.

[31] Laqueur, *Weimar*, pp. 41–8.

[32] Glenda Sluga, *Internationalism in the Age of Nationalism* (Philadelphia, PA, 2013), pp. 56–7.

displacement, war, political repression, or infringements upon their academic freedom. It was also a site at which much criticism was directed by the start of the 1930s, as the limitations of the practices of international intellectual cooperation became apparent. Much practical thinking about the social function of intellectuals was channelled towards Geneva, while the Swiss city was also the site of many organizations and structures that sought to represent intellectual interests in myriad ways.

Beyond the famous and much-publicized work of figures like Julien Benda, the 1920s saw the emergence of a transnational discourse around Europe and North America which pivoted on many of the same questions addressed by the French author. This discourse, inspired in part by the events of the war, took considerable impetus from the post-war humanitarian crisis and the impoverished state in which many intellectual workers found themselves in both victor and vanquished states. It resulted in the establishment of a wide range of national and international unions in the aftermath of the First World War which sought to organize and protect intellectuals as a discrete category. The League of Nations was heavily involved in many of these activities through both the ICIC and ILO. However, by the turn of the 1930s, the onset of economic depression and growing threats to international peace presented a new set of threats to the international intellectual order. The international organization of intellectual life, through the League of Nations, some of its subsidiary committees, as well as other international bodies, can all be seen as the conclusion of the process of post-war emergency relief described elsewhere in this book. The intellectual coordination of the 1920s demonstrated the faith that was placed in intellectual and cultural life as key components of European stability and order, which would be fundamentally challenged by the start of the 1930s.

Thinking about Intellectuals in 1920s Europe

Nicholas Murray Butler, director of the Division of Intercourse and Education at the Carnegie Endowment of International Peace, wrote in 1922 of 'the plight of the intellectuals in Central and Eastern Europe that has so often been brought to our attention'.[33] As has been argued

---

[33] Butler to Henry Pritchett, 4 April 1922, CURBML, Carnegie Corporation of New York (CCNY), III.A.72, Folder 9.

throughout this book, intellectuals were identified as a discrete group in need of humanitarian aid after the First World War. A wide range of schemes were instituted by different organizations to feed, clothe, and provide medical aid and literature to those in need, as well as to rehouse intellectuals who were the victims of war and its aftermath. The practice of post-war humanitarianism demonstrated that the groups being assisted could vary depending on the circumstances in a given institution, city, or country. The language utilized by a range of Anglo-American organizations, was, however, relatively consistent in referring to 'intellectuals' as a distinct category of sufferers; this was not limited to one country or institution, but was common in much post-war humanitarian discourse, both in its public-facing manifestations and in private correspondence. Herbert Hoover stated in 1922 that 'there is no question of the need of the Russian intellectuals' who had 'suffered more than any other class in the Russian debacle'.[34] Fridtjof Nansen published a public appeal that year which identified intellectuals ('les intellectuels' in French) as 'the first to suffer' and appealed to the 'intellectuals of the whole world' to support their Russian colleagues.[35] The utilization of this language by the practitioners of humanitarianism was often at odds with that employed in different nations by these groups themselves.

The identification of intellectuals as a social group was not limited to humanitarian organizations but rather was related to a wider national and international discourse about intellectuals that animated the post-war decades. The historiography of intellectuals tends to focus on a number of salient polemics which emerged in these decades which have been frequently cited, invoked, and debated to the present day.[36] These polemics – and their ongoing fame – reflect the widespread interest in the figure of the intellectual in the inter-war years and, while many emerged from particular national contexts, they spoke to transnational themes.

Perhaps the most famous attempt to define the role of the intellectuals was Benda's *La trahison des clercs*. Benda defined an intellectual as someone who was preoccupied with universal rather than material

---

[34] 'Relief for Russian Men', *Science* 56.1449 (1922), p. 389.
[35] 'Les événements de Russie', *Le Temps*, 7 June 1922, p. 2.
[36] Collini, *Absent Minds*, p. 279; Jeremy Jennings and Tony Kemp-Welch, 'The Century of the Intellectual: From the Dreyfus Affair to Salman Rushdie', in Jennings and Kemp-Welch eds., *Intellectuals in Politics from the Dreyfus Affair to Salman Rushdie* (London, 1997), pp. 1–21.

issues; they were someone who could state, rather grandly, that 'my kingdom is not of this world'.[37] The logic of this focus on the ethereal meant that the political engagement of intellectuals was only justified, according to Benda, in instances where it supported a 'universal' good. According to this definition, intellectuals who spoke out in support of Captain Alfred Dreyfus in 1898 or who those who defended the French republic during the First World War were justified in their action.[38] Benda argued, however, that intellectuals had forsaken their trad-itional position by becoming attached to temporal ideas rather than placing reason above the immediate passions that animated the wider population. He claimed that this traditional intellectual positioning had been challenged in recent times by the adoption by intellectuals of political positions which were often nationalist, xenophobic, or anti-Semitic.[39] To Benda, the *clercs* most guilty of this behaviour were the German intellectuals who supported their state during the First World War.[40] Benda's argument was shaped by a distinct French heritage for intellectual engagement but was soon translated and read far beyond France.[41]

A contrasting but no less influential argument was provided by the Italian writer and Communist Antonio Gramsci in his *Prison Notebooks*. Gramsci took a different approach and explored the social function of the intellectual rather than their cultural and political influence. He concluded that 'all men are intellectuals ... but not all men have in society the function of intellectuals'.[42] Gramsci felt that every social group in society had its intellectuals, being those people who acted as 'permanent persuaders' who upheld the prevailing social and political hegemony.[43] In other words, intellectuals had a social and economic role within their respective societies which did not

---

[37] Julien Benda, *La trahison des clercs* (Paris, 1927), p. 54; Sand, *La fin de l'intellectuel français?*, p. 95.

[38] Winock, *Le siècle des intellectuels*, p. 243.

[39] Winock, *Le siècle des intellectuels*, pp. 238–40.

[40] Benda, *La trahison des clercs*, pp. 66, 68.

[41] In Britain, it was translated as *The Great Betrayal* while in the United States the title was *The Treason of the Intellectuals*. Collini, *Absent Minds*, pp. 288–90. The book was translated into German as *Der Verrat der Intellektuellen*.

[42] Antonio Gramsci, *Selections from the Prison Notebooks of Antonio Gramsci*, edited and translated by Quintin Hoare and Geoffrey Nowell Smith (New York, 1971), pp. 8–9.

[43] Gramsci, pp. 10–12.

necessarily involve them taking a position on pressing cultural matters of the age, nor was it related to a specific vocation, but rather to how they continually reinforced the established order. Gramsci's analysis of the social function of intellectuals recalled the approaches taken by (if not the politics of) many humanitarian organizations in providing intellectual relief in the early 1920s as a means of restoring social order and upholding the dominant hegemony in the successor states of central and eastern Europe.

During the interwar period, there were many diverse definitions of the intellectual and its function being propounded in Germany.[44] In 1929, the Hungarian-born sociologist Karl Mannheim published his book *Ideologie und Utopie* (*Ideology and Utopia*) while teaching in Frankfurt. Mannheim pursued a similar line of enquiry to Gramsci, exploring the question of whether intellectuals could be said to constitute a class. Mannheim drew upon the ideas of his mentor, Alfred Weber, who spoke of a 'socially free-floating intelligentsia'.[45] Mannheim asserted that intellectuals were 'to a large degree unattached to any social class and which is recruited from an increasingly inclusive area of social life'.[46] Unlike older forms of traditional authority, such as that historically exerted by the priesthood, the modern mind and modern intellectuals were 'dynamic, elastic, in a constant state of flux, and perpetually confronted by new problems'.[47] Mannheim claimed that intellectuals had a key role in defending democracy, a task to which they were especially well-suited because of their socioeconomic detachment and ability to see political reality in its totality.[48]

The works of Benda, Gramsci and Mannheim all drew, either implicitly or explicitly, on the distinction between the cultural authority of intellectuals (and its proper application) and their socio-economic position. Beyond these well-known texts, which are often seen to

[44] Phelan, 'Some Weimar Theories of the Intellectual', in *The Weimar Dilemma*, pp. 9–33; Widdig, *Culture and Inflation in Weimar Germany*, pp. 169–95.
[45] Colin Loader, 'Free Floating: The Intelligentsia in the Work of Alfred Weber and Karl Mannheim', *German Studies Review*, 20.2 (1997), p. 217.
[46] Karl Mannheim, *Ideology and Utopia* (first English ed., 1936; new ed., London, 1972), p. 139.
[47] Mannheim, *Ideology and Utopia*, p. 139.
[48] Daniel Bessner, *Democracy in Exile: Hans Speier and the Rise of the Defense Intellectual* (Ithaca, NY, 2018), pp. 23–4.

emanate from particular national contexts, there was a sustained international discussion about the role of intellectuals and intellectual workers both as national and international actors. This was more than just debate; the period following the First World War was marked by the establishment of a number of organizations to safeguard the interests of intellectuals both domestically and internationally. Their very existence constituted an attempt to define and codify the social functions of intellectuals and to enshrine protections for them. The creation of organizations and the debates that surrounded their establishment highlighted a tension between the economic and material standing of those involved in intellectual pursuits on the one hand, and their cultural influence on the other, as did the works of Benda, Gramsci, and Mannheim.

Blackcoats and Brainworkers: Organizing Intellectual Life after the First World War

In 1920 the French author Henri Mugel argued that it would always be easier 'for a street cleaner to make people realize the importance of his work than for Henri Poincaré to make people realize the importance of his'. 'If the streets are not swept for three days', Mugel claimed, 'the result is stench and a threatened epidemic. If no lessons on general physics are given for three days, not one man out of a hundred thousand will suffer.'[49] This stark and rather dramatic rhetoric explained the necessity of recognizing, organizing, and aiding intellectual workers experiencing economic distress in the aftermath of war, as well as the assumed value to be placed on such work. Mugel was not alone in advocating the importance of organizing and protecting workers engaged in intellectual pursuits; across Europe and North America, organizations emerged which sought to protect the interests of those categorized as intellectual workers. Many associations and unions had been formed in the decades prior to 1914 to organize authors, artists, journalists, and others involved in intellectual work; the Belgian internationalists Paul Otlet and Henri La Fontaine were particularly prominent in some of these initiatives.[50] However, following the First World

---

[49] Castrilli, 'International Protection of Intellectual Workers', p. 4. Henri Mugel, 'Manuels et intellectuels', *Paris-Midi*, 24 October 1920, p. 2.

[50] Verbruggen '"Intellectual Workers" and Their Search for a Place within the ILO during the Interwar Period', pp. 276–85; Isabella Löhr, 'Le droit de l'auteur et la

War, a more concerted organization began which used the term 'intellectual worker' as its organizing principle.

The Confédération des travailleurs intellectuels (CTI) was established in France in February 1920. It was a federation of syndicates and associations which sought to represent every intellectual vocation in France.[51] Among the disparate professions represented were journalists, engineers, painters, architects, technicians, scientists, musicians, and authors. They all faced, in the words of the *dreyfusard* writer Romain Coolus, 'an analogous situation', because they earned their living via daily work but the only capital that they possessed was 'that which nature has given them'.[52] More than this, these same intellectual workers had, until the establishment of the CTI, no formal representation and consequently had received no compensation for the damage caused by wartime, a situation which Coolus deemed 'deplorable'.[53] The CTI defined the intellectual worker as someone who drew their means of existence from work in which the effort of the mind dominated that of physical effort, but this definition was not without its critics.[54] The CTI was not the only organization established in France in this period with the purpose of organizing those in intellectual lines of work; indeed, both the Union intellectuelle française and the Compagnons de l'intelligence were formed at around the same time. Meanwhile, both conservative Catholics and the right-wing *Action Française* established their own groups which sought to define intellectuals in a manner more consistent with their respective ideologies.[55]

Many organizations followed the lead of the CTI. In October 1920, a Central Association was founded in Austria under the leadership of Alfons Dopsch, a historian at the University of Vienna. It aimed to

Première Guerre mondiale: un exemple de coopération transnationale européenne', *Le Mouvement Social*, 244 (2013), pp. 67–80.

[51] Chatriot, 'La lutte contre le 'chômage intellectuel', pp. 77–91; MacDonald, *The Intellectual Worker and His Work*, pp. 289–91; Gabriel Galvez-Behar, *Posséder la science: la propriété scientifique au temps du capitalisme industriel* (Paris, 2020), pp. 188–97.

[52] 'Chez les intellectuels', *Comoedia*, 13 February 1920, pp. 1–2.

[53] 'Chez les intellectuels', *Comoedia*, 13 February 1920, pp. 1–2.

[54] Chatriot, La lutte contre le 'chômage intellectuel', p. 79.

[55] Bodleian Libraries Archives and Manuscripts, Oxford (BLAM), MS Gilbert Murray 343/8; MacDonald, *The Intellectual Worker and His Work*, p. 287; Sapiro, 'L'internationalisation des champs intellectuel dans l'entre-deux-guerres', p. 118.

represent professions such as lawyers, doctors, architects, artists, writers, and public and private employees, and held affiliation with 230 professional associations. It stated that its ultimate goal was the creation of an 'International', as 'only international solidarity can bring about a new valuation of intellectual work'.[56] As was the case elsewhere, the issue of how to define intellectual work and workers was contested in Austria.[57] In Britain, the National Federation of Professional, Technical, Administrative and Supervisory Workers (NFPTASW) was founded in 1920 as the equivalent of intellectual workers unions formed elsewhere in Europe. There was a reluctance in Britain to refer to workers of this type as 'intellectual workers', and a range of synonyms was deployed to refer to them, including 'Black Coated' workers, 'brain workers', 'professional workers', and 'mental workers'.[58] By 1923, national organizations had been founded to represent intellectual interests in France, Norway, Netherlands, Czechoslovakia, Switzerland, Belgium, Romania, and Austria.[59]

The situation in Germany was different; here, the formation of associations to protect intellectual workers was framed by hyperinflation and resentment at the severity of the Treaty of Versailles. The Schutzkartell deutscher Geistesarbeiter was founded in July 1923 with the aim of both affirming the value of intellectual work and ensuring good living conditions for intellectual workers in Germany, but also to oppose the 'unbearable burden and treatment by foreign countries' that endangered the German people and its intellectual workers.[60] As it was established during the Franco-Belgian occupation of the Ruhr, the organization's leadership regarded the key issues affecting German intellectuals as

---

[56] 'A World Congress of Intellectual Workers in Vienna', *Neues Wiener Journal*, 13 May 1921, LSF/YM/MfS/FEWVRC/4/3/7/3.

[57] Wasserman, 'The Austro-Marxist Struggle for "Intellectual Workers"', pp. 361–88.

[58] 'Organizing the "Black Coats"', *The Mail*, 9 February 1920, p. 4.

[59] MacDonald, *The Intellectual Worker and His Work*, pp. 287–99. Beyond unions that organized intellectual workers, a number of more specific organizations also emerged in the post-war period, such as the PEN Club, the International Critics' Association, and the International Literary and Artistic Association.

[60] Otto Everling, *Schutzkartell deutscher Geistesarbeiter: Beiträge zu sozialen Fragen der Geistesarbeiter* (Berlin, 1929), p. 17.

THE ILLUSTRATED LONDON NEWS. March 3, 1923.—340

BRITAIN'S "DEVASTATED AREA": DISTRESS AMONG "BLACK COATS."
DRAWN BY OUR SPECIAL ARTIST, STEVEN SPURRIER, R.O.I.

WHERE PRIDE PREVENTS COMPLAINT, AND "KEEPING UP AN APPEARANCE" MAKES THINGS HARDER:
BREAKFAST IN A CLERK'S HOME BEFORE HE SETS OUT TO SEEK EMPLOYMENT.

Figure 6.1 'Britain's "Devastated Area": Distress Among "Black Coats."'
Illustrated London News, March 1923 (© Illustrated London News Ltd/
Mary Evans)

consequences of the post-war settlements. In February 1924, the
Schutzkartell organized a demonstration at the Reichstag which was
attended by President Friedrich Ebert, Chancellor Wilhelm Marx,
and Foreign Minister Gustav Stresemann. The gathering resolved to
remind the world of 'what humanity owes to German science, art
and technology'.[61] Marx spoke of his hope that foreign countries
would not interpret Germany's inability to aid its intellectuals as

---

[61] Otto Everling, *Von deutscher Geistesarbeit und deutscher Wirtschaft* (Berlin,
       1925), p. 13.

evidence of its indifference to their welfare.[62] Otto Everling, the politician and theologian who directed the Schutzkartell, wrote in 1925 that in 'peace without peace', it was easier to rebuild destroyed provinces than cultural life.[63]

Across Europe and North America, many held the conviction that intellectual workers needed to organize in order to defend their position and safeguard their economic status; the arguments made in different national contexts had much in common. Speaking at a meeting of the NFPTASW in 1921, the writer George Bernard Shaw claimed that unemployed mental workers, many of whom were war veterans, were 'starving in the streets'.[64] In the United States, the author John Corbin defined brain workers as those who 'do not labour with their hands and do not control capital' and claimed that they were America's 'forgotten men'.[65] In Germany, the politician Georg Schreiber wrote that the emergency of intellectual workers (*Geistesarbeiters*) extended beyond professors, private docents, and students and encompassed free professions such as doctors, lawyers, artists, poets, filmmakers, writers, composers, journalists, architects, and engineers, all of whom were people who valued quality over quantity in their work.[66] In Switzerland, Ernst Roethlisberger, founder of the Bund der Geistesarbeiter, wrote that 'the intellectual worker, the man of ideas, might reasonably have expected to find himself recognized in all countries as the determining factor in progress and to have gained enormously in prestige' following the war but that 'the contrary is the case'.[67] This was a gendered discourse where, almost exclusively, intellectuals and intellectual workers were assumed to be men.[68]

Most commentators agreed that the war had caused a profound shift in the status of intellectual workers. Vincenzo Castrilli argued that

---

[62] 'Chancellor Comforts German Intellectuals', *The Salt Lake Tribune*, 24 February 1924, p. 3; 'World Called on to Help Germany's Intellectuals', *Brooklyn Daily Eagle*, 25 February 1924, p. 22.

[63] Everling, *Von deutscher Geistesarbeit und deutscher Wirtschaft*, p. 8.

[64] 'The Black-Coated Workers', *The Workers' Dreadnought*, 12 February 1921, p 6.

[65] John Corbin, *The Return of the Middle Class* (New York, 1923), p. 8.

[66] Schreiber, *Die Not der deutschen Wissenschaft*, pp. 108–9.

[67] Castrilli, 'International Protection of Intellectual Workers', p. 7.

[68] Suzanne Grinberg, 'Les travailleurs intellectuels : et les conditions morales et matérielles du travail de la Femme', *C.T.I.: Bulletin de la confédération des travailleurs intellectuels*, 12.37 (1931), pp. 255–7.

post-war reconstruction placed too much emphasis on material rather than intellectual concerns. Allied to crippling post-war inflation, the post-war period saw intellectual workers begin to organize as a corporate group in ways that they had not prior to 1914.[69] In Britain, William MacDonald argued in 1923 that the primary basis of the threat to the position of intellectual workers in the early 1920s was the economic and social conditions created by the war.[70] Writing in the same year, Imre Ferenczi, a Hungarian migration expert who worked for the ILO, claimed that it was only 'under the pressure of the wartime and post-war conditions' that intellectual workers 'became conscious of their situation and grouped together for the defence of their common interests'.[71] There was, however, scepticism about whether intellectuals were suited to union-style organization. One American newspaper wondered whether intellectuals would 'resort or even threaten to resort to strikes and violence in order to achieve their aims'.[72]

The establishment of international bodies to protect the interests of intellectual workers soon followed the creation of national federations. The Confédération internationale des travailleurs intellectuels held its first meeting in Paris in April 1923. Associations from France, Belgium, Romania, Britain, Finland, Austria, and Bulgaria attended as delegates, in addition to observers from a further eleven countries.[73] In his address to the first meeting of the CITI, Romain Coolus noted the challenge of determining who should and should not be included, as definitions varied from nation to nation.[74] The statutes of the CITI stated that its aims were 'to improve the material, moral and social conditions of intellectual workers and to encourage international intellectual cooperation' while membership was only open to organizations from League of Nations member states, meaning that Germany and Russia were excluded.[75] Other organizations with similar goals were

---

[69] Castrilli, 'International Protection of Intellectual Workers', pp. 3–5.

[70] MacDonald, *The Intellectual Worker and His Work*, pp. 161–2, 165.

[71] 'Le chômage des travailleurs intellectuels', 9–11 September 1923, LNA/R1059/13C/30927/30927, p. 1; Christiane Harzig, Dirk Hoerder, and Donna Gabaccia, *What is Migration History?* (Cambridge, 2009), p. 60.

[72] 'Brain Workers Unionize', *Brooklyn Daily Times*, 2 June 1920, p. 4.

[73] 'Les travailleurs intellectuels', *Informations sociales*, 20 April 1923, p. 117.

[74] 'Les travailleurs intellectuels', *Informations sociales*, 20 April 1923, p. 118; 'Intellectual Workers' Federation', *Northern Whig and Belfast Post*, 7 April 1923, p. 9.

[75] CITI statutes, UNESCO/B.IV.17.

formed in this period, such as the International PEN Club, which was seen as a 'literary league of nations', and the Fédération des unions intellectuelles, which sought to create an international atmosphere 'favourable to reciprocal understanding without which it is impossible to realise an ideal of human civilization'.[76] While acknowledging national difference, the proliferation of international organizations demonstrated that many of the challenges facing intellectual workers in this period cut across national borders.

Intellectual Cooperation and the League of Nations

Following its establishment, the League of Nations received proposals from parties across Europe who argued that intellectual work should be a key plank of the new organization's activities. In September 1920, the Third Congress of the UIA resolved that an 'international organiza-tion for intellectual work' should be constituted as one of the organs of the League.[77] The Japanese Association of Teachers wrote in November 1920 to propose the creation of an international education council at the League.[78] The Austrian sociologist Friedrich Hertz wrote from Vienna in November 1920 to suggest the establishment of an International Institute of International Relations in the Austrian cap-ital. Hertz's proposal envisaged a crucial role for intellectuals to coun-teract 'tendencies which tend to poison the mind of the coming generations and to make futile all strivings for peace'.[79] It was widely held that an intellectual organization of some type should come into being within the League.

The decision to establish a body focused on intellectual cooperation was based on proposals received from the UIA and the French Association of the League of Nations respectively, both of which, an official report noted, were 'the outcome of a movement of opinion which has arisen in several countries as a result of the creation of the

---

[76] Tara Talwar Windsor, "Extended Arm of Reich Foreign Policy'? Literary Internationalism, Cultural Diplomacy and the First German PEN Club in the Weimar Republic', *Contemporary European History*, 30.2, (2021), p. 183; 'Union intellectuelle française', BLAM/MS Gilbert Murray 343/8.

[77] 'Report on the international co-ordination of intellectual labour', LNA/R1005/ 13/13875/1139, p. 16.

[78] Y. Shimonaka to League of Nations, 27 September 1920, LNA/R1028/13B/ 8032/8032.

[79] Friedrich Hertz, LNA/R1028/13B/8245/8245, p. 1.

League'.[80] The report posited that there was a growing feeling that the success of the League would require the 'development of the feeling of international solidarity among the nations' which needed to be 'prepared and guided'. This all meant that the League had 'an intellectual duty to fulfil', which required the creation of a commission.[81] The International Committee on Intellectual Cooperation was duly established by the League's Council in January 1922.[82] The committee was initially intended to be a small body, comprising twelve members who were experts in fields such as science and education, to whom the League's Council could refer specific issues.

The French historian and politician Gabriel Hanotaux wrote that those selected by the League's Council for membership of the ICIC were appointed 'in consideration of their personal ability and their reputation in learned circles without any discrimination as to nationality'.[83] While the supposed emphasis on cultural eminence was suggestive of a desire to ensure that transnational intellectual interests were represented, in reality, the membership of the committee reflected the post-war international order. The ICIC was chaired by Henri Bergson, the French philosopher who had been enthusiastic in his partisanship during the First World War, while the Australian-born classicist Gilbert Murray represented Britain, the conservative writer Gonzague de Reynold represented Switzerland, and the Polish-French physicist Marie Curie further added to the committee's eminence. The committee was strongly Eurocentric, with only two non-Western representatives – the Brazilian medic A. de Castro and the Indian political economist D.N. Bannerjee – in its founding cohort.[84] Despite not being a member state of the League, the United States was represented by the astronomer George Ellery Hale. Perhaps the most famous member of the committee appointed in 1922 was Albert Einstein, the theoretical physicist who was catapulted to international celebrity following the experimental verification of his theory of relativity in 1919.[85] Einstein was selected as the German representative in part owing to his fame as a scientist, but

[80] 'Report on the international co-ordination of intellectual labour', p. 16.
[81] 'Report on the international co-ordination of intellectual labour', p. 17.
[82] Irish, 'The "Moral Basis" of Reconstruction?' pp. 785–6.
[83] Laqua, 'Transnational Intellectual Cooperation, the League of Nations, and the Problem of Order', p. 224.
[84] Laqua, 'Transnational Intellectual Cooperation', p. 228.
[85] Aaron Lecklider, *Inventing the Egghead: The Battle Over Brainpower in American Culture* (Philadelphia, PA, 2013), pp. 48–67.

also because, having been a vocal pacifist during the First World War, he was deemed an 'acceptable' face of the former enemy.[86] Germany would remain excluded from membership of the League of Nations until 1926 and thus meaningful collaborations between German institutions and the ICIC did not develop at that time.

The ICIC met in Geneva each August. It initially proposed to undertake a modest work programme encompassing issues such as international bibliography and scientific and university cooperation. By the time of its first meeting in August 1922, these general aims had been superseded by Europe's wider intellectual and humanitarian crisis. The archives of the League of Nations reveal that intellectuals from across Europe and the world looked to the ICIC as an institution that could help them, be they displaced, experiencing hunger, or unable to purchase essential materials because of crippling post-war inflation. Accordingly, the ICIC quickly sought to focus its attention on the state of 'intellectual life' in Europe, sponsoring reports into the situations in Poland and Austria before widening this activity to survey the state of European intellectual life in the years that followed.[87] The ICIC had neither significant financial resources nor a large staff to deal with humanitarian issues in any substantial or sustained way.[88] For this reason, it sought to leverage the fame of its members and its growing moral authority by issuing international appeals on behalf of intellectual life in Austria in 1922 and Hungary in 1924, as well as on behalf of Tokyo Imperial University after the earthquake of September 1923.[89] Following these early initiatives, the ICIC decided that national committees on intellectual cooperation should be established in each member state to act as a conduit between the Geneva body and member states as well as to facilitate bilateral exchanges.[90]

The League's work on international cooperation was further institutionalized in 1924 when the French government offered to establish and fund an International Institute of Intellectual Cooperation, to be based in Paris. This proposal, and the influence which it gave the

---

[86] Danielle Wünsch, 'Einstein et la Commission internationale de coopération intellectuelle/Einstein and the International Commission for Intellectual Cooperation', *Revue d'histoire des sciences*, 57. 2 (2004). pp. 509–20.

[87] 'Intellectual Cooperation: Adoption of the Questionnaire', 1 February 1923, LNA/C-III-II-52–1923-XII.

[88] Stöckmann, *The Architects of International* Relations, p. 131.

[89] Irish, 'The "Moral Basis" of Reconstruction?' pp. 789–93.

[90] Irish, 'The "Moral Basis" of Reconstruction?' p. 797.

French government within the organization, caused much unease among scholars connected with the ICIC, but the offer was formally accepted by the League's Council in late 1924 with the institute officially opening in 1926.[91] The Italian government later contributed two institutes to intellectual cooperation: the International Institute for the Unification of Private Law and the International Educational Cinematograph Institute.[92] In its lifetime, the ICIC had three chairs: Henri Bergson (who held this role until 1925), the Dutch physicist Hendrik Lorentz (1925–28), and Gilbert Murray (1928–1939).

The creation of the different intellectual cooperation mechanisms through the League constituted a response to the wider humanitarian crisis which emerged in Europe following the end of the First World War. Through the establishment of a committee and an institution to deal with intellectual cooperation, the League was also, by definition, contributing to post-First World War discourses regarding the social function of intellectuals. In 1924 René Cassin, the French legal scholar and president of the Union Fédérale veterans group, argued before the assembly of the League of Nations for greater funding for the ICIC. Cassin claimed that intellectuals should be seen as similar to veterans as both groups suffered disproportionately following the war and because both had, in different ways, made the League a reality.[93] Cassin urged greater support of the ICIC 'to defend science in the person of scientists and to stop the reduction in the number of intellectuals across Europe for the betterment of civilization'.[94] An official account produced by the League in 1930 also suggested that the post-war context, and the work of the League, had helped to redefine who an intellectual was. 'It was indeed generally considered that the thinker and the statesman moved in two wholly separate orbits', and that the intellectual was 'out of place, and might even compromise his intellectual integrity, if he

---

[91] Daniel Laqua, 'Internationalisme ou affirmation de la nation? La coopération intellectuelle transnationale dans l'entre-deux-guerres', *Critique internationale*, 52 (2011), pp. 51–67, Renoliet, *L'UNESCO oubliée*, pp. 44–76.

[92] Kathleen Gibberd, *The League in our Time* (Oxford, 1933), p. 194.

[93] These groups were not mutually exclusive.

[94] René Cassin speech, 9 September 1924, AN/382AP/12. For more on Cassin, see Jay Winter and Antoine Prost, *René Cassin: From the Great War to the Universal Declaration* (Cambridge, 2013); Andrew Barros, 'Turn Everyone into a Civilian: René Cassin and the UNESCO Project', in Andrew Barros and Martin Thomas eds., *The Civilianization of War: The Changing Civil-Military Divide, 1914–2014* (Cambridge, 2018), pp. 243–59.

sought to interfere with affairs of state'. The publication claimed that the constitution of the ICIC demonstrated that intellectuals could contribute to government affairs in a productive manner.[95] These examples are two among many that highlight how the League's institutions contributed to a wider discourse about the function of intellectuals. These drew on concerns about the material consequences of war for intellectuals and emphasized the potential for educated experts to inform the study of issues of war and peace in order to guide international public opinion.[96]

Intellectual Workers in the 1920s

There was some overlap in function between the intellectual cooperation bodies of the League of Nations, established to deal with what might be deemed cultural matters, and the work of the International Labour Organization, which had, among other responsibilities, a concern for the economic standing of intellectual workers. Prior to the establishment of the ICIC, Albert Thomas, director general of the ILO, expressed concern about the potential for the duplication of effort between the two bodies. Thomas, a *normalien* and former student of Émile Durkheim, drew a distinction between the economic and social needs of intellectual workers.[97] He was reassured by Nitobe Inazō, one of the League's under-secretaries general, that the resolution establishing the ICIC 'carefully avoids any mention' of intellectual workers and that 'the economic aspect of intellectual workers' was not within the realm of the committee's activities'.[98] When these proposals were put to the League's Council, it determined that intellectual labour was best left to voluntary organizations and that the League would 'do better service to the cause by continuing to help such voluntary exertions than by attempting to organize intellectual labour'.[99] The humanitarian crisis and the response of the ICIC to the impoverished economic condition of scholars in Austria and Hungary meant that it soon began to take an interest in the material, in addition to the cultural.

[95] *League of Nations. Ten Years of World Co-operation* (Geneva, 1930), p. 316.
[96] Stöckmann, *The Architects of International Relations*, p. 149.
[97] Thomas to Nitobe, 13 September 1921, LNA/R1029/13C/15769/14297.
[98] Nitobe to Thomas, September 1921, LNA/R1029/13C/15769/14297.
[99] 'Report on the international co-ordination of intellectual labour', p. 22.

The ICIC never tried to explicitly define who it understood intellectuals to be in the 1920s. By contrast, in 1925 the ILO decided that 'an intellectual worker is one who derives his means of subsistence from work in which mental effort, initiative and personality habitually predominate over physical effort'.[100] This definition was much debated: a report produced by the ILO in 1928 claimed that the definition did not solve the problem of placing intellectual workers into a class, nor did it provide a theoretical definition of who an 'intellectual worker' was. This report stated that 'intellectual workers occupy very varied situations and have very varied functions. Their aspirations, therefore, also vary widely.'[101] The CITI preoccupied itself with identifying issues that cut across national borders such as the rights of scientific inventors, model contracts for intellectuals, resale rights for artists and designers, and freedom of thought.[102] In identifying these cross-cutting issues, it sought to create international protections for intellectual workers.

The issue of intellectual unemployment was a key matter that captured the attention of both the ILO and the ICIC in the 1920s. In 1927, the ILO formed a consultative commission, on which both the CITI and the ICIC had representation, to address transnational problems that impacted intellectual workers, which soon came to focus on unemployment.[103] In 1928, an ILO publication estimated that 40,000 European university graduates were in a critical situation globally owing to unemployment.[104] In the same year, the ILO's Fernand Maurette highlighted the vast number of unemployed intellectual workers in Europe and argued that post-war reconstruction had placed too much emphasis on the material over the intellectual. 'The crisis of intellectual work', Maurette concluded, 'is a salary crisis. Its solution can be found in professional association.'[105] During the Great

---

[100] Verbruggen, '"Intellectual Workers" and Their Search for a Place Within the ILO During the Interwar Period', p. 273.

[101] 'The Progress of Organisation Among Intellectual Workers', *International Labour Review*, 18.4/5 (1928), pp. 530–2.

[102] Louis Gallié, 'Rapport du secrétaire générale, *C.T.I.: Bulletin de la confédération des travailleurs intellectuels*, 12.35 (1931), pp. 176–81; Galvez-Behar, *Posséder la science*, pp. 197–215.

[103] Verbruggen, '"Intellectual Workers" and Their Search for a Place Within the ILO During the Interwar Period', p. 290.

[104] 'The Progress of Organisation Among Intellectual Workers', 529, p. 546.

[105] Fernand Maurette, 'Surproduction du travail intellectuel?', *L'Europe nouvelle*, 10 March 1928, pp. 322–5.

Depression and following the rise of totalitarian regimes, intellectual unemployment became a matter of even greater importance to the CITI, the ILO, and the ICIC.[106]

International reconciliation was also evident in the CITI's international activities in the period following Locarno. In 1926, CITI's fourth annual congress was held in Vienna. At that meeting, German representatives, not yet full members, attended as observers.[107] It was not until 1931 that the Schutzkartell deutscher Geistesarbeiter voted to affiliate to the CITI as its German representative.[108] One of the reasons for the delay was that a number of competing organizations represented different types of professional and intellectual work in Germany, while the CITI wished to work with only one representative group for each nation. Otto Everling formally took his seat on the CITI council as the German delegate in June 1931.[109] Germany's first act as a member of the CITI was for Everling and Louis Gallié to co-present a report on the situation of international workers 'in the face of international economic crisis'.[110] By that point, its annual congress was attended by delegates from Austria, Britain, Belgium, Finland, France, Netherlands, Poland, Czechoslovakia, and Yugoslavia. In the same year, Hungary formed a group to represent intellectual workers in the expectation that they would soon also join the CITI. By 1931, a full eight years into its existence, the CITI still continued to oversee inquiries that sought to clearly define what an intellectual worker was and what different representative bodies stood for, as well as ascertaining what effect intellectual organization had upon issues such as politics, economics, the workers' movement, and public opinion.[111]

One notable protection for the life of intellectuals emerged not from the work of the ICIC, ILO, or CITI, but from the Geneva-based International Committee of the Red Cross. In 1929, the Geneva Convention relative to the Treatment of Prisoners of War included

---

[106] Chatriot, 'La lutte contre le 'chômage intellectuel', pp. 79–91.
[107] M. Siblik, 'Rapport sur le IVème congrès annuel de la confédération international des travailleurs intellectuels.', UNESCO/B.IV.17.
[108] 'Confédération internationale des travailleurs intellectuels', *C.T.I.: Bulletin de la confédération des travailleurs intellectuels*, 12.37 (1931), p. 324.
[109] 'Confédération internationale des travailleurs intellectuels', p. 327.
[110] 'Confédération internationale des travailleurs intellectuels', p. 328. Council meeting of CITI, 21 June 1931, UNESCO/B.IV.17.
[111] 'Commission d'enquête sur le groupement des travailleurs intellectuels en Europe et tout particulièrement en France', UNESCO/B.IV.17, pp. 1–2.

a number of articles that specifically dealt with intellectual relief and wellbeing during conflict. Whereas a wide range of camp libraries, often with very specific research focuses, were set up in internment camps during the First World War for people of intellectual backgrounds, this was not formalized in international law until the 1929 Geneva Convention. Article seventeen established the principle that 'belligerents shall encourage as much as possible the organization of intellectual and sporting pursuits by the prisoners of war'.[112] Article thirty-nine stipulated that 'representatives of the protecting powers and of duly recognized and authorized relief societies may send works and collections of books to the libraries of prisoners, camps'.[113] By contrast, the 1906 Geneva Convention made no reference to the intellectual needs of internees. Heather Jones has argued that the 1929 convention bore much relation to the events of the First World War and the experience of intellectual internees was clearly part of this framing.[114] This was another manifestation of the trend across the 1920s to codify and protect the position of intellectuals as a transnational issue.

The Flickering Lights

When the Sorbonne decided to award Albert Einstein an honorary degree in May 1929, Julien Luchaire, director of the International Institute of Intellectual Cooperation, remarked that it was a 'sign of the times'.[115] The Locarno treaties had ushered in a new era of international cooperation which was symbolized by the fraternization between Gustave Stresemann and Aristide Briand, the respective foreign ministers of Germany and France. In the post-Locarno years, Germany was welcomed back into the international fold, with the

---

[112] Convention relative to the Treatment of Prisoners of War. Geneva, 27 July 1929, Article 17. ihl-databases.icrc.org/applic/ihl/ihl.nsf/ART/305–430018?OpenDocument [accessed 4 August 2022].

[113] Convention relative to the Treatment of Prisoners of War. Geneva, 27 July 1929, Article 39. ihl-databases.icrc.org/applic/ihl/ihl.nsf/ART/305–430040?OpenDocument [accessed 4 August 2022].

[114] Heather Jones, *Violence against Prisoners of War in the First World War: Britain, France and Germany, 1914–1920* (Cambridge, 2011), p. 336. The 1949 Geneva Convention gave further substance to the rights of prisoners to receive intellectual relief.

[115] Luchaire to Einstein, 9 May 1929, UNESCO/A.I.15.

prestigious award to Einstein by France's most eminent university emblematic of this trend. By the time he received his degree six months later in November 1929, the global situation had changed abruptly. Stresemann was dead and a major financial crash had shaken Wall Street which would ultimately lead to a global depression.[116] The lights of Locarno began to flicker.

By the end of the 1920s, international intellectual life, having surmounted the immediate post-war crisis, faced a new set of threats which tested the organizations and practices established over the preceding decade. The depression exacerbated the already difficult economic conditions faced by many members of Europe's middle classes. The rise of authoritarian governments saw European intellectuals face restrictions on their freedom of expression. Finally, the onset of war heralded, as it had during the First World War, the targeting of cultural sites and threats to the lives of intellectuals themselves. Each of these phenomena presented a challenge to the institutions and conventions that had emerged over the prior decade and constituted a threat to both the economic standing of intellectual workers and the assumed cultural authority of intellectuals.

Natural disasters also contributed to late-decade threats to intellectual life. In April 1928, a devastating earthquake struck the Bulgarian city of Plovdiv. Houses, churches, and schools were destroyed, as was the city's public library, the second largest in Bulgaria. As was the case in 1923 following the earthquake in Tokyo, Bulgaria appealed to international sympathy to come to its aid. An international appeal was launched by the 'Cultural and Professional Associations of Bulgaria' which addressed itself in the name of 'the entire intelligentsia of Bulgaria' to 'public opinion of all civilized countries'.[117] The appeal singled out the League of Nations and the Inter-Allied Reparation Commission and asked both to postpone Bulgaria's reparation obligations – stipulated by the Treaty of Neuilly – for at least twenty years. Unlike the early 1920s appeals on behalf of Louvain, Belgrade, or Tokyo, there was no great international clamour to help Plovdiv by the late 1920s. The post-war humanitarian moment had passed.

There was a major reorganization of the work of intellectual cooperation at the League of Nations by the end of the decade which saw the

---

[116] 'La séance de rentrée des facultés', *Le Petit Parisien*, 10 November 1929, p. 3.
[117] 'An Appeal', May 1928. RAC/OMR, Series Q, Box 39, Folder 330.

formation of the Organization for Intellectual Cooperation (OIC). This reorganization was a response to a conviction that intellectual cooperation was undergoing, in the words of the Belgian politician and ICIC member Jules Destrée, a crisis. In 1929, Destrée wrote a series of articles in *Le Soir* which claimed that this crisis was caused by the Eurocentricity of the ICIC, its overemphasis on eminent figures in its initial composition, and because of the French domination of the IIIC.[118] Louis Gallié, head of the CTI, agreed with the diagnosis of crisis. He wrote in 1930 that the work of the ICIC was too reactive and superficial rather than espousing a clear direction of its own. While hinting at the French crisis of faith in intellectuals following Benda's 1927 publication, Gallié argued that 'the crisis of intellectual cooperation was above all a crisis of confidence'.[119] Most parties agreed that the ICIC needed to become a permanent body rather than a committee that met just once annually; accordingly, an executive committee was set up.[120]

This general restructuring of the League's intellectual cooperation bodies led to considerable reflection upon the concept of intellectual cooperation itself. Gilbert Murray, the chair of the ICIC, wrote in 1929 that there had never been 'any authoritative definition of the phrase "intellectual cooperation" as applied to an activity of the League of Nations', and felt that such a definition might be helpful as part of a wider reorganization.[121] Clear definitions of intellectual cooperation were further complicated by linguistic differences. In 1930, Murray claimed that the term 'intellectual cooperation' was a phrase that 'sounds absurd in English, but is all right in French or Italian'. The ICIC chair argued that the term had taken on two different meanings, which he defined as 'a general co-operation of nations in thought and mind as well as in act' and 'a special co-operation among what are called the "intellectuals" of different nations – the teachers, writers, artists, men of science and learning'.[122] Murray claimed that

---

[118] Jules Destrée, 'La crise de la Commission international de Coopération intellectuelle', *Le Soir*, 10 August 1929 and 16 August 1929, in BLAM/MS Gilbert Murray, 275/141, 147.

[119] Louis Gallié, 'La coopération intellectuel au point de vue français', *Bulletin de la confédération des travailleurs intellectuels*, 11.34 (1930), pp. 129–34.

[120] Renoliet, *L'UNESCO oubliée*, pp. 100–9.

[121] Memorandum by Gilbert Murray, c.1929, BLAM/MS Gilbert Murray 276/133.

[122] Broadcast by Murray on 'Intellectual Cooperation', 5 March, 1930, BLAM/MS Gilbert Murray 277/97.

intellectual cooperation really constituted the pooling of 'the best brains of all nations for the common service of all' in order to address complex international problems.[123] In this technical manner the ICIC was, Murray argued, the most 'characteristic instrument' of the League.[124] His colleague on the ICIC, the American physicist Robert Millikan, felt that the committee had erred in seeking to improve conditions for 'that particular class of society which was described under the general heading of intellectual workers' because 'many of our present social ills come from this so-called class struggle'.[125]

The ICIC had begun to be viewed with cynicism by the early 1930s. In his account of the work of the League written in 1933, the Austrian journalist Max Beer wrote with scepticism that 'the intellectual élite' were 'ready to help the League; the splendour of the thought whose rough-cut shape it conceals was great enough to draw the eager masses from their laboratories, their studies, their lecture-rooms and their libraries'. In Beer's account, this same intellectual elite did not have the opportunity to offer their input into meaningful issues relating to international diplomacy. Instead, the journalist claimed that the intellectuals who gathered in Geneva were not permitted to 'go beyond the mediocre sphere of bureaucratic organization, or to push aside the amateurish accumulation of material dealing with the unessentials of intellectual life'. Even in the bespoke agencies that were created to deal with intellectual matters such as the IIIC in Paris or the ICIC in Geneva, 'bureaucrats were the real rulers'.[126]

While a narrative of crisis framed the work of the ICIC by the late 1920s, the committee could lay claim to considerable achievement during this period. The International Studies Conference (ISC), which had its first meeting in Berlin in 1928, was an innovative forum that brought together academics, diplomats, and philanthropists to consider problems in international relations.[127] The ICIC could also point to significant progress in the international protection of cultural property,

---

[123] Gilbert Murray, *The Ordeal of this Generation* (London, 1929), p. 193.
[124] Murray, *The Ordeal of this Generation*, p. 191.
[125] Millikan to Murray, 20 June 1930, BLAM/MS Gilbert Murray 278/11–12.
[126] Max Beer, *The League on Trial: A Journey to Geneva* (London, 1933), pp. 229–33.
[127] Katharina Rietzler, 'American Foundations and the "Scientific Study" of International Relations in Europe, 1910-1940', PhD dissertation, University College London, 2009; pp. 188–241; Ludovic Tournès, *Les États-Unis et la Société des Nations (1914–1946): Le Système international face a l'émergence*

notably through the creation of the International Museums Office in 1926, which organized three key normative international charters between 1931 and 1933.[128] The emphasis placed upon moral disarmament, evident in the ICIC's attempts to reform the content of school textbooks, bore an influence that outlived the interwar period and was formative for many of its participants.[129] Gwilym Davies, a close observer of the League's work on intellectual cooperation, felt that the ICIC's great achievement was to 'bring people together, in the intellectual field, who had not been brought together before' to work together 'disinterestedly for a common end'.[130] The work of intellectuals, viewed as a collective, underpinned these initiatives and many besides; however, in the face of a growing threat to intellectuals and intellectual life, the ICIC was less successful.

The 'crisis' of intellectual cooperation at the League occurred at a time of wider international decline. Around the world, intellectual life was under renewed threat from natural disaster, economic depression, and war. Echoing language that was commonplace in the aftermath of the First World War, in 1932 Karl Mannheim wrote from Frankfurt to his American funders that 'due to the current crisis' his research work 'had almost come to a standstill'.[131] In the same year, the International Student Service, supported by the Carnegie Corporation of New York and the International Institute of Teachers College, set out to research what it regarded as a key postwar problem: the overcrowding of universities and the unemployment

---

d'une superpuissance (Bern: Peter Lang, 2016), p. 295; Stöckmann, *The Architects of International Relations*, pp. 187–93.

[128] François Hartog, *Regimes of Historicity: Presentism and Experiences of Time* (New York, 2017), pp. 183–4; Go Ohba, 'Two Approvals from the 1931 Athens Conference: Anastylosis and International Collaboration for Architectural Conservation: New Evidence', *Conservation and Management of Archaeological Sites*, 19.2 (2017), pp. 99–105; Annamaria Duci, 'Europe and the Artistic Patrimony of the Interwar Period: the International Institute of Intellectual Cooperation at the League of Nations', in Mark Hewitson and Matthew d'Auria eds., *Europe in Crisis: Intellectuals and the European Idea, 1917–1957* (New York, 2015), pp. 227–42.

[129] Barros, 'Turn Everyone into a Civilian', pp. 243–59; Ken Osborne, 'Creating the "International Mind": The League of Nations Attempts to Reform History Teaching, 1920-1939', *History of Education Quarterly*, 56.2 (2016), pp. 213–40.

[130] Davies, *Intellectual Cooperation between the Two Wars*, p. 6.

[131] Karl Mannheim to Edmund E. Day, 13 January 1932, RAC/LSRM, 3.6, Box 61, Folder 660.

of graduates.[132] Walter Kotschnig, the report's author, wrote that behind the 'dry figures' lay the 'misery of a whole generation'.[133] University overcrowding and graduate unemployment were accompanied by a turn to the extreme right among many student organizations in Germany and Austria, which was premised upon the notion that Jews were over-represented in universities and in intellectual professions.[134] This built on rising institutional anti-Semitism in many European institutions in the interwar period and would come to a head in the infamous Nazi law of April 1933.

In his seminal 1927 work, Julien Benda claimed that the proper action of a *clerc* or intellectual was to speak up in defence of issues that were considered to be of universal importance.[135] This kind of intellectual engagement continued to have great force – and divisiveness – in France, where in 1925 a number of mass petitions were published in the name of 'intellectual workers' and 'intellectuals' that both criticized and supported France's war in Morocco.[136] In the 1920s, there was also a greater internationalization of this type of action, with self-styled intellectuals from around the world collectively speaking out in defence of particular issues. This was the case with the Boston-based Italian anarchists Fernando Sacco and Bartolomeo Vanzetti when their murder conviction (and death sentence) was appealed in 1927. Figures such as Albert Einstein, H.G. Wells, George Bernard Shaw, John dos Passos, Marie Curie, Alphonse Aulard, and Victor Basch added their names to an international appeal on behalf of the two men.[137] The French mathematician Jacques Hadamard, a *dreyfusard* and member of the Ligue des droits de l'homme, helped to organize an international appeal and wrote privately that 'since the Dreyfus case, any condemnation of an innocent

---

[132] Walter M. Kotschnig, *Unemployment in the Learned Professions: An International Study of Occupational and Educational Planning* (Oxford, 1937), p. v.
[133] Kotschnig, *Unemployment in the Learned Professions*, p. vi.
[134] Wolfgang Zorn, 'Student Politics in the Weimar Republic', *Journal of Contemporary History*, 5.1 (1970), pp. 128–43.
[135] Benda, *La trahison des clercs*, pp. 54–5.
[136] Sirinelli, *Intellectuels et passions françaises*, pp. 99–102.
[137] Kerry Hinton, *The Trial of Sacco and Vanzetti: A Primary Source Account* (New York, 2004), pp. 47–53; 'Aujourd'hui Sacco et Vanzetti doivent être électrocutés', *Excelsior*, 10 August 1927, p. 3.

man is a thought which we cannot bear'.[138] Francis Dortet issued an 'appeal to American intellectuals' to follow the spirit of the Declaration of the Rights of Man and the Citizen in supporting the condemned men.[139] The decision to execute Sacco and Vanzetti led to protests in cities around the world, from Paris to London to Sydney, many of which were exacerbated by growing anti-Americanism.[140] Riots took place in Geneva during which the League of Nations building was attacked and every window of the council room was smashed.[141]

Benito Mussolini, the fascist leader of Italy, claimed that he had done 'all that was possible within the limits of international relations' to save Sacco and Vanzetti.[142] Seemingly allied to international intellectuals in this instance, Mussolini's actions would further demonstrate the impotence of collective protest and international intellectual organizations just a few years later. In November 1931, Mussolini's government introduced a law that required all university lecturers to take an oath in which they pledged themselves 'to fulfil all academic duties with the purpose of forming active and valiant citizens devoted to the country and to the Fascist regime'.[143] Academics who refused to sign the oath were either removed from their positions or resigned under pressure. In 1932, scholars from around the world directed an international petition not to the Italian government, but at the ICIC and IIIC. It argued that 'this oath involves an intellectual coercion which is incompatible with the ideals of scholars', and for that reason they claimed that the Institute of Intellectual Cooperation should address it.[144] The petition called on the IIIC to consider ways in which the 'intellectual liberty' of Italian professors could be defended and was signed by hundreds of

---

[138] Hadamard to Butler, 12 August 1927. CURBML, Nicholas Murray Butler (NMB) Arranged Correspondence, Box 172.

[139] Francis Dortet, 'L'affaire Sacco & Vanzetti. Un appel aux intellectuels américains', *La Dépêche*, 29 July 1927, p. 1.

[140] Brooke Blower, *Becoming Americans in Paris: Transatlantic Politics and Culture between the World Wars* (Oxford, 2011), pp. 95–6.

[141] 'Riotous scenes at Geneva', *The Times*, 23 August 1927, p. 10.

[142] 'Aujourd'hui Sacco et Vanzetti doivent être électrocutés', *Excelsior*, 10 August 1927, p. 3.

[143] 'The oath of the university professors', *Italy Today, by Friends of Italian Freedom*, 3.2 (1932), p. 1. LNA/R2258/5B/33486/33486.

[144] 'An Appeal to the Committee on Intellectual Cooperation', *Italy Today, by Friends of Italian Freedom*, Supplement to February 1932, March 1932, p. 1. LNA/R2258/5B/33486/33486.

scholars around the world in countries such as Switzerland, Britain, Spain, the United States, Argentina, France, Germany, the Netherlands, and Sweden. Gilbert Murray claimed that the ICIC had received protests 'from so many and such influential quarters'.[145]

The Italian oath issue demonstrated the limits of collective international action; public pressure initiated by intellectuals, no matter how eminent, had little power to alter the policy of another state government. Albert Dufour-Feronce, an under-secretary-general at the League, stated bluntly that one intellectual petition had not been formally acted on by the Secretariat because it was only signed by 'eminent men in the world of science and letters' and did not bear the name of a 'government authority.[146] The secretary to the ICIC, Georges de Montenach, wrote that the ICIC, like the League's Council, had little right to interfere in the internal affairs of sovereign states, a decision that was confirmed by the League's legal section.[147] The situation was made even more difficult as Italy was a member of the League's Council, which had been enthusiastic in its embrace of intellectual cooperation.

In September 1931, Japan invaded the Chinese region of Manchuria. The outbreak of war between two member states of the League of Nations demonstrated that intellectuals and cultural sites would again be targets in conflict and that intellectuals – and the institutions that represented them – would be key figures in seeking to influence international public opinion. In the same month, representatives of Chinese universities sent a telegram to the Sorbonne in Paris. Citing 'the helpless standing of the League of Nations [and] in view of the weakness and unpreparedness of the world public opinion', they called upon 'educators of your country to exert all effort for the cause of justice and righteousness'.[148] Chinese intellectuals again appealed to the Sorbonne in October seeking 'the spirit of justice and humanity of the world's intellectuals against these acts of violence by Japan's soldiers'.[149]

---

[145] Murray to Montenach, 1 January 1932, LNA/R2258/5B/33486/33486.
[146] Albert Dufour-Feronce to S.D. Wicksell, 18 May 1932, LNA/R2258/5B/33486/33486.
[147] Montenach to Murray, 8 January 1932, LNA/R2258/5B/33486/33486.
[148] J. Usang Ly to Sébastien Charléty, 28 September 1931, AN/AJ/16/6966.
[149] 'Appel des intellectuels chinois aux intellectuels du monde entier', circa October 1931, AN/AJ/1/6966.

The outbreak of hostilities in Manchuria demonstrated that modern warfare would take aim at cultural institutions and intellectuals themselves. The historian Luther C. Goodrich arrived in China on a Willard Straight Fellowship in October 1931. He reported a meeting with a missionary in China who recounted that 'one could never tell – when aeroplanes came along high overhead ... how accurate the bombers might be'.[150] In another instance, Goodrich encountered a Chinese archaeologist who had to withdraw from a dig at the ancient capital of the Yin dynasty when 'the soldiers became obnoxious ... choosing his place of operation for target practice'.[151] In May 1932, representatives of four Chinese universities sent a telegram to the ICIC in Geneva urging their intervention following what it called the deliberate targeting of cultural institutions, including a university library, by the Japanese air raids. 'You are requested [to] urge League Council [to] take immediate action for prevention of continuance of such atrocities against civilization'.[152] The accounts of cultural violence brought to mind the events of the First World War, now bolstered by ominous technological advancements. The ICIC, much like international intellectual opinion, was powerless to do much in this instance.

War between Japan and China also upset the post-war humanitarian order. The international effort to help rebuild and restock Tokyo Imperial University in 1923 was built upon sympathy for the victims of the Great Kantō earthquake. Representatives of TIU had maintained regular correspondence with their funders in the United States after the opening of the new library in 1928. In early 1932, Anesaki Masaharu, the TIU librarian and scholar, wrote to John D. Rockefeller, Jr, of his concerns that 'the relationships between your country and ours' could be 'impaired permanently' by Japanese actions in Manchuria.[153] Japan would formally leave the League of Nations in 1933 following the Assembly's vote that the state of Manchukuo had come into existence by force. Japan maintained a place on the ICIC, where they were represented, from 1934,

---

[150] Goodrich Journal, entry for 4–5 April 1932, RAC/IIE, 3.HF.2.13.
[151] Goodrich Journal, entry for 30 May 1932, 1932. RAC/IIE, 3.HF.2.13.
[152] Telegram from Chinese universities to Gilbert Murray, 3 May 1932, UNESCO/ A.1.16.
[153] Anesaki to Rockefeller, 9 March 1932, RAC/OMR, Series G, Box 130, Folder 997.

by Anesaki.[154] Japan's departure from the League in 1933 was mirrored by that of Germany and was striking evidence of the fracturing of the post-Locarno international order.

Conclusion

The figure of the intellectual was the subject of considerable international interest in the decade following the end of the First World War. The economic dislocation that followed the conflict rendered the continuation of intellectual work exceptionally challenging and demonstrated that intellectuals across Europe had much in common materially. The aftermath of war also led to heated discussion about the political and cultural role of the intellectual. While in national settings much ink was spilled regarding the appropriateness of partisanship during the war, at an international level organizations like the League of Nations regarded intellectuals, and their cultural influence, as potential agents of stability and moderators of public opinion.

The 1920s were notable for the proliferation of organizations, established at both national and international levels, which sought to represent the interests of those termed intellectuals. Many of these bodies were a direct outgrowth of the post-war crisis and the material suffering of intellectuals in the face of unemployment, economic distress, or displacement. At the same time, these organizations also represented a conviction that intellectual life too, much like the devastated regions of Belgium and northern France, must be rebuilt, and often explicitly articulated an anxiety that reconstruction privileged material matters over cultural ones. In the immediate post-war years, the potential of intellectuals to influence international public opinion and thus promote peace and stability was widely discussed.

None of this should suggest that a uniform vision of the international function of the intellectual emerged in the 1920s. Tensions were evident between definitions of the intellectual that were primarily based on their material situation and status as part of a workforce, and their cultural function as defenders of universal values. Conflicts were evident, too, between different national framings of the intellectual's role.

---

154 Martin Grandjean, 'Les réseaux de la coopération intellectuelle. La Société des Nations comme actrice des échanges scientifiques et culturels dans l'entre-deux-guerres.' PhD dissertation, Université de Lausanne, 2018, p. 548.

All of this notwithstanding, the proliferation of organizations and publications on the topic suggests that the 1920s saw the internationalization of the idea of the intellectual and that this had its origins in the immediate post-war crisis. By the start of the 1930s, however, it was clear that faith in the restorative potential of intellectual life for European reconstruction and stability was somewhat misplaced; the onset of economic crisis, threats to democracy, and the spectre of war all led many to question what progress had been achieved in the preceding decade. The Spanish philosopher José Ortega y Gasset wrote in 1930 that intellectuals and intellectual life were being undermined by the rise of the 'commonplace' masses.[155] Paul Valéry, who diagnosed the 'crisis of the mind' in 1919, wrote in 1931 that 'it is very evident that, to date, the majority of intellectuals ignore intellectual cooperation. The intellectual does not think of it and does not make use of it.' 'Our cooperation', he concluded ominously, 'only exists in the mortal form of paper'.[156]

---

[155] José Ortega y Gasset, *The Revolt of the Masses* (first ed. 1932; New York, 1957), pp. 16–8. The Spanish edition was first published in 1930.
[156] 'La Création du Comité Permanent des Lettres et des Arts', *Bulletin de la coopération intellectuelle*, 2 (1931), p. 3.

Epilogue: Beyond 1933

In August 1937, the International Committee on Intellectual Cooperation in Geneva received a shocking telegram which described the bombardment of the National Central University in China by Japanese planes. Three tons of explosives were dropped on the campus and machinegun fire transformed the library into a 'beehive'. 'Such deliberate attack [sic] with huge quantities high explosives against university', it exclaimed, 'cannot but be interpreted as threat of destruction to civilization in general'.[1] Japan repeatedly attacked Chinese universities from the air following the re-eruption of conflict in 1937. Graphic and distressing appeals reached European and American intellectuals which urged them to bring these events to wider attention.[2] The Library Association of China wrote to the ICIC to report that 'the magnificent library' of the University of Tientsin 'was razed to the ground' in July 1937 and that a squadron of twenty-seven heavy bombers had dropped one hundred incendiary bombs on the national university of Hunan and the National Tsing Hua university in April 1938 in an attempt to 'eradicate Chinese civilization'.[3] T.L. Yuan, the chairman of the executive board of the Library Association of China, wrote to Gilbert Murray that 'the serious loss of libraries and cultural institutions in China is a hundred times greater than that sustained by Louvain during the Great War'.[4]

Comparisons to Louvain were common by the late 1930s as another global conflict loomed. 'We address universities and centres of culture of the entire world', stated a petition of January 1939, 'to denounce the fact that for the third time, the University of Barcelona has been

---

[1] Chialuen Lo to the Committee on Intellectual Cooperation, 30 August 1937, LNA/R4044/5B/30199/30199.
[2] Telegraph from Chou-Lou to Charléty, 25 October 1938, AN/AJ/16/6966.
[3] 'The destruction of Chinese libraries during Japanese invasion – a preliminary statement', June 1938, LNA/R4044/5B/33187/30199.
[4] Yuan to Murray, 11 June 1938, LNA/R4044/5B/33187/30199.

bombarded'. The authors of this manifesto, twenty-eight academics based at a number of Spanish universities, called on international figures to use their moral authority to prevent the repetition of such violence. The Spanish intellectuals stated that their mission was to 'maintain the cultural flame in our country against the scourge of war'.[5] The emotive language used to describe the deliberate targeting of a university mirrored that used to describe similar events during the First World War. In Paris, René Cassin organized a manifesto by French scholars which stated that the acts of destruction were 'an attack on the civilized world as the burning of Louvain was in 1914'.[6] The fear of attacks on cultural sites drew upon the memory of the First World War and was given further impetus by the conflicts in Spain and China, book burnings in Nazi Germany, and the knowledge that modern technology and the advent of the bomber presented greater destructive potential than had been the case in previous conflicts.[7]

The spectre of Louvain hung not only over Europe, but also the wider world; it was a symbol of both the militaristic excesses of the First World War and the resilience of the self-styled civilized world to rebuild, restore, and overcome. The rebuilt Louvain library was a manifestation of European civilization resurgent, buttressed by American money, and the symbolic epicentre for post-war intellectual reconstruction. When it suffered significant damage at the hands of the German army in May 1940, news reports spoke not only of civilization, but of humanitarianism and philanthropy. One American newspaper headline read that 'Flames of War Again Raze Louvain Library, Rebuilt by U.S. Funds'.[8] By that point, France had again been invaded by the German army but newspapers still reported on the fate of the library; they recounted the role of American philanthropy in the library's

---

[5] 'Manifeste des professeurs d'universités espagnols', 7 January 1939, AN/382AP/23.

[6] Manifesto of French professors, January 1939, AN/382AP/23.

[7] Ovenden, *Burning the Books,* p. 3; Andrew Pettegree and Arthur der Weduwen, *The Library: A Fragile History* (London: Profile Books, 2021), p. 334; Brett Holman, 'World Police for World Peace: British Internationalism and the Threat of the Knock-out Blow from the Air', *War in History,* 17.3 (2010), pp. 313–32.

[8] 'Flames of War Again Raze Louvain Library, Rebuilt by U.S. Funds', *Fresno Bee,* 21 May 1940, p. 4.

interwar reconstruction and informed their readership that it had been 'assassinated again by the barbarians'.[9]

The post-war promise of democracy crumbled in the 1930s. So too, with civil war in Spain from 1936, renewed conflict between Japan and China, and world war commencing in 1939, did the aspiration for peace. Totalitarian states targeted intellectuals, leading to new waves of displacement and a fresh international effort to save those affected. Wartime violence surpassed that of the First World War, creating new humanitarian and cultural crises. Speaking in Chicago in 1939, the British philosopher Bertrand Russell declared that 'in the world as it is now, the intellectual [...] has painfully little influence. Perhaps that was always so'.[10]

***

Feeding the Mind has explored how the intellectual world was rebuilt in the midst of the humanitarian crises that followed the Great War. The intellectual relief of the early 1920s was formative for that which emerged in the 1930s and 1940s when Europe's intellectual life again had to be rebuilt following another global cataclysm. The post-Second World War establishment of the United Nations Educational, Scientific and Cultural Organization (UNESCO) demonstrated that intellectual, cultural, and educational reconstruction would again inform international stabilization following total war. On this occasion it was less Eurocentric, featured less emphasis on Western civilization, and did not see an intellectual elite as crucial to the rebuilding of the world, as had been the case a quarter of a century before. Many of the key framers of the United Nations' (UN) cultural institution were themselves veterans of the League's intellectual cooperation initiatives, intellectual relief initiatives, intellectual exiles, or all three. The response to totalitarianism and the outbreak of world war demonstrated strong continuities of individuals and institutions, if not of the ideas that propounded in the 1920s.

Why this change? Alfred Zimmern argued in 1939 that the post-war years had seen a mood of 'optimism in the English-speaking countries about the future of international relations and of modern civilization as

---

[9] 'L'Université de Louvain n'est plus que ruines ...', *Le Petit Parisien*, 22 May 1940, p. 1.
[10] Bertrand Russell, 'The Role of the Intellectual in the Modern World', *American Journal of Sociology*, 44.4 (1939), p. 493.

a whole' which was 'premature and misplaced'.[11] Zimmern's assertion that the early 1920s were marked by optimism may seem odd. The discourse surrounding civilization in the period was, after all, profoundly bleak. At the same time, politicians, philanthropists, and international organizations placed faith in intellectuals, as symbols and agents of a rational order, to rebuild democratic and peaceful European states. The rescue of intellectual life as an entity was a consequence of a general humanitarian crisis that spanned much of the European continent in the aftermath of the First World War. Intellectual relief simultaneously underpinned the identity of nation states and facilitated international connectedness. This faith was deeply shaken by the collapse of liberal democracies occasioned by the emergence of totalitarian states and the accompanying threat of war.[12]

This epilogue pushes forward to explore how the intellectual relief that emerged between 1933 and 1946 highlights prominent continuities as well as significant differences from that of the 1920s. Post-1933 relief demonstrated a move away from the articulation of threats to intellectuals or intellectual life in humanitarian terms, as had been the case in the 1920s; it also pushed back against programmes, institutions and language that privileged the elite figure of the international intellectual. These differences of emphasis can be seen clearly through an exploration of the international response to the expulsion of Jewish and other intellectuals from Nazi Germany in 1933 and the creation of UNESCO in 1946.

Intellectual Relief in the 1930s

The 'rescue of science and learning' of the 1930s is perhaps the most famous instance of intellectual relief in modern history.[13] The rise to

---

[11] Alfred Zimmern, *The Prospects of Civilization*, Oxford Pamphlets on World Affairs no. 1 (Oxford, 1939), pp. 3–4.

[12] Daniel Bessner has shown how the collapse of democracy in Germany led some to reconsider the potential of intellectuals to educate a wider public. *Democracy in Exile*, p. 17.

[13] Duggan and Drury, *The Rescue of Science and Learning*; Palmier, *Weimar in Exile*; Mitchell G. Ash and Alfons Söllner, eds., *Forced Migration and Scientific Change: Emigré German-speaking Scientists and Scholars After 1933* (Cambridge, 1996); Giuliana Gemelli ed., *The 'Unacceptables': American Foundations and Refugee Scholars Between the Two Wars and After* (Brussels, 2000); Martin Jay, *Permanent Exiles: Essays on the Intellectual Migration from Germany to America* (New York, 1986); Laurel Leff, *Well Worth Saving:*

power of the Nazis in Germany marked an abrupt end to post-Locarno cooperation; Germany left the League of Nations in 1933, ceasing cooperation with the ICIC, and thereafter Adolf Hitler began to unpick the Treaty of Versailles. The Nazi law of 7 April 1933 removed thousands of Jews and opponents of the regime from the civil service and many intellectuals were forced to flee the country.[14] From 1933 into the 1940s, thousands of scholars first fled Germany, then occupied Europe, and many of them were given jobs and homes in institutions across the world.[15] The humanitarian actions of the 1930s have generally been remembered as a success that transformed nations and institutions following the influx of eminent (primarily Jewish) intellectuals from across Europe.[16] This relief was driven by many actors and institutions who had been involved in the work of the early 1920s, but was also a consequence of the failure of some of these same institutions to act decisively in the face of Nazi repression in 1933.

In Geneva, the ICIC received numerous reports that drew attention to the displacement of Jewish scholars and threats to academic freedom in Germany.[17] These issues were, as ICIC chair Gilbert Murray noted privately, 'the kind of subject for which a committee of intellectual cooperation was created'.[18] Yet, as was the case when confronted with stories of Soviet repression of Ukrainian intellectuals in 1924 or the Italian oath in 1931, the organization did not act, deeming it beyond its scope to comment on the internal politics of other countries.[19] In November 1933, a month after Germany left the League of Nations, Hugo Andres Krüss resigned his seat as Germany's representative on the ICIC.[20] Faced with a new crisis for European intellectual life,

American Universities' Life-and-Death Decisions on Refugees from Nazi Europe (New Haven, CT, 2019).

14 Sally Crawford, Katharina Ulmschneider, and Jaś Elsner, 'Oxford's Ark: Second World War Refugees in the Arts and Humanities', in Crawford, Ulmschneider and Elsner eds., *Ark of Civilization*, p. 1.
15 Palmier, *Weimar in Exile*, p. 12.
16 Camurri, 'The Exile Experience Reconsidered', pp. 1–16; H. Stuart Hughes claimed that the influx of refugees led to the 'Deprovincialization of the American mind'. Coser, 'Refugee Intellectuals', p. 65.
17 Magnes to Murray, 8 June 1933, H.W. Tyler to the ICIC, 22 May 1933, LNA/R3991/5B/4953/946.
18 Murray to Montenach, 17 June 1933, LNA/R3991/5B/4953/946.
19 Montenach to Shotwell, 25 July 1933, LNA/R3991/5B/4953/946.
20 Krüss to Murray, 9 November 1933, UNESCO/A.I.15.

a topic which it had studied and towards which it had worked for over a decade, the International Committee on Intellectual Cooperation was unable to act decisively.

Where the ICIC was powerless, other organizations quickly sprang into life, many of which were led by people and institutions with experience of the post-First World War crisis. The Academic Assistance Council (AAC) was established in Britain in May 1933 to aid 'displaced teachers and investigators' from Germany; it was led by Sir William Beveridge, who had chaired the Universities Committee of the Imperial War Relief Fund in the early 1920s.[21] In New York, the Emergency Committee in Aid of Displaced German Scholars was set up in the same month. Backed by the Rockefeller Foundation, it was overseen by Stephen Duggan, director of the Institute of International Education (founded 1919), which had been active in placing refugee Russian scholars following the Bolshevik Revolution.[22] The RF, which had supported so many initiatives in the early 1920s in its previous incarnations, set up three schemes which were cumulatively funded with $1.4 million and brought 295 scholars to safety.[23] The International Student Service, previously known as European Student Relief, assisted German refugee students with funding from the IIE and 'the same faith and energy that we deployed long ago'.[24]

Unlike the general humanitarian crisis of the early 1920s, the situation in the 1930s was primarily related to migration and relief and tended not to portray assistance as a humanitarian act.[25] Instead,

[21] Academic Assistance Council founding statement, May 1933. www.cara.ngo/wp-content/uploads/2015/06/Cara-Founding-Statement.pdf [accessed 1 August 2022]. In 1935 it became known as the Society for the Protection of Science and Learning and, later, the Council for At-Risk Academics. David Zimmerman, 'The Society for the Protection of Science and Learning and the Politicization of British Science in the 1930s', *Minerva*, (2006), 44.1 (2006), pp. 25–45.

[22] Duggan and Drury, *The Rescue of Science and Learning*, pp. 6–7.

[23] Lässig, 'Strategies and Mechanisms of Scholar Rescue: The Intellectual Migration of the 1930s Reconsidered', p. 778.

[24] 'Academic relief of International Student Service for students unable to continue their studies in German universities', RAC, 9. HF.1.25; Rapport Annuel, 1933–1934. AN/61/AJ/101, p. 1.

[25] Lässig, 'Strategies and Mechanisms of Scholar Rescue', p. 782; Isabella Löhr, 'Solidarity and the Academic Community: The Support Network for Refugee Scholars in the 1930s', *Journal of Modern European History*, 12.2 (2014), pp. 231–46; Ash and Söllner, 'Introduction: Forced Migration and Scientific Change after 1933', in Ash and Söllner eds., *Forced Migration and Scientific*

emphasis was placed on the scholarly achievement of eminent individuals and their potential intellectual contribution to a host institution or country. The AAC claimed that its primary aim was to find employment for displaced intellectuals to 'prevent the waste of exceptional abilities exceptionally trained'.[26] The Notgemeinschaft Deutscher Wissenschaftler im Ausland, a relief organization established in 1933 with offices in London, Zurich, and Istanbul, stated explicitly that it was an 'employment agency'; by 1936 it had placed 350 people at institutions across the world.[27] Both the RF and ISS categorized scholars based on their field and scholarly excellence, although the ISS made some allowances for those in greatest need too.[28] The disinclination to use humanitarian language was also evident on the ground. Working as an intermediary between the Notgemeinschaft, Rockefeller Foundation, and IIE, Walter Kotschnig reported in 1936 that American universities were eager to assist displaced German scholars as long as decisions to help were 'made on an academic basis and not one of charity or an action prompted by humanitarian motives'.[29] Given the large numbers of Jewish intellectuals fleeing Germany, the emphasis on scholarly excellence was often a strategy to circumvent American institutional anti-Semitism.[30]

Across Europe, the rise of totalitarianism and the fracture of political life in the 1930s caused a great ideological polarization among intellectuals.[31] Much post-First World War thinking regarded the intellectual as the educator of public opinion in democratic nation states which constituted the liberal international order. With the

---

Change, p. 11; Emily J. Levine, *Allies and Rivals: German-American Exchange and the Rise of the Modern Research University* (Chicago, IL, 2021), p. 223.

[26] AAC founding statement.

[27] RF resolution, 15 May 1935, RAC/RF, SG 1.1., Series 717, Box 2, Folder 12.

[28] Humanities. Deposed Scholars, 1933–1939, 'The Rockefeller Foundation Special Research Aid Fund for Deposed Scholars, 1933-1939', RAC/RF, SG 1.1., Series 717, Box 2, Folder 8; 'Academic relief of International Student Service for students unable to continue their studies in German universities', RAC/IIE 9. HF.1.25; Note sur l'état actuel du fond de secours aux étudiants réfugiés d'Allemagne, 15 February 1935, AN/61/AJ/101.

[29] Walter Kotschnig, 'Situation of and opportunities for displaced German scholars in the United States', RAC/RF, SG 1.1., Series 717, Box 2, Folder 12, p. 3.

[30] Leff, *Well Worth Saving*, pp. 105–13; Levine, *Allies and Scholars*, pp. 223–4.

[31] Heyck, 'Myths and Meanings of Intellectuals in Twentieth-Century British National Identity', pp. 210–1.

demise of democracy, this aspiration receded. During the Spanish Civil War, a famous collectively authored publication argued that 'now, as certainly never before, we are determined or compelled, to take sides'.[32] Intellectuals in the international sphere were increasingly defined by their position on the political spectrum and whether they were right or left, or pro-or anti-fascist. The Spanish Civil War was a key mobilizing moment for this development.[33] At the International Writers' Congress in Valencia in 1937, delegates from around Europe and the world discussed, among other things, what it meant to be an intellectual and to speak out against oppression.[34] Among them was Julien Benda, who argued that the intellectual should 'emerge from his ivory tower to defend the rights of justice against barbarism'.[35] In the same year, the British author George Orwell wrote that 'the fence on which the literary gent sits [. . .] is now pinching his bottom intolerably; more and more he shows a disposition to drop off on one side or the other'.[36]

Intellectuals, and organized intellectual life, were increasingly consumed by Europe's totalitarian turn. The CITI and League of Nations organized a series of events around the theme of 'intellectual cooperation' at the Paris World's Fair in 1937 but the exhibition is best remembered for the symbolic ideological confrontation between the respective Soviet and Nazi pavilions and for the first display of Picasso's *Guernica*, which depicted the horrors of modern war.[37] And when the University of Göttingen celebrated its bicentenary in the same year, the event was boycotted by many international scholars and institutions troubled by the repression of the Nazi government.[38]

---

[32] Louis Aragon, W.H. Auden, José Bergamïn et al., 'The Question', in *Authors Take Sides on the Spanish War* (London, 1937), p. 1.

[33] Tony Judt, *Reappraisals: Reflections on the Forgotten Twentieth Century* (London, 2009), pp. 13–4; Judt, *Past Imperfect: French Intellectuals, 1944–1956* (Berkeley, CA, 1992), p. 19; Julian Jackson, *France: The Dark Years, 1940–1944* (Oxford, 2001), p. 75.

[34] These included the German writer Anna Seghers, the Spanish composer Gustavo Durán, the Dutch writer Jef Last, and the English author Sylvia Townsend. LAC/F/DELTA/RES/204.

[35] Speech of Julien Benda, 4 July 1937, LAC/F/DELTA/RES/204.

[36] George Orwell, *The Road to Wigan Pier* (Harmondsworth, 1966; orig. 1937), p. 185.

[37] UNESCO/B.IV.17; Winter, *Dreams of Peace and Freedom*, pp. 75–98.

[38] Levine, *Allies and Rivals*, p. 213.

The rise of totalitarian regimes led to the targeting of intellectuals across Europe in a bid to silence oppositional voices. Fritz Beck, a key collaborator of the ISS in Germany, was murdered by the SS in the Night of the Long Knives on 30 June 1934, leading to an ISS decision to temporarily suspend relations with German governmental institutions.[39] The Soviet Union took a seat on the ICIC in 1935 having joined the League in the previous year. Soviet involvement overlapped with the worst excesses of Stalin's purges, labelled by one historian as a 'holocaust of the things of the spirit'.[40] In June 1936, Henri Bonnet, director of the Institute in Paris, sent a telegram of condolence to Valerian Obolensky-Ossinsky, the Soviet representative on the ICIC, following the death of the Russian intellectual Maxim Gorky, likely on Stalin's orders.[41] By 1938, Obolensky-Ossinsky was himself a victim of the purges.[42]

The Second World War and UNESCO

The Second World War resulted in cultural and intellectual destruction that far surpassed that of the Great War; Louvain library was a victim again, while the British Museum in London, Prussian State Library in Berlin, and the ancient ruins of Pompeii all suffered differing degrees of damage from aerial bombing raids.[43] Émile Lousse, a professor at Louvain, noted ruefully that owing to the scale and indiscriminate nature of violence in the 1939–45 conflagration, the second burning of the Belgian library aroused comparatively little indignation.[44]

---

[39] Annuel, 1933–1934. AN/61/AJ/101, p. 2. Hitler spoke of his contempt for intellectuals. Richard J. Evans, *The Third Reich in Power, 1933–1939* (London, 2006), pp. 298–9.

[40] Robert Conquest, *The Great Terror: A Reassessment* (London, 1994), p. 307; Norman Naimark, *Stalin's Genocides* (Princeton, NJ, 2010), pp. 99–120.

[41] Bonnet to Obolensky-Ossinsky, 19 June 1936, UNESCO/A.I.68; Conquest, *The Great Terror*, pp. 388–9.

[42] Grandjean, 'Les réseaux de la coopération intellectuelle', p. 549.

[43] Burke, *A Social History of Knowledge II*, p. 146; Nigel Pollard, *Bombing Pompeii: World Heritage and Military Necessity* (Ann Arbor, MI, 2020); Pettegree and der Weduwen, *The Library*, pp. 329–32; Richard Overy, *The Bombing War: Europe 1939–1945* (London, 2013), pp. 472–3. On post-Second World War scientific reconstruction, see John Krige, *American Hegemony and the Postwar Reconstruction of Science in Europe* (Cambridge, MA, 2006).

[44] Émile Lousse, *The University of Louvain during the Second World War* (Bruges, 1946), pp. 50–1.

In contrast to the previous conflict, the Second World War saw the widespread murder of intellectuals, such as that perpetrated by German and Soviet forces in Poland, Ukraine, and elsewhere.[45] In many cases, the targeting of intellectuals was part of a greater crime: the Holocaust.

While the Second World War occasioned unprecedented destruction, it simultaneously effected systematic planning for the post-war world in which post-1918 reconstruction formed a crucial precedent and which culminated in the creation of UNESCO in 1946.[46] Inter-war intellectual institutions fell victim to the war; the ICIC held its last meeting in July 1939 while the Paris-based Institute of Intellectual Cooperation ceased operation following the fall of France in 1940.[47] One of its final acts that year was to issue an international inquiry into the effects of the war on intellectual life to which only a few paltry replies were received.[48]

Discussions of post-war reconstruction gathered pace in wartime on both sides of the Atlantic and reflected upon the failures of the interwar intellectual relief and international cooperation.[49] George F. Zook, president of the American Council on Education, wrote that 'we had the same opportunity twenty-five years ago and we "muffed" it'.[50] In 1943, the Welsh Baptist minister Gwilym Davies urged that 'this time we must succeed where we failed last time', and criticized the League for insufficient funding of intellectual cooperation, which amounted to,

---

[45] Timothy Snyder, *Bloodlands: Europe Between Hitler and Stalin* (London, 2010), pp. 153–6; Gella, 'The Life and Death of the Old Polish Intelligentsia', pp. 22–3; George Sanford, *Katyn and the Soviet Massacre of 1940: Truth, Justice and Memory* (London, 2005).

[46] Charles Dorn, 'The World's Schoolmaster: Educational Reconstruction, Grayson Kefauver, and the Founding of UNESCO, 1942–46', *History of Education*, 35.3 (2006), pp. 297–320; Paul Betts, 'Humanity's New Heritage: UNESCO and the Rewriting of World History', *Past & Present*, 228 (2015), pp. 251–3; H.H. Krill de Capello, 'The Creation of the United Nations Educational, Scientific and Cultural Organization', *International Organization*, 24.1 (1970), pp. 1–30, Renoliet, *L'UNESCO oubliée*, pp. 161–74.

[47] Pernet, 'Twists, Turns, and Dead Alleys', pp. 342–58; Grandjean, 'Les réseaux de la coopération intellectuelle', pp. 510–1.

[48] UNESCO/A.XIII.1.

[49] This was the case with other wartime planning. Jessica Reinisch, 'Internationalism in Relief: The Birth (and Death) of UNRRA', *Past & Present*, Supplement 6 (2011), pp. 258–89.

[50] *Education and the United Nations: A Report of a Joint Commission of the Council for Education in World Citizenship and the London International Assembly* (Washington, DC, 1943), p. v.

in some years, the same as the cost of two Spitfires.[51] The Romanian-born American educationalist Isaac Kandel argued in 1944 that the 'failure of statesmen to unite in utilizing the intellectual resources of the world for the preservation of peace' was a major contributor to war.[52] For Kandel, too much interwar activity concentrated on the elitist cooperation of intellectuals rather than the general promotion of international understanding.[53] A new challenge that emerged during the Second World War was the re-education of German and other Axis-occupied populations from the 'anti-scientific and immoral' methods of the Nazis.[54] As Konrad Jarausch has written, Nazi crimes demanded a 'deeper intervention than that required after 1918'.[55]

The aftermath of the First World War saw an improvised humanitarian intervention largely led by private philanthropy which sought to save the intellectual life of European nations (and 'civilization' itself). By contrast, discussions on intellectual reconstruction during the Second World War were proactive, involved national governments, and considered the problem of education in a more global, rather than European, manner. Moreover, wartime planning built upon the experiences of the preceding decades and mobilized many figures who had been involved in the post-First World War project of intellectual relief and different interwar liberal internationalist projects.[56] A consensus soon emerged that an international organization dealing with educational matters should be formed on the conclusion of the conflict.

The constitution for UNESCO was agreed at a conference held in London in November 1945 where draft proposals, developed over the preceding years, were formalized into a final text. The London conference was attended by representatives from forty-three countries and its composition demonstrated a move away from the elitist Eurocentrism of the early 1920s; delegations came from eleven European, eight

[51] Davies, *Intellectual Co-operation between the Two Wars*, pp. 6, 14.
[52] Isaac Kandel, *Intellectual Cooperation: National and International* (New York, 1944), p.1.
[53] Kandel, *Intellectual Cooperation*, p. 48.
[54] Gilbert Murray, 'Coopération intelletuelle', *L'Avenir* (1944), draft, UNESCO/A.I.35, p. 11.
[55] Konrad Jarausch, *After Hitler: Recivilizing Germans, 1945–1995* (Oxford, 2006), p. 9.
[56] Barros, 'Turn Everyone into a Civilian: René Cassin and the UNESCO Project', pp. 243–59.

Asian, and sixteen central or south American countries.[57] A number of international organizations were also represented, including the ILO, the League Secretariat, and both the ICIC and IIIC. Post-Second World War educational reconstruction and cooperation was an increasingly global aspiration which extended beyond the self-styled centres of civilization in continental Europe.[58]

Many familiar names were among the list of delegates, all of whom had been shaped by the experience of the preceding decades. Léon Blum was a former French prime minister and veteran of France's intellectual foundation myth, the Dreyfus Affair. Other members of the French delegation included Henri Bonnet, former director of the Institute for Intellectual Cooperation, and René Cassin.[59] Gilbert Murray represented the ICIC but brought with him the memory of participation in a committee to send aid to starving students and professors in Vienna after the First World War. The largest delegation was that of the United States, which counted thirty-four members led by the poet Archibald MacLeish. One of the delegation's secretaries was a forty-four-year-old Austrian who had been rendered stateless following the Anschluss of 1938 and who became an American citizen in 1942: Walter Kotschnig.[60]

Kotschnig was a living embodiment of post-war intellectual relief and student self-help. He experienced the worst of the *Hungerkatastrophe* in post-war Austria and made ends meet as an undergraduate in Graz by performing manual labour.[61] By his own account he was 'saved from starving' by 'contributions sent from American students', and this began his interest in student welfare.[62] Kotschnig completed a PhD at Kiel University and took up a position as Assistant Secretary of the European Student Relief in Geneva in 1925

---

[57] 'Conference for the Establishment of the United Nations Educational, Scientific and Cultural Organisation', pp. 9–12. unesdoc.unesco.org/ark:/4 8223/pf0000117626 [accessed 1 August 2022].

[58] Betts, *Ruin and Renewal*, pp. 312–43.

[59] Barros, 'Turn Everyone into a Civilian', p. 257.

[60] Walter M. Kotschnig, 'Quest for Survival', first draft, February 1978, M.E. Grenander Department of Special Collections and Archives (MEGDSCA), University at Albany, State University of New York, Albany, NY, Walter Kotschnig Papers (WKP), Box 1, Folder 6, p. 16.

[61] Biographical note on Dr. Walter Kotschnig, RAC/IIE, 8.HF.2.3.

[62] 'Walter Kotschnig to Give Lecture', *Pomona Progress-Bulletin*, 18 March, 1931, p. 5.

while also working for the League of Nations High Commission for Refugees. He was a key figure who helped to facilitate the placement of refugee scholars in the 1930s and acted as an important link between different committees in Europe and North America. In 1936, Kotschnig and his family moved to the United States. He began working for the State Department during the Second World War to assist in post-war planning.[63] During the war, Kotschnig spoke passionately about the need to establish a United Nations education agency, and attended key planning meetings with other advocates of such an institution.[64] He cautioned against the repetition of the errors of post-First World War relief, such as its being administered by 'bureaucrats' who did not seek to create attitudes 'likely to improve international relations'.[65] Kotschnig was of the opinion that interwar intellectual cooperation was too elitist, too detached, and insufficiently practical.[66]

The creation of UNESCO was notable for what it said about the figure of the intellectual, so widely invoked in the humanitarian discourse of the early 1920s. Many wartime discussions of reconstruction were critical of the elitist detachment implicit in regarding the figure of the intellectual as a guarantor of peace. This idea came to the fore at the London Conference. The Belgian education minister, Auguste Buisseret, argued that the distinction between 'intellectuals and common people' had been eroded under the pressure of wartime occupation, which was, he claimed, 'real intellectual co-operation'.[67] Archibald MacLeish agreed that the war had shown evidence of the willingness of 'soldiers and scientists, intellectuals and devoted women, boys and mature men' to work together.[68] Members of the French delegation disagreed with this line of thinking and sought to emphasize intellectual difference and elitism, evidence for which they saw in the prominence of intellectuals in resistance movements.[69] The philosopher Étienne Gilson argued that 'in all countries occupied by

---

[63] Kotschnig, 'Quest for Survival', MEGDSCA/WKP, Box 1, Folder 6, pp. 6–22.
[64] 'European Author is Fearful of Peace', *The News-Herald*, 14 January 1943, p. 8. HILA, Grayson Kefauver papers (GKP), Box 5, Folder 21.
[65] Walter Kotschnig, *Slaves Need No Leaders. An Answer to the Fascist Challenge to Education* (New York, 1943), p. 163.
[66] Kotschnig, *Slaves Need No Leaders*, p. 257.
[67] 'Conference for the Establishment', pp. 82–3.
[68] 'Conference for the Establishment', p. 41.
[69] James D Wilkinson, *The Intellectual Resistance in Europe* (Cambridge, MA, 1981).

our common enemy, intellectuals have been the vanguard of Resistance'.[70] René Cassin cited the idea, common after the First World War, that intellectuals were both educators and representatives of 'the opinion of the masses'.[71]

The debate about the place of intellectuals in the new institution could be seen in discussions regarding its title. The proposal which emerged through the London-based Conference of Allied Ministers of Education (CAME) called for the creation of an 'Educational and Cultural Organization', whereas a French proposal instead sought a 'United Nations Organization of Intellectual Co-operation'.[72] An American account of the discussions claimed that there was reluctance to use the term 'intellectual' in the title as it was 'one word in French and quite another in English'.[73] The French draft proposal suggested that the organization define the 'rights of intellectuals' and draw up 'international conventions needed for their protection', but this did not make the final version of the constitution.[74] The decision to rebuff the French proposal demonstrated a move away from the institutional legacy of the League of Nations and constituted a renunciation of the intellectual elitism of the interwar years. As Jean-Jacques Mayoux, the final director of the Institute for Intellectual Cooperation, wrote ruefully in 1946, his organization had been saddled with a 'bad reputation'.[75]

Conclusion

The intellectual humanitarianism that followed the end of the First World War belonged to a moment in European history in which the histories of intellectual life and humanitarianism converged. *Feeding*

[70] 'Conference for the Establishment', p. 87.
[71] 'Conference for the Establishment', pp. 91–2.
[72] 'Conference for the Establishment', pp. 1–9. The US and China favoured the title UNESCO, whereas India favoured the French proposal for an 'Intellectual Organisation' of the United Nations.
[73] 'Summary and Analysis of the United Nations Educational, Scientific and Cultural Organization', *"The defences of peace": Documents relating to UNESCO: The United Nations Scientific and Cultural Organisation*, Part II (Washington, DC, 1946), p. 13.
[74] 'Conference for the Establishment', p. 6; *Constitution of the United Nations Educational, Scientific and Cultural Organization, UNESCO, Basic Texts, 2020 Edition* (Paris, 2020), p. 6.
[75] Jean-Jacques Mayoux to Gilbert Murray, 17 June 1946, UNESCO/A.I.16. Salvador de Madariaga, *Victors, Beware* (London, 1946), p. 265.

the Mind has argued that these histories shed an important and reciprocal light onto each other. The post-First World War reconstruction of
intellectual life was a fundamentally conservative act which generally
sought to reconstruct institutions and individual lives as they had been
previously, rather than as they might be in the future. This conservative
vision was built upon widespread anxiety about the fate of civilization,
a term that encompassed both the development of European cultural
achievement and its trappings since the Enlightenment as well as an
imperial and racialized vision of how the world was structured. The
widespread claim that 'civilization' required humanitarian aid was
shorthand for, among other things, the post-war order of liberal nation
states that emerged from the Paris Peace Conference and the threat that
it faced from Bolshevism. In this way, humanitarian aid and the reconstruction of intellectual life were part of the 'recasting' of Bourgeois
Europe, where intellectuals were both symbols and agents of European
civilization.[76]

The myriad schemes to salvage Europe's intellectuals and their institutions in the early 1920s frequently used the language of the 'intellectual' to categorize a particular group who had suffered in the war and
its aftermath. The suffering of those labelled intellectuals transcended
national borders as shared experiences of hunger, poverty, ill-health,
and displacement were experienced across Europe. The ubiquity of
intellectual relief in the early 1920s, as well as the litany of unions
and associations founded in the same decade, suggest a growing
European and American consciousness of the figure of the 'intellectual'
which was rooted in social conditions, traditional elitism, and membership of an international community of democratic nation states.
This would change against the backdrop of the totalitarian polarization of the 1930s, but the 1920s presented a moment in which intellectuals were seen as a Euro-American category in which much hope – and
money – was invested. This vision, however, generally overlooked
those who belonged to no nation-state, as well as (with some excep-
tions) the world beyond Europe and North America. In *La trahison des
clercs*, Julien Benda scarcely mentioned non-European figures, while
membership of the League's ICIC was dominated by European figures
in the 1920s. The establishment of the United Nations and UNESCO
demonstrated a greater commitment to global engagement, a move

[76] Maier, *Recasting Bourgeois Europe*; Rodogno, *Night on Earth*, pp. 3–4.

away from regarding European intellectual elites as the custodians of universal culture, and less emphasis on traditional notions of civilization.[77]

The post-First World War period also reveals much about the contours of modern humanitarianism. The proliferation of many humanitarian agencies, of different sizes and scope, suggests numerous motivations for action. The identification of intellectuals as a discrete category for relief demonstrates that aid was not always given to those with the greatest need in this period, or, at least, not only for those reasons. The events of the early 1920s shed further light upon the development of what has been titled modern humanitarianism, where, it has been claimed, aid became more professionalized, institutionalized, and permanent.[78] While there is evidence of the former, intellectual relief demonstrates that short-lived, small-scale, and amateur initiatives still abounded in this period. Humanitarianism changed in the 1920s but its development was neither linear, nor was it a story of uninterrupted progress.[79]

The issues raised in this book are still pertinent over one hundred years later. War, political repression, economic dislocation, and natural disasters mean that the displacement of people, famine, and the destruction of institutions of knowledge are global issues. Climate change and its consequences mean that this could become much more acute in the future.[80] Forced intellectual migration has remained commonplace in the twentieth and twenty-first centuries, often accompanied by the language of one hundred years prior. In February 2022, days after the Russian invasion of Ukraine which led to the worst displacement of people in Europe for a generation, the French politician Jean-Louis Bourlanges was widely criticized for his comments about refugees fleeing the conflict. The Ukrainian migration was full of 'intellectuals', Bourlanges argued, and was thus of 'great quality from which we can

---

[77] Betts, *Ruin and Renewal*, pp. 1–29. For example, UNESCO's CARE book relief programme spoke of 'mental famine' and provided literature to people in the Philippines, China, India, and Pakistan, as well as Europe. New York Public Library Archives and Manuscripts (NYPLAM), CARE records, Box 4, Folder: Press Conference – Two Europes.

[78] Watenpaugh, *Bread from Stones*, pp. 4–9; Barnett, *Empire of Humanity*, p. 83; Cabanes, *The Great War and the Origins of Humanitarianism*, p. 4.

[79] Scott-Smith, *On an Empty Stomach*, p. 173.

[80] David Wallace-Wells, *The Uninhabitable Earth: A Story of the Future* (London, 2019), pp. 7–8.

profit'. This stood in contrast, it was implied, to refugees from other parts of the world.[81] In the twenty-first century, invocations of 'intellectuals' and 'civilization' often remain shorthand for something else; in this case white Europeans.[82]

Aid to displaced intellectuals is now a matter of global, rather than European concern, as was seen during the Syrian Civil War and the Taliban's return to power in Afghanistan in August 2021 when thousands of intellectuals were placed at risk.[83] A wide range of NGOs and charities now deal specifically with displaced intellectuals and students globally. Some of these, such as the Council for At-Risk Academics (CARA, formerly the AAC) and the Institute of International Education, can trace their origins back to the interwar period.[84] Others, such as the Scholars at Risk Network, were established much more recently.[85] In 2021, UNESCO introduced a 'Qualifications Passport' to facilitate access to higher education for refugees and migrants with prior qualifications.[86] The work of UNESCO and many other organizations proceeds from article 26 of the United Nations' Universal Declaration of Human Rights, which states that education is a human right. The 1989 UN Convention on the Rights of Children added that not only was education a right but that children must have equal opportunity in accessing it.[87] Thus, modern-day intellectual relief is a manifestation of a wider commitment to human rights.

[81] 'Guerre en Ukraine : 'On aura une immigration de grande qualité dont on pourra tirer profit', www.europe1.fr/politique/guerre-en-ukraine-on-aura-une-immigration-de-grande-qualite-dont-on-pourra-tirer-profit-4095961 [accessed 1 August 2022].

[82] Pankaj Mishra, *Bland Fanatics: Liberals, Race and Empire* (London, 2020), pp. 1–9.

[83] Guillaume Tronchet, 'L'accueil des étudiants réfugiés au xxe siècle: un chantier d'histoire globale', *Monde(s)*, 15 (2019), pp. 93–116; 'About Us', www.scholarrescuefund.org/about-us/afghanistan/ [accessed 1 August 2022].

[84] Allan Goodman, 'Lifeline for Refugee Scholars', *Science*, 354.6317 (2016), p. 1207.

[85] '20 Years of Helping Scholars & Promoting Academic Freedom', www.scholarsatrisk.org/wp-content/uploads/2020/12/SAR_20th-Anniversary-Report-2020.pdf [1 August 2022].

[86] 'Successful implementation of the UNESCO Qualifications Passport', en.unesco.org/news/successful-implementation-unesco-qualifications-passport-ensuring-access-higher-education-and [accessed 1 August 2022].

[87] 'Universal Declaration of Human Rights', www.ohchr.org/EN/UDHR/Documents/UDHR_Translations/eng.pdf [accessed 1 August 2022]; 'The United Nations Convention on the Rights of the Child', www.unicef

Knowledge, and the repositories that house it, continue to suffer damage either by unfortunate accident or wilfully destructive act. The 1954 Hague Convention for the Protection of Cultural Property gave greater legal protections to cultural property but deliberate cultural destruction continued.[88] In 1992, the Bosnian National and University Library in Sarajevo was deliberately destroyed during the Yugoslav war with the loss of 1.5 million books.[89] In the twenty-first century, intellectual institutions remain targets of war but also face a new threat: climate change-induced wildfires.[90] Major acts of cultural destruction still elicit global sympathy but institutions can now be rebuilt using modern technology. When part of the library of the University of Cape Town in South Africa was destroyed by fire in 2021, researchers around the world submitted digital scans of items from the library's special collections, which they had previously accessed, in order to begin rebuilding lost knowledge.[91] In a similar manner, a major project in Ireland virtually rebuilt the Public Record Office of Ireland – destroyed in the fighting of the Irish Civil War in 1922 – using digital copies of duplicate documents held in other libraries and archives.[92] International assistance to damaged Ukrainian universities in 2022 ranged from replacement glass for shattered windows to the provision of online lectures from international institutions.[93] Modern technologies afford creative ways of restoring the function of these institutions virtually, if not physically.

The figure of the international intellectual, with their presumed cultural authority, remained the subject of contestation throughout

.org.uk/wp-content/uploads/2010/05/UNCRC_united_nations_convention_on_ the_rights_of_the_child.pdf [accessed 1 August 2022].

[88] Bevan, *The Destruction of Memory*, p. 37.

[89] Michele V. Cloonan and Rebecca J. Knuth, 'Libraries, Archives, and the Pursuit of Access', in Matthew J. Morgan ed., *The Impact of 9/11 on the Media, Arts and Entertainment: The Day that Changed Everything?* (Basingstoke, 2009), p. 181.

[90] Suzanne LaPierre, 'Wildfires Damage Libraries', publiclibrariesonline.org/2020/ 10/wildfires-damage-libraries/ [accessed 1 August 2022].

[91] 'Assisting in Recovery from the UCT Library Fire', sparcopen.org/news/2021/ assisting-in-recovery-from-the-uct-library-fire/ [accessed 1 August 2022].

[92] 'Beyond 2022', beyond2022.ie/?page_id=2#vision [accessed 1 August 2022].

[93] '"Giving Hope": UK Universities Twin with Struggling Ukraine Counterparts', www.theguardian.com/education/2022/may/14/giving-hope-uk-universities-twin-with-struggling-ukraine-counterparts [accessed 1 August 2022].

the twentieth century, with figures such as Raymond Aron, Hannah Arendt, and Edward Said making significant contributions to the debate.[94] That has remained the case in the twenty-first century. The crises of the new millennium, such as the American-led invasion of Iraq in 2003, the COVID-19 pandemic which began in 2020, the Russian invasion of Ukraine in 2022, or the global threat posed by climate change, have all seen the transnational mobilization of intellectuals to make the case for particular courses of action against the backdrop of a growing public scepticism about facts, experts, and intellectuals.[95] As in the 1920s and 1930s, there is much discussion about the proper role of the intellectual or expert in public life, but the twenty-first-century iteration is complicated by the ubiquity of social media, which means that voices speaking from a position of expertise compete against many others in a transnational digital public sphere.[96] As intellectual life, its institutions and practitioners confront an era of new and unsettling threats, their protection remains as important as it was a century ago.

[94] Raymond Aron, *L'opium des intellectuels* (Paris, 1955); Hannah Arendt, *On Violence* (New York, 1969); Edward Said, BBC Reith Lectures, 1993.

[95] Maria Ryan, 'Review Essay: Intellectuals and the "War on Terror"', *Journal of American Studies*, 44.1 (2010), pp. 203–9; Matthew C. Nisbet, 'Disruptive Ideas: Public Intellectuals and their Arguments for Action on Climate Change', *WIREs Climate Change*, 5 (2014), pp. 809–23; Eric Merkley and Peter John Loewen, 'Anti-intellectualism and the Mass Public's Response to the COVID-19 Pandemic', *Nature Human Behaviour*, 5 (2021), pp. 706–15; 'German Thinkers' War of Words over Ukraine Exposes Generational Divide', *The Guardian*, 6 May 2022.

[96] Peter Dahlgren, 'Public Intellectuals, Online Media, and Public Spheres: Current Realignments', *International Journal of Politics, Culture and Society*, 25 (2012), pp. 99–104.

Bibliography

France:
La contemporaine, Nanterre:
Fonds Duchêne, Gabrielle.

Archives nationales, Paris:
Académie de Paris (AJ/16).
Application des traités de paix. Archives de la Commission interalliée des réparations de guerre (AJ/6).
École normale supérieure (61AJ).
Ministère de l'Instruction publique (F17).
Papers of Réné Cassin (382AP).

UNESCO archives, Paris:
Papers of the International Institute of Intellectual Cooperation (AG1 IICI).

Switzerland:
League of Nations Archives, United Nations Library and Archives, Palais des Nations, Geneva:
League of Nations Secretariat Fonds: Intellectual Cooperation and International Bureaux Section.

United Kingdom
Bodleian Libraries Archives and Manuscripts, Oxford:
Papers of Gilbert Murray (MS Gilbert Murray).
Papers of Alfred Zimmern (MS Alfred Zimmern).

British Library, London:
Cecil of Chelwood Papers (additional manuscripts 51071–51204).
Papers of George Nathaniel Curzon, Marquess Curzon of Kedleston (MSS Eur F.112/212).

British Academy Archives, London:
Minutebooks of the British Academy (1912–1919, 1919–1922).

Papers of Sir Israel Gollancz (BAA/SEC/1).
Papers of Sir Frederic Kenyon (BAA/SEC/2).

Library of the Society of Friends, London:
Papers of Friends' Emergency and War Victims' Relief Committee (YM/MfS/FEWVRC).

London School of Economics Archives and Special Collections, London:
Papers of Sir William Beveridge (BEVERIDGE).
Papers of Beatrice and Sidney Webb (PASSFIELD).

The National Archives (United Kingdom), Kew:
Peace Conference: British Delegation, Correspondence and Papers (FO 608)

National Library of Wales, Aberystwyth:
Rev. Gwilym Davies papers (GB 0210 GWVIES).

Parliamentary Archives, London:
Stow-Hill Papers (STH).

Royal Society Archives, London:
New Letter Books (NLB).
Correspondence of Sir Arthur Schuster (MS663).

West Glamorgan Archive Service, Swansea:
Papers of Winifred Coombe-Tennant (D/D T).

United States of America:
American Philosophical Society Archives, Philadelphia:
Franz Boas Papers (MSS.B.B61).

Columbia University Archives, Columbia University, New York:
World War One Collection.

Harvard University Archives, Harvard University, Cambridge, Massachusetts:
Papers of Charles W. Eliot (UAI 15.894).

Hoover Institution Library and Archives, Stanford University, Palo Alto, California:
American Relief Administration Russian Operational Records (23003).
American Relief Administration European Operational Records (23001).
Frank A. Golder papers (xx058).
Grayson N. Kefauver papers (47003).

M.E. Grenander Department of Special Collections and Archives, University at Albany, State University of New York, Albany, New York:
Walter Maria Kotschnig Papers (ger053).

New York Public Library Archives and Manuscripts, New York:
CARE Records (MssCol 470).

Rare Book and Manuscript Library, Columbia University, New York:
Bakhmeteff Archive of Russian and Eastern European, Committee for the Education of Russian Youth in Exile Records, 1914–1939 (Culture (BAR Ms Coll/CERYE).
Carnegie Endowment for International Peace Records (CEIP), Series VII (Projects).
Papers of Nicholas Murray Butler (NMB).

Rockefeller Archive Center, Sleepy Hollow, New York:
Commonwealth Fund Records (FA390).
Institute of International Education Records (FA1289).
International Education Board Records (FA062).
Rockefeller Foundation Records (FA386a).
Laura Spelman Rockefeller Memorial Records (FA061).
Office of the Messrs Rockefeller Records (FA326).

Yale University Divinity Library Special Collections, New Haven, Connecticut:
World Student Christian Federation Records (RG46).

Published Primary Works

Andrews, Fannie Fern, *Memory Pages of My Life* (Boston, MA, 1948).
Apponyi, Albert, ed., *Justice for Hungary: Review and Criticism of the Effect of the Treaty of Trianon* (London, 1928).
Aragon, Louis, W. H. Auden, José Bergamïn et al., 'The Question', in *Authors Take Sides on the Spanish War* (London, 1937), p. 1.
Barbusse, Henri, *Le feu* (Paris, 1916).
Barbusse, Henri, *La lueur dans l'abîme: Ce que veut le Groupe Clarté* (Paris, 1920).
Beer, Max, *The League on Trial: A Journey to Geneva* (London, 1933).
Benda, Julien, *La trahison des clercs* (Paris, 1927).
Bericht der Notgemeinschaft der Deutschen Wissenschaft über ihre Tätigkeit bis zum 31. Marz 1922 (Wittenberg, 1922).
A Book of Belgium's Gratitude (London, 1916).
Bryce, James, *Modern Democracies*, vol. 1 (London, 1921).
Carnegie Endowment for International Peace, Year Book 1921 (Washington, DC, 1921).
The Case of Hungary: A Brief, Submitted by the Committee on Foreign Relations of the Senate of the United States by the Hungarian American Federation (Cleveland, OH, 1919).

The Commonwealth Fund: Second Annual Report of the General Director. For the Year 1919–1920 (New York, 1921).

The Commonwealth Fund: Third Annual Report. For the Year 1920–1921 (New York, 1922).

The Commonwealth Fund: Fourth Annual Report. For the Year 1921–1922 (New York, 1923).

The Commonwealth Fund: Fifth Annual Report. For the Year 1922–1923 (New York, 1924).

Constitution of the United Nations Educational, Scientific and Cultural Organization, UNESCO, Basic Texts, 2020 Edition (Paris, 2020).

Corbin, John, *The Return of the Middle Class* (New York, 1923).

Davies, Alfred T., *Student Captives: An Account of the Work of the British Prisoners of War Book Scheme (Educational)* (London, 1917).

Davies, Gwilym, *Intellectual Co-operation Between the Two Wars* (London, 1943).

'The Defences of Peace': Documents Relating to UNESCO: The United Nations Scientific and Cultural Organisation, Part II* (Washington, DC, 1946).

Delannoy, Paul, *L'Université de Louvain: conférences données au Collège de France en février 1915* (Paris, 1915).

De Madariaga, Salvador, *Victors, Beware* (London, 1946).

De Reynold, Gonzague, *La vie intellectuelle dans les divers pays: Russie. Rapport sur la situation et l'organisation des intellectuels Russes hors de Russie* (Geneva, c1923).

Durkheim, Emile, *The Division of Labour in Society*, introduction by Lewis Coser and translated by W. D. Halls (Basingstoke, 1984).

Education and the United Nations: A Report of a Joint Commission of the Council for Education in World Citizenship and the London International Assembly (Washington, DC, 1943).

Ellwood, Charles A., *The Social Problem: A Reconstructive Analysis* (New York, 1919).

Everling, Otto, *Schutzkartell deutscher Geistesarbeiter: Beiträge zu sozialen Fragen der Geistesarbeiter* (Berlin, 1929).

Everling, Otto, *Von deutscher Geistesarbeit und deutscher Wirtschaft* (Berlin, 1925).

Ferrero, Guglielmo, *The Ruin of the Ancient Civilization and the Triumph of Christianity: with some Consideration of Conditions in the Europe of Today* (London, 1921).

First Report on the Reconstruction of the Tokyo Imperial University Library (Tokyo, 1926).

Fisher, Harold Henry, *The Famine in Soviet Russia, 1919–1923* (New York, 1927).

Fry, Ruth, *A Quaker Adventure: The Story of Nine Years' Relief and Reconstruction* (London, 1926).

Fünfter Bericht der Notgemeinschaft der Deutschen Wissenschaft (Wittenberg, 1926).

Garner, James Wilford, *International Law and the World War*, vol. 1 (London, 1920).

Germanistic Society of America: Report for the Year 1925 (New York, 1925).

Gibberd, Kathleen, *The League in Our Time* (Oxford, 1933).

Godart, Justin, *L'Albanie en 1921* (Paris, 1922).

Gramsci, Antonio, *Selections from the Prison Notebooks of Antonio Gramsci*, edited and translated by Quintin Hoare and Geoffrey Nowell Smith (New York, 1971).

Halecki, Oskar, *Enquiry into the Conditions of Intellectual Life: General Situation* (Geneva, 1923).

Hall, Hubert, *British Archives and Sources for the History of the World War* (London, 1925).

Hinton, Kerry, *The Trial of Sacco and Vanzetti: A Primary Source Account* (New York, 2004).

Hope Simpson, John, *The Refugee Question. Oxford Pamphlets on World Affairs* (Oxford, 1939).

Kandel, Isaac, *Intellectual Cooperation: National and International* (New York, 1944).

Keynes, John Maynard, *The Economic Consequences of the Peace* (New York, 1920).

Koch, Theodore Wesley, *War Libraries and Allied Studies* (New York 1918).

Koch, Theodore Wesley, *Books in the War: The Romance of Library War Service* (New York, 1919).

Kotschnig, Walter M., *Slaves Need No Leaders. An Answer to the Fascist Challenge to Education* (New York and London, 1943).

Kotschnig, Walter M., *Unemployment in the Learned Professions: an International Study of Occupational and Educational Planning* (Oxford, 1937).

Lansing, Robert, *The Peace Negotiations: A Personal Narrative* (New York, 1921).

La paix de Versailles: responsabilités des auteurs de la guerre et sanctions (Paris, 1930).

La paix de Versailles: la Commission de Réparations des Dommages, I (Paris, 1932).

The Laura Spelman Rockefeller Memorial: Report for 1923 (New York, 1924).

The Laura Spelman Rockefeller Memorial: Report for 1924 (New York, 1925).

League of Nations, *Ten Years of World Co-operation* (Geneva, 1930).

Lousse, Émile, *The University of Louvain during the Second World War* (Bruges, 1946).

MacDonald, William, *The Intellectual Worker and his Work* (London, 1923).

Mann, Thomas, *Reflections of a Nonpolitical Man* (New York, 1983).

Mannheim, Karl, *Ideology and Utopia* (first English ed., 1936; new ed., London, 1972).

Miscellaneous Series No. 1 (1920). Economic Conditions in Central Europe (London, 1920).

Montgomery, Walter, *Educational Reconstruction in Belgium: Department of the Interior Bureau of Education, Bulletin, 1921, no. 39* (Washington, DC, 1921).

Murray, Gilbert, *The Ordeal of this Generation* (London, 1929).

Nicolai, Georg Friedrich, *The Biology of War* (New York, 1919).

Nicolae, Iorga, *Histoire des roumains et de leur civilisation* (Paris, 1920).

Nyrop, Kristoffer, *Is War Civilization?* (London, 1917).

Œuvre internationale de Louvain, *La nouvelle bibliothèque de l'université* (Louvain, 1929).

Ortega y Gasset, José, *The Revolt of the Masses* (New York, 1957; first ed. 1932).

Orwell, George, *The Road to Wigan Pier* (Harmondsworth, 1966; orig. 1937).

Papers Relating to the Foreign Relations of the United States: The Paris Peace Conference, 1919, vol. 3 (Washington, DC, 1943).

Papers Relating to the Foreign Relations of the United States: The Paris Peace Conference, 1919, vol. 11 (Washington, DC, 1945).

Rapport du congrès international de femmes (Geneva, 1919).

Recueil des griefs de la minorité hongroise : Dérivant de la violation du traité conclu à Paris le 9 déc. 1919 entre les principales puissances alliées et associées et la Roumanie au sujet de la protection des minorités (Budapest, 1922).

Reed, John, *The War in Eastern Europe* (New York, 1916).

Reiss, R. A., *Rapport sur les atrocités commises par les troupes Austro-hongroises pendant la première invasion de la Serbie* (Paris, 1919)

Reparation Commission. Statement of Germany's Obligations: Under the Heading of Reparations, etc., at April 30th, 1922 (London, 1922).

Report on the British Gift of Books to the Tokyo Imperial University Library, 1923–1933 (London, 1934).

Report of the International Committee of the Red Cross on its Activities During the Second World War, Volume I, General Activities (Geneva, 1948).

The Rockefeller Foundation, Annual Report 1913–14 (New York, 1915).

The Rockefeller Foundation, Annual Report 1917 (New York, 1917).

Rohrbach, Paul, ed., The German Work-Student (Dresden, 1924).

Rolland, Romain, Quinze ans de combat (1919–1934) (Paris, 1935).

Rouse, Ruth, Rebuilding Europe: The Students Chapter in Post-War Reconstruction (London, 1925).

Schreiber, Georg, Die Not der deutschen Wissenschaft und der geistigen Arbeiter (Leipzig, 1923).

Shotwell, James T., At the Paris Peace Conference (New York, 1937).

La Situation du travail intellectuel en Hongrie: réponse à la commission de coopération intellectuelle de la société des nations (Budapest, 1923).

Spengler, Oswald, Der Untergang des Abendlandes: Umrisse einer Morphologie der Weltgeschichte (Munich, 1963; orig. 1918).

Stanojević, Djorje, Le bombardement de l'université de Belgrade (Paris, 1915).

Teleki, Pál, The Evolution of Hungary and its Place in European History (New York, 1923).

Toynbee, Arnold J., The World after the Peace Conference (London, 1926).

Université de Genève, Séance solennelle de distribution des prix de concours, 6 juin 1917. Rapports du recteur et des jurys. (Geneva, 1917).

Veblen, Thorstein, The Higher Learning in America: A Memorandum on the Conduct of Universities by Business Men (New York, 1918).

Vierter Bericht der Notgemeinschaft der Deutschen Wissenschaft (Halle, 1925).

Wells, H. G., Russia in the Shadows (London, 1920).

Zimmern, Alfred, Learning and Leadership: A Study of the Needs and Possibilities of International Intellectual Cooperation (London, 1928).

Zimmern, Alfred, The Prospects of Civilization, Oxford Pamphlets on World Affairs no. 1 (Oxford, 1939).

Secondary Works:

Aiken, Guy, 'Feeding Germany: American Quakers in the Weimar Republic', Diplomatic History, 43.4 (2019), pp. 597–617.

Akhund, Nadine, 'The World of the Carnegie Endowment in the Balkans after World War One: The University Library of Belgrade, 1919-1926', INFOtheca, 12.1 (2011), pp. 3–21.

Amara, Michaël, 'Belgian Refugees during the First World War (France, Britain, Netherlands)', in Peter Gatrell and Liubov Zhvanko eds.,

Europe on the Move: Refugees in the Era of the Great War (Manchester, 2017), pp. 197–214.

Andreyev, Catherine, and Ivan Savický, *Russia Abroad: Prague and the Russian Diaspora* (New Haven, CT, 2004).

Arendt, Hannah, *On Violence* (New York, 1969).

Aron, Raymond, *L'opium des intellectuels* (Paris, 1955).

Ash, Mitchell G. and Alfons Söllner, 'Introduction: Forced Migration and Scientific Change after 1933', in Mitchell G. Ash and Alfons Söllner eds., *Forced Migration and Scientific Change: Emigré German-speaking Scientists and Scholars after 1933* (Cambridge, 1996), pp. 1–19.

Audoin-Rouzeau, Stéphane, and Annette Becker, *14–18: Understanding the Great War* (New York, 2002).

Bailes, Kendall E., 'Natural Scientists and the Soviet System', in Diane P. Koenker, William G. Rosenberg, and Ronald Grigor Suny, *Party, State and Society in the Russian Civil War* (Bloomington and Indianapolis, IN, 1989), pp. 267–95.

Barnett, Michael, *Empire of Humanity: A History of Humanitarianism* (Ithaca, NY, 2011).

Barros, Andrew, 'Turn Everyone into a Civilian: René Cassin and the UNESCO Project', in Andrew Barros and Martin Thomas eds., *The Civilianization of War: The Changing Civil-Military Divide, 1914–2014* (Cambridge, 2018), pp. 243–59.

Baughan, Emily, '"Every Citizen of Empire Implored to Save the Children!" Empire, Internationalism and the Save the Children Fund in Inter-war Britain', *Historical Research*, 86.231 (2013), pp. 116–137.

Baughan, Emily, 'The Imperial War Relief Fund and the All British Appeal: Commonwealth, Conflict and Conservatism within the British Humanitarian Movement, 1920–25', *The Journal of Imperial and Commonwealth History*, 40.5 (2012), pp. 845–61.

Baughan, Emily, 'International Adoption and Anglo-American Internationalism, c 1918-1925', *Past & Present*, 239.1 (2018), pp. 181–217.

Berend, Ivan T., *Decades of Crisis: Central and Eastern Europe before World War II* (Berkeley, CA, 1998).

Berg, A. Scott, *Wilson* (London, 2014).

Bering, Dietz, *Die Intellektuellen: Geschichte eines Schimpfwortes* (Stuttgart, 1978).

Bertrams, Kenneth, 'The Domestic Uses of Belgian–American "Mutual Understanding": The Commission for Relief in Belgium Educational Foundation, 1920–1940', *Journal of Transatlantic Studies*, 13.4 (2015), pp. 326–43.

Bessner, Daniel, *Democracy in Exile: Hans Speier and the Rise of the Defense Intellectual* (Ithaca, NY, 2018).

Betts, Paul, 'Humanity's New Heritage: UNESCO and the Rewriting of World History', *Past & Present*, 228 (2015), pp. 249–85.

Betts, Paul, *Ruin and Renewal: Civilising Europe after the Second World War* (London, 2020).

Bevan, Robert, *The Destruction of Memory: Architecture at War*, 2nd ed. (London, 2016).

Blackburn, Christopher, 'The Rebirth of Poland: American Humanitarianism after the Great War', *Studia Historyczne*, 4.228 (2014), pp. 522–39.

Blom, Philipp, *Fracture: Life and Culture in the West 1918–1938* (London, 2015).

Blower, Brooke, *Becoming Americans in Paris: Transatlantic Politics and Culture between the World Wars* (Oxford, 2011).

Boucher, Ellen, 'Cultivating Internationalism: Save the Children Fund, Public Opinion and the Meaning of Child Relief, 1919–24', in *Brave New World: Imperial and Democratic Nation-Building in Britain Between the Wars*, ed. Laura Beers and Geraint Thomas (London, 2011), pp. 169–88.

Brandow-Faller, Megan, 'The Mobilization of Vienna's Women Artists and the Interwar Splintering of Austrian Frauenkunst', *Austrian Studies*, 21 (2013), pp. 142–62.

Brewis, Georgina, *A Social History of Student Volunteering: Britain and Beyond, 1880–1980* (New York, 2014).

Brewis, Georgina, Norbert Göltz, and Steffen Werther, *Humanitarianism in the Modern World: The Moral Economy of Famine Relief* (Cambridge, 2020).

Budnistskii, Oleg, *Russian Jews between the Reds and the Whites, 1917–1920* (Philadelphia, PA, 2011).

Bullock, Nicholas, and Verpoest, Luc, eds., *Living with History, 1914–1964: Rebuilding Europe after the First and Second World Wars and the Role of Heritage Preservation* (Leuven, 2011).

Burke, Peter, *A Social History of Knowledge, Volume II: From the Encyclopédie to Wikipedia* (Cambridge, 2012).

Burke, Peter, *What Is the History of Knowledge?* (Cambridge, 2016).

Cabanes, Bruno, *The Great War and the Origins of Humanitarianism 1918–1924* (Cambridge, 2014).

Camurri, Renato, 'The Exile Experience Reconsidered: A Comparative Perspective in European Cultural Migration during the Interwar Period', *Transatlantica: Revue d'études américaines. American Studies Journal*, 1 (2014) pp. 1–16.

Canales, Jimena, 'Einstein, Bergson, and the Experiment that Failed: Intellectual Cooperation at the League of Nations', *Modern Language Notes*, 120.5 (2005), pp. 1168–91.

Cassedy, Steven, *To the Other Shore: The Russian Jewish Intellectuals Who Came to America* (Princeton, NJ, 1997).

Chagnon, Marie-Eve, 'American Scientists and the Process of Reconciliation in the International Scientific Community, 1917–1925', in Marie-Eve Chagnon and Tomás Irish, eds., *The Academic World in the Era of the Great War* (London, 2018), pp. 213–32.

Chamberlain, Lesley, *Lenin's Private War: The Voyage of the Philosophy Steamer and the Exile of the Intelligentsia* (New York, 2006).

Charle, Christophe, *Discordance des temps: Une brève histoire de la modernité* (Paris, 2011).

Charles, Schencking, J., 'Giving Most and Giving Differently: Humanitarianism as Diplomacy Following Japan's 1923 Earthquake', *Diplomatic History*, 43.4 (2019), pp. 295–331.

Chatriot, Alain, 'La lutte contre le "chômage intellectuel": l'action de la Confédération des Travailleurs Intellectuels (CTI) face à la crise des années trente', *Le Mouvement Social*, 214 (2006), pp. 77–91.

Chernow, Ron, *Titan: The Life of John D. Rockefeller, Sr* (New York, 1999).

Chickering, Roger, and Förster, Stig, eds., *Great War, Total War: Combat and Mobilization on the Western Front, 1914–1918* (Cambridge, 2000).

Chinyaeva, Elena, 'Russian Émigrés: Czechoslovak Refugee Policy and the Development of the International Refugee Regime between the Two World Wars,' *Journal of Refugee Studies*, 8.2 (1995), pp. 142–62.

Clavin, Patricia, 'The Austrian Hunger Crisis and the Genesis of International Organization after the First World War', *International Affairs*, 90.2 (2014), pp. 265–78.

Cloonan, Michele V., and Rebecca J. Knuth, 'Libraries, Archives, and the Pursuit of Access', in Morgan, Matthew J. ed., *The Impact of 9/11 on the Media, Arts and Entertainment: The Day that Changed Everything?* (Basingstoke, 2009), pp. 181–94.

Cock, A. G., 'Chauvinism and Internationalism in Science: The International Research Council, 1919-1926', *Notes and Records of the Royal Society of London*, 37.2 (1983), pp. 249–88.

Collini, Stefan, *Absent Minds: Intellectuals in Britain* (Oxford, 2006).

Conquest, Robert, *The Great Terror: A Reassessment* (London, 1994).

Cooper, John Milton, *Woodrow Wilson: A Biography* (New York, 2011).

Coser, Lewis, 'Refugee Intellectuals', *Society*, 22.1 (1984), pp. 61–9.

Costigliola, Frank, *Awkward Dominion: American Political, Economic, and Cultural Relations with Europe, 1919–1933* (Ithaca, 1984).

Cox, Mary Elisabeth, *Hunger in War and Peace: Women and Children in Germany, 1914–1924* (Oxford, 2019).

Craig, John E., *Scholarship and Nation Building: The Universities of Strasbourg and Alsatian Society, 1870–1939* (Chicago, IL, 1984).

Crawford, Sally, Ulmschneider, Katharina, and Elsner, Jaś, eds., *Ark of Civilization: Refugee Scholars and Oxford University, 1930–1945*, (Oxford, 2017).

Cullather, Nick, 'The Foreign Policy of the Calorie', *American Historical Review*, 112.2 (2007), pp. 337–64.

Dahlgren, Peter, 'Public Intellectuals, Online Media, and Public Spheres: Current Realignments', *International Journal of Politics, Culture and Society*, 25 (2012), pp. 95–110.

Dăncilă, Andreea, 'The Dynamic of Post-War Political Structures in Multi-Ethnic Regions: Transylvania at the End of 1918', in Burkhard Olschowsky, Piotr Juszkiewicz, and Jan Rydel, eds., *Central and Eastern Europe after the First World War* (Berlin, 2021), pp. 221–28.

Davies, Thomas R., 'The Roles of Transnational Associations in the 1919 Paris Peace settlement: A Comparative Assessment of Proposals and their Influence', *Contemporary European History*, 31.3 (2022), pp. 353–67.

Davies, William, *Nervous States: How Feeling Took Over the World* (London, 2018).

Dialla, Ada, and Alexis Heraclides, *Humanitarian Intervention in the Long Nineteenth Century: Setting the Precedent* (Manchester, 2015).

Dorn, Charles, 'The World's Schoolmaster: Educational Reconstruction, Grayson Kefauver, and the Founding of UNESCO, 1942–46', *History of Education*, 35.3 (2006), pp. 297–320.

Dowdall, Alex, *Communities Under Fire: Urban Life at the Western Front, 1914–1918* (Oxford, 2020).

Drury, Betty, and Stephen Duggan, *The Rescue of Science and Learning: the Story of the Emergency Committee in Aid of Displaced Foreign Scholars* (New York, 1948).

Duci, Annamaria, 'Europe and the Artistic Patrimony of the Interwar Period: the International Institute of Intellectual Cooperation at the League of Nations', in Mark Hewitson and Matthew d'Auria, eds., *Europe in Crisis: Intellectuals and the European Idea, 1917–1957* (New York, 2015), pp. 227–42.

Eilenberger, Wolfram, *Time of the Magicians: The Invention of Modern Thought, 1919–1929* (London, 2020).

Ellis, Heather, and Simone M. Müller, 'Editorial: Educational Networks, Educational Identities: Connecting National and Global Perspectives', *Journal of Global History*, 11.3 (2016), pp. 313–19.

Ermacora, Matteo, 'Assistance and Surveillance: War Refugees in Italy, 1914-1918', *Contemporary European History* 16.4, (2007), pp. 445–59.

Evans, Richard J., *The Third Reich in Power, 1933–1939* (London, 2006).

Fassin, Didier, *Humanitarian Reason: A Moral History of the Present* (Berkeley, CA, 2012).

Fassin, Didier, 'Inequality of Lives, Hierarchies of Humanity: Moral Commitments and Ethical Dilemmas of Humanitarianism', in Ilana Feldman and Miriam Ticktin, eds., *In the Name of Humanity: The Government of Threat and Care* (Durham, NC, 2010), pp. 238–55.

Feldman, Gerald, 'The Politics of Wissenschaftspolitik in Weimar Germany: A Prelude to the Dilemmas of Twentieth-Century Science Policy', in Charles S. Maier ed., *Changing Boundaries of the Political: Essays on the Evolving Balance Between the State and Society, Public and Private in Europe* (Cambridge, 1987), pp. 255–86.

Finkel, Stuart, *On the Ideological Front: The Russian Intelligentsia and the Making of the Soviet Public Sphere* (New Haven, CT, 2006).

Finkel, Finkel, 'Purging the Public Intellectual: The 1922 Expulsions from Soviet Russia', *The Russian Review*, 62.4 (2003), pp. 589–613.

Fitzpatrick, Sheila, *The Cultural Front: Power and Culture in Revolutionary Russia* (Ithaca, NY, 1992).

Flynn, Jeffrey, 'Human Rights, Transnational Solidarity, and Duties to the Global Poor', *Constellations*, 16.1 (2009), pp. 59–77.

Flynn, Jeffrey, 'On the Relatively Recent Rise of Human Dignity', *Anthropological Quarterly*, 89.3 (2016), pp. 895–905.

Forgács, Éva, 'In the Vacuum of Exile: The Hungarian Activists in Vienna 1919–1926', in John Neubauer, Borbála Zsuzsanna Török, and Borbála Zsuzsanna Török, eds., *The Exile and Return of Writers from East-Central Europe: A Compendium* (Berlin, 2009), pp. 109–22.

Fosdick, Raymond B., *The Story of the Rockefeller Foundation* (New York, 1952).

Fox, Robert, *Science Without Frontiers: Cosmopolitanism and National Interests in the World of Learning, 1870–1940* (Corvallis, OR, 2016).

Galvez-Behar, Gabriel, *Posséder la science : la propriété scientifique au temps du capitalisme industriel* (Paris, 2020).

Garsha, Jeremiah J., 'Expanding Vergangenheitsbewältigung? German Repatriation of Colonial Artefacts and Human Remains', *Journal of Genocide Research*, 22 (2020), pp. 46–61.

Gatrell, Peter, *A Whole Empire Walking: Refugees in Russia During World War I* (Bloomington, IN, 2005).

Gatrell, Peter, 'Introduction', in Peter Gatrell and Zhvanko Liubov, eds., *Europe on the Move: Refugees in the Era of the Great War* (Manchester, 2017), pp. 1–22.

Gatrell, Peter, *The Making of the Modern Refugee* (Oxford, 2015).

Gatrell, Peter, *The Unsettling of Europe: The Great Migration, 1945 to the Present* (London, 2019).

Gatrell, Peter, Alex Dowdall, Anindita Ghoshal, et al., 'Reckoning with Refugeedom: Refugee Voices in Modern History', *Social History*, 46.1 (2021), pp. 70–95.

Gelfand, Lawrence E., *The Inquiry: American Preparations for Peace, 1917–1919* (New Haven, CT, 1963).

Gella, Aleksander, 'The Life and Death of the Old Polish Intelligentsia', *Slavic Review*, 30.1 (1971), pp. 1–27.

Gemelli, Giuliana, ed., *The 'Unacceptables': American Foundations and Refugee Scholars Between the Two Wars and After* (Brussels, 2000).

Gerwarth, Robert, *The Vanquished: Why the First World War Failed to End, 1917–1923* (London, 2016).

Gerwarth, Robert, and John Horne, eds., *War in Peace: Paramilitary Violence in Europe after the Great War* (Oxford, 2012).

Geyer, Martin, and Johannes Paulmann, eds., *The Mechanics of Internationalism* (Oxford, 2001).

Gilman, Sander L., *Smart Jews: The Construction of the Image of Jewish Superior Intelligence* (Lincoln, NE, 1996).

Goldstein, Erik, 'Cultural Heritage, British Diplomacy, and the German Peace Settlement of 1919', *Diplomacy & Statecraft*, 30 (2019), pp. 336–57.

Gousseff, Catherine, *L'exil russe. La fabrique du réfugié apatride (1920–1939)* (Paris, 2008).

Guesnet, François, 'Russian-Jewish Cultural Retention in Early Twentieth-Century Western Europe: Contexts and Theoretical Implications', in Jörg Schulte, Olga Tabachnikova and Peter Wagstaff, eds., *The Russian Jewish Diaspora and European Culture, 1917–1937* (Leiden, 2012), pp. 1–8.

Habermas, Jurgen, 'Heinrich Heine and the Role of the Intellectual in Germany', in Jurgen Habermas, ed., *The New Conservatism: Cultural Criticism and the Historians' Debate* (Cambridge, 1989), pp. 71–99.

Hammerstein, Notker, *Die Deutsche Forschungsgemeinschaft in der Weimarer Republik und im Dritten Reich: Wissenschaftspolitik in Republik und Diktatur, 1920–1945* (Munich, 1999).

Harris, Ruth, *The Man on Devil's Island: Alfred Dreyfus and the Affair that Divided France* (London, 2011).

Hartley, Benjamin L., 'Saving Students: European Student Relief in the Aftermath of World War I', *International Bulletin of Mission Research*, 42.1 (2018), pp. 295–315.

Hartog, François, *Regimes of Historicity: Presentism and Experiences of Time* (New York, 2017).

Harzig, Christiane, Dirk Hoerder, and Donna Gabaccia, *What Is Migration History?* (Cambridge, 2009).

Haslam, Sara, 'Reading, Trauma and Literary Caregiving 1914–1918: Helen Mary Gaskell and the War Library', *Journal of Medical Humanities*, 41 (2020), pp. 305–21.

Healy, Maureen, *Vienna and the Fall of the Habsburg Empire: Total War and Everyday Life in World War I* (Cambridge, 2004).

Hewitson, Mark, and Matthew d'Auria, 'Introduction: Europe during the Forty Years' Crisis', in Mark Hewitson and Matthew d'Auria eds., *Europe in Crisis: Intellectuals and the European Idea 1917–1957* (Oxford and New York, 2012), pp. 1–11.

Heyck, Thomas William, 'Myths and Meanings of Intellectuals in Twentieth-Century British National Identity', *Journal of British Studies*, 37.2 (1998), pp. 192–221.

Heyck, Thomas William, *The Transformation of Intellectual Life in Victorian England* (London: Croom Helm, 1982).

Hodder, Jake, 'The Elusive History of the Pan-African Congress, 1919–27', *History Workshop Journal*, 91.1 (2021), pp. 113–31.

Hofmeister, Alexis, 'The Years of 1918–1923 as a Transformative Period of Jewish Politics', in Burkhard Olschowsky, Piotr Juszkiewicz, and Jan Rydel, eds., *Central and Eastern Europe after the First World War* (Berlin, 2021), pp. 281–305.

Hofstadter, Richard, *Anti-Intellectualism in American Life* (New York, 1963).

Holman, Brett, 'World Police for World Peace: British Internationalism and the Threat of the Knock-out Blow from the Air', *War in History*, 17.3 (2010), pp. 313–32.

Horne, John, 'Beyond Cultures of Victory and Cultures of Defeat? Inter-war Veterans' Internationalism', in Julia Eichenberg and John Paul Newman, eds., *The Great War and Veterans' Internationalism* (Basingstoke, 2013), pp. 207–22.

Horne, John, 'Demobilizing the Mind: France and the Legacy of the Great War, 1919-1939', *French History and Civilization: Papers from the George Rudé Seminar*, 2 (2009), pp. 101–19.

Horne, John, 'Introduction: Mobilizing for "Total" War', in John Horne ed., *State, Society and Mobilization in Europe during the First World War* (Cambridge, 1997), pp. 1–17.

Horne, John, 'Reconstruction, Reform and Peace in Europe after the First World War', in Luc Verpoest, Leen Engelen, Rajesh Heynickx et al., eds., *Revival after the Great War: Rebuild, Remember, Repair, Reform* (Leuven, 2020), pp. 297–314.

Horne, John, and Alan Kramer, *German Atrocities 1914: A History of Denial* (New Haven, CT, 2001).

Horowitz, Brian, *Russian Idea-Jewish Presence: Essays on Russian-Jewish Intellectual* Life (Brighton, MA, 2013).

Hoover Institution on War, Revolution, and Peace (Stanford, CA, 1963).

Housden, Martyn, 'White Russians Crossing the Black Sea: Fridtjof Nansen, Constantinople and the First Modern Repatriation of Refugees Displaced by Civil Conflict, 1922–23', *Slavonic and East European Review*, 88.3 (2010), pp.495–524.

Hryn, Halyna, 'The Executed Renaissance Paradigm Revisited', *Harvard Ukrainian Studies*, 27.1–4 (2004/5), pp. 67–96.

Hudgins, Nicole, 'Art and Death in French Photographs of Ruins, 1914–1918', *Historical Reflections / Réflexions Historiques*, 42.3 (2016), p. 51–70.

Ifversen, Jan, 'The Crisis of European Civilisation after 1918', in Menno Spiering and Michael Wintle eds., *Ideas of Europe Since 1914: The Legacy of the First World War* (Basingstoke, 2002), pp. 14–31.

Ifversen, Jan, 'Europe and the Concept of Margin', in Tessa Hauswedell, Axel Körner and Ulrich Tiedau, eds., *Re-Mapping Centre and Periphery: Asymmetrical Encounters in European and Global Contexts* (London, 2020), pp. 27–43.

Iida, Yumiko, 'Fleeing the West, Making Asia Home: Transpositions of Otherness in Japanese PanAsianism, 1905–1930', *Alternatives: Global, Local, Political*, 22.3 (1997), pp. 409–32.

Irish, Tomás, 'Educating Those Who Matter: Thomas Whittemore, Russian Refugees and the Transnational Organisation of Elite Humanitarianism after the First World War', *European Review of History/Revue européenne d'histoire* 28.3 (2021), pp. 441–62.

Irish, Tomás, 'Fractured Families: Educated Elites in Britain and France and the Challenge of the Great War', *Historical Journal*, 57.2 (2014), pp. 509–30.

Irish, Tomás, 'From International to Inter-allied: Transatlantic University Relations in the Era of the First World War, 1905–1920', *Journal of Transatlantic Studies*, 13.4 (2015), pp. 311–25.

Irish, Tomás, 'The "Moral Basis" of Reconstruction? Humanitarianism, Intellectual Relief and the League of Nations', *Modern Intellectual History*, 17.3 (2020), pp. 769–800.

Irish, Tomás, 'National Survival and International Expansion: French Universities and the First World War', in Charlotte A. Lerg and Heike Bungert, eds., *Jahrbuch für Universitätsgeschichte*, vol. 18 (Stuttgart, 2017), pp. 143–62.

Irish, Tomás, 'Scholarly Identities in War and Peace: The Paris Peace Conference and the Mobilization of Intellect', *Journal of Global History*, 11.3 (2016), pp. 365–86.

Irish, Tomás, *The University at War: Britain, France, and the United States, 1914–25* (Basingstoke, 2015).

Irwin, Julia F., *Making the World Safe: The American Red Cross and a Nation's Humanitarian Awakening* (Oxford, 2013).

Irwin, Julia F., 'Taming Total War: Great War-Era American Humanitarianism and its Legacies', *Diplomatic History*, 38.4 (2014), pp. 763–75.

Irwin, Julia F., and Jenny Leigh Smith, 'Introduction: On Disaster', in *Isis*, Focus: Disasters, Science, and History, 1.111 (2020), pp. 98–103.

Jackson, Julian, *France: The Dark Years, 1940–1944* (Oxford, 2001).

Jackson, Peter, *Beyond the Balance of Power: France and the Politics of National Security in the era of the First World War* (Cambridge, 2013).

Jakubowski, Andrzej, *State Succession in Cultural Property* (Oxford, 2015).

Jarausch, Konrad, *After Hitler: Recivilizing Germans, 1945–1995* (Oxford, 2006).

Jay, Martin, *Permanent Exiles: Essays on the Intellectual Migration from Germany to America* (New York, 1985).

Jeffries, Stuart, *Grand Hotel Abyss: The Lives of the Frankfurt School* (London, 2017).

Jennings, Jeremy, ed., *Intellectuals in Twentieth-Century France: Mandarins and Samurais* (London, 1993).

Jennings, Jeremy, and Anthony Kemp-Welsh, eds., *Intellectuals in Politics: From the Dreyfus Affair to Salman Rushdie* (London, 1997).

Johnston, Robert H., *New Mecca, New Babylon: Paris and the Russian Exiles, 1920–1945* (Montreal, 1988).

Jones, Ernest, *Sigmund Freud: Life and Work, Volume Three: The Last Phase, 1919–1939* (London, 1957).

Jones, Heather, 'International or Transnational? Humanitarian Action During the First World War', *European Review of History/Revue européenne d'histoire*, 16.5 (2009), pp. 697–713.

Jones, Heather, *Violence against Prisoners of War in the First World War: Britain, France and Germany, 1914–1920* (Cambridge, 2011).

Josephson, Harold, *James T. Shotwell and the Rise of Internationalism in America* (Cranbury, NJ, 1975).

Judt, Tony, *Past Imperfect: French Intellectuals, 1944–1956* (Berkeley, CA, 1992).

Judt, Tony, *Reappraisals: Reflections on the Forgotten Twentieth Century* (London, 2009).

Kaes, Anton, Martin Jay and Edward Dimendberg, eds., *The Weimar Republic Sourcebook* (Berkeley, CA, 1994).

Kaiga, Sakiko, *Britain and the Intellectual Origins of the League of Nations, 1914–1919* (Cambridge, 2021).

Kenez, Peter, 'Introduction: The Bolsheviks and the Intelligentsia', in Diane P. Koenker, William G. Rosenberg, and Ronald Grigor Suny, eds., *Party, State and Society in the Russian Civil War* (Bloomington, IN, 1989), pp. 239–42.

Kevles, Daniel J., '"Into Hostile Political Camps": The Reorganization of International Science in World War I', *Isis*, 62. 1 (1971), pp. 47–60.

Kimmich, Christoph M., *Germany and the League of Nations* (Chicago, IL, 1976).

King, Edmund G. C., '"Books are More to Me than Food": British Prisoners of War as Readers, 1914–1918, *Book History*, 16 (2013), pp. 246–71.

Kocka, Jürgen, 'The First World War and the "Mittelstand": German Artisans and White-Collar Workers', *Journal of Contemporary History*, 8.1 (1973), pp. 101–23.

Kramer, Alan, *Dynamic of Destruction: Culture and Mass Killing in the First World War* (Oxford, 2007).

Krementsov, Nikolai, and Susan Gross Solomon, 'Giving and Taking Across Borders: The Rockefeller Foundation in Russia, 1919–1928', *Minerva*, 39.3 (2001), pp. 265–98.

Krige, John, *American Hegemony and the Postwar Reconstruction of Science in Europe* (Cambridge, MA, 2006).

Krill de Capello, H. H., 'The Creation of the United Nations Educational, Scientific and Cultural Organization', *International Organization*, 24.1 (1970), pp. 1–30.

Kushner, Tony, 'Local Heroes: Belgian Refugees in Britain during the First World War', *Immigrants & Minorities*, 18.1 (1999), pp. 1–28.

Laqua, Daniel, *The Age of Internationalism and Belgium: Peace, Progress and Prestige* (Manchester, 2015).

Laqua, Daniel, 'Internationalisme ou affirmation de la nation? La coopération intellectuelle transnationale dans l'entre-deux-guerres', *Critique internationale*, 52 (2011), 51–67.

Laqua, Daniel, 'Transnational Intellectual Cooperation, the League of Nations, and the Problem of Order', *Journal of Global History*, 6.2 (2011), pp. 223–47.

Laqua, Daniel, Christophe Verbruggen, and Wouter van Acker, eds., *International Organizations and Global Civil Society: Histories of the Union of International Associations* (London, 2019).

Laqueur, Walter, *Weimar: A Cultural History* (London, 1974).

Lasch, Christopher, *The New Radicalism in America, 1889–1963: The Intellectual as Social Type* (New York, 1965)

Lässig, Simone, 'Strategies and Mechanisms of Scholar Rescue: The Intellectual Migration of the 1930s Reconsidered', *Social Research*, 84.4 (2017), pp. 769–807.

Lecklider, Aaron, *Inventing the Egghead: The Battle over Brainpower in American Culture* (Philadelphia, PA, 2013).

Leff, Laurel, *Well Worth Saving: American Universities' Life-and-Death Decisions on Refugees from Nazi Europe* (New Haven, CT, 2019).

Leonhard, Jörn, *Der überforderte Frieden: Versailles und die Welt, 1918–1923* (Munich, 2018).

Levine, Emily J., *Allies and Rivals: German-American Exchange and the Rise of the Modern Research University* (Chicago, IL, 2021).

Little, Branden, 'An Explosion of New Endeavours: Global Humanitarian Responses to Industrialised Warfare in the First World War Era', *First World War Studies*, 5.1 (2014), pp. 1–16.

Liulevičius, Vėjas Gabriel, *War Land on the Eastern Front: Culture, National Identity, and German Occupation in World War I* (Cambridge, 2000).

Llewellyn, Matthew P., 'Chariots of Discord: Great Britain, Nationalism and the "Doomed" 1924 Paris Olympic Games', *Contemporary British History*, 24.1 (2010), pp. 67–87.

Loader, Colin, 'Free Floating: The Intelligentsia in the Work of Alfred Weber and Karl Mannheim', *German Studies Review*, 20.2 (1997), pp. 217–34.

Löhr, Isabella, 'Coping With a Post-War World: Protestant Student Internationalism and Humanitarian Work in Central and Eastern Europe during the 1920s', *Social History*, 48.1 (2023), pp. 43–64.

Löhr, Isabella, *Globale Bildungsmobilität 1850–1930: Von der Bekehrung der Welt zur globalen studentischen Gemeinschaft* (Göttingen, 2021).

Löhr, Isabella, 'Le droit de l'auteur et la Première Guerre mondiale: un exemple de coopération transnationale européenne', *Le Mouvement Social*, 244 (2013), pp. 67–80.

Löhr, Isabella, 'Solidarity and the Academic Community: The Support Network for Refugee Scholars in the 1930s', *Journal of Modern European History*, 12.2 (2014), pp. 231–46.

Long, Katy, 'Early Repatriation Policy: Russian Refugee Return, 1922-1924', *Journal of Refugee Studies*, 22 (2009), pp. 133–54.

MacMillan, Margaret, *Peacemakers: The Paris Conference of 1919 and Its Attempt to End War* (London, 2001).

Mahmood, Linda, and Vic Satzewich, 'The Save the Children Fund and the Russian Famine of 1921–23: Claims and Counter-Claims about Feeding

"Bolshevik" Children', *Journal of Historical Sociology*, 22.1 (2009), pp. 55–83.

Maier, Charles S., *Recasting Bourgeois Europe: Stabilization in France, Germany, and Italy in the Decade after World War I* (Princeton, NJ, 1975).

Manela, Erez, *The Wilsonian Moment: Self-Determination and the International Origins of Anticolonial Nationalism* (Oxford, 2007).

Marsch, Ulrich, *Notgemeinschaft der Deutschen Wissenschaft: Gründung und frühe Geschichte 1920–1925* (Frankfurt-am-Main, 1994).

Martin, Benjamin G., and Elisabeth Piller, 'Cultural Diplomacy and Europe's Twenty Years' Crisis, 1919–1939: Introduction', *Contemporary European History*, 30 (2021), pp. 149–63.

Maul, Daniel, *The Politics of Service: US-amerikanische Quäker und internationale humanitäre Hilfe 1917–1945* (Berlin, 2022).

Mazower, Mark, 'An International Civilization? Empire, Internationalism, and the Crisis of the Mid-Twentieth Century', *International Affairs*, 82.3 (2006) pp. 553–66.

Mazower, Mark, *Governing the World: The History of an Idea* (London, 2012).

Mazower, Mark, 'Minorities and the League of Nations in Interwar Europe', *Daedalus*, 126.2 (1997), pp. 47–63.

Merkley, Eric, and Peter John Loewen, 'Anti-intellectualism and the Mass Public's Response to the COVID-19 Pandemic', *Nature Human Behaviour*, 5 (2021), pp. 706–15.

Mishra, Pankaj, *Bland Fanatics: Liberals, Race and Empire* (London, 2020).

Mommsen, Wolfgang J., 'German Artists, Writers, and Intellectuals, and the Meaning of War 1914–1918', in John Horne ed., *State, Society and Mobilization in Europe during the First World War* (Cambridge, 1997), pp. 21–38.

Mulder, Nicholas, *The Economic Weapon: The Rise of Sanctions as a Tool of Modern War* (New Haven, CT, 2022).

Nagy, Zsolt, *Great Expectations and Interwar Realities: Hungarian Cultural Diplomacy, 1918–1941* (Budapest, 2017).

Nagy, Zsolt, 'The Race for Revision and Recognition: Interwar Hungarian Cultural Diplomacy in Context', *Contemporary European History*, 30 (2021), pp. 231–47.

Naimark, Norman, *Stalin's Genocides* (Princeton, NJ, 2010).

Nisbet, Matthew C., 'Disruptive Ideas: Public Intellectuals and their Arguments for Action on Climate Change', *WIREs Climate Change*, 5 (2014), pp. 809–23.

Ohba, Go, 'Two Approvals from the 1931 Athens Conference: Anastylosis and International Collaboration for Architectural Conservation: New

Evidence', *Conservation and Management of Archaelogical Sites*, 19.2 (2017), pp. 99–105.

O'Keefe, Roger, *The Protection of Cultural Property in Armed Conflict* (Cambridge, 2006).

Orzoff, Andrea, *Battle for the Castle: The Myth of Czechoslovakia in Europe, 1914–1948* (Oxford, 2009).

Osborne, Ken, 'Creating the "International Mind": The League of Nations Attempts to Reform History Teaching, 1920–1939', *History of Education Quarterly*, 56.2 (2016), pp. 213–40.

Ovenden, Richard, *Burning the Books: A History of Knowledge Under Attack* (London, 2020).

Overy, Richard, *The Bombing War: Europe 1939–1945* (London, 2013).

Overy, Richard, *The Morbid Age: Britain and the Crisis of Civilization, 1919–1939* (London, 2010).

Palmier, Jean-Michel, *Weimar in Exile: The Antifascist Emigration in Europe and America* (London, 2006).

Parmar, Inderjeet, *Foundations of the American Century: The Ford, Carnegie and Rockefeller Foundations in the Rise of American Power* (New York, 2012).

Patenaude, Bertrand, *The Big Show in Bololand: the American Relief Expedition to Soviet Russia in the Famine of 1921* (Stanford, CA, 2002).

Paunović, Miloš, Milan Igrutinovic, Dejan Zec, et al., *Exile in the Classroom: Serbian Students and Pupils in Great Britain during the First World War* (Belgrade, 2016).

Pemberton, Jo-Anne, 'The Changing Shape of Intellectual Co-operation: From the League of Nations to UNESCO', *Australian Journal of Politics and History* 58.1 (2012), pp. 34–50.

Pernet, Corinne A., 'Twists, Turns, and Dead Alleys: The League of Nations and Intellectual Cooperation in Times of War', *Journal of Modern European History*, 12.3 (2014), pp. 342–58.

Pettegree, Andrew and Arthur der Weduwen, *The Library: A Fragile History* (London, 2021).

Phelan, Anthony, ed., *The Weimar Dilemma: Intellectuals in the Weimar Republic* (Manchester, 1985).

Pietsch, Tamson, *Empire of Scholars: Universities, Networks and the British Academic World, 1850–1939* (Manchester, 2015).

Piller, Elisabeth, '"Can the Science of the World Allow This?": German Academic Distress, Foreign Aid and the Cultural Demobilization of the Academic World, 1919–1925', in Marie-Eve Chagnon and Tomás Irish, eds., *The Academic World in the Era of the Great War* (London, 2018), pp. 189–212.

Piller, Elisabeth, *Selling Weimar: German Public Diplomacy and the United States, 1918–1933* (Stuttgart, 2021).

Pipes, Richard, ed., *The Russian Intelligentsia* (New York, 1961).

Pisarri, Milovan, 'Bulgarian Crimes against Civilians in Occupied Serbia during the First World War', *Balcanica*, 44 (2013), pp. 357–90.

Pollard, Nigel, *Bombing Pompeii: World Heritage and Military Necessity* (Ann Arbor, MI, 2020).

Purseigle, Pierre, 'Catastrophe and Reconstruction in Western Europe: The Urban Aftermath of the First World War', in Luc Verpoest, Leen Engelen, Rajesh Heynickx et al., eds., *Revival after the Great War: Rebuild, Remember, Repair, Reform* (Leuven, 2020), pp. 37–53.

Purseigle, Pierre, 'La Cité de demain: French Urbanism in War and Reconstruction, 1914–1928', *French History*, 35.4 (2021), pp. 505–31.

Proctor, Tammy M., 'An American Enterprise: British Participation in US Food Relief Programmes (1914–1923)', *First World War Studies*, 5.1 (2014), pp. 29–42.

Proctor, Tammy, *Civilians in a World at War, 1914–1918* (New York, 2010).

Proctor, Tammy, 'The Louvain Library and US Ambition in Interwar Belgium', *Journal of Contemporary History*, 50.2 (2015), pp. 147–67.

Prost, Antoine, and Jay Winter, *René Cassin: From the Great War to the Universal Declaration* (Cambridge, 2013).

Prott, Volker, 'Tying up the Loose Ends of National Self-determination: British, French and American Experts in Peace Planning, 1917-1919', *Historical Journal*, 57.3 (2014), pp. 727–50.

Rachaminov, Alon, *POWs and the Great War: Captivity on the Eastern Front* (Oxford, 2002).

Racine, Nicole, 'The *Clarté* Movement in France, 1919–21', *Journal of Contemporary History*, 2.2 (1967), pp. 195–208.

Raeff, Marc, *Origins of the Russian Intelligentsia: The Eighteenth Century Nobility* (New York, 1966).

Raeff, Marc, *Russia Abroad: A Cultural History of the Russian Emigration, 1919–1939* (Oxford, 1990).

Rasmussen, Anne, 'Mobilising Minds', in Jay Winter ed., *The Cambridge History of the First World War*, 3 (Cambridge, 2013), pp. 390–418.

Reinisch, Jessica, 'Internationalism in Relief: The Birth (and Death) of UNRRA', *Past & Present*, 210.Supplement 6 (2011), pp. 258–89.

Renoliet, Jean-Jacques, *L'UNESCO oubliéezcu: la Société des Nations et la coopération intellectuelle, 1919–1946* (Paris, 1999).

Richardson, Malcolm L., 'The Political Odyssey of Reinhold Schairer, 1933–1955', *German History*, 39.3 (2021), pp. 377–99.

Rietzler, Katharina, 'Before the Cultural Cold Wars: American Philanthropy and Cultural Diplomacy in the Inter-war Years', *Historical Research*, 84.223 (2011), pp. 148–64.

Rietzler, Katharina, 'Philanthropy, Peace Research, and Revisionist Politics Rockefeller and Carnegie Support for the Study of International Relations in Weimar Germany', *GHI Bulletin Supplement*, 5 (2008), pp. 61–79.

Rietzler, Katharina, 'The War as History: Writing the Economic and Social History of the First World War', *Diplomatic History*, 38. 4 (2014), pp. 826–39.

Ringer, Fritz, *The Decline of the German Mandarins: The German Academic Community, 1890–1933* (Cambridge, MA, 1969)

Rodgers, Daniel T., *Atlantic Crossings: Social Politics in a Progressive Age* (Cambridge, MA, 1998).

Rodogno, Davide, *Night on Earth: A History of International Humanitarianism in the Near East, 1918–1930* (Cambridge, 2021).

Ross, John F. L., 'Fridtjof Nansen and the Aegean Population Exchange', *Scandinavian Journal of History*, 40.2 (2015), pp. 133–58.

Ryan, Maria, 'Review Essay: Intellectuals and the "War on Terror"', *Journal of American Studies*, 44.1 (2010), pp. 203–9.

Said, Edward, 'Intellectual Exile: Expatriates and Marginals', *Grand Street*, 47 (1993), pp. 112–24.

Sand, Schlomo, *La fin de l'intellectuel français? De Zola à Houllebecq* (Paris, 2016).

Sandholtz, Wayne, *Prohibiting Plunder: How Norms Change* (Oxford, 2007).

Sanford, George, *Katyn and the Soviet Massacre of 1940: Truth, Justice and Memory* (London, 2005).

Sapiro, Gisèle, 'L'internationalisation des champs intellectuel dans l'entre-deux-guerres: facteurs professionnels et politiques', in Gisèle Sapiro ed., *L'espace intellectuel en Europe: de la formation des États-nations à la mondialisation XIXe-XXIe siècle* (Paris, 2009), pp. 111–46.

Sasson, Tehila, 'From Empire to Humanity: The Russian Famine and the Imperial Origins of International Humanitarianism', *Journal of British Studies*, 55.3 (2016), pp. 519–37.

Schivelbusch, Wolfgang, *Die Bibliothek von Löwen: eine Episode aus der Zeit der Weltkriege* (Munich, 1988).

Schroeder-Gudehus, Brigitte, 'Challenge to Transnational Loyalties: International Scientific Organizations after the First World War', *Science Studies*, 3.2 (1973), pp. 93–118.

Scott-Smith, Tom, *On an Empty Stomach: Two Hundred Years of Hunger Relief* (Ithaca, NY, 2020).

Seegel, Steven, *Map Men: Transnational Lives and Deaths of Geographers in the Making of East Central Europe* (Chicago, IL, 2018).

Selles, Johanna M., *The World Student Christian Federation 1895–1925: Motives, Methods and Influential Women* (Eugene, OR, 2011).

Shore, Marci, *Caviar and Ashes: A Warsaw Generation's Life and Death in Marxism, 1918–1968* (New Haven, CT, 2006).

Siegelberg, Mira L., *Statelessness: A Modern History* (Cambridge, MA, 2020).

Silverman, Lisa, *Becoming Austrians: Jews and Culture between the World Wars* (Oxford, 2012).

Sirinelli, Jean-François, *Génération intellectuelle: khâgneux et normaliens dans l'entre-deux-guerres* (Paris, 1988).

Sirinelli, Jean-François, *Intellectuels et passions françaises* (Paris, 1990).

Sluga, Glenda, *Internationalism in the Age of Nationalism* (Philadelphia, PA, 2013).

Smith, Leonard V., *Sovereignty at the Paris Peace Conference* (Oxford, 2018).

Smith, James Allen, 'An Internationalism of Beauty: The Rockefeller Restorations in France after the Great War', *The Tocqueville Review/La Revue Tocqueville*, 38.2 (2017), pp. 241–51.

Snyder, Timothy, *Bloodlands: Europe Between Hitler and Stalin* (London, 2010).

Solomon, Susan Gross, ed., *Doing Medicine Together: Germany and Russia between the Wars* (Toronto, 2006).

Solomon, Susan Gross, '"The Power of Dichotomies": The Rockefeller Foundation's Division of Medical Education, Medical Literature, and Russia', in Giuliana Gemelli and Roy MacLeod, eds., *American Foundations in Europe: Grant-Giving Policies, Cultural Diplomacy and Trans-Atlantic Relations, 1920–1980* (Brussels, 2003), pp. 31–52.

Steiner, Zara, *The Lights that Failed: European International History, 1919–1933* (Oxford, 2005).

Sternhell, Zeev, *The Anti-Enlightenment Tradition* (New Haven, CT, 2010).

Stibbe, Matthew, *British Civilian Internees in Germany: The Ruhleben Camp, 1914–18* (Manchester, 2008).

Stöckmann, Jan, *The Architects of International Relations: Building a Discipline, Designing the World, 1914–1940* (Cambridge, 2022).

Stöckmann, Jan, 'The First World War and the Democratic Control of Foreign Policy', *Past & Present*, 249.1 (2020), pp. 121–166.

Surman, Jan, *Universities in Imperial Austria 1848–1918: A Social History of a Multilingual Space* (West Lafayette, IN, 2018).

Thiem, Jon, 'The Great Library of Alexandria Burnt: Towards the History of a Symbol', *Journal of the History of Ideas*, 40.4 (1979), pp. 507–26.

Thompson, John M., *Russia, Bolshevism and the Versailles Peace* (Princeton, NJ, 1966).

Tronchet, Guillaume, 'L'accueil des étudiants réfugiés au xxe siècle: un chantier d'histoire globale', *Monde(s)*, 15 (2019), pp. 93–116.

Todorova, Maria Nikolaeva, *Imagining the Balkans* (Oxford, 2009).

Tooze, Adam, *The Deluge: The Great War and the Remaking of Global Order* (London, 2014).

Tournès, Ludovic, *Les États-Unis et la Société des Nations (1914–1946): Le système international face a l'émergence d'une superpuissance* (Bern, 2016).

Tusan, Michelle, 'Genocide, Famine and Refugees on Film: Humanitarianism and the First World War', *Past & Present*, 237.1 (2017), pp. 197–235.

Verbruggen, Christophe, '"Intellectual Workers" and Their Search for a Place within the ILO during the Interwar Period', in Jasmien van Daele, Magaly Rodriguez García and Geert van Goethem, eds., *ILO Histories: Essays on the International Labour Organization and its Impact on the World during the Twentieth Century* (Berne, 2010), pp. 271–92.

Vernon, James, *Hunger: A Modern History* (London, 2007).

Verpoest, Luc, Engelen, Leen, and Heynickx, Rajesh et al. eds., *Revival after the Great War: Rebuild, Remember, Repair, Reform* (Leuven, 2020).

Vogt, Carl-Emil, 'Fridtjof Nansen et l'aide alimentaire européenne à la Russie et à l'Ukraine bolchéviques en 1921-1923', *La contemporaine*, 3.95 (2009), pp. 5–12.

Vrdoljak, Ana Filipa, 'Enforcement of Restitution of Cultural Heritage through Peace Agreements', in *Enforcing International Cultural Heritage Law*, ed. Francesco Francioni and James Gordley (Oxford, 2013), pp. 22–39.

Wagner, Richard, *Clemens von Pirquet: His Life and Work* (Baltimore, MD, 1968).

Wallace-Wells, David, *The Uninhabitable Earth: A Story of the Future* (London, 2019).

Wasserman, Janek, 'The Austro-Marxist Struggle for "Intellectual Workers": The Lost Debate on the Question of Intellectuals in Interwar Vienna', *Modern Intellectual History*, 9.2 (2012), pp. 361–88.

Watenpaugh, Keith David, 'Between Communal Survival and National Aspiration: Armenian Genocide Refugees, the League of Nations, and Practices of Interwar Humanitarianism', *Humanity*, 5.2 (2014), pp. 159–81.

Watenpaugh, Keith David, *Bread from Stones: The Middle East and the Making of Modern Humanitarianism* (Oakland, CA, 2015).

Watson, Peter, *A Terrible Beauty: The People and Ideas that Shaped the Modern Mind* (London, 2000).

Weitz, Eric D., *A World Divided: The Global Struggle for Human Rights in the Age of Nation-States* (Princeton, NJ, 2019).

Weitz, Eric D., 'From the Vienna to the Paris System: International Politics and the Entangled Histories of Human Rights, Forced Deportations, and Civilizing Missions', *American Historical Review*, 113.5 (2008) pp. 1313–43.

Wertheim, Stephen, *Tomorrow, the World: The Birth of U.S. Global Supremacy* (Cambridge, MA, 2020).

White, Elizabeth, 'A Category "Easy to Liquidate": The League of Nations, Russian Refugee Children in the 1920s and the History of Humanitarianism', in Magaly Rodríguez García, Davide Rodogno, and Liat Kozma eds., *The League of Nations' Work on Social Issues* (Geneva, 2016), pp. 201–16.

Whitfield, Stephen J., 'Franz Boas: The Anthropologist as Public Intellectual', *Society*, 47.5 (2010), pp. 430–8

Widdig, Bernd, *Culture and Inflation in Weimar Germany* (Berkeley, CA, 2001).

Wilkinson, James D., *The Intellectual Resistance in Europe* (Cambridge, MA, 1981).

Williams, Robert C., *Culture in Exile: Russian Emigrés in Germany, 1881–1941* (Ithaca, NY, 1972).

Windsor, Tara Talwar, '"The Domain of the Young as the Generation of the Future": Student Agency and Anglo-German Exchange after the Great War', in Marie-Eve Chagnon and Tomás Irish, eds., *The Academic World in the Era of the Great War* (London, 2018), pp. 163–87.

Windsor, Tara Talwar, '"Extended Arm of Reich Foreign Policy"? Literary Internationalism, Cultural Diplomacy and the First German PEN Club in the Weimar Republic', *Contemporary European History*, 30.2, (2021), pp. 181–97.

Winock, Michel, *Le siècle des intellectuels* (Paris, 1999).

Winter, Jay, *The Day the Great War Ended, 24 July 1923: The Civilianization of War* (Oxford, 2022).

Winter, Jay, *Dreams of Peace and Freedom: Utopian Moments in the Twentieth Century* (New Haven, CT, 2006).

Winter, Jay, *The Great War and the British People* (London, 1985).

Wohl, Robert, *The Generation of 1914* (Cambridge, MA, 1979).

Wolff, Larry, *Inventing Eastern Europe: The Map of Civilization on the Mind of the Enlightenment* (Stanford, CA, 1994).

Wolff, Larry, *Woodrow Wilson and the Reimagining of Eastern Europe* (Stanford, CA, 2020).

Wright, Alex, *Cataloguing the World: Paul Otlet and the Birth of the Information Age* (New York, 2014).

Wünsch, Danielle, 'Einstein et la Commission internationale de coopération intellectuelle / Einstein and the International Commission for Intellectual Cooperation', *Revue d'histoire des sciences*, 57. 2 (2004). pp. 509–20.

Zimmerman, David, 'The Society for the Protection of Science and Learning and the Politicization of British Science in the 1930s', *Minerva*, (2006), 44.1 (2006), pp. 25–45.

Zorn, Wolfgang, 'Student Politics in the Weimar Republic', *Journal of Contemporary History*, 5.1 (1970), pp. 128–43.

Newspapers and Periodicals

American Journal of International Law
American Journal of Sociology
The Anaconda Standard
Les Annales : Politiques et littéraires.
ARA Bulletin
Arbeiter Zeitung
L'Art libre
The Athenaeum
The Atlantic Monthly
L'Attaque
L'Avenir
Berliner Tageblatt
Boston Transcript
Bridgeport Times and Evening Farmer
Brooklyn Daily Eagle
Brooklyn Daily Times
Bulletin de la coopération intellectuelle
Bulletin de la vie artistique
Bulletin of the American Library Association
Bulletin of the John Rylands Library
Bulletin Yougoslave
C.T.I. : Bulletin de la confédération des travailleurs intellectuels
La Chronique des Arts
Columbia University Quarterly
Comoedia
The Contemporary Review
Current History
The Czechoslovak Review
Dayton Daily News
La Dépêche
L'Écho de Paris
Edinburgh Evening News
L'Europe nouvelle
Evening Star
Excelsior

Le Figaro
Foreign Affairs
Fortnightly Review
Fresno Bee
Le Gaulois
Greenville Daily News
L'Humanité
L'Illustration
The Indianapolis News
The Indianapolis Star
Informations sociales
L'information universitaire
L'intermède: Camp de Würzburg
International Labour Review
The International Supplement of the Imperial University News
Isis
Italy Today, by Friends of Italian Freedom
The Japan Advertiser
Journal des Débats
Journal officiel de la République française, Débats parlementaires
Journal of the British Institute of International Affairs
The Mail
Le Matin
Nashville Tennessean
Neue Freie Presse
Neues Wiener Journal
Neues Wiener Tagblatt
Newcastle Daily Chronicle
The News-Herald
New York Times
New York Tribune
Northern Whig and Belfast Post
Oeuvre internationale de Louvain
Paris-Midi
Le Petit Parisien
The Plain Speaker
Pomona Progress-Bulletin
Proceedings of the British Academy
Recueil de documents étrangers
Reichspost
Revue des bibliothèques
Revue des deux mondes
Revue de Hongrie
Revue internationale de l'enseignement
Richmond Times-Dispatch

Russian Life
The Salt Lake Tribune
San Pedro Daily Pilot
Science
Scientific American
The Scotsman
The Scranton Times
Sheffield Daily Telegraph
Le Soir
The Times
Le Temps
Transactions of the Royal Historical Society
University of California Chronicle
Washington Post
Welsh Outlook
Wisconsin State Journal
The Workers' Dreadnought
Yorkshire Post

Unpublished Theses:

Grandjean, Martin, 'Les réseaux de la coopération intellectuelle. La Société des Nations comme actrice des échanges scientifiques et culturels dans l'entre-deux-guerres', PhD dissertation, Université de Lausanne, 2018.

Laker, Robert, 'Geneva in Motion: Winifred Coombe Tennant's Experiences at the Third Assembly of the League of Nations', MA diss., Swansea University, 2020.

Multanen, Elina Hannele, 'British Policy Towards Russian Refugees in the Aftermath of the Bolshevik Revolution', PhD diss., School of Slavonic and East European Studies, University College London, 2000.

Rietzler, Katharina, 'American Foundations and the "Scientific Study" of International Relations in Europe, 1910-1940', PhD diss., University College London 2009.

Websites:

'About Us', www.scholarrescuefund.org/about-us/afghanistan/ [accessed 1 August 2022].

Academic Assistance Council founding statement, May 1933. www.cara.ngo/wp-content/uploads/2015/06/Cara-Founding-Statement.pdf [accessed 1 August 2022].

'Assisting in recovery from the UCT library fire', sparcopen.org/news/2021/assisting-in-recovery-from-the-uct-library-fire/ [accessed 1 August 2022].

'Beyond 2022', beyond2022.ie/?page_id=2#vision [accessed 1 August 2022].

Conference for the Establishment of the United Nations Educational, Scientific and Cultural Organisation', unesdoc.unesco.org/ark:/48223/pf0000117626 [accessed 1 August 2022].

Convention relative to the Treatment of Prisoners of War. Geneva, 27 July 1929, Article 17. ihl-databases.icrc.org/applic/ihl/ihl.nsf/ART/305–430018?OpenDocument [accessed 4 August 2022].

Convention relative to the Treatment of Prisoners of War. Geneva, 27 July 1929, Article 39. ihl-databases.icrc.org/applic/ihl/ihl.nsf/ART/305–430040?OpenDocument [accessed 4 August 2022].

'Convention (IV) respecting the Laws and Customs of War on Land and its annex: Regulations concerning the Laws and Customs of War on Land. The Hague, 18 October 1907', ihl-databases.icrc.org/applic/ihl/ihl.nsf/Treaty.xsp?action=openDocument&documentId=4D47F92DF3966A7EC12563CD002D6788 [accessed 1 August 2022]

'"Giving Hope": UK Universities Twin with Struggling Ukraine Counterparts', www.theguardian.com/education/2022/may/14/giving-hope-uk-universities-twin-with-struggling-ukraine-counterparts [accessed 1 August 2022].

'Guerre en Ukraine : "On aura une immigration de grande qualité dont on pourra tirer profit"', www.europe1.fr/politique/guerre-en-ukraine-on-aura-une-immigration-de-grande-qualite-dont-on-pourra-tirer-profit-4095961 [accessed 1 August 2022].

LaPierre, Suzanne, 'Wildfires Damage Libraries', publiclibrariesonline.org/2020/10/wildfires-damage-libraries/ [accessed 1 August 2022].

The London Manifesto, 1921, www.jpanafrican.org/docs/vol8no4/8.4–8-1921Pan.pdf [accessed 1 August 2022]

'Successful implementation of the UNESCO Qualifications Passport', en.unesco.org/news/successful-implementation-unesco-qualifications-passport-ensuring-access-higher-education-and [accessed 1 August 2022].

'The United Nations Convention on the Rights of the Child', unicef.org.uk/wp-content/uploads/2010/05/UNCRC_united_nations_convention_on_the_rights_of_the_child.pdf [accessed 1 August 2022].

'Universal Declaration of Human Rights', *www.ohchr.org/EN/UDHR/Documents/UDHR_Translations/eng.pdf [accessed 1 August 2022].

The Versailles Treaty, 28 June 1919, avalon.law.yale.edu/subject_menus/versailles_menu.asp [accessed 1 August 2022].

'20 Years of Helping Scholars & Promoting Academic Freedom', www.scholarsatrisk.org/wp-content/uploads/2020/12/SAR_20th-Anniversary-Report-2020.pdf [1 August 2022].

Index

Academic Assistance Council (AAC), 232, 233, 243
aid workers: descriptions of deprivation, 131; expertise, 82; on impact of aid, 84; in intellectual kitchens, 65; involvement in book relief, 91, 116–17; on needs of intellectuals, 10, 50, 81
Allies: blockade of Central Powers, 41, 51, 53; defence of Western 'civilization', 4, 17, 23, 155, 156; post-war intellectual connections, 162; reparations policy, 42
Alsace and Lorraine, 150–1, 175
American Library in Paris, 97
American Red Cross (ARC), 43
American Relief Administration (ARA): administration of Commonwealth Fund money, 46; aid to Austria, 53, 63, 65; aid to Russia, 40, 55, 57, 69–70, 80, 82–3, 138; establishment and function, 42; Germany excluded from activities, 60; intellectual relief, 9; refugee aid, 121, 145; use of distribution networks for book relief, 94
American Section of European Student Relief (ASESR), 75, 80
Andrews, Fannie Fern, 37
Anesaki, Masaharu, 183, 185, 186, 224
Anglo-American University Library for Central Europe (AAULCE), 95–6, 98
anti-intellectualism, 197–8
anti-Semitism, 68, 69, 135, 201, 221, 233
Apponyi, Albert, 77, 103, 106
ARA see American Relief Administration (ARA)
Arbeitsmittel-Beschaffungs-Ausschuss (AMBA), 92, 98–9, 105

archives, destruction/displacement of, 2, 35, 39–40, 158, 244
Arnesen, Emily, 28
art, 28, 34, 35, 60, 149
artists, 3, 10, 24, 52, 64, 91
artworks, 33, 158, 176, 177
Asia, 24
Austria: anti-Semitism, 69, 221; archival records, 39; book relief to, 88, 90, 96, 98–9, 109, 183; *Büchernot* (book emergency), 89, 118; Commonwealth Fund assistance, 63; cultural destruction in Serbia, 158, 165–7, 169; exclusion of Jews from universities, 135; hunger crisis, 51, 53–4, 238; hyperinflation, 89, 90; ICIC and, 211; intellectual organizations, 204–5, 208; intellectual relief to, 8, 43–5, 59, 63–7, 78, 92, 105; international reintegration, 108; Jewish refugees in, 142; Mittelstandshilfe, 73; Quakers in, 43, 70, 83, 90, 142; sharing of university collections, 35; supply of books to other nations, 88; terminology used to describe intellectuals, 197; threatened by civilizational decline, 105
Austrian army, 2, 165, 167, 170
Austrian intellectuals: accounts of suffering, 53–4, 61, 192; attendance at intellectual kitchens, 64–7; categories of intellectuals, 80; economic status, 213; effect of book crisis on, 96, 98–9; justification for assistance, 12, 59; material sacrifices, 74; physical appearance, 77; response to aid, 76, 83
Austro-Hungarian Empire, 146, 165

275

Printed in the USA
CPSIA information can be obtained
at www.ICGtesting.com
LVHW011554301223
767616LV00005B/206